trick

American gene
ias

93

ANGLO-AMERICAN GENERAL ENCYCLOPEDIAS 1703-1967

A Historical Bibliography

ANGLO-AMERICAN

GENERAL

ENCYCLOPEDIAS

A Historical Bibliography

1703–1967

By S. Padraig Walsh

R. R. Bowker Company

NEW YORK • LONDON • 1968

Foreword

●●

It is one thing to have a guide to current, frequently promoted encyclopedias. The rub is to identify obsolete works which themselves appear on the doorstep or in the supermarket. This problem arises more often than is comfortable for the community librarian. And if he cannot identify the encyclopedia, there goes the omniscience which he has steadily been developing among his patrons.

So here it is, a guide to some 419 English-language encyclopedias under many titles, since these works have a habit of reappearing. From *Adair's New* to *Zell's Popular,* on both sides of the Atlantic, the whole panorama of efforts to summarize mankind's most significant knowledge is displayed. Bibliographically, it is a prodigious achievement. Only one who has worked with encyclopedia literature over several decades can appreciate what documentary sleuthing was involved.

It took a Padraig Walsh to follow up his *General Encyclopedias in Print,* an annual, discriminating guide to the contemporary encyclopedia scene, with this fine retrospective effort.

As one surveys Walsh's descriptions he recognizes how significantly the English-language encyclopedists on both sides of the ocean have contributed to the development of this literary form. Too often contemporary encyclopedists have been underestimated by scholars, and the impromptu essayist on the subject inevitably falls back on Diderot or Pliny. In fact, the former was a bad example of objectivity—the cornerstone of free world encyclopedia building. Indeed, both British and American encyclopedists have often revealed that they are the equal of their illustrious predecessors.

Of course there have been many bad examples of encyclopedia making in recent years. The ratio of "recommended" to "not recommended" in the U.S. *Subscription Books Bulletin* since 1930 proves that fact. But even this very high occurrence of unfavorable judgments shows an awareness on the part of English-language encyclopedists of the meaning of encyclopedism. The quantity and quality of encyclopedia criticism alone attests to the greater sophistica-

v

tion of this age, and particularly of the English-language encyclopedists in the art and science of creating examples of the encyclopedia form of great excellence. To verify this assertion one has only to read Walsh.

The notes are no less remarkable than the scholarship that went into verifying the entries. Some describe a work in a few short sentences. Other annotations, like the essay on the *Britannica,* truly underwrite the subtitle of Walsh's work. To all of this are added appendices that identify encyclopedists and their co-workers as well as encyclopedia publishers and their distributors. A third appendix provides a working bibliography on the encyclopedia; and a fourth the historical outline of the English-language encyclopedia's development. Finally, there is a forum on our good encyclopedias which reveals some of the dimensions of British and American awareness of the art.

Librarians have needed a tool such as this for a long time.

                                                                    Louis Shores

Contents

• •

Introduction

• •

The Beginning—and Later

Almost exactly 300 years ago, in the County of Shropshire in England, in either 1666 or 1667, the exact year is uncertain, there was born one John Harris who, in adult life, became a well-known divine and author, having previously obtained a Master of Arts Degree from St. John's College, Cambridge, in 1691, and a Doctor's Degree in Divinity at Lambeth in 1706. In 1696 he had become sufficiently well known to be elected a Fellow of the Royal Society, and went on to become its Secretary in 1709. Harris was the author of several works of relative importance at that time, and was the subject of another, the *Picture of a High Flying Clergyman* (1716), where he was held up to ridicule by a bitter critic and contemporary, a Rev. Charles Humphreys. Harris died at the age of 53 (or 54) on September 7, 1719, and, despite his several writings, died a pauper.

Insofar as we are here concerned, Harris will be forever remembered as the editor of the *Lexicon Technicum; or, An Universal Dictionary of Arts and Sciences,* which is generally accepted to be the first alphabetically-arranged encyclopedia to be published in the English language, although in actual fact, a similar work by an unknown compiler, the *Universal, Historical, Geographical, Chronological and Classical Dictionary* had been issued a few months earlier in 1703. To Harris, however, is credited the beginning of the English-language encyclopedia, and now, for the first time, a general reference work was made available to the general public, or at least to that segment of society who could read only English and could afford to purchase the important new work. Prior to 1704, encyclopedias had been published in Britain, but were available only in Latin or French, and were exclusively designed for the aristocratic and literate society of 17th- and 18th-century England.

By modern standards, the *Lexicon Technicum* is a poor and curious work, but at that time it represented an undeniably important step forward. The

original edition in 1704 was contained in one large folio volume and emphasized the practical and scientific subjects of that time at the expense of the
humanities. In those far off days it was still possible for one person to compile
a reasonably well-rounded encyclopedia and even to write a considerable part
of it himself, making minimal use of subject specialists and turning to them
only for the most intricate topics. Harris was sufficiently well educated to have
done much of the work himself, but in fact, and this was a revolutionary step
forward, he recruited contributions from the greatest scholars of the day. His
connections through the Royal Society were, of course, invaluable to him, and
the *Lexicon Technicum* is one of the first examples of an editor drawing on the
resources of experts, and to John Harris goes the credit for innovating the
modern and now quite essential system of obtaining contributions from inter-
nationally established specialists. There can be no doubt that, although the
Lexicon Technicum was in itself relatively short-lived (the last edition was
published in 1736), it exerted a considerable influence not only on the development of the English-language encyclopedia, but also on the development
of foreign-language works; particularly the French publications, which now
borrowed not only from Harris, but from the succeeding and improving British
encyclopedias; a complete reversal of what had been taking place less than
a century earlier.

After the *Lexicon Technicum* came the important and influential *Cyclopaedia*
of Ephraim Chambers in 1728, which in its turn prompted the appearance in
1771 of the ever-famous *Encyclopaedia Britannica,* one of the most authoritative
encyclopedias ever to be published anywhere in the world, which is today
the largest and oldest English-language encyclopedia in existence. The British-
produced encyclopedias gained in strength and authority throughout the 18th
century, and among the most important works to be published during that
period were: Temple Henry Croker's *The Complete Dictionary of the Arts and
Sciences* (1764), an outrageous plagiarization of the *Cyclopaedia* of Ephraim
Chambers; *A General Dictionary, Historical and Critical* (1734), which was an
expanded English translation of Bayle's fine French *Dictionnaire Historique et
Critique;* and the *Encyclopaedia Perthensis* (1796), a large, but somewhat
pretentious, compilation which claimed that it would supersede the use of all
other works of reference. This, it is believed, was afterwards transported to
the United States and distributed as the *New and Complete American Encyclopaedia,* a title even more pretentious than the original claim.

The tempo of production quickened perceptibly in the 19th century. This
was perhaps the most creative period in the history of English-language
encyclopedias, during which great strides forward were made both in the
compilation of the works and in their technical production. In 1802, the *New
Cyclopaedia,* which was an enlargement and improvement of Ephraim
Chambers's *Cyclopaedia,* appeared. The *New Cyclopaedia* was edited by
Abraham Rees, who had also worked on the later editions of the *Cyclopaedia.*
The next major and particularly important work to be published was the
ambitious, but commercially unsuccessful, *Encyclopaedia Metropolitana* in
1817, and this was followed, in 1827, by the *Encyclopaedia Edinensis,* under
the editorship of James Millar, who had previously edited the fourth edition

of the *Encyclopaedia Britannica*. Similar to, but more popular in approach than the *Britannica*, the *Edinensis* entered the market in the face of fierce competition from the established works, and despite its popular appeal, failed as a saleable item.

Until this time the business of encyclopedia publishing had been virtually a British monopoly, and what few works were available in the United States were either imports or reprints of the original British encyclopedias, although, by clever changing of titles and format, they were not always recognized as such. The monopoly was ended in 1829, when the *Encyclopaedia Americana* was published in Philadelphia. This was the first American encyclopedia in the accepted sense, but even this was edited by Francis Lieber, a 29 year-old German immigrant, who had previously worked on that reputable German encyclopedia, the *Konversations Lexikon*. It was, in fact, the seventh edition of this fine work which formed the base for this still popular American encyclopedia. Meanwhile, in Britain, in addition to several lesser works, there appeared Charles Knight's useful and successful *Penny Cyclopaedia*, which eventually evolved into the compact and scholarly *Everyman's Encyclopaedia* of the present time. The pendulum swung back to the United States in 1851, where the good *Iconographic Encyclopaedia* was published under the editorship of Spencer Baird. This was again actually a translation from a German work by J. G. Heck, but considerably expanded and adapted to meet American requirements. This work indicated the growing awareness of the need for an American-produced encyclopedia, but it was not until 1858 that the first true American work appeared. Unlike its predecessors, this owed nothing to any other encyclopedia, British or European. This was the scholarly *New American Cyclopaedia*, edited by Americans throughout under the editorial direction of George Ripley and Charles Anderson Dana, two journalists of great repute throughout the English-speaking world. A success from the outset, it was a work of such importance that even today, more than a century later, it is still useful to historians for its authoritative biographical articles. It continued in existence until 1884, and annual updating supplements were issued until 1903, almost 50 years after it first appeared.

Several other important works were published during the second half of the 19th century, both in Britain and in the United States. The most significant was *Chambers's Encyclopaedia* (1860), one of the best works ever produced, and named after its originators, the publishing brothers, William and Robert Chambers of Edinburgh. The work has changed ownership at least twice since then, and is now in its fourth edition. Today, it is easily the largest of the British-produced encyclopedias. In 1880, it was exported to the United States and reprinted as the *Library of Universal Knowledge*. This in turn was substantially revised to become the fine *International Cyclopaedia* of 1898, and this, in its turn, formed the base from which was compiled and published the great *New International Encyclopedia* of 1902; regarded by many as the finest encyclopedia in English ever to be published. This has long since been out of print, although vestiges of it may still be discerned in the small and popular *Funk & Wagnalls Standard Reference Encyclopedia* of the present time. Other works of importance which were published during the second half of the 19th century were *Johnson's New Universal Cyclopaedia* (New York, 1876); Robert Hunter's *The Encyclopaedic Dictionary* (London and New York, 1879); and *The Century Dictionary* (*and Cyclopaedia*) (New York, 1889).

The 20th century has seen an even greater influx of new titles, and the growing dominance of the American publishing industry. From 1900 onwards, the number of new works emanating from American presses increased steadily, while the number of British-produced works proportionately decreased.

In the United States, the following titles were most significant: *Hill's Practical Encyclopedia* (1901), although not an impressive work itself, it later appeared under a variety of titles and furnished a starting point from which *The World Book* (1917) developed; the *New International Encyclopedia* (1902), which has already been mentioned; the *Students Reference Work* (1902), which was to play an important role in the publication of *Compton's Pictured Encyclopedia* twenty years later; the *Americana* (1907), a reconstituted edition of the original *Encyclopaedia Americana* of 1829 (it afterwards reverted back to the original title); the *Book of Knowledge* (1912), which was to be a great favorite with children for another half century; the *American Educator Encyclopedia* (1919), which also owed much to *Hill's Practical Encyclopedia*; *Compton's Pictured Encyclopedia* (1922), which became a great rival of the *World Book Encyclopedia,* and which still ranks along with it as one of the best encyclopedias for children; the *Lincoln Library of Essential Information* (1924), an exceptionally well-compiled repository of general information topically arranged in one volume; the *Britannica Junior* (1934), a good work for younger children; the immensely popular one-volume *Columbia Encyclopedia* (1936); the *American People's Encyclopedia* (1948), an excellent intermediate work, the great new *Collier's Encyclopedia* (1949), immediately acclaimed as one of the best adult encyclopedias; the *Encyclopedia International* (1963), the first completely new encyclopedia of importance for more than a decade; the *Grolier Universal Encyclopedia* (1965), a smaller work which was drawn from the same basic material as the *Encyclopedia International;* the *New Book of Knowledge* (1966), an entirely new and significant work for younger children, which replaced the older and long popular *Book of Knowledge.* And then, finally, in 1967, came the *Merit Students Encyclopedia,* yet another carefully planned work created especially to meet the needs of elementary grade students, and put out by the publishers of the scholarly *Collier's Encyclopedia.*

In Britain, a marked decline both in quantity and quality quickly became apparent. There were a number of reasons for this, not least being the intervention of two economically serious World Wars, and, of course, a smaller market than in the growing United States. Until the beginning of the 20th century, Britain was, of course, the home publishing base of the *Encyclopaedia Britannica,* but even this long established work ran into grave financial difficulty which seriously threatened its continued existence. It was rescued from almost certain demise by two farseeing Americans, Horace E. Hooper and James Clarke, who eventually obtained control, and it has now been American-owned for more than 50 years. Even so, there were a number of new encyclopedias published in the United Kingdom which were of significance, and perhaps the most important of these was *The Harmsworth Encyclopaedia* (1905), which was afterwards published in the United States as *Nelson's Encyclopaedia* (1906) and where it was re-issued intermittently until the early 1940's. Important also was Arthur Mee's *Children's Encyclopaedia* (1908), which was exported to North America and adapted to American needs and interests and re-published as the enormously popular *Book of Knowledge* (1910) for more than 50 years. Another significant title was the small *The Everyman Encyclopaedia* (1913). This is the second largest of the British-produced encyclopedias of the present time, and is now in its fifth edition (1967). *Harmsworth's Universal Encyclopaedia* appeared in 1920, and as with several other British works, this was later issued in the United States in a revised edition, first as *Doubleday's Encyclopedia* (1931) and afterwards as the *Grolier Encyclopedia* (1944–1960). It was not until 1930 that any other work of any importance was published, and this was the popular *Newnes Pictorial Knowledge* (1936), which was succeeded in 1960 by the eight-volume *Newnes Popular Encyclopaedia.* Meanwhile, the excellent one-volume *Hutchinson's Twentieth Century Encyclopaedia* had been published in 1948, and the major British work for older children, the *Oxford Junior Encyclopaedia,* had commenced publication in 1949. A smaller work for children had been published in 1961 as *Black's Children's Encyclopedia,* but this was greatly overshadowed by the twelve-volume *Children's Britannica,* first published in 1961, as the British counterpart of the American-oriented *Britannica Junior.* A weekly encyclopedia, that is, an encyclopedia which is being issued in weekly sections over a period of three years, is *Purnell's New English Encyclopaedia,* which commenced in 1965. This, however, under new ownership, was re-issued in an eighteen-volume format as the *New Caxton Encyclopaedia* in 1966. A move which is perhaps indicative of the growth of the encyclopedia publishing industry in the United Kingdom, was the issuance, in 1966, of an International edition of the American *World Book Encyclopedia,* in which the basic work has been revised by British editors to conform to British and other English-speaking countries' requirements.

The continuing and ever increasing demand for good new encyclopedias ensure that there are even more significant works in the offing throughout the world, and not only in English. The public is no longer content with revised editions of older encyclopedias, and is becoming more and more discriminating in its demands. Even the scholarly *Encyclopaedia Britannica,* for example, has been subjected to severe criticism in recent years for its unchanging inclusion of outdated and inaccurate articles, especially in a best selling work *The Myth of the Britannica,* by Dr. Harvey Einbinder. It may well be that we shall in the quite near future see the demise of seemingly ageless favorites. The long popular *Book of Knowledge* in the United States, and its counterpart in Britain, the *Children's Encyclopaedia,* have been phased out of existence prior to the launching of updated versions such as the *New Book of Knowledge* (1966).

Scope of This Work

Since the *Lexicon Technicum* in 1704, this compiler has recorded a total of more than 400 titles of a general encyclopedic nature in the English language although, to be sure, a considerable number of these are re-titled editions and versions of earlier works. It was not always easy, however, to determine which titles should be included in a history of encyclopedias as well as those to be excluded and there are, the compiler is well aware, a number of titles omitted which other authorities would have deemed worthy of inclusion, and conversely, there are titles included which others would have considered either non-encyclopedic or so insignificant as not to warrant mention.

There are, for example, many excellent dictionaries which contain a great deal of general and specific encyclopedic information. The two outstanding instances are the monumental thirteen-volume *Oxford English Dictionary,* as well as its several abridgements, and the equally informative American *Webster's Third New International Dictionary,* and its abridgements. And there are, in addition, several other larger dictionaries which supply encyclopedic information either within their single alphabetical listings of words or in the form of reference supplements, and a particularly outstanding example of the latter type is the recently published *Random House Dictionary of the English Language,* which contains a substantial amount of brief information not only in its main text, but also in its almost 400 pages of supplementary appendices.

To compound the problems of inclusion and exclusion, there is an intermediate category of work which is usually referred to as the encyclopedic dictionary, which combines brief definitive entries for words with longer, more explanatory articles on the words which apply to things, i.e., peoples, places, animals, etc. And if this is not enough, there had to be taken into consideration also those several great works on a particular subject or group of related subjects which, in addition to their primary purpose, contain a great deal of general information. Particularly notable examples of these would be such scholarly publications as the *New Catholic Encyclopedia,* the *Jewish Encyclopedia,* and the *Encyclopedia of the Social Sciences,* and there are, of course, many others of a similar category.

Because of this multiplicity of borderline cases, it became necessary to lay down relatively inflexible guidelines for inclusion and exclusion, and of these the three most pertinent were (a) that the works in question were classified as general encyclopedias in one or more of the several sourcs consulted, and primarily the *National Union Catalog* of the Library of Congress, and the *British Museum Catalogue.* Also consulted, especially for the more modern titles, were the *British National Bibliography,* the *American Book Publishing Record,* and again for both older and more recent titles, the *United States Catalog* and its successor, the *Cumulative Book Index,* the *Reference Catalogue of Current Literature* (now *British Books in Print*) and the *English Catalogue,* all of which recorded titles not to be found elsewhere. In addition to these, the compiler also referred to the card and printed catalogs of the larger American and British public libraries, including the New York Public Library, and the Glasgow and

Westminster Public Libraries, as well as several other university and special collections. Whenever possible a direct physical examination of titles was implemented but this, desirable though it was, proved impractical in most instances and, in some instances, due to the lack of availability, quite impossible. In the main, and especially where a direct examination was not possible, extensive reference was made to previously published reviews and evaluations, and to such other bibliographic data as was available. Last, but by no means least, trade catalogs issued by individual publishers were consulted whenever possible; (b) that they were in fact vended as general encyclopedic works, although they may not have been classified as such in one or more of the above sources. The publishers' trade catalogs were often useful in this respect, and the files of old newspapers carrying advertisements were again a decisive factor in determining the inclusion or exclusion of a number of titles; (c) that the word "Cyclopedia" or "Encyclopedia" was incorporated into the title, except, of course, where the remainder of the title specifically included a finite subject. But this third criteria posed other problems and required qualification. It could not, for example, be applied to the earliest publications, which used the term "Dictionary" rather than "Encyclopedia". In the early days, the term "Dictionary", as then used, was quite correct and, in fact, the term "Cyclopedia" (or "Encyclopedia") was not used until the *Encyclopaedia Britannica* incorporated it into its title in 1771. At the present time, the word "Dictionary" means a reference work which is concerned with the meanings and spellings of words *per se*, whereas by an "Encyclopedia" is meant a work which provides information about the things that words represent. There is no encyclopedic work on the market at the present time which does in fact use the old term "Dictionary", which has long since become obsolete in this respect. Thus, if the *Lexicon Technicum; or, An Universal Dictionary of Arts and Sciences* were being published today, the sub-titling would certainly be changed to . . . *or, Encyclopedia of Arts and Sciences,* which would be more readily comprehended by the 20th-century reader.

Although there is a distinct difference between works which are primarily dictionaries and those which are primarily encyclopedias, there still remained a very definite possibility that those dictionaries which included the words "Cyclopedia", "Encyclopedia" or "Encyclopedic" in their titles could still have been misconstrued as general encyclopedic works of reference (and perhaps vended as such). In such cases, it was decided to include these borderline publications as encyclopedic works, rather than to exclude them as the dictionaries which they properly are. Thus, the reader will find included herein, the *Century Dictionary and Cyclopedia,* and the *Encyclopaedic Dictionary* of Robert Hunter, but not the equally important and informative *Oxford English Dictionary* or *Webster's Third New International Dictionary,* principally on the premise that these latter are not vended as encyclopedias, and their titles are not such that they could even remotely be regarded as such by even non-professionals.

There remains but one class of work which could have been excluded but which is in fact included, and this is the many handbooks of general and miscellaneous information, usually arranged non-alphabetically, and which as a general rule provide information of a more practical "how-to-do-it" character, rather than the more abstract and scholarly articles of the all-purpose multi-volume encyclopedias. Provided that they did and do deal with a wide range of general topics rather than restricted to more specific topics, these have been regarded, if not exactly encyclopedic, as at least falling into a category of encyclopedia supplements. Notable examples of such works are the annual *Information Please Almanac,* its main competitor, the *World Almanac,* and the British *Whitaker's Almanac* and *Pears Cyclopaedia.*

The Arrangement of Encyclopedias

Encyclopedias are generally regarded as alphabetically arranged repositories of general knowledge, but this has not always been so nor does it necessarily mean that they have to be arranged in this manner. In fact, the most favored method in the early days was the logical or systematic, in which all subjects of a like nature were brought together so that, for example, the *related* articles on "Animals" and "Zoos" would be brought together under a broad subject category. Few non-alphabetical works are still in existence and of those that are, none cater to the erudite adult. The alphabetically arranged encyclopedia, on the other hand, would artificially place the two obviously connected articles on "Animals" and "Zoos" at the opposite ends of the alphabet, and in the largest works, they could be as many as thirty or more volumes apart. Probably the most outstanding example of a systematically arranged encyclopedia was the great *Encyclopaedia Metropolitana,* the concept of which was evolved by the poet, Samuel Coleridge. Yet, despite the clear logic and great merit of this work, it was commercially unsuccessful, simply because it is easier to find information in an alphabetically arranged encyclopedia. There can be no doubt now but that the alphabetically arranged encyclopedia, which was first introduced in the 18th century, has now almost completely ousted the systematically arranged work as the most favored method of presentation, and this is clearly indicated by the recent publication of the alphabetically arranged *New Book of Knowledge* to replace the older, non-alphabetically arranged *Book of Knowledge.*

The Revision and Updating of Encyclopedias

Encyclopedias, when they were first produced in England, were almost exclusively the prerogative of the wealthy and educated classes, due primarily to their relatively high cost and the scholarly nature of their contents. As such, they were not planned with such care as they are in modern times and, for the first century at least, concerned themselves mainly with the arts and sciences and only gradually introduced more popular information, such as biographies and the description of places. Biographies of living people, for example, were not included until about 1800, as this, naturally, would have entailed more frequent revision and updating; a great inconvenience to the early publishers and editors. At that time, it will be appreciated, the whole field of human knowledge was very much smaller than it is now, and as the rate of expansion was slower in proportion, the problems of updating were by no means as acute as they are today. The change, when it came, was sudden, precipitated first by the Industrial Revolution and then the tremendous explosion of knowledge and technological advancement of the 20th century; an explosion which is billowing outwards at an ever increasing rate and with still accelerating momentum.

Encyclopedias which were once good for twenty years and even longer found their useful life becoming shorter and shorter, and the complacent attitude towards revision and updating was compelled to change. The scrutinizing of articles and their revision when necessary now became essential features of the commercially successful encyclopedia. The editorial staffs, instead of being recruited and assembled for each edition, now had to be maintained on at least a skeleton permanent basis, and those encyclopedias which ignored the trend and failed to conform, even the very good ones, soon began to litter the wayside of progress. At the present time, for example, out of the approximately 400 titles which have been recorded, barely 50 are still in existence, and by far the greater number of these came into being during the last half-century, and a not inconsiderable number within the last decade.

Radically changed also are the methods of compilation. Whereas, years ago, a handful of good editors and specialist contributors could produce a well-rounded general encyclopedia, it is now essential, if a really good and successful work is to be produced, to recruit a large and highly qualified staff of specialists, and contributions solicited not from a few but from thousands of highly qualified experts in every branch of science, technology and the humanities. Practically every single word in every single article has to be scrutinized not once in ten or more years, but virtually from day to day to detect the changes in meaning and application, and with thousands of new words coming into use in the English language every year (and thousands more becoming obsolete), this is a vital factor. Since the days of John Harris, just about everything in the encyclopedia publishing industry has changed and is continuing to change. Today's editor in chief is not the scholarly and erudite part-time editor of two hundred years ago who could write a great deal of the material himself, but a highly specialized, high speed administrator, one who can plan an encyclopedia to cover the widest possible range of human knowledge within very restricted confines; for, while knowledge itself is now reputed to be doubling itself every ten years, the physical boundaries of an encyclopedia cannot expand proportionately without making it prohibitive in cost.

The Selling of Encyclopedias

The days when it was not only possible, but practical, to secure sales by subscription well in advance of publication, enabling an exact and accurately predetermined print order and profit, are gone forever. Today, encyclopedias are sold by extensive promotional advertising through every imaginable media of communication, and through high pressure door-to-door salesmanship. Regrettably, this latter, all too frequently, has been of an unethical nature and has, at times, been so dishonest that the industry, as a whole, has been castigated. This is readily understandable in the case of inferior works, which were deliberately designed for a short life and a quick profit. It is much less understandable, and unforgivable, when the same questionable tactics have been employed in the sale of better quality works, and yet this is the case. Instance after instance occurs of the less scrupulous salesman being much more concerned with a quick and handsome bonus by selling what is basically a good encyclopedia to a totally unsuited purchaser, and this is a criticism which, unfortunately, can penetrate to the higher echelons of some of the best known publishers.

For the most part, and certainly it is true of all the major works, today's encyclopedias are geared to meet the needs and requirements of specific age groups, or are designed for a certain purpose, as distinct from the earlier works, which were designed to be all things to all people. The discriminating publisher of the mid-20th century, for example, does not just publish an encyclopedia. Now he must plan and orient it to a particular age group, especially the school grades, and this usually involves a careful study of school curricula, the interests and requirements of the group whom it is intended to serve, and even more careful research of the market to determine its saleability and profit probabilities.

The launching of a new encyclopedia at the present time is an exceedingly expensive proposition, and will only be considered and entered into if all the pertinent factors add up to a handsome and continuing profit. This does not mean, however, that quality is a secondary consideration to quantity. On the contrary, hard headed publishers and editors are only too fully aware that they can succeed only if they do produce a work of quality. If they do not, the demand is such that their competitors most certainly will, and this is a good and healthy augury for the future.

The Future

There is a vast chasm separating the *Lexicon Technicum* of 1704 and today's modern top quality encyclopedias, which are marvels of human ingenuity, skill and enterprise. And what does the future hold in store for us? Undoubtedly, a great deal. The present-day works are being continuously improved. Although the individual personal touches of editorial directors will never be completely subjugated, there can be no question but that the computerized encyclopedia is already well within sight; evolving new methods of compilation of almost infallible accuracy and an ever quickening updating of all important subject material. And, who knows, the logic of the computer may even swing the pendulum back from alphabetical to systematic arrangement by facilitating the compilation of indexes of meticulous and unerring exactitude.

Time will tell of these and related developments, but one very probable outcome will be the eventual demise of the inferior encyclopedias. For such could not possibly keep pace with the giants of the industry, who can more readily invest enormous sums in such progress, an outlay which, in the long term, must result in ever better and ever less expensive encyclopedias proportionate to their content.

ACKNOWLEDGEMENTS

Many people, too numerous to mention each individually, have contributed directly and indirectly to this work and, at times, even unknowingly. At the risk of invidiousness, however, I am compelled in all honesty and sincerity to single out for heartfelt thanks, Dr. Louis Shores, Dean Emeritus of the Florida State University Library School, for his expert and constructive advice and always encouraging suggestions; Mr. Robert L. Collison, Librarian of the British Broadcasting Corporation, again for his invaluable advice, and also for blazing the trail for me with his important *Encyclopaedias: their History Throughout the Ages* (Hafner, 1964 and 1966); and Mr. Robert A. Landau, of the R.R. Bowker Company, who so superbly edited the manuscript throughout, and whose vigilance brought to my attention many grievous discrepancies and omissions. And last, but certainly by no means least, I wish to express to my wife, Violet, and my two sons, Robert and Peter, my sincere gratitude for their unflagging patience during the past two years, and for the practical assistance which they gave me from time to time.

S. Padraig Walsh

Historical Bibliography

· ·

A DAIR'S NEW ENCYCLOPEDIA; a new and up to date reference work for home, school and office . . . with 50 full page maps. New York: World Syndicate Publishing Co., Inc., c.1923. 5v. 20 cm. Editor in Chief: Francis Joseph Reynolds (1867–1937).

As far as can be ascertained, this work was published once only, in 1923. No reviews are traceable and there is no positive indication from extant bibliographic records of its relationship to any other encyclopedia. There can be little doubt, however, that it is either a reprint or an adapted version of the *New World Encyclopedia* (1919), which was itself a reprint of the *New World Wide Cyclopedia* (1918). These, in turn, were derived directly from the *People's Cyclopedia* (1914) and the *Everybody's Cyclopedia* (1911–1912), all of which were published by the Syndicate Publishing Co.

It is within the bounds of probability that the work originated even earlier with the *Crown Encyclopedia and Gazetteer*, first published in 1903, and reissued in 1905 (with the addition of a dictionary) as the *Continental Encyclopedia*. It is significant that Reynolds was afterwards "assistant editor" of a revived edition of the *New World Wide Cyclopedia* (1928), in which the editor in chief was named as George Jotham Hagar (1847–1921), who had edited many of the previous titles. Since Hagar had been dead several years when the *New World Wide Cyclopedia* was issued in 1928, it is obvious that the actual editor must have been Reynolds, and he was, in fact, named as the editor of the succeeding editions, beginning with the *Times Encyclopedia and Gazetteer* in 1929 which, in 1930, 1932 and 1934 was reissued as the *Twentieth Century Encyclopedia* by the World Syndicate Co.

The work was finally issued in 1937 as the *World's Popular Encyclopedia*, with further editions in 1940 and 1942, although Reynolds' name is not included in the two later editions.

1

AITON'S ENCYCLOPEDIA; a practical work of reference for the
home, school and library . . . Minneapolis: Welles Bros. & Co., 1910. 5v.
26cm. Editor: George Briggs Aiton (b.1856).

Aiton was an Inspector of Schools in Minnesota at the turn of the century
and he conceived his idea of a popular home and school encyclopedia through
his experience and contact with children.

It was only published once under his direction, however, and when it re-
appeared in 1912, it was retitled the *Standard Reference Work*, and expanded to six volumes under the imprint of the Interstate Publishing Co.,
with Harold Melvin Stanford as chief editor. The work met with some success, and further editions were issued in 1913, 1915 and 1917 (when it was
expanded to seven volumes) under the imprint of the original publishers,
Welles Bros. & Co. By 1922, the work had expanded to ten volumes, the
last two of which were supplementary study and reading guides, and this
edition was published by the Standard Education Society.

In 1930, the work was rebuilt and retitled the *New Standard Encyclopedia*, and all subsequent editions to the present time have been published
under this title. In 1923, however, the work had been published for only
one edition as the *National Encyclopedia for the Home, School and Library*,
under the imprint of the National Encyclopedia Corp.

AMERICAN ANNUAL CYCLOPAEDIA AND REGISTER
OF IMPORTANT EVENTS . . . embracing political, civil, military
and social affairs, public documents, biography, statistics, commerce, finance,
literature, science, agriculture and mechanical industry. (Vols. 1–14, 1861–
1874) New York: D. Appleton & Co., 1862–1875. 14v. 25cm.

This very useful annual compilation of important data was designed to
supplement the *New American Cyclopaedia* (1858–1863) and the *American
Cyclopaedia* (1873–1884). After 1875, it was retitled *Appleton's Annual
Cyclopaedia*, and continued publication under that title until 1903. It is invaluable as a record of its time.

THE AMERICAN CYCLOPAEDIA; a popular dictionary of general
knowledge. New York: D. Appleton & Co. 1873–1876. 16v. 26cm. Editors:
George Ripley (1802–1880) and Charles Anderson Dana (1819–1897).

More than 300 contributors assisted in the compilation of this excellent
encyclopedia, one of the best of its times. It was not a completely new
work, however, but was in fact a thorough revision of the *New American
Cyclopaedia* (1858–1863), compiled by the same editors and also published
by Appleton. A second edition was published in 1883 and 1884, revision
being implemented by the provision of supplements at the end of each
volume. A "General and Analytical Index," compiled by T. J. Conant, was
published separately in 1884, and an annual supplement, *Appleton's Annual
Cyclopaedia* (1861–1903), served to update the main text. No further editions of the work, which is still valuable historically, were published after

1884, although the publishers continued to update the work with their annual supplement until 1903.

Appleton remained active in the field of encyclopedia publishing with their *Johnson's Universal Cyclopaedia* (1893–1897), the *Universal Cyclopaedia* (1900–1905) and *Appleton's New Practical Cyclopaedia* (1910–1920).

One of the editors, Charles Anderson Dana, was a friend of Abraham Lincoln and was the second Secretary of War in the Lincoln administration during 1864 and 1865. He was also the editor of the *New York Sun* from 1868 to 1897, and he is particularly remembered for his famous letter "Is There a Santa Claus?" in reply to the query of a little girl.

As a portrait of its time, the *American Cyclopaedia* is of great value for its coverage of the Civil War and the Reconstruction periods, as well as its otherwise unobtainable biographies.

THE AMERICAN EDUCATOR; completely remodelled and rewritten from the original text of the "New Practical Reference Library", with new plans and additional material. Peace Edition. Chicago: Ralph Durham Co., 1919. 8v. 24cm. Editor in Chief: Ellsworth Decatur Foster (1869–1936). Editor for Canada: James Laughlin Hughes (1846–1935).

The history of this reference work (currently published as the *American Educator Encyclopedia*) is interesting in that it was, at one time, related to the *World Book Encyclopedia*, both works being, for a short period, issued by the same publisher. The title page of the original edition quite clearly states that the work is remodelled from the *New Practical Reference Library* (1907), but its origin can be traced back still further to 1901, when a work entitled *Hill's Practical Encyclopedia*, in four volumes, was published under the imprint of the Chicago Book Co. In 1902, the same work was published by the firm of Dixon & Hanson as *Hill's Practical Reference Library of General Knowledge*, and further editions were issued in 1904 and 1905. In 1907, however, Dixon & Hanson retitled the work the *New Practical Reference Library*, and this was re-issued in 1911 under the imprint of the Dixon-Hanson-Bellows Co. Another edition was published in 1912 (with an expansion to six volumes) and this appeared under the imprint of the Hanson-Bellows Co. Further editions followed in 1913 (with Foster listed as an associate editor), 1914, 1915, and 1917, when the publisher's imprint reads the Hanson-Roach-Fowler Co.

It is of particular interest to note that the same firm published the first edition of the *World Book* in the same year, with Ellsworth D. Foster as general editor. The two works, while similar in some respects, were in most respects different and certainly, from 1920 onwards, pursued a quite independent course of development.

The *American Educator*, in its own right, was published in a revised edition in 1922 and was published simultaneously in Canada as the *Dominion Educator* (afterwards the *New General Encyclopedia*), although the names of the editors were reversed for the Canadian edition. In the edition which followed in 1923, the subtitling was changed to read "a new and thoroughly modern reference work designed to meet the needs of every age." Further editions followed in 1924, 1925 and 1926 when the name of the publishers was changed to the Bellows-Durham Co.

A period of revision and redevelopment beginning about 1927 was completed with new editions in 1929 and 1930, when the work was expanded to ten volumes. In 1931, the work was acquired by the United Educators Inc., and all subsequent editions, beginning with that of 1932, when the word "Encyclopedia" was added to the title, have appeared under their imprint.

Since 1932, the *American Educator* has been published regularly under a policy of continuous revision, although with little expansion, as the present day work is little larger than the earlier editions. It is not known how long Foster was associated with the work, but he was certainly connected with the *World Book Encyclopedia* in the later 1920's. It is known that in 1941, the editor in chief was Lorimer Victor Cavins (b.1880), although he had been preceded by a number of associate and managing editors. Since 1955, however, the work has been edited by the present editor in chief, Everett Edgar Sentman.

There have been few major changes in the work over a number of years, apart from improved format and presentation, although in 1957, the set was available in either 10 or 14 volumes, the larger format including supplementary material on Nature, Recreation, Hobbies, and a Study Guide. This was omitted from the 1965 edition, and the work is now available only in a 14-volume set, which does not include the supplementary material of earlier editions.

The *American Educator Encyclopedia* is, today, one of the better small, family encyclopedias published in the United States. Unfortunately, however, the merits of the work are marred by a series of complaints against the distributors in connection with their sales tactics. A "Cease and Desist" order was issued in 1938 by the Federal Trade Commission (Docket #3349) and further complaints were recorded in 1939 (Docket #3428) and 1942 (Docket #4554), and although these complaints were directed against the vendors of the work, as distinct from the publishers themselves, or against the quality of the work, they have undoubtedly done considerable harm to the reputation of the encyclopedia, and have probably mitigated against its acceptance by the most authoritative educational authorities.

• References:

Subscription Books Bulletin, January 1930; July 1934; April 1938; January 1943; July 1950.
Booklist and Subscription Books Bulletin, April 15, 1958; December 15, 1965.

AMERICAN EDUCATOR AND LIBRARY OF KNOWL-EDGE; containing concise and exhaustive articles upon science, arts and mechanics, etc. . . . . Philadelphia: National Publishing Co., 1902. 738 p. 25cm.

A small, insignificant and poorly produced one-volume work which has been issued, in an identical format, or in whole or in part with additional material, under several other titles. No editor is named, but it is known that the original compiler was Henry Davenport Northrop (1836–1909), who had compiled and edited the *Standard Cyclopedia* in 1897, which was subsequently issued as the oddly named *X-Rays of Intellectual Light* (1899); the *Standard American Book of Knowledge* (1900), the *20th Century Cyclopedia of Universal Knowledge* and *World's Book of Knowledge* (1901), the *New Century Cyclopedia of Universal Knowledge* (1902), the *American Home Educator and Book of Universal Knowledge* (1903) and the *Standard Library of Knowledge* (1904), all of which were issued under the imprint of the National Publishing Co.

Despite the similarity in titles, this work has no connection whatsoever with the much larger *American Educator*.

AMERICAN FAMILY ENCYCLOPEDIA; a concise and comprehensive reference work, especially planned, compiled and written for school, college, office and home use. New York: Books Inc., 1963. 8v. (1496p.) 22cm. Editor in Chief: Charles Ralph Taylor (b.1877). Managing Editor: Lewis Mulford Adams.

Although the title was new in 1963, this work in itself most certainly was not. It was first published in 1938 as the *New American Encyclopedia* and was probably derived in part from the *World Wide Illustrated Encyclopedia*, a multi-volume work edited by Taylor and published by the same company in 1937.

The work has had an unsatisfactory history, having appeared in several different formats over a period of almost thirty years, and in at least one instance, in 1953, the encyclopedic material was also contained in *Webster's Unified Dictionary and Encyclopedia*.

The title of *New American Encyclopedia* was transferred to an entirely different work in 1963 (albeit published by the same firm) and the present title adopted to give the semblance of a new work. Although the work is described as being in eight volumes, it is of such small content, it can and has been accommodated in single- and four-volume editions also.

AMERICAN HOME EDUCATOR AND BOOK OF UNIVERSAL KNOWLEDGE . . . being a complete treasury of knowledge on scientific, historical, artistic and all important subjects. Philadelphia: National Publishing Co., 1903. 738p. 25cm. Compiler: Henry Davenport Northrop (1836–1909).

Unquestionably, a re-issue of the one-volume *American Educator and Library of Knowledge* (1902), which was itself derived from the *Standard Cyclopedia* (1897), *X-Rays of Intellectual Light* (1899), the *Standard American Book of Knowledge* (1900), the *20th Century Cyclopedia of Universal Knowledge* and *World's Book of Knowledge* (1901), all of which were compiled by Northrop and published by the National Publishing Co. The work seems to have terminated with the issuance of the *Standard Library of Knowledge* in 1904.

AMERICAN HOME ENCYCLOPEDIA OF USEFUL KNOWLEDGE, by Marshall Everett (*pseud.*) . . . a complete library of universal knowledge . . . showing the newest and most wonderful inventions and the world's great progress in science and commerce. Chicago: Columbia House, 1908. 336p. 24cm. Compiler: Henry Neil (b.1863).

A small and virtually valueless one-volume work which had first been published in 1905 as *Everett's Encyclopedia of Useful Knowledge* under the imprint of the Bible House, and which was re-issued in 1907 as the *Columbia Encyclopedia of Useful Knowledge*. The only distinguishing feature of the work is that it is the only known instance of an encyclopedia being compiled under a pseudonym.

AMERICAN HOME LIBRARY; a book of interesting and useful information for home and school, with 300 illustrations. Steubenville, Ohio: Union Publishing House, 1930. 666p. 24cm. Editors: Oliver W. Bateman and Cloyce Benjamin Ulery (b.1889).

A small one-volume compendium of practical rather than academic usefulness, and of limited subject coverage. Further printings were registered in 1951 and 1953, but the work now seems to have been discontinued.

AMERICAN INTERNATIONAL ENCYCLOPEDIA; a comprehensive reference work. Unabridged. New York: American International Encyclopedia, 1950. 16v. 21cm. Editor in Chief: William Dodge Lewis (b.1870).

A direct descendant of the much older *Winston's Encyclopedia* (1909) and its successor, *Winston's Cumulative Loose Leaf Encyclopedia* (1912–1942), both of which were published under the imprint of the John C Winston Co., a well-known producer of dictionaries. In 1942, Winston sold the publishing rights to their encyclopedic works to a New York distributor who re-issued it in 1942 as the *Encyclopedia Library*, in 12 volumes, with a further printing in 1943.

Over the years, the original quality of the work had deteriorated badly and when the Knickerbocker Press issued it for supermarket consumption in 1950 as the *American International Encyclopedia*, it was a very inferior work, containing only some 3½ million words. William Dodge Lewis had become editor of *Winston's Cumulative Loose Leaf Encyclopedia* in 1934, and his name was continued in the later editions and the retitled versions, but it is most unlikely that he was actively concerned with these.

• Reference:
Subscription Books Bulletin, January 1950; July 1951.

AMERICAN OXFORD ENCYCLOPEDIA FOR HOME AND SCHOOL. New York: Little & Ives Inc., 1965. 14v. 26cm. Editor in Chief: William T. Couch (b.1901).

This is intended to be an American adaptation of the well-known and authoritative *Oxford Junior Encyclopaedia,* published in Britain from 1948 to 1954 and later, rewritten in part and expanded to meet American needs and interests, but basically still the *Oxford Junior Encyclopaedia.* Publication began in late 1964, based on the second edition (1964) of the *Oxford Junior Encyclopaedia,* and was scheduled for publication in 1965, but in the summer of that year, publication was suspended due to financial difficulties.

The publishers state that the suspension is only a temporary measure, with further volumes scheduled for 1966. After such a dismal start, however, it appears unlikely that the work, which did show signs of being a worthwhile contribution to the field of general knowledge, will ever be completed.

The editor in chief, William Couch, had previously edited *Collier's Encyclopedia* from 1951 until about 1960 but, as far as is known, is no longer associated with the project.

AMERICAN PEOPLES ENCYCLOPEDIA; a comprehensive, modern-minded reference work. Chicago: The Spencer Press, 1948. 20v. 26cm. Editor in Chief: Franklin Julius Meine (b.1896).

This was a completely new work when it was first published in 1948, although it was based, to some extent, on the older *Nelson's Encyclopaedia,* first published in 1905, and with a terminal copyright date of 1940, the last edition being edited by Meine. Although the older work was used for background material, the *American Peoples Encyclopedia* was in itself a much superior work, with a good list of contributing authorities, signed articles, excellent writing and production.

For several years the work was sold exclusively through the mail order house of Sears, Roebuck & Co., and despite this apparent restriction, it rapidly won wide acceptance as a reliable and relatively inexpensive adult encyclopedia for home and library use. Unfortunately, during the 1950's, the selling methods used to vend the work contravened the regulations of the Federal Trade Commission, who, in 1958, issued a "Cease and Desist" order against Sears, Roebuck (Docket #7081), who immediately waived all rights and ceased to sell the work through their retail outlets. With this main source of selling closed, the quality of the work was immediately affected and revision, which had been one of the work's strong points, became so ineffective that the recommendation of the American Library Association's Subscription Books Committee, which had been awarded to the set in 1953, was withdrawn in 1961.

In 1962, however, The Spencer Press was acquired by Grolier Inc., who immediately, under the editorial direction of Dr. Lowell A. Martin (formerly Dean of the Library School at Rutgers University), instituted a major revision, including the provision of an analytical index, and, by 1965, the work had been restored to its former acceptable authority and again obtained an endorsement from the Subscription Books Committee.

After the first edition of the work in 1948, the set was revised and published annually until 1956, but no further editions were published until 1962, when it first appeared under the Grolier imprint. Since then, with

Edward Humphrey as editor in chief, it has been published annually and, as with all major encyclopedias, a year book is available to keep the previous editions up-to-date. Oddly, the title *American Peoples Encyclopedia* had been used in 1946 for a small 144-page publication, with Meine as editor, which was, however, simply a reprint of the "Dictionary of General Information" which comprised a section of *Webster's Encyclopedic Dictionary*, compiled by the same editors.

• References:
Subscription Books Bulletin, April 1949; October 1953.
Booklist and Subscription Books Bulletin, January 1, 1965.

AMERICAN REFERENCE LIBRARY; Chicago, circa 1931.

Bibliographic details for this work seem to be nonexistent. In 1931, however, it was known to be the subject of a "Cease and Desist" order issued by the Federal Trade Commission against the Co-Operative Book Co. (Docket #1551), in which it was found that the respondent had sold the set known as the *American Reference Library* up to 1927, and thereafter known as the *Source Book*.

In 1932 a "Cease and Desist" order (Docket #1371) was issued against the Perpetual Encyclopedia Corp. and others for deceptive selling practices. Apparently the vendor, who actually purchased the sets from the Perpetual Encyclopedia Corp., represented the work to be recent, although it had in fact been first published in 1913 as the *Home and School Reference Work*, and was subsequently marketed as the *National Encyclopedia*, the *Perpetual Loose Leaf Encyclopedia* and the *North American Reference Book*, and perhaps other unrecorded titles also.

AMERICANA; a universal reference library, comprising the arts and sciences, literature, history, biography, geography, commerce etc., of the world. Issued under the editorial supervision of the "Scientific American." New York: Scientific American Compiling Department, 1907. 16v. 26cm. Editors: Frederick Converse Beach (1848–1918) and George Edwin Rines (b.1860).

The *Encyclopedia Americana* was first published in 1829–1833 in 13 volumes and further editions appeared in 1838, 1848 and 1849, after which it lapsed. Towards the end of the century, however, determined efforts were made to revive the original work and, as a result, the *Encyclopedia Americana* re-appeared in 1902, in 16 volumes, under the imprint of R. S. Peale & Co., and with Beach, then editor of *Scientific American*, as editor in chief.

Another edition was issued in 1903–1904, but this appeared under the imprint of the Americana Co., with George Edwin Rines as managing editor of volumes 8–16. Yet another edition appeared between 1903 and 1906, but this was now under the imprint of the *Scientific American*, and when they re-issued the work in 1907, the word "Encyclopedia" was dropped from the title, and it was known simply as the *Americana* for a number of years.

Another edition was issued in 1911, when it was increased in size to 20 volumes, and another in 1912, when two additional volumes of supplementary updating material increased the set to 22 volumes. With this edition, however, the connection with *Scientific American* was severed, and when the work next appeared in 1918–1920, it was under its original title, and has remained so ever since. Its association with *Scientific American* was of considerable benefit to the work and the influence of the editors can still be discerned through the work's extensive treatment of scientific and technical subjects.

Beach had severed his connection with the work at the same time as the *Scientific American*, but his associate, Rines, continued and he was editor in chief of the re-named edition of 1918–1920. Curiously, Rines was also the managing editor of the 1911 edition of the *United States Perpetual Encyclopedia*, a 30-volume work, which had the same subtitling "a library of universal knowledge", as later editions of the *Encyclopedia Americana*, but the connection, if any, is obscure.

THE ANGLO-AMERICAN ENCYCLOPEDIA (or CYCLO-PEDIA); a standard work of reference in art, literature, science, history, geography, commerce, biography, discovery and invention. New York and London: Anglo-American Encyclopedia Co., 1911. 50v.

A search of the various bibliographic tools, which should have recorded an entry for this work, failed to elicit clear information on the origins of this work. Collison, however, describes it briefly.

The subtitling of the work is, however, identical in every respect to that of the 25-volume *Werner Encyclopedia*, which was published in Akron, Ohio, in 1909, under the imprint of the Werner Co., and it is believed that this was, in turn, printed from pirated plates of the ninth edition of the *Encyclopaedia Britannica*, with additional material.

ANGLO-AMERICAN ENCYCLOPEDIA AND DICTION-ARY; a comprehensive encyclopedia of the arts, sciences, history, biography, geography and general literature; comprising also a practical and exhaustive work of reference to the English language, giving the full definitions, the origin, pronunciation and use of words. Philadelphia: Avil Printing Co., 1902. 12v. 26cm.

Not to be confused with the *Anglo-American Encyclopedia* (or *Cyclopedia*) published in London in 1911, this is actually two quite separate works bound into one for sales purposes. Volumes 1–5 comprise an alphabetically arranged encyclopedia, and it is believed that this is, in fact, the five-volume supplement to the *Encyclopaedia Britannica* published by Werner, at Akron, Ohio, in 1900. The remaining seven volumes comprise a dictionary, although it has not been ascertained which one this actually is.

Another edition was issued in 1904 by the Globe Publishing Co., and in 1906, it was re-issued under the imprint of J. A. Hill & Co., New York, who simultaneously issued Volumes 1–5, separately, as the *New American Comprehensive Encyclopedia*. The true origin of the work is complicated and confused still further by the issuance of further editions under the imprint of the Fifth Avenue Library Society, and the Werner Co.

APPLETON'S ANNUAL CYCLOPAEDIA AND REGISTER OF IMPORTANT EVENTS . . . embracing political, military and ecclesiastical affairs, public documents, biography, statistics, commerce, finance, literature, science, agriculture and mechanical industry. v.1. 1861. New York: D. Appleton & Co., 1876–1903. 42v. 25cm.

This is a continuation of the *American Annual Cyclopaedia*, which Appleton published from 1862 to 1875, which comprised the first 14 volumes of the complete set. These annual works formed a valuable supplement to the *New American Cyclopaedia* (1858–1863) and its successor, the *American Cyclopaedia* (1873–1883). Three cumulative indexes were published, one for the first 15 volumes (1861–1875); another for the next 20 volumes (1876–1895) and a final index for the last seven volumes (1896–1902), by which time the main work had gone out of print.

These annual supplements are of considerable value historically, especially for their detailed coverage of a turbulent period in the history of the United States.

APPLETON'S NEW PRACTICAL CYCLOPEDIA; a new work of reference based upon the best authorities, and systematically arranged for use in home and school. New York: D. Appleton & Co., 1910. 6v. 25cm. Editors: Marcus Benjamin (1857–1932); Arthur Elmore Bostwick (1860–1942); George Jotham Hagar (1847–1921); Gerald Van Casteel.

Although Appleton had long been associated with the publishing of encyclopedias (*New American Cyclopaedia; American Cyclopaedia; Johnson's Universal Cyclopaedia* and the *Universal Cyclopaedia*), their *New Practical Cyclopedia* was a much smaller and quite new and different work. Further editions were issued in 1913, 1915 and 1920, when a supplementary history of World War I was included.

It evidently lapsed after the 1920 edition, although it was still being sold many years later and became the subject of a "Cease and Desist" order issued by the Federal Trade Commission in 1929 (Docket #1540) against the David B. Clarkson Co. for misrepresentation of the actual selling price.

In 1930 the work re-appeared in 10 volumes as the *New Universal Encyclopedia*, under the imprint of Foster, Temin & Oliver, in a very shabbily produced version. All of the original editors were listed in this edition as members of the Editorial Board, although one of them at least, Bostwick, protested the use of his name.

Perhaps the best known of the editors was Bostwick, a former Librarian of Congress, who subsequently edited *Doubleday's Encyclopedia* (1931). Another of the editors, George Jotham Hagar, was simultaneously editor of the *New Standard Encyclopedia* (1906), but this was a quite different work issued by another publisher

APPLETON'S UNIVERSAL CYCLOPAEDIA *see* UNIVER-SAL CYCLOPAEDIA

AUSTIN'S NEW ENCYCLOPEDIA OF USABLE INFOR-MATION. New York: Parke, Austin & Lipscomb, 1948. 1634p. 26cm. General Editors: Lewis Copeland and Lawrence W. Lamm.

This is not an encyclopedia in the true sense of the word, but rather a compilation of practical "how-to-do-it" information interspersed with some general and miscellaneous material. The work was arranged in three distinct sections—Home, Business, and Self Improvement and Recreation, and, while it may have had some merit for homemakers, it was inadequate as a work of reference, despite quite a good index.

It was probably an expansion of an earlier work edited by Copeland and issued as the *Handy Encyclopedia of Useful Information*. In 1951, the work was acquired by the J.G. Ferguson Co., who re-issued it under the title of the *Everyday Reference Library*, and further editions followed in 1954 and 1957. Beginning with the 1959 edition, a three-volume format was adopted and editions, with minor revisions, have appeared at regular intervals since.

BASIC EVERYDAY ENCYCLOPEDIA; prepared by the Reference Department of Random House. New York: Random House, 1954. 574p. 26cm. Editor: Jess Stein.

Published once only in 1954, although still being sold many years later, this compact and well-condensed one-volume desk encyclopedia contains almost a million words and some 12,500 subject entries. The entries are, of necessity very brief, but the information is well selected and well edited, and it has proved to be a popular inexpensive work for many years, despite its lack of up-to-date material.

• Reference:
Subscription Books Bulletin, July 1955.

BEETON'S ENCYCLOPAEDIA OF UNIVERSAL INFOR-MATION. London: Ward, Lock, 1879–1881. 4v. 23cm. Compiler: Samuel Orchart Beeton (1831–1877).

A topically arranged work containing some 50,000 brief articles, Volumes 1 & 2 deal with Geography, Biography and History; Volumes 3 & 4 deal with Science, Art and Literature.

Although the work appears to be original, it should be noted that Beeton is credited as being the compiler of a work entitled the *Dictionary of Uni-*

versal Information, which was published under the Appleton imprint. No actual date of publication is recorded, but as it was listed in the *American Catalogue* for 1876, it clearly predates the present title.

Beeton is not known to have been associated with any other encyclopedic works, but the publishers, Ward, Lock, had many years earlier published the *Family Cyclopaedia* (1859), which may well have provided Beeton with the background material for his works.

BLACKIE'S MODERN CYCLOPAEDIA OF UNIVERSAL INFORMATION; a handy book of reference on all subjects . . . with numerous pictorial illustrations and a series of maps. London and Glasgow: Blackie & Son, 1889–1890. 8v. 24cm. Editor: Charles Annandale (1843–1915).

The development and subsequent history of this work is one of the most complicated series of changes of titles, editors and publishers which can be envisaged.

Ostensibly, the work was new when first published in 1889, but it was almost certainly derived from, or closely influenced by, the much older *Popular Encyclopaedia* (1841–1893), which had been edited by Annandale since 1882. It was re-issued by Blackie in 1896–1897 in the same format, but in 1901, under the imprint of the Gresham Publishing Co., a work entitled the *New Popular Encyclopaedia* was issued in 14 volumes under the editorship of Annandale, and this was in fact a new and revised edition of the *Popular Encyclopaedia.* But, in 1906, Gresham published the *Modern Cyclopaedia of Universal Information,* in eight volumes, which was also under the editorship of Annandale.

The similarity of titles, size and editorship, indicates that the sets, if not the same, are closely related. This is bewildering in itself, but the situation is further complicated by the issuance in the United States, under the imprint of Gebbie & Co., of the *New Cabinet Cyclopaedia and Treasury of Knowledge* (1891–1892), edited by Annandale, but with the articles relating to America revised and edited by Ainsworth Rand Spofford (1825–1908). This is quite clearly the American reprint of *Blackie's Modern Cyclopaedia,* and the last 1899 edition was also published by Brown, Eager & Hull as the *New National Cyclopaedia and Treasury,* again with Annandale and Spofford as editors.

In 1901, Gebbie reappeared on the scene and re-issued the work in eight volumes as the *XX Century Cyclopaedia and Atlas.* Subsequently, in 1903, under the imprint of E.R. Dumont, two volumes of a dictionary of living Americans and two volumes containing a dictionary of the English language were added to the original eight volumes, and it was again retitled as the *New Twentieth Century Cyclopaedia and Dictionary.* Thereafter it seems to have passed from publisher to publisher until 1905, when it reverted to its original eight-volume format and re-appeared under two different publishers' imprints as the *New and Complete Universal Self Pronouncing Encyclopedia.* Yet again, in 1906, under the imprint of the Thompson Publishing Co., it was re-issued as the *New Cosmopolitan Encyclopedia,* although this edition omitted Spofford, who died in 1908, as one of the editors.

As far as can be ascertained from the records available, the work terminated its American existence in 1912 with the publication of the nine-volume *National Encyclopedia of Reference,* published under the imprint of the Standard Bookbinding Co., some six years after the last issue of its British counterpart.

The complexity and multiplicity of titles under which it was issued can be gauged from the fact that Annandale is credited with the editorship of no less than 12 multi-volume works, and Spofford with six.

BLACK'S CHILDREN'S ENCYCLOPEDIA; illustrated by Marjorie Falla and others. London: Adam & Charles Black, April, 1961. 12v. 25cm. Editors: William Worthy and R. J. Unstead.

First published in 1961, this is one of the better works for children published in Britain. It is also available in two- and four-volume editions, but apparently only the 12-volume set is equipped with an index. Well written and attractively produced, the encyclopedia was compiled by two former schoolteachers, versed in the reference requirements of children. In 1964, "Look It Up" supplements, with answers, were provided for self study and school use.

This is the only modern encyclopedia published by the old and well established firm of A. & C. Black, but they had, between 1842 and 1903, been closely connected with the publication of the 7th, 8th, 9th and 10th editions of the *Encyclopaedia Britannica.*

• Reference:
Library Association Record, October 1961.

BOOK OF GENERAL KNOWLEDGE. London: English Universities Press, 1938. 362p. 19cm. Editor: Ronald Russell Martin (b.1891).

A small and well compiled handbook of general knowledge, although much too brief for any but casual use. Further editions were issued in 1939, 1943 and 1949, but by 1956 it had been superseded by a larger and different work, the *Teach Yourself Concise Encyclopedia.*

BOOK OF KNOWLEDGE (British); a pictorial treasury of reading and reference for young and old. London: Waverley Book Co., 1959. 6th edition. 8v. Editor: Gordon Stowell.

This work should not be confused, despite some relationship in ownership, with the larger and quite different American 20-volume *Book of Knowledge,* first published in 1912. The 1959 edition of the British work is described as being the sixth, although it was in fact first published in 1922 and afterwards as *Cassell's Book of Knowledge,* the *Waverley Book of Knowledge,* the *Hammerton Book of Knowledge,* and from 1938 to 1953, under the imprint of the Waverley Book Co., as the *New Book of Knowledge.*

The earlier editions were edited by Sir John Hammerton, who had been editorially associated with some dozen encyclopedic works from 1920 until his death in 1949. The 1959 edition of the *Book of Knowledge,* one of the best medium-sized British encyclopedias, was considerably improved over earlier issues, and a new feature was the provision of a "Fact Index". In style, it approaches the concept of a popular adult encyclopedia, while retaining its general usefulness for school work in the later age groups.

The subtitling, "To inspire ambition, to stimulate the imagination, to provide the inquiring mind with accurate information told in an interesting style and thus lead into the broader fields of knowledge—such is the purpose of this work" is identical in every respect to the subtitling of the original 1922 edition of *Compton's Pictured Encyclopedia*. The works of 1966 are markedly different from each other in most respects, but the resemblance of the present day *Book of Knowledge* to earlier editions of *Compton's* is unmistakable.

• Reference:
Library Association Record, October 1961.

THE BOOK OF KNOWLEDGE (American); the children's encyclopedia; with an introduction by John H. Finley. New York: The Grolier Society, 1912. 24v. (5776p.) 24cm. Editors in Chief: Arthur Mee (1875–1943) and Holland Thompson (1873–1940).

Now more than 50 years old, this topically-arranged encyclopedia for boys and girls has long been and still is a firmly established favorite of American youth. First published in 1912, it was primarily a reprint of the famous British *Children's Encyclopaedia*, published in London between 1908 and 1910 by the Educational Book Co., but with such adaptations, by Holland Thompson, as would make it useful to American users. Over the years the original British emphasis has been eliminated and the work today is regarded as almost uniquely American.

Editions of the *Book of Knowledge* have appeared regularly during the past half-century under a policy of continuous revision, and occasionally with changes of format, e.g., 10 or 12 volumes instead of 20. It was not until 1929 that Mee was displaced as editor by Thompson, or rather this was when Thompson's name preceded Mee's on the title page, although, in the 1943 Canadian edition, Mee was still being listed as editor in chief. Ellen V. McLoughlin (b.1893) became managing editor in 1941 and continued in that position until 1960 when John D. Tedford was appointed.

In 1966 the *Book of Knowledge* was replaced by the completely reorganized *New Book of Knowledge*, and it will be remembered only as a landmark in encyclopedia publishing. Similarly, its British counterpart, which is also owned by Grolier Inc., is being phased out of existence, and will not be available after 1970.

• References:
Subscription Books Bulletin, January 1932; July 1935; January 1941; July 1947; April 1953.
Booklist and Subscription Books Bulletin, December 1, 1958; February 1, 1960.

THE BOYS AND GIRLS ENCYCLOPAEDIA. London: Odhams Press, 1960. Editor: Jeanne Seguin.

A small one-volume work containing simple information for younger users. The date of publication is given as 1960, but it is probably a revision or adaptation of several other one-volume children's encyclopedias published by Odhams over a number of years.

BRITANNICA JUNIOR; an encyclopaedia for boys and girls, prepared under the supervision of the editors of the "Encyclopaedia Britannica". Chicago, New York and London: Encyclopaedia Britannica Inc. 1934. 12v. 26cm. Editor: Franklin Henry Hooper (1862–1940). Associate Editor: Walter Yust (b.1894).

The idea of a junior version of the famous *Encyclopaedia Britannica* had been mooted for years, but it was not until 1934 that the idea was implemented. Even then, the first *Britannica Junior* was not an original work, but a revision and re-modelling of a work entitled *Weedon's Modern Encyclopedia*, which had been published in an eight-volume format only three years previously by the S. L. Weedon Co. Further editions are recorded for 1937 and 1938, when Yust became editor in chief of both works. Since 1940 it has been published annually under a policy of continuous revision, and was expanded to 15 volumes, its present format, in 1947. Harry S. Ashmore became editor in 1961, but the present editor is W. R. Dell.

The work is one of the most popular of American encyclopedias for children, but differs from any other known work in that the index is contained in the first volume instead of the more orthodox last. Short fact entries are incorporated into the index, and the arrangement of the volumes is such that each contains all the entries for one or more letters of the alphabet. It should be noted that the *Britannica Junior* is the American junior version of the *Encyclopaedia Britannica*, and is not the same as, although not dissimilar to, the *Children's Britannica*, published in London in 1960, and designed for British school children.

• References:

Subscription Books Bulletin, January 1935; July 1939; October 1943; April 1948; January 1953.
Booklist and Subscription Books Bulletin, February 1, 1959.

THE BRITISH CYCLOPAEDIA OF ARTS AND SCIENCES, manufactures, commerce, literature, history, geography, politics, biography, natural history, biblical criticism and theology, on the basis of the German "Konversations-Lexikon", with such additions as will adapt it to the present state of science. London: Orr & Smith; Philadelphia: T. Wardle, 1833–1835. 2v. 24cm. Compiler: Charles Frederick Partington (d.1857).

The success of the famous German encyclopedias of the eighteenth and nineteenth centuries had led to a great deal of imitation, and the rather grandiloquently entitled *British Cyclopaedia* was just one of these. To be fair, this is stated on the title page of the work, a practice which was not always the case.

The compiler, Charles Partington, was a scientist by profession and in his lifetime had done a great deal to educate the working classes of his day in the more popular scientific and technical subjects. He wrote much of this encyclopedia himself and the work, generally, was a quite useful adult encyclopedia with a popular approach.

There is no record of further editions except for an entry in the British Museum Catalogue, which lists an edition in ten volumes, published between 1835 and 1838. This comprised two volumes on the arts and sciences, three volumes on geography, two volumes on biography and three volumes dealing with natural history. It has no connection whatsoever with the similarly entitled *British Encyclopaedia* of 1809.

• Reference:
Collison, Encyclopedias: Their history throughout the ages.

THE BRITISH ENCYCLOPAEDIA, or, Dictionary of Arts and Sciences. Comprising an accurate and popular view of the present improved state of human knowledge. Illustrated with elegant engravings by Messrs. Lowry and Scott. London: Longman, Hurst, Rees & Orme, 1809. 6v. 22cm. Compiler: William Nicholson (1753–1815).

This work was commissioned primarily in opposition to a somewhat similar work, *A Dictionary of Arts and Sciences,* which had been published in 1806, the editor of which was supposed to be Dr. George Gregory, Prebendary of St. Paul's. A well-known scientist and inventor, William Nicholson, was thereupon named as editor of the new *British Encyclopaedia.* In actual fact, however, neither Gregory nor Nicholson were active in the compilation of the rival works, and in actuality, both were edited by the same person, not named in any bibliographic records, but known to be a well-informed scholar by the name of Jeremiah Joyce (1763–1816).

The *British Encyclopaedia* proved to be the more successful of the two and although no further editions are recorded as having been published in Britain, it enjoyed success in North America. The first American edition appeared in seven volumes in 1816–1817 under the Mitchell & Ames imprint, and two 12-volume editions were published by Mitchell, Ames & White in 1818 and then again in 1819–1821. The latter edition also appeared in the same years under the Ingram & Lloyd of Nashville, Tenn. imprint.

Although the titles are very similar, the *British Encyclopaedia* is evidently not connected with the *British Cyclopaedia* of 1833, nor with a much more modern work, *The British Encyclopaedia,* published in ten volumes by the Odhams Press in 1933.

• Reference:
Collison.

BRITISH ENCYCLOPAEDIA (Odhams 1933) *see* CONCISE ENCYCLOPAEDIA

BRITISH UNIVERSITIES ENCYCLOPAEDIA. London, 1935. A special re-issue of the 1935 edition of *Chambers's Encyclopaedia,* and the last to be published under the imprint of William and Robert Chambers. In every respect identical to the better known work, it appeared once only under this title.

BUFTON'S UNIVERSAL CYCLOPAEDIA; Multum in Parvo; a comprehensive, accurate and dependable storehouse of universal knowledge, treating history, geography and invention, embracing over 16,000 subjects . . . all subjects treated in plain simple language with cross references, and over 2,000 illustrations, maps, charts and gazetteer. Kansas City: Bufton Publishing Co., 1919. 4v. 27cm. Editor: William A. Colledge (1859–1927) Associate Editor: Paul Ingebrikt Neergaard (b.1884). Managing Editor: James D. Bufton (b.1884).

As far as can be ascertained, this work was first published in 1919, although this is open to some doubt, and it may well have been a revision of a much older work, the *Universal Cyclopaedia and Dictionary* (1898), although Colledge was connected, as joint editor, with yet another work, the 12-volume *New Standard Encyclopedia* in 1906. In any event *Bufton's Universal Cyclopaedia* was a very inferior work and eventually, about 1928, the publishing rights were acquired by the Mutual Publishing Co., Kansas City, who re-issued it in 1929 as the *Library of Knowledge,* under the editorship of Neergaard.

At about this time, the Federal Trade Commission took an interest in the titles, and the result of their inquiry is detailed in their Docket #1571, dated December 18, 1931. In spite of the deterrent, however, publication of the work continued, and it was re-issued in an eight-volume edition in 1936 under the imprint of American Surveys Inc., and again, in 1937, the Executives Guild, Kansas City, published an identical set under their imprint. It was undoubtedly sold for years afterwards by various distributors, but the 1937 edition is the last recorded issue.

THE CABINET CYCLOPAEDIA. London, 1829–1849. 133v. Editor: Dionysius Lardner (1793–1859).

One of the most remarkable encyclopedias ever published in the English language, it was published over a period of twenty years in 133 small, handy-sized volumes, the small format lending itself to the adjective of "Cabinet".

The editor of this unusual work, which was filled with really excellent articles by the leading authorities of the time, had himself contributed articles to the *Encyclopaedia Edinensis* and the *Encyclopaedia Metropolitana,* principally on scientific matters. He was elected to the Chair of Natural Philosophy and Astronomy at what is now the University College, London in 1827. Lardner, although severely criticized by his contemporaries, did an excellent editorial job.

• Reference:
Collison.

CAMBRIDGE ENCYCLOPAEDIA. Montreal: Cambridge Society Ltd., 1934. 13v. Editor: Athelstan Ridgway.

Although bearing the imprint of a Canadian publisher, this work was actually printed in Britain and the contents, except for some minor variations, is identical to the 1931–1932 edition of the well-known *Everyman's Encyclopaedia*, published by Dent in London and Dutton in New York.

Some color plates of negligible value were added to each volume and the binding was embellished with a maple leaf for attraction and, for good measure, an atlas volume was added to the 12 volumes of text.

In effect, the work was a very good one, but it was retailed in Canada at an unjustifiably high cost, almost twice as much as the original edition had sold for in the United States.

• Reference:
Subscription Books Bulletin, July 1935.

CASSELL'S BOOK OF KNOWLEDGE *see* BOOK OF KNOWLEDGE (British)

CASSELL'S CABINET CYCLOPAEDIA, etc. London: Cassell & Co., 1904. 1358p. 20cm.

A small single, octavo-volume compendium of general knowledge containing a considerable amount of brief information. Authorship of the work is uncertain, but it was almost certainly a revision of earlier one-volume encyclopedias published by Cassell.

As far as is known, it has no connection with the very much larger *Cabinet Cyclopaedia* of Dionysius Lardner.

CASSELL'S CONCISE CYCLOPAEDIA . . . with numerous illustrations. London: Cassell & Co., 1883. 1340p. 20cm. Editor: William Heaton.

One of the earliest of the compact, one-volume informational handbooks which were developed to meet the rising demand for this type of work towards the end of the century. Containing brief entries for more than 12,000 subjects, this handy little work proved to be exceedingly popular, and further editions were published in 1888, 1896 and 1899. It is so similar in size to *Cassell's Cabinet Cyclopaedia* (1904) that it is probable that the two works are the same.

CASSELL'S ENCYCLOPAEDIA OF GENERAL INFORMATION; with colored plates and maps and numerous full page engravings Special edition. London: Cassell & Co., 1908. 10v. 22cm.

Actually a re-issue of *Cassell's Storehouse of General Information,* a four-volume work published by Cassell in 1891–1894. No editors are given for either title, and the origin of the work is difficult to trace. As the work seemed to enjoy some popularity as an inexpensive family encyclopedia, it seems surprising that it was not published after 1908.

CASSELL'S MINIATURE CYCLOPAEDIA. London: Cassell & Co., 1888. 764p. 20cm. Compiler: Sir William Laird Clowes (1856–1905).

Following the pattern set for one-volume handbooks of information so successfully initiated by Larousse, this compact little work contained no less than 30,000 brief articles of a dictionary nature.

A second edition was issued in 1898, but this type of work never quite achieved the success in Britain that Larousse had in France.

CASSELL'S MODERN ENCYCLOPAEDIA; a new dictionary of universal knowledge. London: Cassell & Co., 1934. 1024p. 22cm. Editor: Sir John Alexander Hammerton (1871–1949).

Not an original work, this one-volume encyclopedia had been published the previous year as the *Modern Encyclopaedia* under the imprint of the Amalgamated Press. Both appear to be abridged versions of the *Concise Universal Encyclopaedia* (1930–1931), which was itself derived from *Harmsworth's Universal Encyclopaedia* of 1920.

CASSELL'S POPULAR EDUCATOR; a complete encyclopaedia of elementary, advanced and technical education. New and revised edition. London and New York: Cassell, Petter & Galpin, c.1910. 8v. 26cm. Original Editor: R. Wallace.

Despite its subtitling, this work is more in the nature of a course of self-education than a systematically arranged encyclopedia.

The 1910 printing appears to be an expanded edition from the six-volume issues, first between 1852 and 1855, and afterwards 1867–1870, 1872–1875, 1876–1879 and 1884. The work has also been known simply as the *Popular Educator*.

CASSELL'S STOREHOUSE OF GENERAL INFORMA-TION. London: Cassell & Co., 1891–1894. 4v. 22 cm.

A small work of negligible value. No editors are listed and the authority of the work is questionable. It was re-issued in a ten-volume edition in 1908 under the title of *Cassell's Encyclopaedia of General Information*.

CATHOLIC ENCYCLOPEDIA FOR SCHOOL AND HOME. New York: McGraw-Hill, 1965. 12v. 25cm. Editor in Chief: Msgr. John H. Harrington.

Although this work is primarily an encyclopedia designed for Catholic schools and homes, it does contain a considerable amount of general information presented in an unbiased form. The work was completely new in 1965 and it is the intention of the publishers to revise it continuously. Major Catholic encyclopedias have been published previously, but this is the first to be directed towards students and presented in a popular style eminently suitable for lay readers.

The work is arranged alphabetically, is well illustrated and includes an excellent 86-page bibliography as an appendix. The material is drawn from that assembled for the much larger *New Catholic Encyclopedia*, which is scheduled for publication in 1967.

THE CAXTON ENCYCLOPAEDIA. London: Caxton Publishing Co., 1960. 6v. 25cm.

This work may be a revision and expansion of the *World of the Children*, a four-volume work published by Caxton in 1948, with a second edition in 1957. In 1961 it was re-issued as the *Caxton World of Knowledge*.

Caxton commenced publication in March, 1966, of a new 18-volume work, the *New Caxton Encyclopedia*, but this is a re-issue of *Purnell's New English Encyclopaedia*, which had previously been issued in some 200 weekly parts, beginning in January, 1965.

CENTURY BOOK OF FACTS; a handbook of ready reference, embracing history, biography, government, law . . . and useful miscellany. Springfield and Chicago: King-Richardson Co., 1902. 681p. 24cm. Compiler: Henry Woldmar Ruoff (1867–1935).

The most remarkable feature of this one-volume work is that despite its mediocrity, it has remained in existence for more than 60 years. It is, in all probability, basically the same work as the *Universal Manual of Ready Reference*, published in 1904 by the Richardson Co., and also compiled by Ruoff, which has the same method of topical or subject arrangement and almost the same number of pages. Further editions of the *Century Book of Facts* were issued in 1905, with an expansion to 726 pages, 1906 and 1908. In an edition of 1909, however, the title was amended to read the *New Century Book of Facts*, with an expansion to 1,117 pages and with a new editor, and it has been published under this title ever since.

Of interest is the career of the original compiler. In 1908 he was the editor of the *Standard Dictionary of Facts*, a similar work, which preceded the *Lincoln Library of Essential Information*. In 1911 he was listed as the editor in chief of the *Volume Library*, and many years later, the editor of the *Circle of Knowledge*. All these works have two features in common. They are all handbooks of reference and all are arranged in a systematic subject arrangement. The *Volume Library*, like the *New Century Book of Facts*, is still in existence as *Cowles Comprehensive Encyclopedia*.

THE CENTURY DICTIONARY; an encyclopedic lexicon of the English language. New York: The Century Co., 1889–1891. 6v. 33cm. Editor: William Dwight Whitney (1827–1894).

Although, in fact, a dictionary, this excellent work contained so much encyclopedic information, it was frequently consulted for more factual information than would normally be found in a language dictionary. It was, and still remains, an invaluable source for historical information, particularly for topics of American interest, although it has been out of print for more than half a century.

The first edition, which in many ways compared favorably with the *Oxford English Dictionary*, was issued between 1889 and 1891 and was described as being six volumes in twenty-four. In 1895, it was re-issued in a ten-volume edition, of which volumes 1–8 comprised the dictionary proper, while volumes 9 and 10 contained a useful dictionary of names and a world atlas. Further editions, either in the eight-volume format or in the combined ten-volume edition, were issued in 1899, 1901, 1902, 1903 and 1904.

Beginning with the 1901 edition, however, the title and subtitling read, *The Century Dictionary and Cyclopaedia; a work of universal reference in all departments of knowledge, with a new atlas of the world.* Between 1906 and 1909, the work was re-issued in 12 volumes, of which the last two were supplements to the main work. Publication of the work terminated in 1911 with the issuance of a revised and enlarged 12-volume edition.

CHAMBERS'S CONDENSED ENCYCLOPEDIA; a dictionary of universal knowledge for the people. Revised edition. New York: A. L. Burt, 1895. 698p. 19cm. Editor: D. T. Stuart.

A small and useful compact work of ready reference which followed the vogue for this type of handbook towards the end of the nineteenth century.

According to the title page, it was revised and edited by D. T. Stuart, which clearly indicated prior publication, although no records could be traced for earlier editions under this title. It is, however, almost certainly derived from *Chambers's Information for the People* (1857), which preceded the larger *Chambers's Encyclopaedia* by only three years, and was probably assembled from the same basic material. The subtitling of this small work and that of the larger encyclopedia is identical.

CHAMBERS'S ENCYCLOPAEDIA; a dictionary of universal knowledge for the people (on the basis of the latest edition of the German "Konversations-Lexikon"). London: W. & R. Chambers, 1860–1868. 10v. 26cm. Editors: Andrew Findlater (1810–1885) and John Merry Ross (1833–1883).

One of the largest and most famous encyclopedias in the English language and currently, if the American-owned *Encyclopaedia Britannica* is excepted, the major British general reference encylopedia. It should not, however, be confused with the much earlier *Cyclopaedia* (1728) of Ephraim Chambers, which was an entirely different project. The new work took its title from the name of its publishers, the Edinburgh firm of William and Robert Chambers who, shortly before, had published their useful smaller work, *Chambers's Information for the People,* which was probably derived from the same basic material. The new work was edited by two well-known Scottish educators and it immediately won a world-wide reputation for scholarship and reliability. This has remained an integral feature of the work for a century despite commercial pressures; a policy which has won for the original publishers and their successors universal respect and confidence.

It also achieved popularity in the United States and editions were published there by Little, Brown and by Lippincott between 1869 and 1870. Further editions of *Chambers's Encyclopaedia* were published in 1874, when a supplement and an index were also provided, and this was followed by a revised edition in 1878. This latter edition was reprinted in the United States as the *Library of Universal Knowledge* (1880–1881), with additions by American editors, and this in turn provided the foundations on which the fine *International Cyclopaedia* (1898) and the *New International Encyclopedia* (1902) were built. Meanwhile, in Britain, further editions were published in 1888–1892, 1897–1898, 1901, 1904–1905 and 1908, the latter with a preface by David Patrick (1849–1914). It was not until 1923, however, that a new edition, still in ten volumes, was issued, which listed Patrick, although he had died some ten years earlier, and William Geddie as editors. This was followed, 12 years later, by the publication of a new edition, but the authority of this was marred by still listing Patrick (now dead for twenty-one years) as editor. This 1935 edition was also issued in a special edition entitled the *British Universities Encyclopaedia*.

In 1944, the publishing rights were acquired from Chambers by the firm of George Newnes Ltd., who had been publishing smaller one-volume works for some ten years before. Under the editorship of Margaret D. Law, the work was thoroughly revised and a completely new edition in 15 volumes was launched in 1950, and this was followed by revised editions in 1955 and 1959. Mrs. Law relinquished her position in 1963 and was succeeded by M. Vibart Dixon. The present editor is M. G. de St. V. Atkins. Unlike most of the major encyclopedias *Chambers's* was not, in recent years, published annually or at frequent intervals under a policy of continuous revision. Instead, the publishers adopted a program of complete revision at intervals of approximately five years, and issued both loose leaf supplements at the end of each volume, and the excellent *Chambers's Encyclopaedia World Survey*, first published in 1952. This supplement was issued at intervals of approximately two years until 1959, when it took on the frequency of annual publication.

In 1966 the encyclopedia was acquired by the Pergamon Group of Companies based in Oxford, and when the new edition, extensively revised, was issued in 1966, it was published under the imprint of the Pergamon Press. For all practical purposes, however, the editorial work had been completed by the previous owners. Although it bore an imprint of 1966, the work of assembling the material must have taken some considerable time, as little of the material in the main body of the work was dated later than 1963. The new publishers have since announced their intention of revising the encyclopedia more frequently than in the past, and the possibility of a North American edition by 1970 has been mentioned.

Of interest also is the editorial activity of one of the original editors, John Merry Ross, who edited the *Globe Encyclopaedia* (1876–1881) and its successors, the *Students Encyclopaedia* (1883) and the *Illustrated Globe Encyclopaedia* (1890–1893), all of which may well have been greatly influenced by the larger work.

• References:

Collison.

Subscription Books Bulletin, April 1930; April 1951.

Booklist and Subscription Books Bulletin, December 15, 1956, January 1, 1968.

CHAMBERS'S INFORMATION FOR THE PEOPLE; a popular encyclopaedia. Philadelphia: J. B. Smith Co.; Edinburgh: W. & R. Chambers, 1857. 2v. 25cm. Editors: William Chambers (1800–1883) and Robert Chambers (1802–1871).

A forerunner of the much larger *Chambers's Encyclopaedia* of 1860–1868, this smaller work was probably derived from basically the same material, and provided the publishers with the experience needed to publish their major project. The bibliographic records indicate that the brothers had edited this work themselves and there is no doubt that they did take an active part in its compilation. The lion's share of the work, however, is probably more attributable to Andrew Findlater (1810–1885), the Scottish educator and one time headmaster of Gordon's Hospital at Aberdeen, who later edited the *Chambers's Encyclopaedia*. The smaller work, however, continued to exist separately and independently and further editions were published in 1858, 1860, 1874, and 1880, with publication simultaneously in the United States by the firms of J. B. Smith, J. L. Gibson and Lippincott.

THE CHAMPLIN ENCYCLOPEDIA. Chicago: Consolidated Book Publishers Inc., 1946. 12v. 23cm. Original Compiler: John Denison Champlin (1834–1915): Editor: Lincoln MacVeagh (b.1890).

This was not really an encyclopedia, even in a very general sense, but a collection of hitherto separate works first published in the late nineteenth century and brought together as an encyclopedic set for commercial purposes in 1946.

Volumes 1 and 2 contained information on persons, volumes 3 and 4 on places and events, volumes 5 and 6 on literature, art and mythology, volumes 7 and 8 on plants and animals and volumes 9–12 dealt with science and invention. No index was provided, which certainly obviated whatever value the work might otherwise have had.

The separate works had first been brought together in 1924 as the *New Champlin Cyclopedia for Young Folks*, in optional six- and twelve-volume sets, under the editorship of Lincoln MacVeagh, and although these were quite extensively revised from the various books published between 1863 and 1905, it was a poor source of reference. The publishers issued reprints in 1947 and 1950, but it has since gone out of print.

• Reference:

Subscription Books Bulletin, July 1948.

CHANDLER'S ENCYCLOPEDIA; an epitome of universal knowledge, with contributions from a large number of eminent scientists. Illustrated by colored maps and engravings. New York: P. F. Collier, 1898. 3v. 29cm. Editor: William Henry Chandler (1841–1906).

This is the first of several encyclopedias to be published under the well-known Collier imprint. The work was published once only under this title and must have had a very limited success. The compiler is recorded as the editor of one other encyclopedic publication, the *New Complete Condensed Encyclopedia* and, as this was issued several years after his death, it is, in all probability, a reprinting of the earlier work.

CHILDREN'S BRITANNICA. London: Encyclopaedia Britannica, 1960–1961. 12v. 25cm. Editor: John Armitage.

This is quite a different publication from the *Britannica Junior,* although the two works have a common purpose in that both are designed for younger children not yet capable of coping with the much more advanced *Encyclopaedia Britannica.* In style and presentation, and even to some extent in appearance, the two works have similarities, but these apart, the *Children's Britannica* is predominantly British, whereas the *Britannica Junior* is specifically American. Although perhaps expensive in relation to similar encyclopedias designed for British school children, this is an excellent work, accurate, attractive and well produced. A yearbook has been available to supplement the work since 1961. The editor, John Armitage, is also the London editor of the *Encyclopaedia Britannica.*

• Reference:
Library Association Record, October 1961.

THE CHILDREN'S ENCYCLOPAEDIA. London: The Amalgamated Press, 1908–1910. 8v. 25cm. Editor: Arthur Mee (1875–1943).

Undoubtedly, the most successful and most loved of any encyclopedia for children published in Britain. It commenced publication in serial form in 1908 and met such a need, it was immediately reprinted in book form in 1910. It was successful not only in Britain but in other English-speaking countries, and by 1912 arrangements had been made to publish it in the United States as the *Book of Knowledge* which, like its British counterpart, won wide and immediate acceptance with children and parents. Both works are still in existence and retain their popularity seemingly without any sign of this diminishing over the years, although it should be noted that the *Book of Knowledge* developed independently and has long since shed its British origins.

Arthur Mee's *Children's Encyclopaedia* has been published steadily for more than fifty years. Unfortunately, few of the printings appear to have been recorded. The Library of Congress, for example, lists only the 1925 edition in ten volumes and another edition in 1953, although the 1960 printing, under the imprint of the Waverley Book Co. is described as the 28th edition. From the evidence available, it appears that the work has also been published under alternative titles from time to time, such as the *Harmsworth's Children's Encyclopaedia,* and *Mee's Children's Encyclopaedia.*

Although acquired by the Grolier Society Ltd. in 1963, it appears that, like the American *Book of Knowledge* it has served its purpose. It is now so outmoded in design and content that it is being gradually phased out of existence, and will not be available after 1970.

• Reference:
Library Association Record, October 1961.

THE CHILDREN'S ENCYCLOPEDIA. Illustrated by Hamilton Greene. New York: A. S. Barnes, 1959. 1147p. 26cm. Editor: Chandler Whipple.

Not to be confused with the multi-volume British *Children's Encyclopaedia*, this is a small one-volume work of somewhat indifferent quality, containing some 3,000 entries. Large, heavy, awkward and badly produced, its in-print existence was very brief.

CHILDREN'S EVERYTHING WITHIN; a complete library of knowledge and good reading for boys and girls. London: George Newnes Ltd., 1939. 608p. 22cm. Compiler: Arthur Courland Marshall.

A small one-volume work, abridged from *Newnes Golden Treasury* (1933), and *Newnes Everything Within* (1933), but simplified for children. All three titles were compiled by Marshall and published by Newnes.

CHILDREN'S GUIDE TO KNOWLEDGE (British); an account of the story of man—what he has found out about life, himself and his surroundings and the things he has achieved in science and the arts. London: Odhams Press, 1949. 512p. 23cm. Advisory Editor: William Tom Williams (b.1884).

One of a large number of one-volume encyclopedias for children published by Odhams Press since 1932. Attractive enough, and popular for casual browsing, but of very limited reference usefulness. A work with an identical title was published in New York in 1957, but there is no evidence that the works are in any way connected.

CHILDREN'S GUIDE TO KNOWLEDGE (American); New York: Published for the Parents Institute by special arrangement with Stravon Publishers, 1957. 258p. 26cm.

Not related to the British work of the same title, this is a very small and simple one-volume handbook of general knowledge for children, topically arranged.

CHILDREN'S HOME EDUCATOR AND TREASURY OF KNOWLEDGE; a new and enlarged edition of the "Treasury of Knowledge", with illustrations and plates. London: Waverley Book Co., 1936. 2v. (912p.) 22 cm. Editor: Arthur William Holland.

A search of the extant bibliographies failed to reveal an earlier edition of this work as the *Treasury of Knowledge* in recent times. It is, however, possibly a revision of *Maunder's Treasury of Knowledge and Library of Reference*, first published in two volumes in 1830 and reprinted at intervals up to 1873.

CHILDREN'S ILLUSTRATED ENCYCLOPEDIA OF GENERAL KNOWLEDGE; a reference book and school companion for boys and girls. New York: Philosophical Library, 1957. 480p. 22cm.

Although with an American imprint, this is actually a British publication. It had previously been distributed in the United States as the *Encyclopedia for Boys and Girls* in 1944, with S. Johnson as editor, and is a reprint of one of the many similar one-volume encyclopedias for children published by Odhams Press, London.

CHILDREN'S PICTORIAL ENCYCLOPEDIA. New York: W. H. Wise, 1948. 630p. 26cm. Advisory Editor: Henry B. Gilbert.

A small and unimportant one-volume work for children, perhaps derived from similar British works.

CHILD'S FIRST ENCYCLOPAEDIA. London: Odhams Press, 1964. 6v. 24cm.

Apparently a new work by the publishers, although possibly derived from the eight-volume *Modern Encyclopaedia*, published by Odhams in 1961. One of the most active organisations in encyclopedia publishing, Odhams are credited with more than 20 different titles, although several of them are undoubtedly identical reprints, retitled for sales purposes.

CIRCLE OF KNOWLEDGE; essential facts of everyday interest in nature, geography, history, travel, government, science, invention, education, language, literature, fine arts, philosophy, religion, industry, biography, human culture and universal progress. Easy to read, easy to understand, easy to retain. Chicago: John A. Hertel Co., 1934. 1103p. 25cm. Editor in Chief: Henry Woldmar Ruoff (1867–1935).

A topically arranged one-volume handbook of general information, supplemented by a detailed index. In itself, the work was of relatively poor quality, especially in competition with the similarly arranged *Lincoln Library of Essential Information*, a far superior compilation.

According to one authority, the *Circle of Knowledge* was in existence in 1928, at which time it was being issued by the American Educational Association, who were probably also the publishers of the *Volume Library*, another very similar work. Ruoff, many years earlier, had edited the *Century Book of Facts* (afterwards the *New Century Book of Facts*); the *Volume Library* (now *Cowles Comprehensive Encyclopedia*) and the *Standard Dictionary of Facts*, a work which preceded and probably influenced the *Lincoln Library* of later years. Of interest is the striking similarity between all these titles. Ruoff had been associated, directly or indirectly, with all of these, and it is not without significance that three of them are still in existence.

• Reference:
Subscription Books Bulletin, January 1930.

THE CLEAR TYPE ENCYCLOPAEDIA. London and Glasgow: Collins, 1935. 316p. 22cm. Editors: John Maxey Parrish and John Redgwick Crossland (b.1892).

Yet another of the many small, inexpensive encyclopedias of general knowledge for children published in Britain. This work has been published under a number of different titles, e.g., *Laurel and Gold Encyclopaedia* (1935) and the *Standard Encyclopaedia* (1937), while variations of it have appeared as the *New Gem Encyclopaedia* (1935) and *An Encyclopaedia of General Knowledge* (1938). Parrish and Crossland have also jointly edited several other larger works from which the *Clear Type Encyclopaedia* undoubtedly evolved.

COLLIER'S ENCYCLOPEDIA; New York: Collier, 1949–1951. 20v. 28cm. Editorial Director: Frank Webster Price (b.1901); Editor in Chief: Charles Patrick Barry (b.1902); Advisory Editor and Library Consultant: Louis Shores.

One of the major encyclopedias in the English-speaking world, *Collier's Encyclopedia* was a completely new project when it commenced publication in 1949, and was an entirely different work from earlier encyclopedias published by Collier from 1902 to 1950; *Collier's New Encyclopedia* (1902–1929) and the *National Encyclopedia* (1932–1950). The new work was several years in the making and its development was aided inestimably by the foresight of the president of the P. F. Collier Co. in seeking the advice of the American Library Association in the fashioning of the encyclopedia. Acting upon their advice, Collier's appointed Dr. Louis Shores, librarian and authority on reference books, as advisory editor.

Successful from the outset, *Collier's Encyclopedia* immediately won an international reputation for scholarship, reliability and readability, and it rightly ranks today as one of the foremost encyclopedias in the world.

Operating under the now almost universally adopted system of continuous revision, the encyclopedia has been published annually, with frequent interim printings, since the completion of the initial edition in 1951. Of the original editorial staff, neither Barry nor Price are now associated with the work. William Terry Couch (b.1901) replaced Barry as editor in chief from 1951 to 1960, and Dr. Shores became the editor in chief as well as library consultant.

About 1960, another important editorial change took place. William D. Halsey was appointed editorial director. Halsey was a well-known and experienced editor who had earlier, in collaboration with Clarence D. Barnhardt, compiled the invaluable *New Century Cyclopaedia of Names.* Under the direction of these two authorities, *Collier's Encyclopedia* was thoroughly revised and expanded to 24 volumes with the edition of 1962.

The present-day *Collier's* contains almost 20,000 pages and almost as many illustrations and maps. In number of words it ranks third in size, only the *Encyclopaedia Britannica* and the *Encyclopedia Americana* being larger. Two especially notable features of the work are its enormously detailed index of more than 400,000 entries (the largest of its kind), and its excellent classified bibliography of some 12,000 titles, citing films and other materials as well as books, which is valuable as a selective buying guide and a course of reading and study. A particularly fine yearbook, *Collier's Encyclopedia Yearbook*, was available as an updating supplement, even before completion of the first edition, which is particularly useful for its inclusion of a survey of research in progress. At the time of writing, basically the same editorial staff, under the direction of William Halsey, are engaged in the compilation of a new junior encyclopedia.

• **References:**
Collison.
Subscription Books Bulletin, July 1950; July 1952.
Booklist and Subscription Books Bulletin, December 15, 1959; February 15, 1963.

COLLIER'S NEW ENCYCLOPEDIA; an entirely new and original work containing a greater number of titles than any other similar compendium, with articles by over 300 contributors. New York: Collier, 1902. 16v. 25cm.

Despite its similarity of title, this is in no way connected, except in an ancestral sense, with *Collier's Encyclopedia* (1949) a larger and superior work also published by Collier. *Collier's New Encyclopedia*, although never one of the front ranking encyclopedias, enjoyed a fair measure of popularity and remained in existence for almost 30 years. From 1902 the work was reprinted frequently, but it was not until about 1921 that it appeared to undergo extensive revision, when it was issued in 10 volumes, and with a new subtitling "a loose-leaf and self revising reference work". Further editions were published in 1926 and 1928, with a terminal edition in 1929, when a supplemental 64-page question manual for home study was also provided.

Rather oddly, no editors could be found listed for any editions of the work, but it may well have been compiled initially under the editorship of Henry Mitchell McCracken (1840–1918) who had edited the ten-volume *University Encyclopedia of Twentieth Century Knowledge*, also published in 1902 under the Collier imprint, and possibly the same work. Since 1905 the encyclopedia had been supplemented by *Collier's Self Indexing Annual* but after 1921, this service appears to have been incorporated into the main work as an integral part of the loose leaf revision service. No further editions of the work were published after 1959 and it was replaced in 1932 by the *National Encyclopedia*.

• Reference:

Subscription Books Bulletin, January 1931.

COLLINS CONCISE ENCYCLOPAEDIA *see* CONCISE ENCYCLOPAEDIA

COLLINS NEW AGE ENCYCLOPAEDIA *see* NEW AGE ENCYCLOPAEDIA

COLUMBIA ENCYCLOPEDIA; compiled and edited at Columbia University. New York: Columbia University Press, 1935. 1949p. 31cm. Editor in Chief: Clarke Fisher Ansley (1869–1939).

From the year of its first publication this magnificent work has been universally regarded as the definitive one-volume encyclopedia in the English language. Unlike most major encyclopedias, it is not published annually under a policy of continuous revision, but is completely revised at intervals of approximately 15 years, although updating supplements are issued in the interim to keep the preceding edition relatively up to date.

The work was reprinted in 1936, 1937, 1938 and 1940, in which year it incorporated a supplement of events covering the period, 1935–1939. Further printings were issued in 1942, 1944 and 1946, each incorporating supplements, but also available separately for the convenience of purchasers of earlier editions. A second edition, completely revised and expanded to 2203 pages was issued in 1950 under the editorship of William Bridgwater and Elizabeth J. Sherwood, and reprints of this, incorporating supplements, were issued in 1953, 1956 and 1959. The third and present edition was published in 1963, again under the editorial direction of William Bridgwater, whose co-editor was now Seymour Kurtz.

Special versions of the second and third editions were published in five volumes by the Parents Magazine Educational Press. These multi-volume editions differed only from the regular version in that additional illustrative material was included.

The *Columbia Encyclopedia* is an amazingly compact work and a very scholarly and successful attempt to bridge the gap between the large learned encyclopedias and the smaller more popular family works. A particularly notable feature of the work is the extensiveness of its bibliographical references, the third edition citing some 40,000 titles. The present edition, containing some 7½ million words and some 75,000 entries, is larger than many multi-volume works.

An abridged version of this excellent work, compiled by the same editorial staff, has been published by the Viking Press as the *Columbia-Viking Desk Encyclopedia*.

• References:

Subscription Books Bulletin, October 1935; January 1939; January 1947; July 1951.

Booklist and Subscription Books Bulletin, October 1, 1959; May 15, 1964.

THE COLUMBIA ENCYCLOPEDIA OF USEFUL KNOWLEDGE, by Marshall Everett (*pseud.*) . . . showing the newest and most wonderful inventions and the world's great progress in science and commerce. Chicago: Columbia House, 1907. 336p. 24cm. Compiler: Henry Neil (b.1863).

Little better than a hack work, this very small and unimportant work bears no relation to the authoritative *Columbia Encyclopedia* (1935), nor to the Columbia University Press. It had previously been published as *Everett's Encyclopedia of Useful Knowledge* in 1905 and was subsequently re-issued as the *American Home Encyclopedia of Useful Knowledge* in 1908.

COLUMBIA-VIKING DESK ENCYCLOPEDIA; compiled and edited at Columbia University by the staff of the "Columbia Encyclopedia". New York: Viking Press, 1953. 1092p. 27cm. Editor in Chief: William Bridgwater.

An extremely well-edited, condensed version of the second edition of the *Columbia Encyclopedia* (1950), containing, in some 31,000 entries and 1½ million words, basic essential information for home, student, and office use.

Revised editions were issued in 1954 and 1960, both in regular trade editions and special editions for book clubs. In 1965, it was issued in an inexpensive paperback edition, which represents quite a remarkable value, although some of the information had, by that time, become dated. A new edition, based on the third edition of the *Columbia Encyclopedia* (1963) is in preparation.

• References:
Subscription Books Bulletin, April 1954.
Booklist and Subscription Books Bulletin, February 15, 1961.

COLUMBIAN CYCLOPAEDIA. New York: Funk and Wagnalls, 1899. 39v. 18cm. Editor: Richard Gleason Greene (1829–1914).

Several encyclopedias have been published under the Funk and Wagnalls imprint during the past century, but the first of these was the *Columbian Cyclopaedia*, the only recorded entry for which is contained in the *American Catalogue* of 1895–1900. The work appears to have consisted of 38 volumes of text, as the last volume is recorded as being a world atlas.

As no copies of the work could be found for a physical examination, no firm tracing of its history is possible. Of interest, however, and perhaps of significance, is the fact that the editor, Richard Gleason Greene, is also listed as the editor, in 1906, of the *New Imperial Encyclopedia and Dictionary,* which had previously been published in 1903 as the *Imperial Encyclopedia and Dictionary*. Subsequently, in 1909, these latter titles were re-issued as the *United Editors Encyclopedia and Dictionary* and again in 1911 as the *United Editors Perpetual Encyclopedia*, this last title being in 30 volumes as against the 40 volumes of all the previous titles. It is unfortunate that this work was not available for examination as it may well have solved a complicated situation in respect of all these titles.

THE COMPACT ENCYCLOPAEDIA. London: Gresham Publishing Co., 1927. 6v. 22cm. Editors: Richard Ferrer Patterson (b.1888) and John Dougall.

An abridged and revised edition of the *New Gresham Encyclopedia* (1921–1924), edited by two of the three original editors of the earlier work, and compressed to approximately half the size of its 12-volume predecessor. This was the last encyclopedia to bear the Gresham imprint. Several years earlier they had published the *New Popular Encyclopaedia* (1901) and the *Modern Cyclopaedia* (1906–1907). Another abridgement of the work was published by Collins in 1933 as the *Concise Encyclopaedia*.

THE COMPLETE DICTIONARY OF ARTS AND SCIENCES, in which the whole circle of human learning is explained, and the difficulties attending the acquisition of every art, whether liberal or mechanical, are removed, in the most easy and familiar manner. The theological, philological, and critical branches by the Rev. Temple Henry Croker . . . The medicinal, anatomical, and chemical, by Thomas Williams . . . The mathematical by Samuel Clark . . . and the other parts by several gentlemen particularly conversant in the arts and sciences they have undertaken to explain. Coventry: John Jones, 1764–1766. One large folio volume. Compilers: Temple Henry Croker (1730–c.1790) Thomas Williams, Samuel Clark.

To a large extent, this curious work is a plagiarization of the famous *Cyclopaedia* of Ephraim Chambers, and this is almost openly admitted in the preface to the work. The work is unusual, also, in that it was the first encyclopedia to be published in an English province, although there was, at that time, a flourishing publishing business in Coventry. Beginning in April 1765, the work was issued in 150 parts of three sheets each and when completed comprised some 450 large folio sheets bound into one volume.

The chief editor, Temple Henry Croker, was at one time Chaplain to the Earl of Hillsborough. He afterwards became engaged in commerce with a conspicuous lack of success, filed papers in bankruptcy, emigrated to the West Indies and died there about 1790 in obscurity.

• Reference:
Collison.

COMPLETE LIBRARY OF UNIVERSAL KNOWLEDGE . . . showing the newest conditions of industry, commerce, invention, science, art, literature, philsosophy, etc. Chicago: Monarch Pub. Co., 1904. 702p. 24cm. Editor in Chief: Ferdinand Ellsworth Cary (b.1848).

A poorly produced one-volume handbook of general information published simultaneously as the *New Idea Self Instructor* (1904). It was re-issued several years later in a revised and enlarged edition as the *Knowledge Book* (1915) the *Knowledge Library* (1918) and the *New Knowledge Library* (1919).

THE COMPLETE REFERENCE HANDBOOK; basic knowledge for home, school and office. New York: Stravon Publishers, 1964. 720p. 27cm. Editors: Frank Alweis and others.

A small one-volume handbook of miscellaneous and practical information, providing historical and factual material on the United States, the United Nations, philosophy, religion, art, grammar and other subjects.

THE COMPREHENSIVE PICTORIAL ENCYCLOPEDIA; new edition, with 32 pages of illustrations and maps in full color. Cleveland and New York: World Publishing Co., 1942. 1262p. 24cm. Editor in Chief: Nella Braddy Henney (b.1894).

With only minor revisions, this is a reprint of a work first published in the United States in 1934, as *Facts*, by Doubleday, Doran & Co., and this was itself probably adapted from a British work, *Routledge's Universal Encyclopaedia*, also published in 1934. It had previously been published in a one-volume format as the *New Concise Pictorial Encyclopedia* in 1938. Subsequently, under the imprint of another publisher, it was re-issued in four volumes as the *World Home Reference Encyclopedia* in 1951.

Originally, the work was a quite useful compilation of brief factual information, but lack of revision quickly led to it being regarded as unreliable, and its success was even further obviated by the practice of issuing it under different titles.

COMPTON'S PICTURED ENCYCLOPEDIA . . . to inspire ambition, to stimulate the imagination, to provide the inquiring mind with accurate information told in an interesting style, and thus lead into broader fields of knowledge, such is the purpose of this work. Chicago: F. E. Compton & Co., 1922. 8v. 26cm. Editor in Chief: Guy Stanton Ford (b.1873).

One of the two leading encyclopedias for children published in the United States, *Compton's Pictured Encyclopedia* was first published in an eight-volume format in 1922, five years after the successful launching of its nearest rival, the *World Book Encyclopedia*. The work was immediately successful, and in the edition of 1924 it was expanded to 10 volumes, and by 1932 had grown to its present size of 15 volumes.

Like most major encyclopedias, the work is published annually under a policy of continuous revision and, under a vigorous team of editors, it has improved continuously over the years. It differs from its old rival, the *World Book Encyclopedia*, in that *Compton's* presents its information in much longer articles, relying on an index to pinpoint more specific information. *Compton's* also includes briefer entries in its "Fact-Index", a feature in which it has pioneered. The *World Book*, on the other hand, includes all its entries, brief and detailed in one alphabetical arrangement, as do most encyclopedias, and more nearly approaches the concept of an adult encyclopedia. Both works have their merits and their advocates, however, and libraries, at least, seem to prefer to have both works available for their patrons. *Compton's* has pioneered in several areas of encyclopedia publishing, and two particularly praiseworthy features are (a) its now quite widely imitated "Fact-Index" which incorporates brief dictionary type entries and tables into the general index and (b) the unit letter system of arrangement, in which all the entries for one or more letters of the alphabet are contained in one volume.

Changes in the work since its commencement have been relatively few. Guy Stanton Ford remained as editor in chief until 1961, and he was succeeded by Charles Alfred Ford, who, in turn, was succeeded by Donald Lawson in 1964. In 1962, however, a major change took place when the F. E. Compton Co. was acquired by Encyclopaedia Britannica Inc., and, although it continues under the older name, F. E. Compton is now a subsidiary and a part of the Encyclopaedia Britannica group of publications. *Compton's Pictured Encyclopedia* (the words "and Fact-Index" were added in 1940), was an entirely new project when it was first published in 1922 after several years of preparation.

It is of interest, however, to note that this was by no means the first encyclopedic work to be published by F. E. Compton, a well-known American educationalist. From 1909 to 1920, he had published the useful five-volume *New Students Reference Work*, and this, along with another publication entitled *Pictured Knowledge* (1916), must certainly have provided the basic experience and material from which the new work emerged.

A thoroughly good encyclopedia, *Compton's* has always been one of the first choices as an encyclopedia for children, and its bibliographies, divided into books for younger, more advanced readers, and teachers and parents, are of exceptional usefulness. Currently, the work is supplemented by the *Compton Yearbook*, but in the earlier years of its existence, the supplements were published monthly as *Compton's Pictured Newspaper*.

When first published in 1922, *Compton's* was published simultaneously in Britain as the *Book of Knowledge* or *Cassell's Book of Knowledge*. The present day editions of the two works are not the same, although the *Book of Knowledge*, now published by the Grolier Society, bears a striking resemblance to earlier editions of *Compton's*. The title page of the British publication still carries the wording "To inspire ambition, to stimulate the imagination . . ." which appeared on the original editions of *Compton's*.

• References:

Subscription Books Bulletin, October 1932; January 1935; July 1939; October 1943; October 1947; January 1953.
Booklist and Subscription Books Bulletin, April 15, 1959; October 15, 1963.

CONCISE ENCYCLOPAEDIA; with an introduction by Cyril Norwood. London: Collins, 1933. 10v. 22cm. Editor: John Maxey Parrish.

This is a revised edition of the *New Gresham Encyclopedia* (1921–1924), and the *Compact Encyclopaedia* (1927) both issued under the imprint of the Gresham Publishing Co. Containing brief, unsigned articles, the work was mediocre in quality and compared poorly with the new edition of *Everyman's Encyclopaedia* also published in 1932. The firm of Odhams issued the *British Encyclopedia* in ten volumes in 1933, which appears to be identical to this work.

• Reference:
Subscription Books Bulletin, April 1935.

THE CONCISE ENCYCLOPEDIA; a library of world knowledge, complete in 8 volumes; illustrated with nearly 1,200 drawings, 250 half tones, 64 maps and 8 lithographs, made expressly for this work. New York: W. H. Wise & Co., 1937. 8v. 22cm. Editor: Alexander Hopkins McDannald (1877–1948).

This very useful little encyclopedia, containing brief but pertinent information on some 25,000 subjects, had previously been issued as the *Modern Encyclopedia* (1933–1937) in a one-volume format, but with less entries. The original work had been compiled by the staff of the *Encyclopedia Americana*, under the supervision of McDannald, who was then the editor in chief of the larger work.

In 1940, the work, in a 15-volume edition, re-appeared under the imprint of the Unicorn Press, and this was sold through supermarkets at 70¢ per volume on a weekly basis. Reverting back to its original one-volume format, the work was then re-published by Wise as the *New Modern Encyclopedia*, with Frank Webster Price (b.1901) as general editor. The last printing of this, at one time useful desk encyclopedia, is recorded as 1949.

• Reference:
Subscription Books Bulletin, October 1937.

THE CONCISE POCKET ENCYCLOPAEDIA. London: Asprey & Co., 1925. 718p. 17cm. Revision Editor: Warwick Wyatt Crouch.

A very small pocket-sized work, with dictionary type entries. It is probably a revision of the *Pocket Encyclopaedia*, first published by Sampson, Low in 1888.

CONCISE UNIVERSAL ENCYCLOPAEDIA. London: Amalgamated Press, 1930–1931. 1458p. 25cm. Editor: Sir John Alexander Hammerton (1871–1949).

A condensed version of *Harmsworth's Universal Encyclopaedia*, a nine-volume work first issued in 1920, which was itself derived from a much earlier work. Sir John Hammerton is credited with the editorship of several other works, some of which are probably re-issues or revisions of the *Concise Universal Encyclopaedia*.

CONSOLIDATED ENCYCLOPEDIA. London and Toronto: Consolidated World Research Society, 1939. 10v. 24cm.

The copyright to this work is held by the Standard Education Society, who are the publishers of the *New Standard Encyclopedia*. Except for some minor changes to meet the needs of English and Commonwealth users, the material appears to be identical. Not too well done, no further editions have been recorded since 1939.

CONSOLIDATED WEBSTER COMPREHENSIVE ENCYCLOPEDIC DICTIONARY; a library of essential knowledge. Chicago: Consolidated Book Publishers, 1954. 1600p. 26cm. Editor in Chief: Franklin Julius Meine (b.1896).

Not a true encyclopedia but a miscellany of general information derived from a variety of other publications, including material from *Webster's Enclopedic Dictionary* (1941–1942), *Webster's Columbia Concise Dictionary* (1939), the *Modern Family Garden Book* (1935) and a work entitled the *Theory and Practice of Photography*. The work had previously been published as the *Webster's Comprehensive Encyclopedic Dictionary* (1941), and the *Library of Essential Knowledge* (1942), this latter title being re-issued in 1954.

The work was poorly produced and badly arranged in 13 separate sections, but without either an index or a table of contents. In abridged versions, by omitting one or more of the sections, it has also been issued as the *Consolidated Webster Encyclopedic Dictionary* (1954), *Webster's Columbia Encyclopedic Dictionary* (1940) and *Webster's Encyclopedic Dictionary* (1941).

• Reference:
Subscription Books Bulletin, December 15, 1957.

CONSOLIDATED WEBSTER ENCYCLOPEDIC DICTIONARY; a library of essential knowledge. Chicago: Consolidated Book Publishers, 1954. 1400p. 26cm. Editor in Chief: Franklin Julius Meine (b.1896).

An abridged version of the *Consolidated Webster Comprehensive Encyclopedic Dictionary* (1954). First published in 1940 as *Webster's Columbia Encyclopedic Dictionary*.

CONTINENTAL ENCYCLOPEDIA; a reference library of universal knowledge, embracing over 400 illustrations and over 65,000 subjects, all brought down to date of publication. New York: The Success Co., 1905. 8v. 19cm. Editor: Charles Leonard Stuart (b.1868).

The claim of this work to treat over 65,000 subjects is more readily accepted when it is realized that volumes 7 and 8 comprise a dictionary of the English language, the entries of which are undoubtedly claimed in the count.

In fact, this work is a re-issue of the five-volume *Crown Encyclopedia and*

Gazetteer, first published in 1903, under the imprint of the Christian Herald. In 1908, it was re-issued as the *New Century Reference Library* in an identical eight-volume format. Stuart was afterwards the joint editor of the *Current Cyclopedia of Reference* (1909), *Everybody's Cyclopedia* (1911) and the *People's Cyclopedia* (1914), all of which are directly related to the *Continental Encyclopedia.*

CONVERSATIONS-LEXICON (Brockhaus) *see* BRITISH CYCLOPAEDIA OF ARTS AND SCIENCES, CHAMBERS'S ENCYCLOPAEDIA, ENCYCLOPAEDIA AMERICANA

COWLES COMPREHENSIVE ENCYCLOPEDIA—THE VOLUME LIBRARY. New York: Cowles Educational Books, 1963. 2425p. 24cm. Editor: Benedict A. Leerburger, Jr.

A one-volume handbook of general information which originated as the *Volume Library* in 1911, and last published under that title in 1962, when it was acquired by the present publishers, thoroughly revised and re-titled with the edition of 1963. Although the work has been in existence for more than 50 years, it has never achieved the success of the work it most closely resembles, the *Lincoln Library of Essential Information.* Since being acquired by Cowles, however, it has been extensively revised and vastly improved over earlier editions.

The arrangement of the work is topical and is, in effect, a condensation of several texts on different subjects into one volume.

CROWN ENCYCLOPEDIA AND GAZETTEER; a reference library of universal knowledge, embracing 500 illustrations and over 65,000 subjects, all brought down to the date of publication . . . with 96 colored maps. New York: Christian Herald, 1903. 5v. 18cm. Editor: Charles Leonard Stuart (b.1868).

This work was first copyrighted in 1903 and apparently has no pre-history, although in view of later developments, this is an assumption which is open to some doubt. The claim of the publishers to include 65,000 subjects in the work appears to be extravagant in view of the relatively small size of the set, and this could only be achieved if the entries were of a very brief dictionary-type nature. The encyclopedia, with the addition of a two-volume dictionary, was issued in eight volumes in 1905 as the *Continental Encyclopedia,* under the imprint of the Success Co., and this same arrangement was repeated when the work was issued under yet another title, the *New Century Reference Library,* in 1907, by a Philadelphia-based publisher.

Charles Stuart was afterwards listed as joint editor of the *Current Cyclopedia of Reference* (1909), the *Everybody's Cyclopedia* (1911) and the *People's Cyclopedia* (1914). This latter title was re-published as the *New World Wide Cyclopedia* (1918), and this was once again under the imprint of Christian Herald, which was re-issued by another publisher in 1928 and afterwards became, in turn, the *Times Encyclopedia and Gazetteer*, the *Twentieth Century Encyclopedia* and the *World's Popular Encyclopedia*. Most of the titles appeared under the imprint of the Syndicate or World Syndicate Publishing Co., with whom the Christian Herald was evidently closely associated.

THE CULTURAL LIBRARY. New York: Parents Magazine Educational Press, 1965. 10v. 26cm. Editor: George Dinsmore Stoddard (b.1897).

This is the recently adopted title of a work which had first been published from 1914 to 1931 as *Our Wonder World*, and which subsequently became the *New Wonder World* (1932–1958), the *New Wonder World Encyclopedia* (1959–1961) and the *New Wonder World Cultural Library* (1962–1964). From 1914 to 1958 the work had been published by the George L. Shuman Co., but was acquired by Parents Magazine in the latter year, considerably revised and re-issued in a changed format in 1959.

The work is a topically arranged compilation of general knowledge and, until recently at least, has enjoyed a fair measure of success and endorsement.

CURRENT CYCLOPEDIA OF REFERENCE. New York: Syndicate Publishing Co., 1909. 8v. 20cm. Editors: Charles Leonard Stuart (b.1868) and Charles Smith Morris (1833–1922).

While the origins of this work, one of the many poor encyclopedias published at the turn of the century, are clouded by the switching of titles, editors and publishers, there can be little doubt that it is directly descended from the *Crown Encyclopedia and Gazetteer* (1903), the *Continental Encyclopedia* (1905), and the *New Century Reference Library* (1907), all of which were edited by Stuart, although appearing under the imprints of different publishers or distributors. The work was afterwards evidently continued as the *Everybody's Cyclopedia* (1911) and the *People's Cyclopedia* (1914), edited jointly by Stuart and George Jotham Hagar for the Syndicate Co., and these were followed by several other titles culminating with the *World's Popular Encyclopedia* in 1942.

It is doubtful if Charles Morris, who is known to have edited several other encyclopedias for the Syndicate Publishing Co., had any real hand in this work, and his name was probably used by the publishers for prestige and sales purposes.

THE CURRENT ENCYCLOPEDIA; a monthly record of human progress, containing the latest information on history, science, philosophy, literature, legislation, politics, industry, religion, education, art, etc., prepared by a national staff of contributors. Chicago: Modern Research Society and Current Cyclopedia Co., 1901–19?? 2v. 27cm. Editors: Samuel Fallows (1835–1922) and Edmund Buckley.

One of the earliest attempts to publish an encyclopedia in the form of a monthly publication, the whole accumulating into a series of yearbooks or bound volumes. The effort was evidently short-lived and only two volumes, covering the period from July, 1901 to April, 1902 are recorded under this title. It is believed, however, that a work called *Progress* was merged with the *Current Encyclopedia* and the publication continued as *The World Today*. One of the editors, Samuel Fallows, later edited the *Human Interest Library*, a topically arranged work for children, in 1914.

CYCLOPAEDIA: or, An universal dictionary of arts and sciences, containing an explication of the terms and an account of the things signified thereby in the several arts, liberal and mechanical, and the several sciences, human and divine, compiled from the best authors. London: James and John Knapton, 1728. 2v. 40cm. Compiler: Ephraim Chambers (c.1680–1740).

Although not the first true encyclopedia in the English language, this is certainly one of the most important and one of the most famous, not so much for its own qualities, but for the great influence it exerted upon the future development and making of encyclopedias. Chambers, a map reader by profession, was probably inspired by the *Lexicon Technicum* of John Harris some 25 years previously, but his *Cyclopaedia* considerably broadened the coverage of the *Lexicon Technicum* to include more of the humanities. A particularly notable feature of the new work was the elaborate and sometimes intricate system of cross references, an innovation of Chambers which was quickly adopted by other editors and publishers. The merit of the *Cyclopaedia* was immediately recognized by the leading scholars of the day and, as a result, Chambers was elected to membership in the Royal Society, in 1729, just one year after his work was first published.

A second edition was published in 1738 by the firm of D. Midwinter, who also published the third edition in 1739, the fourth in 1741 (Chambers had died in 1740) and the fifth in 1746. In 1742, the work was published in Dublin in a so-called fifth edition, although this was actually a pirated reprint of the fourth edition of 1741. So popular was the work, it was translated into Italian and published in a nine-volume edition in Venice in 1748–1749 as the *Dizionario Universale delle Arti e delle Scienze*, and this was revised and issued in a six-volume edition between 1762 and 1765.

Meanwhile, in London, a seventh edition was published by the firm of W. Innys in 1751–1752, and this was followed by a two-volume supplement in 1753. This latter was edited by a well-known and respected mathematician, George Lewis Scott (1708–1780), but it was severely criticized and rather harshly condemned by other scholars as worthless. It was not until 1778 that a further edition of the now aging *Cyclopaedia* was printed. This in a five-volume format, four of which contained textual material, the fifth containing plates and an index, was issued under the imprint of W. Strahan, London. The editor of this new five-volume edition was Abraham Rees (1743–1825) who incorporated the criticized supplements of Scott into the original compilation of Chambers under one alphabetical arrangement. In 1786–1788, a new edition was issued under the imprint of J. F. and C.

Rivington, containing a great deal of new material, and this was re-issued in 1788–1791.

Although the *Cyclopaedia* is now but a landmark in the history of encyclopedia publishing, its impact and influence upon later generations was incalculable. It directly influenced the famous French *Encyclopédie* of Diderot, and the *New Cyclopaedia* compiled by Abraham Rees and published between 1802 and 1820. Rees had, of course, edited the 1778 and subsequent editions of the *Cyclopaedia* and his new work was quite openly based upon and modelled on the work of Chambers. Less directly, the pioneering example of the *Cyclopaedia* stimulated the publication of the *Encyclopaedia Britannica* and many subsequent works.

The *Cyclopaedia* of Ephraim Chambers is sometimes confused with the modern *Chambers's Encyclopaedia,* but there is no connection whatsoever between these two fine works.

• Reference:
Collison.

CYCLOPEDIA, DICTIONARY AND ATLAS OF THE WORLD; a handbook of necessary information for teachers and students, and for home, school and office . . . illustrated with numerous engravings, charts and an atlas of the world, including a map of each state of the Union. Springfield: Hampden Publishing Co., 1909. 976p. 24cm. Editor in Chief: Charles Smith Morris (1833–1922).

A compendium of miscellaneous information, supplemented by a dictionary and an atlas. The work is an amplification of an earlier series of publications comprised in whole or in part of the encyclopedic material in this title. These are the *Popular Compendium of Useful Information,* the *Twentieth Century Cyclopedia of Practical Information* and the *World Encyclopedia* (all of which were published in 1901); the *Golden Treasury of Useful Information* and the *World's Best Knowledge and How to Use It,* both of which were published in 1902. Charles Morris edited all of these and other similar one-volume works.

DAILY EXPRESS ENCYCLOPAEDIA; including 3,500 illustrations with atlas and gazetteer index. London: Daily Express Publications, 1934. 9v. 22cm.

A small, but quite useful encyclopedia, designed for low income families in the depression years. The set was obtained by clipping coupons from the *Daily Express* newspaper for a specified number of weeks; a form of subscription which was in vogue before the Second World War. The sets offered were usually of inferior quality.

It is unlikely that the *Daily Express Encyclopaedia* was an original compilation, but no record can be found of its publication under any other title.

A DICTIONARY OF ARTS AND SCIENCES. London, 1806–1807. 2v. Editor: Dr. George Gregory (1754–1808).

This publication is the result of a curious situation which arose at the beginning of the nineteenth century. Although Gregory is named as the editor of this work, he played little actual part in its compilation, primarily because of his involvement with cathedral duties as the Prebendary of St. Paul's.

The actual editing was done by a scholar by the name of Jeremiah Joyce who, at the same time, was editing the similar but somewhat larger *British Encyclopaedia,* a work which had been originally commissioned in opposition to Gregory's work. Thus, although the two works were bitter rivals, they were in fact compiled by the same anonymous editor. The *British Encyclopaedia* was the more successful commercially and no further editions of *A Dictionary of Arts and Sciences* were published.

• Reference:
Collison.

DICTIONARY OF SCIENCE, LITERATURE AND ART; comprising the history, description and scientific principles of every branch of human knowledge, with the derivation and definition of all the terms in general use. The various departments edited by eminent literary and scientific gentlemen. London: Longmans, 1842, New York: Harper & Bros., 1844. 1352p. 25cm. Editor in Chief: William Thomas Brande (1788–1866). Associate Editor: Joseph Cauvin.

In its day a highly successful one-volume encyclopedia of general, but scholarly information. Further printings of the work were made in 1845, 1847, 1848 and 1851, and a revised second edition, expanded to 1,423 pages, was published in 1852.

Upon the death of Brande in 1866, the work was reissued in three volumes, with Sir George William Cox (1827–1902) as assistant editor. A new and final edition was published in 1875 by Longmans.

DICTIONARY OF U.S. HISTORY *see* ENCYCLOPAEDIC DICTIONARY OF AMERICAN HISTORY

DICTIONARY OF UNIVERSAL INFORMATION *see* BEETON'S ENCYCLOPAEDIA OF UNIVERSAL INFORMATION

DOMINION EDUCATOR. Peace edition. Toronto: P. D. Palmer & Co., 1919. 8v. 24cm. Editors in Chief: James Laughlin Hughes (1846–1935) and Ellsworth Decatur Foster (1869–1936).

The Canadian edition of the *American Educator,* with the names of the editors reversed, and published under the imprint of the Canadian distributor of the work. In later years, to avoid the impression that the work was produced in Canada, the title was changed to the *New General Encyclopedia* (1935).

DOUBLEDAY'S ENCYCLOPEDIA; written by leading authorities in every branch of knowledge . . . containing many illustrations from all parts of the world. Garden City, N.Y.: Doubleday, Doran & Co., 1931. 10v. 24cm. Editor: Arthur Elmore Bostwick (1860–1942). Managing Editor: Asa Don Dickinson (b.1876). Associate Editor: Nella Braddy Henney (b.1894). Foreign Editor: Sir John Alexander Hammerton (1871–1949).

This is a thorough and successful American adaptation of the popular British *Harmsworth's Universal Encyclopaedia,* first published in 1920, but which was in itself based to some degree on *The Harmsworth Encyclopaedia* of 1905. The new work, however, contained several thousand new articles and omitted those least useful to American readers, and it had a particularly good index. It won immediate acceptance by librarians and educators as an "in between" set which could be used by both students and parents.

The editor in chief of the American edition was Arthur Elmore Bostwick, a well-known librarian, who had earlier been joint editor of *Appleton's New Practical Encyclopedia* (1910). Further editions of *Doubleday's Encyclopedia* were published in 1932, 1936 (with an expansion to 11 volumes), 1938, 1940, 1941 and 1943.

By 1940, however, the work had dropped out of favor due to an inadequate policy of revision and in 1943, the set was acquired by Grolier Inc., who re-issued it in 1944 as the *Grolier Encyclopedia,* under which title it was published until 1964, when it was discontinued.

Much of the encyclopedic material had, in the meantime, formed the major part of a work entitled the *Unified Encyclopedia* (1960–1964), which combined the entries from the *Grolier Encyclopedia* with longer, simplified articles from another Grolier publication, the *Richards Topical Encyclopedia.*

• References:
Subscription Books Bulletin, April 1931; July 1932; October 1940; January 1943.

EDINBURGH ENCYCLOPAEDIA; conducted by David Brewster . . . with the assistance of gentlemen eminent in science and literature. Edinburgh: Blackwood, 1808–1830. 18v. 24cm. Editor: Sir David Brewster (1781–1868).

Paradoxically, one of the most important and one of the least successful of the great British encyclopedias of the eighteenth and nineteenth centuries, the *Edinburgh Encyclopaedia* was noted for its excellent scientific articles, several of which were written by the editor, a great scientist in his own right. Originally, the work was intended to comprise 12 volumes but, with the increase in new discoveries in science, it eventually grew to 18 volumes, the first being issued in 1808, and the last in 1830.

The work was highly accurate, authoritative and, for its time, contemporary. More than 150 well-known authorities contributed to the originality and selectiveness of the articles. Like the *Encyclopaedia Britannica,* with which it compared favorably, it originated in Edinburgh, as did other great encyclopedias. Unlike the *Britannica,* however, it was not a successful commercial venture, and no further editions were printed of this worthy contribution to general knowledge.

• Reference:
Collison.

*ENCYCLOPAEDIA AMERICANA; a popular dictionary of arts, sciences, literature, history, politics and biography, brought down to the present time, including a copious collection of original articles on American biography, on the basis of the 7th edition of the German "Conversations-Lexicon". Philadelphia: Carey, Lea & Carey, 1829–1833. 13v. 23cm. Editor: Francis Lieber (1800–1872). Assistant Editors: Edward Wigglesworth (1804–1876), Thomas Gamaliel Bradford (1802–1887) and Henry Vethake (1792–1866).

Although the titles are identical, this work, the first encyclopedia to be compiled and published in the United States, is in no way connected with the *Encyclopaedia Americana* published by J. M. Stoddart between 1883 and 1889, which was a supplement to the American reprintings of the ninth edition of the *Encyclopaedia Britannica.*

The compiler of this original *Encyclopaedia Americana* was not himself an American, but a young German exile, who had earlier been associated in Germany with the Brockhaus *Conversations Lexicon.* Basing the new encyclopedia on the seventh edition of that great work, as would the Chambers brothers in 1860, Lieber adapted it to American requirements most successfully. Reprints and revisions of the work, which had won immediate acceptance, appeared in 1835 and 1836, and in 1838 a new edition was published under the imprint of Thomas, Cowperthwaite & Co., and reprints and revisions of this were issued in 1848, 1849, 1858 and later. Additionally, in 1848, a supplementary volume, edited by Henry Vethake, was issued, increasing the set to 14 volumes. But in the latter half of the century, with all the original editors dead, the work lapsed and remained out of print for several years.

It was not until the very end of the century that interest in the original work was revived, and determined efforts were made to bring it back into print. A completely new edition, based upon, but largely remodelled from Lieber's work, was planned. This was published in 1902 under the imprint

* NOTE: For ease of reference and arrangement, titles beginning with the words "Encyclopaedia" and "Encyclopedia" are listed as though both were spelled in the same manner.

of R. S. Peale & Co., who had earlier been associated with a pirated reprint of the ninth edition of the *Encyclopaedia Britannica* and who had also published a less significant work in 1883 as *Peale's Popular Educator and Cyclopedia of Reference.* Not only was the new edition a complete and thorough revision and expansion of the original, it was also retitled as:

ENCYCLOPEDIA AMERICANA; a general dictionary of the arts and sciences, literature, history, biography, geography, etc., of the world. New York and Chicago: R. S. Peale & Co., 1902. 16v. 26cm. Editor in Chief: Frederick Converse Beach (1848–1918). Assistant Editors: Nathan Haskell Dole (1852–1935), Edward Thomas Roe (b.1847) and Thomas Campbell-Copeland.

The editor in chief of the new work was Frederick Converse Beach, then the editor of the highly reputable *Scientific American,* a factor which was to have a lasting influence on the *Encyclopedia Americana.* The success of the revised edition was immediate and, between 1903 and 1906, further editions were issued, one under the imprint of the Americana Co., and the latter under the imprint of the Scientific American Compiling Department. Managing editor of the later issues was George Edwin Rines (b.1860), who, some years later, edited the *United Editors Perpetual Encyclopedia.*

A major change took place in the edition of 1907, when the word "Encyclopedia" was dropped from the title leaving the work simply entitled *Americana,* and all the editions from then until 1912 were so entitled. With Beach now firmly directing the editorial content of the work, assisted by the Scientific American Compiling Department, the editions from 1902 to 1912 in particular, were especially strong in the fields of science and technology and, in fact, these features are still dominant in present-day editions. *Scientific American* continued to publish the work, and with the 1911 edition, the set was increased in size to 20 volumes, and two supplementary volumes were added in 1912 to bring the work up to 22 volumes.

Another important change in the development of the *Encyclopedia Americana* took place in 1912, when its connection with the *Scientific American* was severed. From then until 1918, the work was thoroughly revised and eventually published, in 1918 and 1920, once again as the *Encyclopedia Americana.* This edition increased the size of the set to 30 volumes, George Edwin Rines being responsible for the editorial revision. Although the title had now reverted to the original, the work is still, even today, referred to simply as the *Americana,* just as, indeed, the *Encyclopaedia Britannica* is simply referred to as the *Britannica,* status symbols for both works.

From 1920 until his death in 1948, the *Encyclopedia Americana* was edited by Alexander Hopkins McDannald (1877–1948), who was also responsible for the first *Americana Annual* in 1923, an exceptionally fine annual supplement which has appeared annually ever since. Further editions of the work were published at regular intervals from 1922 until about 1936, since when it has been published annually under a policy of continuous revision. With the edition of 1943, an entirely new and detailed alphabetic index was provided, replacing the "Reader's Guide" or classified index, of preceding editions, which vastly increased the set's value as a source of reference. Apart from this, only relatively minor innovations have been introduced, although the work has naturally been kept abreast of current developments through its comprehensive revision policy.

When McDannald ceased to be the editor of the work he was succeeded by Dr. Lavinia Dudley, who guided the editorial policy from then until 1963. At the beginning of 1964, Dr. Dudley retired from the position, but remained an Editor Emeritus. She was succeeded by David C. Whitney (formerly managing editor of the *World Book Encyclopedia*), but his stay was relatively short, and, since 1965, George Cornish, who had earlier edited the *Encyclopedia International* has taken over the reins of editorship.

The *Encyclopedia Americana* is unquestionably one of the best and largest encyclopedias in the English language at the present time and, in size, ranks second only to the *Encyclopaedia Britannica*. Special features of the work are its histories of individual centuries, its reviews and summaries of outstanding works of literature and music and, of course, the special attention it pays to topics of American interest, although its subject coverage is truly international. The *Americana Annual,* like the parent set, is considered to be one of the best encyclopedic publications available. Both publications appear under the imprint of the Americana Co., but for many years now, the company has been a subsidiary of Grolier Inc.

- **References:**

Collison.

Subscription Books Bulletin, January 1932; October 1936; October 1939; July 1941; October 1943; October 1945; April 1951.

Booklist and Subscription Books Bulletin, June 1959; June 1964.

ENCYCLOPAEDIA BRITANNICA; or, A dictionary of arts and sciences, compiled upon a new plan. In which the different sciences and arts are digested into distinct treatises or systems; and the various technical terms, &c. are explained as they occur in the order of the alphabet. Illustrated with one hundred and sixty copperplates. By a Society of Gentlemen in Scotland. In three volumes. Edinburgh: A. Bell & C. Macfarquhar, 1771. 3v. 27cm. Editor: William Smellie (1740–1795).

Throughout the English speaking world and, for that matter, anywhere in the world, the *Encyclopaedia Britannica* is by far the most famous encyclopedia in the English language and, at present at least, the largest. It has not always been so, however. Its beginnings were moderate enough and when it commenced publication, in parts, in 1768, no one could have envisaged its phenomenal growth over the next 200 years.

The first edition of the *Britannica* was issued in 100 parts over a period of three years, and when it was completed in 1771, it comprised only three rather large volumes containing a total of 2,670 pages—a small enough set by present-day standards. This famous work was the result of a splendid collaboration between three Scotsmen (the "Society of Gentlemen") who were influenced and inspired by the triumph of the famous French *Encyclo-pédie* of Diderot and by the success, even earlier, of the great *Cyclopaedia* of Ephraim Chambers. The three collaborators were Andrew Bell (1726–1809), an engraver, Colin Macfarquhar (c.1745–1793), a printer, and the first editor of the work, William Smellie (1740–1795), a scholar who undertook the responsibility of editorship at the remarkably early age of twenty-eight.

The new encyclopedia, benefiting from the experience of Chambers, and the shortcomings of Diderot's attempt, was planned to include some 45 principal subjects, supported by another 30 quite lengthy articles and numerous brief entries, complemented by a fairly extensive series of cross references to the principal topics, all under the now widely adopted alphabetical arrangement innovated by the *Lexicon Technicum* in 1704.

Some of the articles in the first edition of the *Britannica*, especially those on the more important sciences, extended to more than 100 pages. The new *Britannica* was produced at, for those early days, a quite remarkable speed. In all, 100 parts were issued, the first appearing in December, 1768 (at a cost of 6d. per part in a regular paper edition, or 8d. per part on a superior quality paper). The first volume was completed in 1769, the second in 1770 and the third and final volume in 1771, Andrew Bell contributing the 160 copperplate engravings. The three volumes were reprinted in London in 1773, under the imprint of Edward and Charles Dilly, but the names of the three collaborators were omitted from the title page, and this was almost certainly a pirated reprint, the first of very many which were to plague the publishers for more than a century afterwards.

The first edition was, not surprisingly, only a moderate success. Unlike the magnificent editions which were to be published later, the original work was an odd mixture of fact and fiction. For instance, the articles on medical subjects were exact and thorough, but along with these appeared old wives' tales, superstition, and prejudice. On the whole, the work, as a source of reference, was poorly balanced.

Despite this somewhat inauspicious start, however, a second edition was planned almost immediately. Smellie, however, declined to continue as editor and Bell and Macfarquhar chose as his successor James Tytler (c.1747–1805), who had a miscellaneous background in theology, practical aeronautics, medicine and unsuccessful writing. Oddly enough, like Smellie, he was a very young man to take on such a responsible editorial task, and he was only twenty-nine when he began compiling the second edition in 1776. Like the first, the revised edition was issued in parts, the first of which appeared in June, 1777, the whole being completed in 18 parts by September, 1784. Much larger than the first edition, the second comprised ten large quarto volumes, 8,595 pages, and 340 copperplate engravings. This much improved edition appeared under the imprint of J. Balfour, Edinburgh, although in fact Bell and Macfarquhar were still primarily the publishers. Several improvements were implemented in the second edition, including a tripling of the number of principal articles and the indexing of the longer of these, the grouping of all maps together under the article on "Geography" and, an important innovation, the inclusion of historical and biographical articles. Additionally, in the final volume was a 200-page appendix which included botanical tables and a substantial bibliography. It was this second edition, rather than the first, which really brought the *Encyclopaedia Britannica* to the forefront of encyclopedia publishing. From that time onwards no work of merit could limit its coverage to the exact arts and sciences, the second edition setting the style for the inclusion of the biographies of living people and the wider world of knowledge. James Tytler, to whom much credit is due for the much improved second edition, was not associated with later editions of the *Britannica,* and all that is certainly known about him is that he was forced to flee Scotland because of his political writings and died obscurely in 1805 in Salem, Mass.

Weekly numbers of the third edition first appeared in 1787. This was planned to be completed in 300 parts, the first of which was issued in 1788, the whole to be contained within 15 large quarto volumes, embellished with some 360 plates. In actual fact, however, when the third edition was eventually completed ten years later in 1797, it comprised no less than 18 volumes, containing almost 15,000 pages and 542 plates. Basically, the third edition was an enlargement of the second, and there were not as many startling improvements, although a notable development was the more detailed treatment of the history of individual countries. For the most part, however, the earlier articles were repeated without change. Thus, although Tytler was no longer associated with the work, his influence was still apparent. Credited with the editing of the third edition were Macfarquhar and George Gleig (1753–1840), Bishop of Brechin. Macfarquhar edited Volumes 1–12 and Gleig Volumes 13–18. Gleig also edited a two-volume supplement to the third edition in 1801, under the imprint of Thomson Bonar, and a second edition of this supplement, again in two volumes, was printed in 1803.

This third edition was also published in the United States, under the imprint of Thomas Dobson of Philadelphia, with the simple title of *Encyclopaedia.* This was issued in parts between 1790 and 1797 and completed in 1798 in 18 volumes, with a three-volume supplement being issued in parts between 1800 and 1803.

The fourth edition was begun in 1800 and completed in 1810 in 20 quarto volumes, comprising 16,035 pages and 581 plates. This was published under the imprint of Andrew Bell, but curiously, as he did not possess the copyright, the fourth edition did not include the articles from the two-volume supplement edited by Gleig for the third edition. In fact, most of the fourth edition was a reprint, with additions, of the third, although it did contain a full account of Jenner's introduction of vaccination for cowpox (1796) and some important articles on mathematics by Professor A. R. Wallace.

By this time, all three originators of the *Britannica* were dead, the last surviving member, Andrew Bell, dying in 1809, just before completion of the fourth edition. Editorship of the fourth edition is credited to Dr. James Millar, a physician and surgeon, but his actual contribution to both the fourth and fifth editions was relatively insignificant. On the death of Andrew

Bell, the question of ownership and publishing rights became a crucial issue, and an intended reprint of the fourth edition in 1810 was postponed pending a settlement. Negotiations for the sale of the *Britannica* had begun in 1810 between the heirs of Andrew Bell and an enterprising young Edinburgh bookseller and publisher, Archibald Constable (1774–1827), and the purchase was eventually completed in 1814. As a result, the intended reprint of the fourth edition became instead the fifth edition, and this was published in 1817, under the imprint of Constable, in 20 volumes, containing more than 16,000 pages and 582 plates.

Constable also embarked upon the publication of a six-volume supplement, to be issued in half-volume parts. The first of these appeared in December, 1816, and the last in 1824. This important supplement added 669 articles, 4,933 pages, 9 maps and 125 plates to the main work, and included biographies of people who had died during the preceding 30 years. It also included three preliminary dissertations and an invitation, for the first time, to foreign scholars to contribute articles. Even more important, however, was Constable's innovation of printing the initials of the contributors at the end of the more important articles, and the provision of a key to the initials in each volume. The editor of the supplement was Macvey Napier (1776–1847), a young Scottish librarian and scholar, who was adept in obtaining the services of the most noted authorities of the day. The supplement updated not only the fifth edition, but the so-called sixth edition, which was, to all intents and purposes, merely a reprint of the fifth, with some new articles and the correction of errors. This, as did the fifth edition, appeared under Constable's imprint, who published 20 volumes between 1820 and 1823. Editorship of the sixth edition is credited to Charles Maclaren (1782–1866), owner and editor of the influential *Scotsman*, but his actual contribution to the work is minimal, being confined chiefly to minor revisions of the historical and geographical articles.

By this time, the *Encyclopaedia Britannica* had achieved an international reputation. The new seventh edition, in particular, with the brilliant Mcvey Napier at the editorial helm, marked a very definite advance. Constable, whose contribution to the success of the *Britannica* was of incalculable value, had died in 1827, and the publishing rights were then acquired by Adam Black, founder of the present-day firm of A. & C. Black of Edinburgh and London. Publication of the seventh edition, under the imprint of A. & C. Black, commenced in 1830, and was eventually completed in 1842. It comprised 21 quarto volumes containing 17,101 pages and 506 plates.

By far the most notable feature of the seventh edition was the introduction of a general index to the complete work, previous editions being indexed only for the principal articles. The index, which was contained in a supplementary volume of 187 pages, was compiled by Robert Cox, and although not a good index, as judged by present-day standards, it was an instant success. This devotion of the last volume to an index to the *Encyclopaedia Britannica* has remained a feature of the work to the present time, and the principle has been imitated since by many other encyclopedias.

According to the title page, the eighth edition contained extensive improvements and additions but, in actual fact, the introduction of more "efficient" editorial policies was responsible for some inadequate editing, with some important articles being drastically reduced, and many others suffering because of lack of proper revision. Again published under the imprint of A. & C. Black, the first volume of the eighth edition was issued in 1853, and when publication was completed in 1860, it comprised almost 18,000 pages in 21 quarto volumes, and in 1861, a substantially improved index volume was added. The editor of the eighth edition was Dr. Thomas Stewart Traill (1781–1862), a professor of medical jurisprudence at Edinburgh University. Himself a substantial contributor, it was not unnatural that articles devoted to scientific and medical subjects were prone to unequal treatment.

The ninth edition of the *Britannica* is perhaps the most famous of all. It was in this that several important innovations were introduced, and it was this edition also which was pirated so widely in the United States. For this deservedly acclaimed edition, Adam and Charles Black engaged as editor Thomas Spencer Baynes (1823–1887), a well-known philosopher and journalist, and a professor at the Scottish University of St. Andrews. The appointment in itself marked a significant change in policy. From its inception in 1768, the *Britannica* had been edited by a Scotsman, but Baynes, although closely connected with Scotland, was born in England, and he thus became the first "foreign" editor of the work.

Publication of the great ninth edition commenced in 1875 and was completed thirteen years later, in 1888, in 24 volumes of text, plus the now well-established index volume, which contained 20,504 pages and over 16,000 articles. Its high level of scholarship, authenticity, and originality of thought were immediately lauded. The illustrative material in the ninth edition was much more numerous and vastly superior in quality to all the preceding editions. Other important innovations were the addition of birth and death dates to the biographical articles, the individual indexes and substantial bibliographies to the major articles, and the inclusion of practical articles to relate the contents to the requirements of everyday life.

Although Baynes is credited with most of the editorship of this vastly improved new edition, he had, to all intents and purposes, relinquished the actual editing of the work by 1881 because of ill-health, and indeed died in 1887 just a year before publication of the work was completed. One of the contributors to the ninth edition, William Robertson Smith (1846–1894) had joined Baynes as co-editor in 1880, and he took over as chief editor in 1881, seeing the work through to completion. The work was so successful that about 10,000 sets were subscribed for in Britain (a large number in those days), but five times that number were sold in the United States (published and sold in 1878–1889 by Charles Scribner's Sons). In addition to these, an even larger number of pirated reprints were also sold in the rest of North America.

It was this ninth edition also which was reprinted and issued by the influential British newspaper. *The Times* in 1898 on an installment basis. This was an amazing and revolutionary development in sales techniques and is almost certainly the first known employment of time payment or hire-purchase in the selling of books in Britain. The scheme was engineered by two enterprising Americans, James Clarke and Horace Everett Hooper (1859–1922), who had developed their selling methods in the rough-and-tumble American subscription set business. So successful were these two practical men that they almost succeeded in gaining control of *The Times* itself, and they, without question, can be credited with rescuing that newspaper from dire financial straits, and guarantying the continuance of the *Britannica*. The achievement of these two men is even more marked when one realizes that *The Times* edition of the *Britannica* was issued no less than ten years after the original date of publication, by which time, even in those slower moving days, much of the work was already dated.

Even while the ninth edition was being sold, a tenth edition was in preparation, and the pending publication of this was announced in 1899. This was not in fact a new edition, however, but the addition of 11 new volumes to supplement the preceding ninth edition, and these, although in effect constituting in themselves a quite independent library of reference dealing with recent events and developments, were numbered as Volumes 25–35. Volume 34 contained a collection of maps, while Volume 35 was an index volume which indexed not only the supplement but the entire 32 volumes of text, containing some 600,000 entries. The eleven-volume supplement was issued under the imprint of A. & C. Black, and under the joint editorship of Sir Donald Mackenzie Wallace (1841–1919), Arthur Twining Hadley (1856–1930) and Hugh Chisholm (1866–1924). By far the major part of the editorial work was directed by Chisholm, however, who was also the editor of the *St. James's Gazette*. The first volume of the supplement was printed and published in 1902 and the set was completed with the publication of the eleventh volume a year later. Significantly, for the first time, an American editor, Franklin Henry Hooper (1862–1940), Horace Hooper's brother, was appointed with an editorial office in New York.

Excellent though the supplement was, however, it could only be considered as a stopgap to update the now aging ninth edition, and, as soon as it was completed, work commenced in 1903 on the preparation of an eleventh edition, for which most of the text was to be thoroughly revised and rewritten. Hugh Chisholm, who had so brilliantly edited the "tenth" edition, was appointed editor in chief, with the historian, Walter Alison Phillips (1864–1950) as his chief assistant editor. The Scottish origins of the *Britannica* had by this time largely disappeared, but the American influence, initiated by Clarke and Hooper, was becoming more and more evident.

At one time, it appeared that the eleventh edition would be published under the imprint of *The Times*, but the attempt by Clarke and Hooper to wrest control had failed and, after protracted negotiations, the copyright and control of the *Britannica* passed from the firm of A. & C. Black to the Syndics of the University of Cambridge in 1910, although to all practical intent, ownership of the work had now passed to American interests. The editorial work on the eleventh edition was largely done in London, but the American office, under Franklin Hooper, concerned itself with ensuring that the *Britannica* would be comprehensible to the average reader. In fact, the eleventh edition was the last to be produced entirely in Britain. Its British connection, nevertheless, remains very strong to the present day, and is a classical and splendid example of Anglo-American accord in the field of encyclopedia publishing. Of interest, in this regard, is the imprint on the title page of the eleventh, which gives the place of publication as New York, by the Encyclopaedia Britannica, Inc., although the verso of the title page states clearly that the work is "Copyright in all Countries subscribing to the Berne Convention by the Chancellor, Masters and Scholars of the University of Cambridge".

Even to this day, the eleventh edition of the *Britannica* is considered to be the finest edition of the work ever published, and ranks as one of the greatest encyclopedias ever published anywhere in the world. Three "firsts" in the publication of the massive eleventh edition are worthy of note: it was the first edition to be issued complete at one time; the first to be printed on an opaque India paper, instead of the familiar coarse paper of the earlier editions; and the first to be dedicated jointly to both the reigning sovereign of Great Britain and the President of the United States. The work was eventually published in 1910 and 1911 in 29 volumes, the last of which was the now indispensable index. The amount of revision which was implemented in the eleventh edition was truly massive and amounted to what was virtually a re-organization of the entire contents. The long monographic articles of the ninth and earlier editions were broken down into more specific units and the 17,000 articles of the preceding edition were redistributed under more than 40,000 more specific; more current and popular headings for speedier reference. In 1913, the publishers also made available a 443-page handbook which grouped the various articles together under 66 courses of study for self-education purposes.

With more than 75,000 sets of the eleventh edition sold, the *Britannica* had probably attained the height of its popularity, but this was even further augmented in 1916, when the publishers issued a much smaller edition, called the *Handy Volume Encyclopaedia Britannica*, photographically reduced from 8¾" × 11¾" to 6½" × 8½", and this was sold at less than half the cost of the larger and almost prohibitively priced original printing, mostly in America on the installment plan by Sears, Roebuck. Apart from the inconvenience of the much finer print, the reduced volume issue was identical in all other respects, and its immense popularity can be measured from the fact that by the time it was withdrawn from sale in the middle 1920's, more than 200,000 sets had been distributed. Less successful, however, was the idea of binding two volumes into one in the larger format, with narrower margins, of which about 25,000 copies were sold.

The twelfth edition, appearing in 1922, like the tenth was merely an extension of its predecessor, adding three volumes, numbered 30–32, to the 29 volumes of the eleventh edition. These three volumes dealt with the period from 1910 to 1921, and the events and developments preceding, during and shortly after the First World War. To a large extent, they dealt primarily with the campaigns of the war and other historical developments.

Some attention, however, was also paid to the fields of science and technology, particularly where the war had accelerated development, but the humanities were virtually ignored. The supplement was edited mostly by Chisholm, but Horace Hooper, whose last publication this was to prove, took a close interest in its preparation. Temporarily, it stimulated the sales of the eleventh edition, now 12 years old, but it was clearly designed to be but an updating supplement pending the preparation of a completely new edition. A two-volume special supplement to the *Brittanica* appeared in 1924. Entitled, *These Eventful Years: the twentieth century in the making as told by many of its makers,* the volumes dealt with important developments in various fields.

However, the continuing demand for the *Britannica* produced not a new edition, but another stopgap issue, the so-called thirteenth edition. Work on this had begun in 1925, with James Louis Garvin (1868–1947) as editor, but it was too hastily produced in a complete set of 32 volumes to be much more than a reprinting of the eleventh and twelfth editions. Volumes 1–28 were edited by Chisholm, and to all intents and purposes this was a reissue of the famous eleventh edition, but the three additional volumes, 30–32, were edited by Garvin. A further printing was made available in 1926 in which the 32 volumes were telescoped into 16. Significantly, in this edition, or at least in the supplement to it, the American contribution exceeded the British and the supplementary volumes were actually printed in the United States.

The last numbered edition of the *Britannica* was the fourteenth. The preparation of this had begun even before the thirteenth had been published, and it was eventually published in 1929 in 24 volumes, a format which the work has retained to the present time. Since 1929, the set has been revised under the now commonly practiced policy of continuous revision, and issues have been published at regular annual intervals since the fourteenth edition was published. Editor in chief of this was James Louis Garvin, editor of the influential *Observer,* with Franklin Henry Hooper retaining his appointment as American editor. Shortly afterwards, Garvin terminated his association with the *Britannica,* and from at least 1936 the editor's preface was being signed by Hooper, the first American editor in chief. Since then, the editor in chief has always been an American. By 1939, Walter Yust (b.1894), formerly an associate editor, was being designated as editor in chief, and he in turn was succeeded about 1960 by Harry S. Ashmore. Later in the 1960's, Warren E. Preece became the chief executive editor, assisted by John Armitage as the London editor.

In common with all major encyclopedias, the *Britannica* is updated by an annual supplement, the *Britannica Book of the Year,* which has been published annually since 1950. In actual fact, it had first been published in 1938, but further issues were suspended from 1939 to 1949, during and shortly after the Second World War, although an omnibus volume covering the years 1937–1941 was published in 1943. For the period, 1939–1949, the publishers issued a multi-volume work entitled *Ten Eventful Years,* a well-compiled survey of the events and developments of the period. The

1938 edition of the *Britannica Book of the Year* was by no means, however, the first updating supplement to be issued. Long before, in 1913, with Hugh Chisholm as editor, the company had issued the *Britannica Yearbook*, which was intended to be a biennial supplement to the eleventh edition, but in this instance, World War I intervened and the project was not resumed after the cessation of hostilities. In October, 1933, another attempt was made to update the fourteenth edition and the subsequent printings by the issuance of a periodical publication variously entitled *World Today* and the *Britannica Bulletin*. This was intended to be published about five times each year, containing new and supplementary articles, written by Brittanica authors under the supervision of the editorial staff. Never a success, the publication was replaced in 1938 by the *Britannica Book of the Year*.

Since the Second World War, the *Encyclopaedia Britannica* has been reprinted in Britain for the British consumer market, and the British editorial contribution to the work has risen substantially for the past 20 years, although it has been American-owned for well over half a century and, despite its British origins and influence, the head office in Chicago still retains overriding editorial authority. On the other hand, however, the two junior versions are each produced in their own countries, the *Britannica Junior* being distinctly American, and the *Children's Britannica* decidedly British.

No history of the *Britannica* would be complete without at least a brief description of the extensive pirating which plagued the work, and the ninth edition in particular, between 1875 and 1905. Actually, the pirating was still going on until quite recently, and only within the past few years, pirated editions were being printed in Formosa, one of the countries which does not recognize international copyright. The most important pirating, however, is that which occurred in the United States, when at least 12 unauthorized printings of A. & C. Black's ninth edition were issued by several American printers and publishers over a period of 30 years. Until 1891, the lack of an international copyright agreement between England and the United States led to unrestrained acts of literary piracy. Either country could, and did, print the best works of the other without compensation or authorization, and would be quite within the law in doing so. Naturally, the publishers on both sides of the Atlantic were not slow to grasp such saleable opportunities, and by no means the least of these was the excellent ninth edition of the *Britannica*.

The first of the pirated printings appeared in 1875, and continued through 1889, under the imprint of J. M. Stoddart, Philadelphia, in 24 volumes, which used the same title as the Edinburgh edition. This same edition appeared again in 1884 under the imprint of Roger Sherman, who issued yet another edition in 1896. In 1883, again under the imprint of Stoddart, a work was published entitled *Stoddart's Encyclopaedia Americana; a companion to the Encyclopaedia Britannica (ninth edition) and to All Other Encyclopedias*. This was a four-volume abridgment of the first Stoddart printing and it was re-issued in 1884 under the imprint of Hubbard Bros. The contents were limited almost entirely to topics of American interest

Due to the lack of need of initial capital, the pirated reprints could be sold at a considerably lower cost than the original, and this highly profitable business attracted other publishers. In 1888, under the imprint of Henry G. Allen, a five-volume set was issued, which, however, was largely identical to *Stoddart's Encyclopaedia Americana,* but with an extra volume of updating material. In comparison with the other pirated reprints, this was a poorly produced work.

Then, in 1890, appeared a ten-volume set entitled the *Americanized Encyclopaedia Britannica,* which was published in Chicago by the Belford-Clarke Co. One of the oddest facts about this particular edition is that the second partner in the firm was James Clarke who, along with Horace Hooper, had been involved in *The Times* printing of the ninth edition in London in 1898, and both, with others, were partners in the Clarke Co. which at one time owned the *Britannica.* The Belford-Clarke reprint related itself more closely to the original than any other reprint in that it included all the subjects in the Edinburgh edition. However, when any given subject was of little or no interest, the text was either condensed or omitted entirely, but the subject listing was retained, with a reference to the appropriate volume and page of the original Edinburgh edition. Conversely, topics of American interest were given more extensive treatment than in the original.

In the following year, 1891, a firm by the name of R. S. Peale & Co., of Chicago, issued a 12-volume work (described as 24 volumes in 12) under the title of *American Revisions and Additions to the Encyclopaedia Britannica.* This is perhaps the most important reprint of all and is certainly one of the best known. The publishers cleverly eluded any possibility of action against them by omitting all articles with individual copyrights (a scheme devised by the Encyclopaedia Britannica Co.) and substituted these with similar articles by American writers. Nevertheless, the work, which was reproduced photographically, was to all intents and purposes, an exact facsimile of the Edinburgh edition. Shortly afterwards, Peale made an arrangement with the Werner Co., Akron, Ohio, to continue with the reprints, and such was the output of these publishers, they soon overshadowed the works of other American reprinters. In 1895, the Werner Co. reprinted the R. S. Peale edition, to which they added new maps, some original American articles, plus other minor revisions and additions. An editor was appointed for this newest reprint named William Harrison De Puy (1821–1901), but his contributions amounted to little, despite the claim of the Werner Co. that he had spent 12 years studying the *Britannica* before rewriting it for the American public. Two years later, in 1897, the Werner Co. issued a new supplement in five volumes, which was edited by Day Otis Kellogg (1796–1874) and Willis Fletcher Johnson (1857–1931), and this was re-issued in 1900 and 1901 as the "Twentieth Century Edition", which became Volumes 25–29 added to the earlier Peale reprint in 24 volumes. In 1902 an index volume was issued to bring up the number of volumes to 30 and, in addition, a separately published guide to systematic readings for self-education purposes became a new thirty-first volume.

A less well-known reprint is the 29-volume work published under the imprint of Maxwell Sommerville of Philadelphia, in 1891 and again in 1894. These were comprised of the first Stoddart reprint, the four volumes of the Hubbard abridged edition and a separate volume of appendices. The Stoddart edition was also reprinted in 1884 and again in 1896 by Roger Sherman, Philadelphia, who had in fact printed the original Stoddart edition, and this must have been a reciprocal arrangement since the names of both appear as copyright claimants. The Sherman printing differed from the Stoddart only in that the reprint was bound two volumes in one, or 12 large volumes in all.

In 1896, a *New Americanized Encyclopaedia Britannica* was published under the imprint of A. F. Shelden & Co., a Chicago based publisher. Except for the imprint, however, this was identical to the 12-volume reprint by Peale in 1891 and the earlier Belford-Clarke printing of 1890.

Only two further pirated editions have been definitely recorded. The first of these was issued by the Saalfield Publishing Co., which like the Werner Co. with which it was closely associated, was based at Akron, Ohio. This appeared in 1904, but it is apparently identical to the Werner reprint, except that the Saalfield edition is in 12 volumes, of which Volumes 1–8 constituted the main work, the supplementary volumes being contained in Volumes 9–12. Lastly, appeared a 15-volume edition in 1905, issued under the imprint of the Riverside Publishing Co., Chicago. This edition was comprised of the ten volumes of the Belford-Clarke printing with the five-volume supplement issued by the Werner Co. in 1897.

The extraordinary circumstance about these many pirated editions is that in several instances, the abridgments, omissions, additions and revisions which were implemented actually improved upon the Edinburgh edition, and this was especially true insofar as the American consumer market was concerned. The Stoddart printing, for example, was much more popular in the United States than the original Edinburgh edition. This is chiefly due to the fact that Stoddart compiled his own index to the *Britannica,* which was far more detailed than the original. Because of this, the Stoddart edition is still retained and respected in many American libraries. Today, of course, the *Encyclopaedia Britannica,* despite its origins and title, is to all intents and purposes, a major American encyclopedia with an international coverage, and it is still today, as it was almost two hundred years ago, the largest encyclopedia in the English language.

• References:

Collison.
Kogan, H. The Great EB.
Einbinder, H. The Myth of the Britannica.
Library Quarterly, October 1963.
Subscription Books Bulletin, January 1930; October 1936; October 1939; July 1941; October 1945; April 1951.
Booklist and Subscription Books Bulletin, February 1, 1957, December 15, 1961, December 1, 1967.

ENCYCLOPAEDIA EDINENSIS, or, Dictionary of arts, sciences and literature. Edinburgh: J. Anderson, Jr., 1827. 6v. 27cm. Editor: James Millar (1762–1827).

Like the *Britannica,* Scottish in origin, the *Encyclopaedia Edinensis* was planned as a much more popular work, while retaining a great deal of scholarly erudition in its articles. The compilation of the work had begun in 1816, and James Millar, who had edited the fourth and part of the fifth editions of the *Britannica,* was responsible for its planning and editing, and the scholarship of the work can be measured by the fact that Millar had himself contributed extensively to earlier editions of the *Britannica.*

Despite its popular appeal, the work proved unsaleable and no further editions are recorded. A factor in its failure may have been its relatively large format; the vogue at the time being for the more compact and convenient octavo printings.

• Reference:
Collison.

ENCYCLOPEDIA FOR BOYS AND GIRLS; a modern reference book. New York: Philosophical Library Inc., 1944. 396p. Compiler: S. Johnson.

A very small one-volume work, quite inadequate, despite its title, as a source of reference. The work was arranged topically, with simple writing and presentation.

The work is British in origin and was probably published in the United States by arrangement with Odhams Press, although no clue to this is contained on the title page or elsewhere. In 1957, it appeared in the United States as the *Children's Illustrated Encyclopedia of General Knowledge.*

ENCYCLOPEDIA INTERNATIONAL. New York: Grolier Inc., 1963–1964. 20v. 27cm. Editor in Chief: George A. Cornish.

One of the most recent encyclopedias to be published and one of the very few new major works since the Second World War, the publishers claim that it took more than four years to prepare and cost more than four million dollars to compile and publish. Designed to stand between sets for children and the larger more comprehensive works, the *Encyclopedia International* is aimed primarily at the reference requirements of junior and senior high school students in the United States, although its coverage is international in scope. In parts, however, the work is certainly adult enough, and a particularly noteworthy feature is the inclusion of much practical information for domestic use.

Well written, with a high degree of accuracy, excellent diagrams and other illustrative material, the work has won immediate acceptance by educators and librarians and appears destined to become a major source of reference in its own particular sphere of interest. A detailed index accompanies the set, and well selected bibliographies accompany some 2,000 of the work's 35,000 subject articles. A useful feature is the inclusion of a study guide with many major articles. The high degree of authority is indicated by the listing of some 2,000 subject specialists as contributors.

When it first appeared in 1963 the *Encyclopedia International* replaced a much smaller work, the *Grolier Encyclopedia,* which was discontinued in the same year, but, apart from common ownership, the two works are in no way related. What is directly related to the *Encyclopedia International,* however, is the *Grolier Universal Encyclopedia,* a very successful abridgement in ten volumes (approximately half the size) published in 1965. In the abridged edition some articles were omitted and others abbreviated. Also omitted was the index, which was replaced by an excellent system of cross references.

In common with most present day encyclopedias the *Encyclopedia International* is published annually under a policy of continuous revision and an updating annual supplement is provided. The editor of the work, George Cornish, has also edited the *Encyclopedia Americana* since 1965.

• Reference:
Booklist and Subscription Books Bulletin, December 15, 1963.

ENCYCLOPEDIA LIBRARY; a comprehensive reference work . . . illustrated with photographs, maps, drawings and color plates, including 7 color plates from the famous J. L. G. Ferris collection of American historical paintings. New York: Encyclopedia Library Inc., 1942. 12v. 24cm. Editor in Chief: William Dodge Lewis (b.1870).

One of the many small multi-volume encyclopedias often encountered in supermarkets in the 1950's and afterwards. Although in twelve volumes, these were very thin, and in actual content, some three and a half million words, this work was much smaller than a number of good one-volume encyclopedias.

First published under this title in 1942, the work is in fact already thirty years old, and had first appeared as *Winston's Cumulative Loose Leaf Encyclopedia* in 1912, under which title it had been published regularly until 1942, in which year the publishing rights were sold by John C. Winston to the New York firm of the Knickerbocker Press. A further printing of the *Encyclopedia Library* was issued in 1943, and it appears to have terminated with its re-issue, in 1950, as the *American International Encyclopedia.*

ENCYCLOPAEDIA LONDINENSIS; or, Universal dictionary of arts, sciences and literature . . . embellished by . . . engravings. London, 1810–1829. 24v. 26cm. Compiler: John Wilkes (1727–1797). Editors: John Jones and Greville Jones.

The extant information about this quite large encyclopedia is surprisingly scant. In size at least, it apparently equalled the *Encyclopaedia Britannica* of the same period, and was, in fact, four volumes larger. But the only traceable information is contained in the Catalogue of the British Museum, and this is but a bare bibliographic entry. Equally little is known about John Wilkes, who is recorded as the compiler of the work, although his death occurred a full 13 years before commencement of publication, the actual editing being implemented by two unknown editors with identical surnames and probably related.

Clearly, however, if the work had been of any considerable merit, it would have been more fully described in one of the few histories available.

Undoubtedly, of course, the rivalry of such well established works as the *Britannica* and other fine sets of the period would have mitigated against its success, but it is surprising that an encyclopedia of this size, published over a period of 20 years, has such an obscure background and history.

ENCYCLOPAEDIA METROPOLITANA; or, Universal Dictionary of knowledge, on an original plan: comprising the three-fold advantage of a philosophical and an alphabetical arrangement with appropriate engravings. London: B. Fellowes, 1817–1821 and F. & J. Rivington, 1822–1845. 29v. 29cm. Planner: Samuel Taylor Coleridge (1772–1834). Editors: Thomas Curtis, Edward Smedley (1788–1836), Hugh James Rose (1795–1838) and Henry John Rose (1800–1873).

This was one of the finest encyclopedias ever published but, for a number of reasons, it was never commercially successful, and never achieved any worthwhile degree of popularity; an essential factor in the life of a reference work. There can be little doubt that one of the reasons for its failure was the inordinately long-time—almost 30 years—it took to complete publication, from the first part in 1817 to the last in 1845. A second and decisive reason was its departure from the fashion of the time, when it abandoned the easily understood alphabetical arrangement to the less easily comprehended but more logical systematic order. And last, but not least, was the undeniable popularity of the well established *Britannica*. Whatever the major cause, however, it certainly could not be attributed to lack of quality, as the contents were written by most of the leading scholars of the day.

The original editor of the work was Thomas Curtis (who was afterwards to edit the *London Encyclopaedia*), but after only six of the 59 parts had been issued, Edward Smedley, who had contributed extensively to the famous *Penny Cyclopaedia* assumed the position of chief editor in 1822, and he continued in that position until his death in 1836. The editorial responsibility was then assumed by Hugh James Rose, Principal of King's College, London, but his editorial reign was cut short after only two more years on his sudden death at the early age of forty-three in 1838. Hugh Rose was then succeeded by his brother Henry John Rose, who saw the work through to completion.

The text of the *Encyclopaedia Metropolitana* was contained in 28 large quarto volumes, with a twenty-ninth volume comprising an index to the complete work. Over the 28 years of its turbulent changes in publication and editorship, the *Metropolitana* was actually issued in 59 parts, or about two parts to each volume. The first six parts were published under the imprint of B. Fellowes, but the remainder, from 1822 to 1845, were issued by the firm of F. & J. Rivington.

The first volume of the work contained not only the usual and familiar introduction to the purpose and use of the encyclopedia, but a learned dissertation by Samuel Taylor Coleridge on a "Preliminary Treatise on Method." Coleridge had in fact planned the *Encyclopaedia Metropolitana* and had based his systematic order of the contents on an evolutionary system. Coleridge's own actual contribution to the work was, however, relatively insignificant, although recent research has led to the discovery of evidence that he may well have had more to do with it than has hitherto been supposed.

Shortly after completion of the original edition in 1845, the firm of J. J. Griffin, London, issued a second edition between the years 1848–1858. Griffin, however, discarded the large quarto format in favor of the more convenient "cabinet" octavo size, and the complete work was contained in 40 such volumes, with an altered sub-titling, "A system of universal knowledge, on a methodical plan projected by Samuel Taylor Coleridge". The amount of revision in the second edition was small, but both editions were very well illustrated for those days, and contained scholarly and authoritative articles on a wide variety of subjects which are still historically valuable.

• Reference:
Collison.

ENCYCLOPEDIA OF GENERAL KNOWLEDGE. London: Wm. Collins & Son, 1938. 512p. Editors: John Maxey Parrish and John Redgwick Crossland (b.1892).

A small one-volume compendium of general knowledge, simply presented for children, of little reference value, but interesting to browse through. The work had previously been published as the *New Gem Encyclopedia* in 1935.

Both Parrish and Crossland had also edited several other one-volume encyclopedias, most of which were published by Collins, and all of which bore a close resemblance to each other.

ENCYCLOPAEDIA OF MODERN KNOWLEDGE (Hammerton). London: Amalgamated Press, 1936–1937. 5v. (2888p). 22cm. Editor: Sir John Alexander Hammerton (1871–1949).

Judging from the number of works ostensibly edited by Sir John Hammerton—12 at least—he must be considered one of the most prolific of modern encyclopedia editors. His first recorded work is the older *Harmsworth's Universal Encyclopaedia,* first published in 1920, and this was also issued under the imprint of the Amalgamated Press, and this earlier title, or at least an abridged version of it, was issued in 1930 as the *Concise Universal Encyclopaedia,* and again, in 1934, as the *Modern Encyclopaedia,* and simultaneously as *Cassell's Modern Encyclopaedia.*

The present title is undoubtedly a re-issue, revised and perhaps abridged of *Harmsworth's Universal Encyclopaedia.* Subsequently, in 1951 and again in 1959, a much enlarged edition was published as the *New Universal Encyclopaedia.*

ENCYCLOPAEDIA OF MODERN KNOWLEDGE (Speck & Hetherington). London: Ward, Lock, 1965. 1v. Editors: Gerald E. Speck and John Hetherington.

Although the title is identical, and although both works are published in Britain, this, and Hammerton's *Encyclopaedia of Modern Knowledge* are completely different works.

This smaller work is a one-volume encyclopedia containing a limited amount of general knowledge for children.

It was previously issued in 1954 as the *Junior Pictorial Encyclopaedia* and in 1956 was titled the *Wonder Book Encyclopaedia,* all three titles being edited by Speck and published under the Ward, Lock imprint.

ENCYCLOPAEDIA PERTHENSIS; or Universal dictionary of knowledge, collected from every source, and intended to supersede the use of all other English books of reference. Illustrated with plates and maps. Perth: C. Mitchell, 1796–1806. 23v. 22cm. Editor: Alexander Aitchison.

This somewhat pretentious work was first issued in weekly parts between 1796 and 1806, and eventually republished in 23 bound volumes in the latter year. The *Perthensis* is unusually bold in its claims that it would supersede the use of all other works of reference in the English language. The claims bore little relation to the facts, however, and the work met with little success, although a second edition was published, again in weekly parts, between 1807 and 1816, which, like the first, was re-issued in 24 bound volumes in 1816, the last volume being a supplement to the earlier text.

It is believed that the work was also published in the United States as the *New and Complete American Encyclopaedia,* although no concrete evidence could be found to verify this.

ENCYCLOPAEDIC CURRENT REFERENCE; a compendium of the world's recent progress on the arts, sciences, history, biography, and general literature. Boone and Chicago: Holst Publishing Co., 1906. 2v. 26cm. Editor: Bernhart Paul Holst (1861–1939).

This small work is clearly similar to an earlier work, the *Teacher's and Pupil's Cyclopaedia,* published between 1902 and 1907, which in turn became the *New Teacher's and Pupil's Cyclopaedia* in 1910, the *International Reference Work* in 1923, the *Progressive Reference Library* in 1928, the *World Scope Encyclopedia* in 1945, the *New American Encyclopedia* and other titles in 1964.

Encyclopaedic Current Reference, however, was somewhat smaller than the other titles and it was more probably intended to be an abridged edition or updating supplement.

THE ENCYCLOPAEDIC DICTIONARY; a new and original work of reference to all the words in the English language, with a full account of their origin, meaning, pronunciation and use. With numerous illustrations. London and New York: Cassell, Petter, Galpin & Co., 1879–1888. 14v. 27cm. Editor: Robert Hunter (1824–1897).

Not an encyclopedia in the accepted sense of the word, but a large dictionary which contained a considerable amount of encyclopedic information in a manner similar to that employed by the *Oxford English Dictionary* and *Webster's International Dictionary*.

The work is sometimes referred to as *Lloyd's Encyclopaedic Dictionary*, from the name of the publisher who re-issued it in 1895. Subsequently, the work was published by the Syndicate Publishing Co. in 1901 as the *Imperial Dictionary and Cyclopaedia* (7v.), and as the *International Dictionary and Cyclopaedia*, in either three or eight volumes. A year previously, the same company had issued the work in a six-volume format as the *International Encyclopaedia and Dictionary*.

ENCYCLOPAEDIC DICTIONARY OF AMERICAN REFERENCE. Boston, 1901. 2v. Editors: John Franklin Jameson (1859–1937) and James William Buel (1849–1920).

The title of this work is quite misleading as the contents are concerned only with a history of America in dictionary arrangement, with scarcely any general information. It had previously been issued, more accurately, as ε *Dictionary of U.S. History* in 1894.

ENCYCLOPEDIC LIBRARY OF KNOWLEDGE. New York: International Readers League and Periodical Publishers Service Bureau, Inc. 1944. 8v. 21cm. Editor: Charles Ralph Taylor (b.1877).

A compendium of poorly arranged and badly dated miscellaneous general information in brief form, which was originally intended to be published in parts for supermarket sales. The enterprise was apparently a failure, as no further editions are recorded. The material in the encyclopedia section of the intended set was also published in the *New American Encyclopedia* (1938 also edited by Taylor.

THE ENGLISH CYCLOPAEDIA; a new dictionary of universal knowledge. London: C. Knight, 1854–1870. 22v. Editor: Charles Knight (1791–1873).

Sometimes popularly referred to as "Knight's Cyclopaedia", after the name of its editor and publisher, the arrangement of this work (which was to form the base many years later from which *Everyman's Encyclopaedia* was launched) was in eight volumes devoted to the Arts and Sciences, six volumes to Biography, four volumes to Geography and four volumes to Natural History, a total of 22 volumes. A supplement in four volumes, one to each of the four main sections, was published between 1869 and 1873, together with a synoptical index.

The work was derived from and modelled on the famous *Penny Cyclo-paedia* (1833–1843) which was also compiled and published by Charles Knight, and this latter title was re-issued between 1850 and 1853 in an abridged two-volume edition as the *Imperial Cyclopaedia.*

No further issues of the *English Cyclopaedia* are recorded, but certainly *Everyman's Encyclopaedia* of 1913–1914, in 12 volumes, constituted a thorough revision and rewriting of Knight's classical work. The work has also been erroneously confused with a work entitled the *English Encyclo-paedia,* which is, however, an entirely different encyclopedia, published many years before (1802), and long before the *Penny Cyclopaedia* from which the *English Cyclopaedia* is derived.

• Reference:
Collison.

THE ENGLISH ENCYCLOPAEDIA; being a collection of treatises and a dictionary of terms, illustrative of the arts and sciences. London: G. Kearsley, 1802.

This work must not be confused with the *English Cyclopaedia* described above, with which it has no apparent connection, predating that title by more than fifty years.

Regrettably little information is available about this earlier work, but in size and general description it closely resembles the reference work en-titled *Pantologia,* also published by Kearsley, a London bookseller, in 1813, the preparation of which had begun in 1802.

ENQUIRE WITHIN UPON EVERYTHING. 1v. London, 1856.

A very popular one-volume handbook of general and miscellaneous in-formation which was first published in 1856 and frequently thereafter until its terminal edition in 1952.

In size and content it approximated the even more popular *Pears Cyclo-paedia,* although it never achieved the same degree of authority and com-prehensiveness.

EVERETT'S ENCYCLOPEDIA OF USEFUL KNOWL-EDGE . . . a complete library of universal knowledge . . . showing the newest and most wonderful inventions and the world's great progress in science and commerce. Chicago: Bible House, 1905. 336p. 24cm. Compiler: Marshall Everett (*pseud.* of Henry Neil, b.1863).

One of the very small compendiums of miscellaneous information which abounded at the turn of the century. Of popular but limited usefulness, the work had previously been published in 1901 as the *American Home En-cyclopedia of Useful Knowledge* and this was re-issued in 1907 as the *Columbia Encyclopedia of Useful Knowledge.* The latter title is in no way related to the present day *Columbia Encyclopedia.*

The small work's only claim to fame rests in the fact that this is the only known instance where an editor has cloaked his identity under a pseudonym.

EVERY AMERICAN'S ENCYCLOPEDIA *see* TIMES EN-
CYCLOPEDIA AND GAZETTEER

EVERYBODY'S CYCLOPEDIA; a concise and accurate compi-
lation of the world's knowledge, prepared from the latest and best authorities
in every department of learning; including a chronological history of the
world . . . a treasury of facts . . . a statistical record . . . assisted by a
corps of eminent editors, educators, scientists, inventors, explorers, etc. New
York: Syndicate Publishing Co., 1911. 5v. 20cm. Editors in Chief: Charles
Leonard Stuart (b.1868), George Jotham Hagar (1847–1921).

This encyclopedia has appeared under so many different titles, both before and after the one under discussion, that it is almost impossible to exactly determine its origin, although its subsequent history is clearer.

The first work with which Charles Leonard Stuart is identified is the
Crown Encyclopedia and Gazetteer, published in five volumes in 1903 under
the imprint of Christian Herald, a publisher closely connected with the
Syndicate Publishing Co. This was followed in 1905 by the *Continental
Encyclopedia,* under the imprint of the Success Co. (probably a distributor)
which was in eight volumes, the latter two of which, however, constituted
a dictionary. The encyclopedic material in these two earlier titles is quite
identical. Then, in 1907, again in eight volumes, and again under the editorship of Stuart, it was re-issued as the *New Century Reference Library,* under
the imprint of the National Press Association, which, like the Syndicate
Publishing Co., was based at Philadelphia.

Everybody's Cyclopedia is apparently a re-issue of the three earlier titles,
but minus the dictionary supplement. In addition, for this title, Stuart had
as his joint editor, George Jotham Hagar, who was to figure more prominently in subsequent titles. With both men still named as editors, the work
was re-issued under yet another title in 1914 as the *People's Cyclopedia.*
Stuart's connection with the encyclopedia apparently ended with this edition,
but with Hagar continuing as editor in chief, the set was published in 1918
as the *New World Wide Cyclopedia,* and a second edition of this was published in 1928, although Hagar had died seven years previously.

In the interim period, however, the work had been issued in 1919 both
as the *World Wide Cyclopedia* and the *New World Encyclopedia,* both of
the last two titles appearing under the imprint of the Christian Herald. In
all probability, the work was re-issued in 1923 as *Adair's New Encyclopedia.*
This was also published by the Syndicate Publishing Co., but the editor in
chief was named as Francis Joseph Reynolds, who was listed as an assistant
editor of the 1928 edition of the *New World Wide Cyclopedia,* but as Hagar
was then dead, he must have been in fact the chief editor. This is confirmed
by Reynolds being listed as the editor in chief of yet another title, the
Times Encyclopedia and Gazetteer in 1929 which, yet again, was published
under the imprint of the Syndicate Publishing Co. With Reynolds as editor,
this was re-issued in 1930 as the *Twentieth Century Encyclopedia,* further
editions appearing in 1932 and 1934. This, in its turn, was re-titled the

World's Popular Encyclopedia in 1937, with further editions in 1940 and 1942, although Reynolds is not listed as editor of the two last editions, having died in 1937.

The confusion resulting from these rapidly changing titles is compounded still further by the fact that the three principal editors have been connected with several other encyclopedic works, most of which, however, were published under the imprint of the Syndicate Publishing Co., or its successor, the World Syndicate Publishing Co.

• Reference:
Subscription Books Bulletin, July 1930.

E V E R Y B O D Y ' S   E N C Y C L O P E D I A ; compiled with the assistance of a large corps of specialists and experts. Chicago: De Bower-Chapline Co., 1909. 1367p. 28cm. Editor: Charles Higgins.

A fairly large quarto one-volume encyclopedia of general information, and in no way related to the similarly named multi-volume *Everybody's Cyclopedia*, published two years later.

For sales purposes the work was published simultaneously as the *La Salle Extension University Encyclopedia* and as the *Webster's Universal Encyclopedia*, all identical in content and all bearing the De Bower-Chapline imprint. In 1910 the work was re-issued in a much smaller format as the *Modern Universal Encyclopedia* and again in 1913 as the *Home and Office Reference Book of Facts*.

The name of Charles Annandale was associated with the two latter titles, but his actual contribution appears to have been the loaning of his name for prestige purposes.

E V E R Y B O D Y ' S   E N C Y C L O P E D I A   F O R   E V E R Y D A Y   R E F - E R E N C E ; a compendium of necessary information for home, school and office. Philadelphia, 1907. 490p. 25cm. Editor in Chief: Charles Smith Morris (1833–1922).

A small, unimportant, poorly compiled compendium of general information which had earlier been published under at least four different titles in 1901: *Popular Compendium of Useful Information; The Twentieth Century Cyclopedia of Practical Information; The World Encyclopedia*, and the *Handy Cyclopedia of Common Things and Biographical Dictionary*.

In the year following, these were all re-issued as the *Golden Treasury of Useful Information* and the grandiloquently titled *World's Best Knowledge and How to Use It*. Several of the titles differed in size and appeared under different imprints, but basically they were the same, the copyright to all the titles being owned by the John C. Winston Co. Finally, in 1909, the work was re-issued as the *Cyclopedia, Dictionary and Atlas of the World*.

E V E R Y B O D Y ' S   E V E R Y D A Y   R E F E R E N C E   B O O K   F O R   H O M E   A N D   O F F I C E. London: Granville Press, 1905. 984p. 27cm.

A modest one-volume encyclopedia containing topically arranged practical

and general information, of interest only in that it subsequently had a more
illustrious history. Later in the same year of its original issue it was re-titled
Pannell's Reference Book for Home and Office, and a second edition under
this title was published in 1906.

Shortly afterwards, the copyright passed into the keeping of Thomas and
Edwin Chater Jack, London and Edinburgh, and they republished it as
Jack's Reference Book for Home and Office from 1908 until 1929. The last
recorded issue of the work is in 1936, when it appeared under the imprint
of Thomas Nelson & Sons.

The firm of T. C. and E. C. Jack had earlier been associated with the
Globe Encyclopaedia of Universal Information (1876–1881) and in 1913
they also published another one-volume encyclopedia, *The New Encyclopaedia,* but this does not appear to be connected with *Jack's Reference Book,*
a work which enjoyed a fair measure of popularity for many years.

EVERYDAY KNOWLEDGE; a book of ready reference on matters of
interest, with plates. London: Modern World Press, 1936. 567p. 21cm.

Little information about this small one-volume work is available. Published once only, no editors are recorded, and the publisher is not, as far
as can be ascertained, connected with any other encyclopedic work.

EVERYDAY REFERENCE LIBRARY; an encyclopedia of useful
information. Chicago: J. G. Ferguson Co., 1951. 1634p. 26cm. Editors: Lewis
Copeland and Lawrence W. Lamm.

Although this work does contain a considerable amount of general information it is, more accurately, a compendium of practical and useful "how-to-
do-it" type of information.

From 1951 to 1957, the work was published in a single volume format,
but since then it has been available in a subscription edition of three volumes, each devoted respectively to Home, Business and Leisure.

Prior to its publication under the Ferguson imprint in 1951, it had been
published in 1948 as *Austin's New Encyclopedia of Usable Information,*
under the imprint of Parke, Austin & Lipscomb, but this, in turn, was
probably a revised and enlarged edition of the *Handy Encyclopedia of Useful Information,* edited by Lewis Copeland and published by the Blakiston
Co. in 1946 and 1947.

THE EVERYMAN ENCYCLOPAEDIA. London: J. M. Dent;
New York: E. P. Dutton & Co., 1913–1914. 12v. 17cm. Editor: Andrew
Boyle.

One of the great small encyclopedias of all time, this compact little work
represented a thorough revision and rewriting of the *English Cyclopaedia*
of 1854 (sometimes referred to as *Knight's Cyclopaedia* because of the name
of the publisher), which itself had been modelled on the famous *Penny
Cyclopaedia* published between 1833 and 1843.

Small in size, with few illustrations, but remarkably reasonable in cost, the *Everyman Encyclopaedia* was an instant success. The articles, arranged alphabetically, were short and specific, but highly accurate and scholarly. Unlike most modern encyclopedias, it is not reprinted frequently, but appears in completely new editions at irregular intervals.

A second edition, again in 12 volumes, but with a slightly altered title (viz., *Everyman's*) and a supplementary atlas volume as an optional purchase, was issued in 1931–1932, with Athelstan Ridgway as editor. This revised and enlarged edition contained nearly 7 million words and 50,000 articles in its more than 9,000 pages, and was considered to be one of the best encyclopedias of its day. The reputation of this excellent work was marred somewhat by the publication in Canada in 1934 of the *Cambridge Encyclopaedia,* which was printed with only minor variations from the plates of the 1931 edition of *Everyman's,* although this reprint retailed at almost twice the cost of the original.

A third edition, again under the editorship of Athelstan Ridgway, was published by Dent in London and Macmillan in New York, in 1950, which maintained the high quality of its predecessors.

The fourth edition, although now out of print, was published in London by Dent in 1958. In the same year the work was published in the United States by Macmillan, but with a variation in title, as the *Macmillan Everyman's Encyclopedia*.

A new fifth edition was published in May, 1967. Although comprised of the same basic format of 12 volumes, and about 8 million words, the new edition was substantially revised, and an appreciable increase in the amount of illustrative material was evident. The type face was also increased in size by about one-third, which was a considerable aid to ease of readability.

• References:
Collison.
Subscription Books Bulletin, July 1930.

EVERYONE'S CYCLOPAEDIA. Glasgow: David Bryce & Son, 1907. 720p. 22cm.

A small one-volume collection of miscellaneous information of no reference value, but popular for casual browsing. No editors or compilers are listed.

FACTS; the new concise pictorial encyclopedia, with an introduction by John Erskine. Garden City: Doubleday, Doran & Co., 1934. 4v. 24cm. Editor in Chief: Nella Braddy Henney (b.1894), British Editor: Lawrence Hawkins Dawson (b.1880), European Editor: Richard Friedenthal (b.1896).

This four-volume encyclopedia, first published in the United States in 1934, was a well compiled and well condensed work containing some 30,000 concise entries. It enjoyed considerable success for a number of years as a source of brief information on a wide variety of topics. Although no acknowledgement is made, *Facts* is almost certainly derived or adapted from the British one-volume work, *Routledge's Universal Encyclopaedia*, also published in 1934. A clue to its origin is provided in the listing of Lawrence H. Dawson as the British editor of *Facts*, who was, in fact, the editor in chief of the British work.

In 1938, again under the imprint of Doubleday, the work was revised and re-issued in a single-volume format as the *New Concise Pictorial Encyclopedia*. Shortly afterwards the publishing rights were acquired by the World Publishing Co., based at Cleveland (previously the Syndicate Publishing Co.), and they re-published the work, again in a single-volume format, as the *Comprehensive Pictorial Encyclopedia* in 1942, listing William Hendelson as the editor of revisions.

Reverting to its original four-volume format, the work was finally published in 1951 as the *World Home Reference Encyclopedia*, under the editorship of Eugene M. Fisher, but now under the imprint of the Consolidated Book Publishers. By this time, however, the original quality of the work had deteriorated to a marked degree and it was discontinued shortly afterwards.

• Reference:
Subscription Books Bulletin, July 1934.

THE FAMILY CYCLOPAEDIA; being a complete treasury of useful information on all subjects bearing upon the common interests and daily wants of mankind, etc. London: Ward, Lock, 1859. 350p.

One of the earliest small, one-volume encyclopedias of general knowledge, in vogue in the second half of the nineteenth century. Ward, Lock have long been noted for their publication of one-volume works, at least five being recorded under their imprint during the past one hundred years.

The editorship and compilation of this small work is anonymous, but portions of it may well have been incorporated into *Beeton's Encyclopaedia of Universal Information*, published by Ward, Lock some twenty years later.

FUNK AND WAGNALLS NEW STANDARD ENCYCLOPEDIA OF UNIVERSAL KNOWLEDGE, prepared by an editorial staff of experts and specialists, with the help of leading scholars, scientists, and men of affairs of the English-speaking world. New York and London: Funk & Wagnalls Co., 1931. 25v. 15cm. Editor: Francis (Frank) Horace Vizetelly (1864–1938).

The unusual circumstance about this neat, compact, well edited and well printed encyclopedia is that it was originally designed to be offered as a premium with subscriptions to *Literary Digest*. For many years it was not available for individual sale.

This desirable home and desk encyclopedia was original only up to a point, however, and several of the articles were extracted and condensed from the large and authoritative *New International Encyclopedia,* which Funk & Wagnalls had acquired in 1931. Almost certainly also, much of the historical material must have been derived from the earlier 25-volume *Funk and Wagnalls Standard Encyclopedia of the World's Knowledge,* first published in 1913. Indeed, the origins can possibly be traced still further back to 1899, when Funk & Wagnalls published an encyclopedic reference work in 38 volumes, with a thirty-ninth volume as an atlas supplement, which was known as the *Columbian Cyclopaedia.* Additionally, just before the issuance of the work under discussion, Funk & Wagnalls had issued a ten-volume set (probably an abridgement) known as the *Pocket Library of the World's Essential Knowledge.*

Despite these probable antecedents, however, the *Funk & Wagnalls New Standard Encyclopedia* was so thoroughly revised as to be essentially a new work. Certainly, through the depression years, it was a wonderful bargain as a low cost encyclopedia, and its value was accentuated by the provision, in 1935 and 1937, of an extra twenty-sixth volume containing an index and a course of study. Further editions of the main work were made available in 1934, 1935, and 1937, but from then, coinciding with the demise of the *Literary Digest,* it was not re-issued until 1942, when it appeared, by arrangement with Funk & Wagnalls, under the imprint of the Unicorn Press.

By now, however, the set was no longer contingent upon a subscription to the journal and could be purchased at retail, or through supermarkets, at $1.00 per volume, with an alternative de luxe edition also available at $1.50 per volume. Trouble cropped up for the new publishers, however, and, as a result of complaints, the Federal Trade Commission issued a "Cease and Desist" order against the company in 1950 (Docket #5488) on the grounds of false representation and disparagement of competitive sets.

Subsequently the work was thoroughly revised and considerably enlarged by Joseph Laffan Morse (b.1902) and published in 36 volumes in 1949–1950 as the *New Funk & Wagnalls Encyclopedia,* with a further edition in 1952. The size of the work probably mitigated against sales and, beginning in 1954, the set was again reduced to its original format of 25 volumes, but with yet another change of title to the *Universal Standard Encyclopedia,* and a further edition, still under the imprint of the Unicorn Press, was issued in 1957–1958. In 1959, the publishers changed their company name to the Standard Reference Works Publishing Co., and the title of the encyclopedia to *Funk & Wagnalls Standard Reference Encyclopedia,* under which title the work has appeared annually since 1960, with Morse continuing as editor in chief.

• References:

Subscription Books Bulletin, April 1932; January 1936; January 1945.

FUNK AND WAGNALLS STANDARD ENCYCLOPEDIA OF MODERN KNOWLEDGE. New York: Standard Reference Works Publishing Co., 1959. 3936p. 31cm. Editor: Joseph Laffan Morse (b.1902).

A very large and very useful one-volume encyclopedia based on the 25-

volume *Universal Standard Encyclopedia* issued by the same publishers. Only one printing is recorded despite its rather obvious claims to be a particularly useful one-volume source of reference.

FUNK & WAGNALLS STANDARD ENCYCLOPEDIA OF THE WORLD'S KNOWLEDGE. New York and London: Funk & Wagnalls Co., 1913. 25v. 16cm.

No editors are recorded for this work, and its origins are rather uncertain, but it was probably derived or adapted from the 38-volume *Columbian Cyclopaedia*, published by Funk & Wagnalls in 1899. Some of the historical material was probably also contained in the *Pocket Library of the World's Essential Knowledge*, a ten-volume set published by the same company in 1929, and the *Funk and Wagnalls New Standard Encyclopedia of Universal Knowledge*, published in 25 volumes in 1931.

FUNK & WAGNALLS STANDARD REFERENCE ENCYCLOPEDIA. New York: Standard Reference Works Publishing Co., 1959. 25v. 22cm. Editor in Chief: Joseph Laffan Morse (b.1902).

First published under this title in 1959, the work is derived directly from the *Funk & Wagnalls New Standard Encyclopedia of Universal Knowledge*, published between 1931 and 1943, its successor, the *New Funk & Wagnalls Encyclopedia*, issued from 1949 to 1952, and finally, the *Universal Standard Encyclopedia*, from 1954 to 1958.

Since 1959 the work has been published annually with sufficient revisions to keep it relatively up to date, and is one of the few sets sold through food and department stores which has earned approval as a useful and inexpensive work for home use. For an encyclopedia in the lower price range, the work is exceptionally well compiled, well edited and well written. The subject coverage is also remarkably comprehensive within the scope of its 7 million words. The list of contributors is small, but good, and some of the contributed articles are signed.

Indirectly, the work is descended from the famous *New International Encyclopedia*, many of the original articles having been condensed from that work, acquired by Funk & Wagnalls in 1931. The work does, however, lack adequate illustrative material; color illustrations, in particular, being confined to one frontispiece plate in each volume.

• Reference:
Booklist and Subscription Books Bulletin, July 1, 1962.

A GENERAL DICTIONARY, historical and critical; in which a new and accurate translation of that of Mr. Bayle is included, and interspersed with several thousand lives never before published. London: G. Strahan, 1734–1741. 10v. Compiler: Thomas Birch (1705–1766).

The compiler of this quite useful work was a historian of some repute, the rector of the small town of Ulting in Essex and secretary of the Royal Society from 1752–1765. Basically, the work is an English translation of an outstanding French encyclopedia in two volumes, the *Dictionnaire Historique et Critique,* printed in Rotterdam in 1697 and compiled by the French philosopher, Pierre Bayle (1647–1706). Birch, however, expanded Bayle's work by including several thousand biographies, most of which he had written himself.

The work was moderately successful and a second edition in five volumes was published between 1734 and 1738 by the firm of J. J. Knapton, who had achieved publishing fame by being the first to publish the famous *Cyclopaedia* of Ephraim Chambers only six years previously.

• Reference:
Collison.

GLOBE ENCYCLOPAEDIA OF UNIVERSAL INFORMA-TION. Edinburgh: T. C. Jack, 1876–1881. 6v. 25cm. Editor: John Merry Ross (1833–1883).

John Merry Ross was a Scottish educationalist who had been the principal assistant to Andrew Findlater in the compilation of the first edition of *Chambers's Encyclopaedia,* published between 1860 and 1868. With this valuable experience as a background, it is not unreasonable to assume that the *Globe Encyclopaedia* was considerably influenced by the larger work, and an indication to this is perhaps provided by the publication in the United States of a "Globe" edition of *Chambers's Encyclopaedia,* by Lippincott, in five volumes.

In 1883, under the imprint of Hodder & Stoughton, the work was re-issued in an identical six-volume format as the *Student's Encyclopaedia of Universal Knowledge.* Ross died in the same year, but despite this, his name still appeared as editor in yet another re-issue of the work as the *Illustrated Globe Encyclopaedia,* published in London by Virtue & Co. between 1890 and 1893 in six volumes.

GOLDEN BOOK ENCYCLOPEDIA. New York: Simon & Schuster, 1959. 16v. 27cm. Compiler: Bertha Morris Parker.

A gaudily illustrated encyclopedia of general knowledge for younger children. Although the work is described as being in 16 volumes, each of these is comprised of less than one hundred pages, and several one-volume encyclopedias for children are, in fact, larger. Although possibly of use to stimulate reading interests in children, it is much too limited for actual reference use, containing, as it does, only about 1,300 subject entries, treated briefly and simply. An index is provided, but this again is altogether too limited, although a "Reading and Study Guide" is more usefully compiled.

The work is mediocre, and the word encyclopedia is perhaps inapplicable to such a limited general coverage. However, it is attractive in appearance and appeals to younger children and in this respect may be of some value, especially at the low cost of the edition which is usually available through supermarkets at about $1.00 per volume. A second edition, but very little revised, was issued in 1961.

• Reference:
Booklist and Subscription Books Bulletin, January 15, 1960.

THE GOLDEN ENCYCLOPEDIA; illustrated by Cornelius De Wit. New York: Simon & Schuster, 1946. 125p. Compiler: Dorothy Agnes Bennett (b.1909).

Not a reference tool, but a small and very simply worded and illustrated compendium of miscellaneous information for younger children. With an extremely limited subject coverage arranged under 170 broad headings, and an index which contains less than one thousand references, the work can be considered only as a very simple introduction to the use of more comprehensive works.

In 1963 it was revised and enlarged under the editorship of Jane Werner Watson and re-titled the *New Golden Encyclopedia*.

GOLDEN ENCYCLOPAEDIA FOR CHILDREN, with plates. London: British Books, 1934. 2v. (756p.) 22cm. Editors: John Redgwick Crossland (b.1892) and John Maxey Parrish.

No relation to the similarly named American work, this is a small simplified encyclopedia for younger children.

It had previously been issued in 1933 as the *Wonder Encyclopaedia for Children* and was subsequently re-issued in 1940 as the *Modern Illustrated Encyclopaedia*.

Crossland and Parrish have jointly edited several other small encyclopedias, most of which were based upon, or adapted from their first joint publication, the *New Standard Encyclopaedia*, published in 1932.

GOLDEN HOME AND HIGH SCHOOL ENCYCLOPEDIA. New York: Golden Press, 1961. 20v. (2999p.) 27cm. Editor in Chief: Virginia Sarah Thatcher (b.1917).

Another in the series of "Golden" books inaugurated by Simon & Schuster and afterwards published under the imprint of the Golden Press, this, the most ambitious work in the series, was planned to meet the needs of high school students and also to serve as a source of popular reference for home use. Primarily, it is designed for sale through food supermarkets at a very low cost, although a hard bound edition is also available.

The bibliographical description of the work as being in 20 volumes is misleading, as each of these is barely 150 pages in length. The entire contents could have been contained in one large volume and the work is by no means as inexpensive as it might seem in comparison, costwise, with larger one-volume encyclopedias such as the *Columbia* or the *Lincoln Library*.

The most striking feature of the work is the profuse use of color, but this is often overdone, at times to the point of gaudiness. While it may have some interest as a set to glance through casually at idle moments, its reference value is strictly limited.

The editor in chief of the work, Virginia Thatcher, was simultaneously editor of a larger work, the *Universal World Reference Encyclopedia,* which is in no way related to the *Golden Home and High School Encyclopedia.*

• Reference:
Booklist and Subscription Books Bulletin, September 15, 1963.

GOLDEN PATHWAY TO A TREASURY OF KNOWL-EDGE. London: International University Society, 1931. 8v. 22cm.

A rather insignificant compendium of general instruction usually sold on a subscription basis from door to door in Britain. The work is more in the nature of a self-educator than an encyclopedia.

A second edition was published in 1934, with the place of publication moved to Nottingham. A third edition was issued just before the war in 1939, but since then the work appears to have gone out of print although the publishers are themselves still active.

GOLDEN TREASURY OF KNOWLEDGE. New York: Golden Press, 1961. 16v. 27cm. Editor in Chief: Margaret Bevans (b.1917).

A very small and inexpensive work, comprised of 16 thin volumes, lavishly illustrated in color, but containing less than half a million words in the text. The arrangement of the work is topical, and it is designed as a source of browsing for very young children.

As a work of reference it has no value, but could have some use as an inexpensive source of motivation for retarded readers.

GOLDEN TREASURY OF USEFUL INFORMATION . . . and handy dictionary of common things. Philadelphia: International Publishing Co., 1902. 606p. 25cm. Editor in Chief: Charles Smith Morris (1833–1922).

A small one-volume work which has been issued under a bewildering variety of titles and formats, either identical in content, or adapted and abridged from an earlier work, the *Twentieth Century Cyclopedia of Practical Information,* first published in 1901. In the same year abridged editions were issued as the *Popular Compendium of Useful Information,* the *World Encyclopedia,* and the *Handy Cyclopedia of Common Things.*

In 1902, the work was issued as the *World's Best Knowledge and How to Use It.* Later, in 1907, it was re-issued as *Everybody's Encyclopedia for Everyday Reference* and finally, in 1909, as the *Cyclopedia Dictionary and Atlas of the World.*

GREAT ENCYCLOPAEDIA OF UNIVERSAL KNOWL-EDGE, with 1,100 illustrations and a 22 page supplement of famous characters in drama and fiction. London: Odhams Press, 1948. 1146p. 22cm.

The firm of Odhams has published a considerable number of one- and multi-volume encyclopedias since the *New Standard Encyclopaedia* appeared under their imprint in 1932. No editors are given for this work, but it is very probably a re-issue of the *New Illustrated Universal Reference Book*, published in 1933 and *Universal Knowledge A–Z*, published in 1938.

GRESHAM ENCYCLOPAEDIA *see* CONCISE ENCYCLOPAEDIA

GROLIER ENCYCLOPEDIA. New York: Grolier Society, 1944. 11v. 24cm. Editor: Silas Edgar Farquhar (1887–1948).

First published under this title in 1944, the *Grolier Encyclopedia* was in fact a re-titling of the older *Doubleday Encyclopedia*, first published in 1931, which was itself an American adaptation of *Harmsworth's Universal Encyclopaedia*, first published in Britain between 1920 and 1923.

The publishing rights to the *Doubleday Encyclopedia* were acquired by the Grolier Society in 1941, although an actual change in title did not take place until the edition of 1944. Prior to the Grolier take over, the work had been edited by Arthur Elmore Bostwick, but with the change of ownership, the editorial responsibility had passed to Silas Farquhar, who had previously edited the *New Human Interest Library* (1925–1930), the *Volume Library* (1931–1932), the *World Book Encyclopedia* (1933–1939) and the *Modern Library of Knowledge* (1940).

From the time of its acquisition by Grolier in 1941 until the last printing of the work in 1963, the *Grolier Encyclopedia* was published annually under a policy of continuous revision, but this was not always as well implemented as it should have been and, eventually, in 1963, it was discontinued as a major product of the Grolier Society.

Farquhar died in 1948, and Kenneth D. Sultzer became the managing editor. He was succeeded by Nunzia A. Buongiorno in 1954. In the 1959 and later editions, Ellen Veronica McLoughlin (b.1893) was listed as editor. From 1944 to 1947 the set was in 11 volumes, the last of which constituted a general index and an atlas, but the latter volume was omitted from later editions.

Both as the *Doubleday Encyclopedia* and as the *Grolier Encyclopedia* the work attained only a limited acceptance by educators and librarians, never arising above a grade of fair quality, and, during the 1950's it declined in popularity due mostly to the appearance of newer and better encyclopedias in the same general price range. Shortly before its demise in 1963, however, a considerable amount of the encyclopedic entries were extracted and reprinted, with some revision, in a work entitled the *Unified Encyclopedia*, which was an unusual merger of two distinct and differently arranged sets, the *Grolier Encyclopedia*, and the topically arranged *Richards Topical Encyclopedia* under one alphabetical arrangement.

The *Grolier Encyclopedia* should not be confused with the *Grolier Uni-*

versal Encyclopedia which is an abridged and condensed version of the *Encyclopedia International,* an entirely different reference work owned and distributed by the same publishing group.

• References:
Subscription Books Bulletin, January 1945; October 1953.
Booklist and Subscription Books Bulletin, February 15, 1960.

THE GROLIER UNIVERSAL ENCYCLOPEDIA. New York: Grolier Inc., 1965. 10v. 25cm. Editorial Director: Lowell A. Martin. Editor in Chief: William Morris. Managing Editor: Herbert Kondo.

One of the newest medium-sized encyclopedias on the market the *Grolier Universal Encyclopedia* is an exceptionally well-edited condensed version of its parent, the 20-volume *Encyclopedia International,* first published by the same company in 1963.

Designed to meet the need for a low cost work to serve the needs of the entire family, the *Grolier Universal* is approximately 60% the size of the parent set, containing some 5 million words and dealing with about 25,000 subject entries. It differs from the larger work mainly in that cross references are substituted for the comprehensive index of the *Encyclopedia International.*

Further economies were effected by the omission of bibliographies and the reduction in the number of illustrations and maps. Despite these abridgements, the work is a very useful concise encyclopedia in its own right and has won official acceptance as a low priced ready reference encyclopedia especially useful for multiple use in schools and where more comprehensive and expensive sets cannot be afforded.

• Reference:
Booklist and Subscription Books Bulletin, January 15, 1965.

HAMMERTON BOOK OF KNOWLEDGE *see* BOOK OF KNOWLEDGE (British)

HANDY CYCLOPEDIA OF COMMON THINGS AND BIOGRAPHICAL DICTIONARY. Philadelphia, 1901. 200p. 24cm. Editor: Charles Smith Morris (1833–1922).

A much reduced version of the *Twentieth Century Cyclopedia of Practical Information,* also published in 1901. With additional material, the work has been issued under a wide variety of titles between 1902 and 1909.

HANDY CYCLOPEDIA OF THINGS WORTH KNOWING; a manual of ready reference. Chicago: A. J. Dubois, 1911. 382p. 17cm.

A very small handbook of miscellaneous, but interesting information. Despite its sub-titling, it was far from being a manual of ready reference. No editors are listed and the work was probably compiled, somewhat inexpertly, by the publisher's own staff.

HANDY ENCYCLOPEDIA OF USEFUL INFORMATION.
Philadelphia: P. Blakiston Co., 1946. 438p. 21cm. Editor: Lewis Copeland.

In itself, this small work is only a haphazard compilation of practical and general information for the home, and can hardly be considered a general encyclopedia. A revised edition was issued in 1947, but the copyright to the work was acquired in the same year by the firm of Parke, Austin & Lipscomb.

In 1948 they re-issued the work in a very much revised and enlarged format as *Austin's New Encyclopedia of Usable Information,* with Copeland as editor. Shortly afterwards the publishing rights were acquired by the J. G. Ferguson Co. of Chicago, who re-issued it in 1951 as the *Everyday Reference Library.* Since 1957, the work has been in three volumes, devoted to Home, Business and Recreation respectively.

THE HARMSWORTH ENCYCLOPAEDIA; Everybody's Book
of Reference. London: Amalgamated Press Ltd., and Thomas Nelson & Sons, 1905–1906. 8v. 22cm. Editor: George Sandeman.

This very good encyclopedia of its day was published serially from 1905 and completed in eight bound volumes in 1906. More than half a million copies were sold almost immediately.

It is interesting to note that while it was being published in Britain jointly by the Amalgamated Press and Thomas Nelson, an adapted and enlarged edition, prepared under the editorship of Frank Moore Colby (1865–1925) was being published in 12 volumes in the United States as *Nelson's Encyclopaedia.*

In Britain, a second edition of the *Harmsworth Encyclopaedia* was issued in 1906, but in 1911, it was being published there also as *Nelson's Encyclopaedia,* and, in all probability, the *Harmsworth Universal Encyclopaedia* (1920–1923) was based to some extent on the earlier title.

Containing some 50,000 brief but well written articles, the work proved immensely popular in the United States as well as in Britain, and the work developed further in North America as *Nelson's Perpetual Looseleaf Encyclopedia* in 1917, with a further printing in 1920. Several years elapsed before a new edition was published in 1937 as the *Nelson Complete Encyclopedia,* which was finally re-issued in 1940 as *Nelson's Encyclopedia: Unabridged* and *Nelson's New Looseleaf Encyclopedia.* By then, however, the work had deteriorated considerably in quality, and no further editions have been recorded, although the background material was used to compile the very good *American People's Encyclopedia* in 1948.

• Reference:
Collison.

HARMSWORTH'S CHILDREN'S ENCYCLOPAEDIA *see* CHILDREN'S ENCYCLOPAEDIA

HARMSWORTH'S UNIVERSAL ENCYCLOPAEDIA. London: Amalgamated Press, 1920–1923. 10v. 22cm. Editor: Sir John Alexander Hammerton (1871–1949).

Although there is no clear indication or acknowledgement, this work, originally issued in Britain in serial form from 1919, was almost certainly based upon the *Harmsworth Encyclopaedia,* published by the same company in 1905, although it was by no means as popular as its predecessor.

The most interesting aspect of this reference set is that, in 1931, the firm of Doubleday, Doran & Co. revised and adapted it for American use. It was re-published in the United States as the *Doubleday Encyclopedia,* and for several years enjoyed a fair measure of success; yet another instance of Anglo-American accord in the field of encyclopedia publishing.

In 1944, *Doubleday's Encyclopedia* was re-titled the *Grolier Encyclopedia,* under which it was published until it went out of print in 1963, although a considerable amount of the material was incorporated into the *Unified Encyclopedia* (1960–1965).

Meanwhile, in Britain, an abridged edition of the *Harmsworth Universal Encyclopaedia* was published in 1930–1931 as the *Concise Universal Encyclopaedia,* and this was followed by other condensed versions in 1933 as the *Modern Encyclopaedia* and again in 1939 as *Cassell's Modern Encyclopaedia.* In 1936, a five-volume work, edited by Hammerton, and entitled the *Encyclopaedia of Modern Knowledge,* appears to be a more direct descendant. Quite definitely, however, the ten-volume *New Universal Encyclopaedia* first published in 1951 (with a new edition in 1959) under the imprint of the Educational Book Co., is a revision of the original *Harmsworth's Universal Encyclopaedia.*

• References:
Collison.
Subscription Books Bulletin, April 1931.

HARPER'S BOOK OF FACTS; a classified history of the world, embracing science, literature and art. New York: Harper & Bros., 1895. 1000p. 27cm. Compiler: Joseph H. Willsey. Editor: Chorlton Thomas Lewis (1834–1904).

A quite useful one-volume encyclopedia dealing with a wide variety of subjects from a historical viewpoint. A second edition, with a slightly different sub-titling, was published in 1906.

The work is probably derived from the *Dictionary of Science, Literature and Art,* published by Harper in 1844, with a last recorded edition in 1875.

HAYWARD'S KEY TO KNOWLEDGE. Chicago and New York: Americana Corp., 1931. 9v. 23cm. Editor: Alexander Hopkins McDannald (1877–1948).

This topically arranged work is described as "A comprehensive and systematic presentation of practical and essential knowledge written in an interesting and instructive way for children and youth". The work had a very short existence, apparently being published once only and disposed of immediately. It was rather poorly produced and the lack of an index also mitigated against its usefulness, although far more inferior works were in existence both before and after.

The publishers were also the owners and distributors of the *Encyclopedia Americana,* which this "Key to Knowledge" was probably intended to supplement. The editor, McDannald, was also the editor of the *Americana.* Each of the nine volumes dealt with a broad subject area and was complete within itself.

• Reference:
Subscription Books Bulletin, April 1935.

HILL'S PRACTICAL ENCYCLOPEDIA; the student's library of general knowledge, with guideposts and a reading index. Compiled under the supervision of Thomas E. Hill, assisted by a large corps of eminent writers on special subjects. Chicago: The Chicago Book Co., 1901. 4v. 24cm. Supervisor: Thomas Edie Hill (1832–1915). Editor: L. Brent Vaughan (b.1873)

The history of this work is particularly interesting in that it throws some light on the later development of two of the leading home and school encyclopedias in the United States at the present time.

At the same time that *Hill's Practical Encyclopedia* was being issued under the imprint of the Chicago Book Co., it was also being issued by the Caxton Co. of Chicago, as the *School Library Encyclopedia,* although with a different sub-title and omitting Hill as the supervising editor.

Both works were issued again in 1902 under the same imprints but, simultaneously, the work was also published as *Hill's Practical Reference Library of General Knowledge,* under the imprint of Dixon & Hanson, Chicago and Toledo, and the work continued under this latter title, with editions in 1904 and 1905. With the exception of the titles and prefaces, all three works were identical.

HILL'S PRACTICAL REFERENCE LIBRARY OF GENERAL KNOWLEDGE; compiled under the supervision of Thomas E. Hill, assisted by a corps of eminent writers on special subjects. Chicago and Toledo: Dixon & Hanson, 1902. 4v. 24cm. Supervising Editor: Thomas Edie Hill (1832–1915). Editor: L. Brent Vaughan (b.1873). Revision Editor: William Francis Rocheleau.

This is a continuation of *Hill's Practical Encyclopedia* (1901–1902) and the *School Library Encyclopedia* (1901–1902), which appeared under the imprints of two other publishing companies. Further editions of the *Practical Reference Library* were published in 1904 and 1905, both of which listed William Francis Rocheleau as editor of revisions.

In 1907 Dixon & Hanson made two important changes—they increased the size of the work to five volumes and re-named it the *New Practical Reference Library*, with Rocheleau now listed as an associate editor. A further edition followed in 1911, although the imprint of the publishers now read the Dixon-Hanson-Bellows Co.

At about this time, Dixon broke away from the company to compile an entirely different work of reference, and evidently Rocheleau went with him, as he was listed as the editor in chief of the *Home and School Reference Work*, published by the Dixon-Rucker Co. in 1913. The previous year another edition of the *New Practical Reference Library* was issued, under the imprint of the Hanson-Bellows Co., and this increased the set to six volumes. Further editions under the Hanson-Bellows imprint followed in 1913, 1914 and 1915, in which year we find recorded as one of the editors, Ellsworth Decatur Foster (1869–1936).

It was in 1917, however, that the most significant change of all took place, when the work was issued under the imprint of the Hanson-Roach-Fowler Co., who were also the original publishers, in the same year, of the *World Book*, and both works were published under the same imprint again in 1918, but thereafter the two works developed along quite independent lines.

Despite the common ownership for this short period, the *World Book* was not a continuation of the *New Practical Reference Library* although prepared initially by basically the same editorial staff, and this is made quite clear by the issuance, in 1919, of the *American Educator*, which was directly derived from the *New Practical Reference Library*.

HOME AND OFFICE REFERENCE BOOK OF FACTS; a superb volume of universal knowledge, with illustrations and pronunciations, compiled with the assistance of a large corps of experts and specialists. Philadelphia: National Publishing Co., 1913. 632p. 21cm. Editors: Charles Higgins, Charles Annandale (1843–1915) and H. D. Lovett.

A small one-volume work with a pretentious title, abridged from several earlier works edited by Higgins as the *La Salle Extension University Encyclopedia*, the *Webster's Universal Encyclopedia* and *Everybody's Encyclopedia*, all of which were published in 1909 by the De Bower-Chapline Co.

In 1910 the work was also issued as the *Modern Universal Encyclopedia*. Annandale's name was probably used for prestige purposes, as his contribution was undoubtedly minimal.

HOME AND SCHOOL REFERENCE WORK. Chicago: Dixon-Rucker Co., 1913. 6v. 25cm. Editor in Chief: William Francis Rocheleau. Assistant Editor: Loran D. Osborn (b.1863).

In or about 1910, a publisher by the name of H. N. Dixon, who had previously been associated with the firm of Dixon and Hanson, publishers of *Hill's Practical Reference Library*, began compiling a new encyclopedia, and engaged as his editor in chief, William Francis Rocheleau, who had also been connected with *Hill's Practical Reference Library.* Dixon's new work was completed and published in a six-volume set in 1913, five of the volumes containing encyclopedic material, the sixth a Course of Study, Methods and an Index.

The work was poor by the standards of the time, but a second edition was issued in 1915, with an expansion in size to seven volumes. Around about 1922, Dixon sold the publishing rights to the Perpetual Encyclopedia Corp., and they, in 1924, re-issued the work as the *Source Book,* in ten volumes, and still with Rocheleau as editor. Under this title it went through several editions, but it was always a poor work, and it ceased publication in 1936.

For a while, the set was also sold (at the same time as the *Source Book*) as the *Home and School Reference Work,* and the *American Reference Library,* and probably several other titles also. In such instances, the distributors would obtain the work from the Perpetual Encyclopedia Corp. and then provide different title pages under their own imprints.

HOME CYCLOPEDIA OF NECESSARY KNOWLEDGE
. . . carefully prepared by eminent specialists. Chicago and Philadelphia: John C. Winston Co., 1902. 500p. 25cm. Editors: Charles Smith Morris (1833–1922), Alice A. Johnson, Mrs. Jeanette McKenzie Hill (1852–1933), Henry Hartshorne (1823–1897).

A small poorly produced one-volume encyclopedia of miscellaneous information. Re-issued in 1905 as the *Home Educator in Necessary Knowledge.* Both works were probably adapted from a one-volume encyclopedia compiled by Morris in 1901 as the *Twentieth Century Cyclopedia of Practical Information.*

HOME EDUCATOR IN NECESSARY KNOWLEDGE . . .
carefully prepared by eminent specialists. Philadelphia: Foster Publishing Co., 1905. 500p. 25cm. Editors: Charles Smith Morris (1833–1922), Alice A. Johnson, Jeanette McKenzie Hill, Henry Hartshorne (1823–1897).

A re-issue of the *Home Cyclopedia of Necessary Knowledge* first published in 1902.

HOME LIBRARY MANUAL AND CYCLOPEDIA *see* STANDARD AMERICAN BOOK OF KNOWLEDGE

HOME LIBRARY OF KNOWLEDGE *see* BUFTON'S UNIVERSAL CYCLOPEDIA

HOME LIBRARY OF USEFUL KNOWLEDGE; a condensation of 52 books into 1 volume, constituting a complete cyclopedia of reference, historical, biographical, scientific and statistical; embracing the most improved and simple methods of self instruction in all branches of popular education. Chicago: Home Library Assn., 1886. 830p. 27cm. Editor: Richard S. Peale.

The new title for a work which commenced publication in 1883 as *Peale's Popular Educator and Cyclopedia of Reference*, with further editions in 1884 and 1885. A second and final edition was published by Peale in 1887.

In a very large format, the work was designed as a series of courses of self-study in the various arts and sciences. In some ways it is reminiscent of the one-volume *Lincoln Library* and *Cowles Comprehensive Encyclopedia* of the present time.

THE HOME TEACHER; a cyclopaedia of self-instruction. London: W. Mackenzie, 1886–1888. 1440p. 26cm. Editor: Samuel Neil (1825–1901).

A large one-volume work of reference, comprehensive and quite useful in its day, although published only once. The firm of W. Mackenzie, London and Glasgow, had previously published the well accepted *National Encyclopaedia* in 1867.

HOME UNIVERSITY ENCYCLOPEDIA; an illustrated treasury of knowledge, with special plates and articles and departmental supervision by 462 leading editors, educators and specialists in the United States and Europe. Revised edition. New York: University Society Inc., 1941. 15v. 23cm. Editor: Charles Ralph Taylor (b.1877). Advisory Editor: Carl Clinton Van Doren (1885–1950).

This work is reputed to be based on *Nelson's Encyclopaedia*, first published in 1905 and last revised in 1934. In parts, it does appear to lean heavily on the older work, but poor editing and hasty abridgements resulted in a much poorer work than might otherwise have been the case.

Although first copyrighted under this title in 1941, the encyclopedia had previously been published in 1935 as the *New York Post World Wide Illustrated Encyclopedia*, which was re-titled the *World Wide Illustrated Encyclopedia* in 1937, and the *University Illustrated Encyclopedia* in 1938. For a while, the set was sold simultaneously under all three titles.

The *Home University Encyclopedia* has been printed from time to time with very little revision. A "second" edition was published in 1961, when the work was reduced in size to 12 volumes, and this was followed by another printing in 1962, with Sherman Day Wakefield (b.1894) as joint editor.

The set is still being retailed by the Publishers Co., Washington, but as there has been little or no improvement since the original edition, it is doubtful if it will remain in print for any length of time.

THE HOW AND WHY LIBRARY; little questions that lead to great discoveries . . . school studies made as fascinating as fiction for children and readers of all ages. Includes articles on the origin and evolution of life, based on the conclusions of eminent scientists. Chicago: F. E. Compton & Co., 1913.

2v. (655p.) 25cm. Compiler: Mrs. Eleanor Stackhouse Atkinson (1863–1942).

More of an anthology than an encyclopedia, but included in this survey because of its close relationship to other encyclopedic works, the *How and Why Library* first appeared as Volume 5 of the *New Students Reference Work* in 1912, and continued as a supplement to that work until 1934. It was also available separately, however, and, until 1934, could be obtained in either a single-volume or two-volume format.

In 1934 the work was expanded to three volumes, under the imprint of L. J. Bullard & Co., who had acquired it from the S. L. Weedon Co. In the same year two additional volumes, compiled by George Willis Diemer (b.1885), were made available. Further printings were issued regularly until 1951, when the set was expanded to six volumes, with a final edition in 1959.

Shortly afterwards, the work was acquired by Field Enterprises who incorporated it into their *Childcraft,* a 16-volume anthology for children.

• References:

Subscription Books Bulletin, April 1935; April 1942.

HUMAN INTEREST LIBRARY; visualized knowledge. Chicago: Midland Press, 1914. 4v. 24cm. Editors: Bishop Samuel Fallows (1835–1922) and Henry Woldmar Ruoff (1867–1935).

A somewhat haphazard anthology of general information for children arranged in a topical manner, each volume dealing with a broad subject area. Further printings were issued in 1922, 1924 (with an expansion to five volumes), 1925, and 1926, by which time the work was being edited by Silas Edgar Farquhar (1887–1947).

In 1928, under Farquhar's direction, the work was substantially revised and expanded to six volumes and retitled the *New Human Interest Library.* In 1933 the set was expanded to seven volumes (the last volume being a reader's guide), and this format was continued with the printings of 1935 and 1937.

No copyrights appear to have been issued since prior to the war, although this inferior work is still in print and is currently being retailed under the imprint of the Publishers Co.

HUTCHINSON'S PICTORIAL ENCYCLOPAEDIA. London: Hutchinson & Co., 1936–1937. 3v. 25cm. Editor in Chief: Walter Hutchinson (d.1950). Assistant Editors: Athelstan Ridgway and Eric J. Holmyard (b.1891).

A very useful medium-sized British encyclopedia compiled and published by the chief executive of the publishing firm. Assisting him in the compilation and editing of this popular work were Athelstan Ridgway and Eric John Holmyard, both of whom had been responsible for the editorial direction of the 1931 edition of the *Everyman's Encyclopaedia.*

The outbreak of hostilities in 1939 probably prevented a re-issuance of the work, but it probably provided the basic material from which a newer work, *Hutchinson's Twentieth Century Encyclopaedia,* was published in 1948.

HUTCHINSON'S NEW 20th CENTURY ENCYCLOPE-DIA. New York: Hawthorn Books. London: Hutchinson & Co., 1965. 1119p. 23cm. Editor: Edith M. Horsley.

A revision and re-titling of *Hutchinson's Twentieth Century Encyclopaedia,* first published in Britain in 1948. This excellent one-volume encyclopedia, containing more than one million words in 19,000 subject entries, is now in its fourth British edition, although the 1965 printing was the first to appear under an American imprint.

• Reference:

Booklist and Subscription Books Bulletin, March 1, 1966.

HUTCHINSON'S TWENTIETH CENTURY ENCYCLO-PAEDIA. London: Hutchinson & Co., 1948. 1024p. 23cm. Editor: Walter Hutchinson (d.1950).

One of the best of the smaller British one-volume encyclopedias, this excellent desk source of reference has long been a favorite in Britain. Although basically a new work in 1948, it owed more than a little to *Hutchinson's Pictorial Encyclopaedia,* a three-volume work issued by the same company in 1936, and also edited by Walter Hutchinson, the chief executive of the firm.

The original editor died in 1950 and the second edition in 1952 and the third edition in 1955 were revised by Edith M. Horsley. When the work entered into its fourth edition in 1965, the title was altered slightly to *Hutchinson's New 20th Century Encyclopedia,* with Edith M. Horsley as editor.

I SEE ALL . . . the world's first picture encyclopedia. London: Amalgamated Press, 1928–1930. 5v. (3008p.) 25 cm. Editor: Arthur Mee (1875–1943).

The claim of the publishers that this was the world's first pictorial encyclopedia may not be completely valid, but there is no doubting that it was certainly one of the first to set a new pattern in encyclopedia publishing. In this work illustrations predominate by far, the idea being to provide a comprehensive illustration rather than separate unrelated details. Only a few words of text accompany each illustrated subject.

Arthur Mee, the editor of this work, is better known for his famous *Children's Encyclopaedia,* first published in 1910 and shortly afterwards adapted for American readership as the *Book of Knowledge* in 1912.

ICONOGRAPHIC ENCYCLOPAEDIA OF SCIENCE, LIT-
ERATURE AND ART; systematically arranged by J. G. Heck. Translated from the German, with additions, and illustrated by five hundred steel
plates, containing upwards of 12,000 engravings. New York: R. Garrigue,
1851. 4v. (plus a two-volume atlas) 26cm. Compiler: Johann Georg Heck. Editor: Spencer Fullerton Baird (1823–1887).

An "Anglicized" edition of the fine *Bilder Atlas* of Brockhaus, but revised
and enlarged by American specialists under the editorship of Spencer Baird.
The arrangement of the work was systematic, each volume being devoted to
a broad subject area, with separate indexes at the end of each volume.

A new and enlarged edition, in seven volumes, but excluding the atlas, was
published between 1886–1890 by the Iconographic Publishing Co., Philadelphia. Previous to that a six-volume edition appeared in 1857, but the publisher's imprint is unavailable.

• Reference:
Collison.

ILLUSTRATED ENCYCLOPEDIA; based on an encyclopedia of
the famous Librairie Larousse. New York: Grosset & Dunlap, 1959. 295p.
30cm. Compiler: René Guillot (b.1900).

A very simple and colorful one-volume collection of elementary general
knowledge for younger children. It was adapted for American usage from a
French work entitled *L'Encyclopédie Larousse des Enfants*, first published
in Paris in 1956.

ILLUSTRATED ENCYCLOPEDIA OF KNOWLEDGE; pre-
pared and edited by the National Lexicographic Board. De Luxe edition. Brooklyn: Premiumwares, 1954–1955. 20v. 24cm. General Editor: Albert H. Morehead.

According to the title page, this work was prepared by the important
sounding "National Lexicographic Board," of which Albert H. Morehead (a
contributor to the *Encyclopaedia Britannica*) is chairman and general editor.
The work, however, was extremely poor and was, apparently, designed to
be offered as a premium through chain and department stores and food
supermarkets, and, in at least one instance, it was offered as an inducement
to purchase a television set.

In 1955 it was also issued as the *Illustrated Home Library Encyclopedia*,
with an additional twenty-first volume containing an atlas and gazetteer,
under the imprint of the Educational Book Guild. Later, in 1958, now
under the imprint of the Bobley Publishing Corp., it was re-titled the
Illustrated World Encyclopedia, under which title it was still being retailed
through mail order catalogs in 1966.

All three works were "compiled" by the National Lexicographic Board,
who were also responsible for a quite different work, the *New Wonderbook
Cyclopedia* in 1954.

ILLUSTRATED ENCYCLOPEDIA OF THE MODERN WORLD. New York: Little & Ives Co., 1956. 20v. 28cm. Editor in Chief: Franklin Dunham (b.1892).

Except for the addition of a two-volume atlas and gazetteer, this work is identical to the *New Pictorial Encyclopedia of the World,* also edited by Dunham, and published in 1954 under the imprint of the Pictorial Encyclopedia Corp. Based on the same material, Little and Ives issued in 1961, the 20-volume *Little and Ives Illustrated Ready Reference Encyclopedia,* again under the editorship of Dunham.

All three sets were sold through supermarkets in inexpensive editions. Poorly produced, and limited in content, the works were of little value even in their cheapest editions. The illustrative material was chosen from the Otto L. Bettman Archives and from the collection maintained by International News Photos.

ILLUSTRATED GLOBE ENCYCLOPAEDIA. New edition. London: Virtue & Co., 1890–1893. 6v. 27cm. Editor: John Merry Ross (1833–1883).

A new printing rather than a new edition, this work had previously been issued as the *Globe Encyclopaedia* between 1876–1881 and as the *Student's Encyclopaedia of Universal Knowledge* in 1883.

John Merry Ross had previously been associated with Andrew Findlater in the compilation of the first edition of *Chambers's Encyclopaedia* between 1860–1868.

• Reference:
Collison.

ILLUSTRATED HOME LIBRARY ENCYCLOPEDIA; prepared and edited by the National Lexicographic Board. Guild edition. New York: Educational Book Guild, 1955. 21v. 23cm. Editor: Albert H. Morehead.

With the addition of an atlas volume, this is an exact reprint of the *Illustrated Encyclopedia of Knowledge,* a poorly produced work published in 1954 by Premiumwares for distribution through general retail outlets. In 1958, the work was acquired by the Bobley Publishing Corporation, who re-issued it in an improved format as the *Illustrated World Encyclopedia.* These three identical works, and a similar 12-volume work, the *New Wonder Book Cyclopedia of World Knowledge,* were prepared by the National Lexicographic Board, whose chairman and general editor is Albert H. Morehead.

The work is small and limited in usefulness, each of the 20 volumes being thinner than is necessary, containing only some 5,000 articles in about 1½ million words, a figure considerably below the minimum desirable to provide reasonable subject coverage.

• Reference:
Booklist and Subscription Books Bulletin, October 15, 1956.

ILLUSTRATED WORLD ENCYCLOPEDIA; prepared and edited by the National Lexicographic Board. Literary Treasures edition. New York: Bobley Publishing Corporation, 1958. 21v. 24cm. Editor: Albert H. Morehead.

A continuation, but improved and enlarged, of the *Illustrated Home Library Encyclopedia* (1955) and its predecessor, the *Illustrated Encyclopedia of Knowledge* (1954), all of which were prepared by the National Lexicographic Board under the general direction of Albert Morehead. The "Literary Treasures" edition includes useful synopses of the most outstanding literary works required in school curricula.

Despite its considerable improvement over the earlier editions, the latest issues of the *Illustrated World Encyclopedia* are still not accepted by educators and librarians. The publishers claim that the work now contains more than 15,000 classroom subjects and 11,000 illustrations. The work, unlike most major encyclopedias, can be purchased through department stores and mail order catalogs at quite a low cost.

• Reference: Booklist and Subscription Books Bulletin, November 15, 1960.

THE IMPERIAL CYCLOPAEDIA (based on the *Penny Cyclopaedia*). Sub-division: The Cyclopaedia of the British Empire. London: Charles Knight, 1850–1853. 2v. 22cm. Editor: George Long (1800–1879).

The publication of this relatively small work is traceable directly to the famous *Penny Cyclopaedia*, published by Charles Knight from 1833 to 1843, edited by George Long.

The *Imperial Cyclopaedia* was not a re-issue of the earlier work, however, but a much smaller condensation, dealing primarily with subjects pertinent to the interests of the far flung British Empire at that time.

IMPERIAL DICTIONARY AND CYCLOPAEDIA *see* ENCYCLOPAEDIC DICTIONARY

THE IMPERIAL ENCYCLOPAEDIA, or, dictionary of the sciences and arts, comprehending also the whole circle of miscellaneous literature etc. London: J. & J. Cundoe, 1812. 4v. 27cm. Editors: William Moore Johnson and Thomas Exley (1775–1855).

Not to be confused with Knight's *Imperial Cyclopaedia* of 1850, this is a poor and rather amateurish attempt to compete with the more scholarly productions of the day, such as the *Encyclopaedia Britannica*, which were then being published in ever increasing quantity to meet public demand.

Johnson was an unknown curate at the small town of Henbury in Gloucestershire, but Exley was quite a well-known mathematician. Neither were qualified to compile a really scholarly work of general knowledge, and no further editions of the work are known to have been issued.

• Reference: Collison.

IMPERIAL ENCYCLOPEDIA AND DICTIONARY; a library of universal knowledge and an unabridged dictionary of the English language under one alphabet. New York: H. G. Allen & Co., and the Gilbert Publishing Co., 1903. 40v. 19cm.

Something of a mystery work, the only record of this work's existence is provided in the United States Catalog for the period. No editors are listed, and there is no indication of where the dictionary material emanated from.

It can be determined with some accuracy, however, that the editor of the work was Richard Gleason Greene (1829–1914) who, a few years previously, in 1899, had edited the similarly sized *Columbian Encyclopedia,* published by Funk & Wagnalls in a 39-volume set, and it seems more than probable that the *Imperial Encyclopedia and Dictionary* is a re-issue of this. This is confirmed by the appearance, in 1906, of the *New Imperial Encyclopedia and Dictionary,* again in 40 small volumes, with which Greene is quite definitely associated as editor in chief, and which appeared under the imprint of the Pacific Newspaper Union, San Francisco.

Again, in 1909, under the imprint of the United Editors Association, the work was published in 40 small volumes as the *United Editors Encyclopedia and Dictionary,* and finally, in 1911, in an enlarged format of 30 volumes, the United Editors Association re-issued the work as the *United Editors Perpetual Encyclopedia.* In this last edition, however, the managing editor is given as George Edwin Rines (b.1860), who, at the same time, was associated with the *Encyclopedia Americana.* Curiously, the sub-titling, "a library of universal knowledge", was not only identical in all four works, but was also used in the 1918 edition of the *Encyclopedia Americana.*

The idea of merging dictionary and encyclopedic articles was not novel and other works had adopted a similar arrangement, but the idea was to be revived in the mid-twentieth century by a work known as the *Unified Encyclopedia.*

IMPERIAL REFERENCE LIBRARY; comprising a general encyclopedia of literature, history, art, science, invention and discovery; a pronouncing dictionary of the English language, etc. With nearly four thousand illustrations. Edited and compiled with the assistance of more than 200 specialists in the various departments. Philadelphia: Syndicate Publishing Co., 1901. 6v. 29cm. Editor in Chief: Charles Smith Morris (1833–1922).

This work has appeared under so many different titles over a relatively short period that its actual origin and eventual development are difficult to trace.

It can be determined with some certainty, however, that it is a direct re-issue of the *Universal Cyclopaedia and Dictionary,* with Morris as editor, published under the imprint of the National Book Concern in 1898. This was followed in 1899 by the *International Reference Library,* in an identical format, but now under the imprint of L. J. Smith & Co. In 1900, yet another publisher or distributor, the Dictionary and Cyclopaedia Co., issued an edition entitled the *Universal Reference Library,* except that this was in eight volumes instead of six, the last volume being an atlas.

In 1901, the same year in which the *Imperial Reference Library* was issued, an apparently identical work, although with different sub-titling, was published as the *Twentieth Century Encyclopaedia.* The *Imperial Reference Library* was itself re-issued in 1907 and 1910, which coincided with further editions of the *Twentieth Century Encyclopaedia.*

Thereafter, the history of the set is less clear, but it may well have been the forerunner of *Winston's Encyclopedia,* published in 1909 under the joint editorship of Morris and Spofford.

INFORMATION PLEASE ALMANAC atlas and yearbook. New York: Doubleday, 1947. 1v. 20cm. Planned and Supervised by Dan Golenpaul Associates. Editor: John Kieran.

Annual compendium of current events and statistics. Available in both hard and soft cover. Similar to the American *World Almanac* and the British *Whitaker's Almanac,* although it has some features not available in the other works.

INTERNATIONAL AMERICAN ENCYCLOPEDIA. Chicago: International American Co., c.1943.

No copyright appears to have been issued for this work and no copies could be found for examination. It may have been an inverted title for the *American International Encyclopedia,* a small 20-volume work which was being retailed through supermarkets at about the same time.

INTERNATIONAL CYCLOPAEDIA; a compendium of human knowledge, revised with large additions. New York: Dodd, Mead & Co., 1898. 15v. 25cm. Editors: Harry Thurston Peck (1856–1914), Selim Hobart Peabody (1829–1903) and Charles Francis Richardson (1851–1913).

One of the great encyclopedias in the English language, the *International Cyclopaedia* has an intriguing history.

In 1884, Dodd, Mead & Co. acquired the plates of an earlier work entitled the *Library of Universal Knowledge,* published from 1880–1881 under the imprint of the American Book Exchange, New York. However, the *Library of Universal Knowledge* was not in itself an original work, but a reprint of the 1880 edition of *Chambers's Encyclopaedia,* which, in turn, like the *Encyclopaedia Americana* before it, was based on the German *Conversations-Lexicon.* Thus, the *International Cyclopaedia* and *Chambers's Encyclopaedia* were closely related to each other at this stage and were basically the same, although, to be sure, the copious revisions and additions which were effected both in the *Library of Universal Knowledge* and the *International Cyclopaedia,* drew the two great works further and further apart.

No sooner had the *International Cyclopaedia* been published, however, than another massive revision was implemented, and a completely new edition, expanded to 17 volumes, was published by Dodd, Mead between 1902–1904 as the *New International Encyclopedia*, universally considered to be the best encyclopedia of its time, containing, as it did, more than 80,000 highly authoritative and scholarly articles.

Further editions were published in 1904, 1905, 1907 (when the work was expanded to 20 volumes), 1909, and 1911. These were followed by a second revised edition, in 23 volumes, between 1914–1917, and this was re-issued in 1923, when a popular edition in 13 volumes was also made available.

The last recorded edition of this great work, still valuable for its historical articles, was in 1935, when it appeared, under the imprint of Funk & Wagnalls, in 25 volumes, the last two of which were supplementary.

INTERNATIONAL DICTIONARY AND CYCLOPAEDIA *see* **ENCYCLOPAEDIC DICTIONARY**

INTERNATIONAL ENCYCLOPEDIA AND DICTION-ARY. London and Glasgow: Collins, 1936. 2v. 22cm.

A small and insignificant encyclopedia of general knowledge combined with an elementary dictionary, one of a series of similar works issued by the same publisher over a number of years.

INTERNATIONAL LIBRARY OF REFERENCE; a compendium of universal knowledge, comprising a general encyclopedia of literature, history, art, science, invention and discovery . . . with nearly four thousand illustrations . . . compiled and edited with the assistance of more than two hundred specialists in various departments. St. Louis: L. F. Smith & Co., 1899. 6v. 29cm. Editors: Charles Smith Morris (1833–1922), Daniel G. Brenton and John F. Hurst.

A re-issue, but under a different imprint, of the *Universal Cyclopaedia and Dictionary*, first published in 1898. In 1900, it was re-issued as the *Universal Reference Library* and subsequently, from 1901 to 1910, it was issued simultaneously as the *Imperial Reference Library* and the *Twentieth Century Encyclopaedia*.

Morris, either singly or in association with other editors, compiled several other multi-volume encyclopedias, culminating with the *Winston's Encyclopedia* in 1909, which may have been a development of the earlier titles.

INTERNATIONAL REFERENCE WORK; a library of history, geography, biography, biology, literature, economics, civics, art, sciences, discoveries, explanations, explorations, inventions, commerce, etc . . . prepared by over 100 leading educators of the world. Chicago and Boone: Holst Publishing Co., 1923. 10v. 25cm. Editor in Chief: Bernhart Paul Holst (d.1939). Associate Editors: Hill McClelland Bell (1860–1927), Ruric Neval Roark (1859–1909).

This work was by no means original, as it was basically a re-issue of a much older work (with many articles reprinted verbatim) entitled the *Teacher's and Pupil's Cyclopaedia*, published by Holst between 1902–1904 in a four-volume edition, although there is some evidence that an unrecorded edition was published in three volumes in 1895. A two-volume abridgement of the earlier work was published in 1906 as *Encyclopaedic Current Reference*. In 1910, the main work was revised and re-titled the *New Teacher's and Pupil's Cyclopaedia*, with an expansion in size to five volumes. This was followed in 1911 by two other versions, one in a single-volume edition, the *Unrivalled Encyclopedia*, and the other in a two-volume format, the *Practical American Encyclopedia*, both of which appeared under the imprint of the W. B. Conkey Co., who were, in fact, the printers to Holst.

Further editions of the *New Teacher's and Pupil's Cyclopaedia* were published at irregular intervals until 1927, and, from 1923 to 1927, the identical work was offered as the *International Reference Work*, except that the latter title contained two additional volumes on "Practical Home and School Methods", which were also retailed separately. Subsequently, as a result of the investigation by the Federal Trade Commission, the two works were merged under one title and re-appeared in 1928 as the *Progressive Reference Library*, under which title it was published until 1939, the year of Holst's death. In 1945, the publishing rights were acquired by a New York publisher, who re-issued the work (with the deceased Holst listed as editor), in 1945, as the *World Scope Encyclopedia*, which was published annually until 1964.

This, in turn, was acquired by Publishers Co., who re-issued it in the same year as the *New American Encyclopedia*, the *World University Encyclopedia*, and, by arrangement with a Florida distributor, as the *World Educator Encyclopedia*. Additionally, in 1954, the same work was issued for supermarket consumption as the *New World Family Encyclopedia* and the *Standard International Encyclopedia*.

The poor quality of the work, under all its earlier titles, is evidenced by the listing, in 1927, of an associate editor who had been dead since 1909.

INTERNATIONAL'S WORLD REFERENCE ENCYCLO-PEDIA. New York: International Readers League and Publishers Periodical Service Bureau, 1942. 10v. 21cm. Editor in Chief: Franklin Julius Meine (b.1896). Former Editor in Chief: Walter Miller (b.1864).

Although first published under this title and format in 1942, the basic material from which it was assembled was formerly copyrighted as the *Standard American Encyclopedia* in 1937, which was, itself, a poorly revised edition of a work of the same title published in 1912. The *Standard American Encyclopedia* was re-issued in 1939, 1940, and 1941, in which year Meine edited the work, which was now under the imprint of the Consolidated Book Publishers.

The *International's World Reference Encyclopedia* was apparently a stopgap issue for distribution by another vendor, and offered as a premium with certain newspapers (as was the *Standard American Encyclopedia*), although another edition was issued in 1944.

Subsequently, in 1945, and again under the imprint of the Consolidated Book Publishers, the work was retitled the *Universal World Reference Encyclopedia*, under which title it has appeared regularly since 1945, with a substantial improvement from earlier issues.

J ACK'S REFERENCE BOOK FOR HOME AND OFFICE; an encyclopaedia of general information, a medical, legal, social, educational and commercial guide, and an English dictionary. Late "Pannell's Reference Book". New and enlarged edition. London and Edinburgh: T. C. & E. C. Jack, 1908. 1088p. 22cm.

A new, enlarged and thoroughly revised edition of *Pannell's Reference Book for Home and Office* and *Everybody's Everyday Reference Book for Home and Office*, both published in 1905 by the Granville Press, London. Although small in content, *Jack's Reference Book* was a very useful and very popular one-volume compendium of general and practical information, similar in size, appearance and content to the more useful *Pears Cyclopaedia*.

During its lifetime it was revised and reprinted several times, and did not become extinct until the mid-1930's. The last recorded edition was published by Thomas Nelson & Sons in 1936.

JOHNSON'S NEW UNIVERSAL CYCLOPAEDIA; a scientific and popular treasury of useful knowledge, with numerous contributions from writers of distinguished eminence in every department of letters and science in the United States and Europe. New York: Alvin J. Johnson & Sons. Pittsburgh: W. D. Cummings, 1876–1878. 4v. 28cm. Editors in Chief: Frederick Augustus Porter Barnard (1809–1889) and Arnold Henry Guyot (1807–1884).

A very well compiled encyclopedia in its original edition, and particularly useful for its coverage of scientific subjects, although the quality of the work deteriorated rapidly in later years. A "revised" edition, splitting the four volumes into eight, was issued in 1884, although no revisions of note had been implemented.

In 1893, omitting the word "New" from the title (a reversal of the usual practice), the work was substantially revised and re-titled *Johnson's Universal Cyclopaedia*. This edition, under the competent editorship of Charles Kendall Adams, President of Cornell University, was issued in parts until its completion in 1897. A curious feature of this printing is that, before publication had been completed, the publishing rights had been acquired by the firm of D. Appleton & Co., with the result that three volumes bore the Appleton imprint, while the remaining five carried the Johnson imprint.

In a new edition in 1901, Johnson's name was omitted from the title, and the work, now expanded to 12 volumes, was published simply as the *Universal Cyclopaedia*. Further editions followed in 1902, 1903 and 1905.

JOHNSON'S UNIVERSAL CYCLOPAEDIA; a new edition, prepared by a corps of 36 editors, assisted by eminent European and American specialists. New York: D. Appleton & Co. and Alvin J. Johnson & Co., 1893–1897. 8v. 28cm. Editor in Chief: Charles Kendall Adams (1835–1902).

A thoroughly revised edition of *Johnson's New Universal Cyclopaedia,* first published in four larger volumes between 1876 and 1878, and re-issued in eight (split) volumes in 1884. For the new 1893 edition, the word "New" was dropped from the original title. While publication was proceeding, the publishing rights to the work were acquired by the firm of D. Appleton & Co., with the curious result that Volumes 1, 5 and 8 bear the Appleton imprint, whereas Volumes 2, 3, 4, 6 and 7 (the first to be published) were issued under the Johnson imprint. Editor of the new edition was Charles Kendall Adams, the then President of Cornell University.

In 1900, Johnson being no longer associated with the work, his name was omitted from the title, and the set, revised and expanded to twelve volumes, was published in 1901 simply as the *Universal Cyclopaedia,* although it was not infrequently referred to as *Appleton's Universal Cyclopaedia,* after the name of its new publisher. Publication continued until a terminal edition in 1905, but the death of Adams in 1902 necessitated a change of editor and, from 1902 until the final printing, revisions were effected by Rossiter Johnson (1840–1931).

• Reference:
Collison.

JUNIOR PEARS ENCYCLOPAEDIA. London: Pelham Books, 1961. 702p. 18cm. Editor: Edward Blishen.

A simplified version of the famous and very useful *Pears Cyclopaedia* designed for younger users. Like its parent volume, it is being published annually.

JUNIOR PICTORIAL ENCYCLOPAEDIA. London: Ward Lock, 1959.

A small encyclopedia for children, simply written and presented, containing a considerable amount of illustrative material. It has previously been issued as the *Wonder Book Encyclopaedia* in 1956 and was re-issued in 1965 as the *Encyclopaedia of Modern Knowledge.*

JUNIOR WORLD ENCYCLOPAEDIA: Special edition. London: Low & Marston, 1960. 16v. 27cm. Editor: M. D. Carter.

In sixteen volumes, but all very thin and small. The work is designed for children, and is apparently derived from the "Golden" series of encyclopedias published in the United States, although a fair amount of revision for British use is evident.

• Reference:
Library Association Record, October 1961.

K NOWLEDGE; the weekly color encyclopaedia. London: Purnell, 1961–1965. 18v. Editor: John Chancellor.

The first weekly part of this elementary encyclopedia was issued on January 9, 1961, and further parts were made available on a weekly basis at 2/- (about 30¢) each. Primarily, the work is designed for children between the ages of eight and twelve, but in parts it reads more like an adult encyclopedia. On the basis of weekly issues, it takes almost four years to complete the set, but in January of each year, the work commences from the first number again, differing only in the color of the masthead. Although the idea of issuing an encyclopedia in parts is as old as encyclopedia publishing itself, it is only in recent years that the practice has been revived, and the improvements in printing techniques mean that such works can now be produced in a much more attractive format than hitherto.

Upon completion, *Knowledge* is contained in 12 or 16 fairly bulky volumes, providing a quite reasonable subject coverage for younger children. The bindings are not, of course, as substantial as those in regular encyclopedias, but, with care, will stand up to fair wear and tear. The most striking feature of the work is the exceptional quality of the colored illustrative material. This is mostly Italian in origin, although the work itself is decidedly British.

In 1965, Purnell launched a work entitled *New Knowledge,* which is similar in several ways, but differs in that the contents are differently arranged. In 1966, Purnell also commenced publication of the *Purnell's New English Encyclopaedia* which is apparently derived from the same basic material. This is also being retailed through bookstores in weekly parts, but, at the same time, the Caxton Publishing Co. are issuing a more strongly bound set as the *New Caxton Encyclopaedia,* beginning late in 1966.

THE KNOWLEDGE BOOK; science, invention, discovery, progress . . . supplemented by a series of review questions for students . . . embellished and illuminated by over 600 photographic half tone illustrations and colorplates. Marietta: G. A. Millikan Co., 1915. 764p. 24cm. Editors: Ferdinand Ellsworth Cary (b.1848), Emory Adams Allen (b.1853), Thomas Herbert Russell (b.1862).

Very probably a re-issue of the *Complete Library of Universal Knowledge* and the identical *New Idea Self Instructor,* both of which were published in 1904 by the Monarch Book Co. of Chicago, and both of which were edited by Cary. The 1915 edition was probably revised by Allen and Russell.

In 1918 the work was re-issued as the *Knowledge Library* and finally in a much expanded edition as the *New Knowledge Library* in 1919.

THE KNOWLEDGE LIBRARY; science, invention, discovery, progress . . . supplemented by a series of review questions for students . . . embellished and illuminated with over 650 photographic half tone illustrations and color plates. Marietta: G. A. Millikan Co., 1918. 764p. 24cm. Editors: Ferdinand Ellsworth Cary (b.1848), Emory Adams Allen (b.1853) and Thomas Herbert Russell (b.1862).

An identical reprint of the *Knowledge Book,* published in 1915 by the same company. In 1919, in an expanded edition, it was re-issued as the *New Knowledge Library.* It was probably based on or derived from the *Complete Library of Universal Knowledge* and the *New Idea Self Instructor,* both issued in 1904.

KONVERSATIONS LEXIKON *see* CONVERSATIONS LEXICON (Brockhaus)

LA SALLE EXTENSION UNIVERSITY ENCYCLOPEDIA; compiled with the assistance of a large corps of specialists and experts. Chicago: De Bower-Chapline Co., 1909. 1367p. 28cm. Editor: Charles Higgins.

A fairly large comprehensive one-volume work with many brief entries, also published simultaneously in 1909 as *Everybody's Encyclopedia* and *Webster's Universal Encyclopedia.*

In 1910, Higgins is recorded as the joint editor of the *Modern Universal Encyclopedia,* which is probably an abridgement of the three earlier works and this was re-issued in 1913 as the *Home and Office Reference Book of Facts.*

LAUREL AND GOLD ENCYCLOPEDIA. London and Glasgow: Collins, 1935. 316p. 22cm. Editors: John Redgwick Crossland (b.1892) and John Maxey Parrish.

A small encyclopedia for children, of browsing interest rather than reference usefulness. It was published simultaneously as the *Clear Type Encyclopaedia,* and is abridged from the *Golden Encyclopaedia for Children,* first published in 1934, and several other similar works compiled by Crossland and Parrish.

LEXICON TECHNICUM; or, an universal English dictionary of arts and sciences. London: John Harris, 1704. folio. Compiler: John Harris (1667?– 1719).

Generally considered to be the first alphabetically arranged English general encyclopedia, although, in fact, a work entitled, *Universal, Historical, Geographical, Chronological and Classical Dictionary,* by an anonymous compiler, published only a few months previously in 1703, is an alphabetically arranged work of reference.

Not in itself a great encyclopedia, the *Lexicon Technicum* is historically important in that Harris, a scientist of repute and a Fellow of the Royal Society, started the trend towards the domestic production of encyclopedias in Britain. Up to this time, publishers had been translating French encyclopedias for use in the British Isles, but Harris did such a fine job that, within a short time, the situation completely reversed itself, and the foremost French encyclopedias were based on the better English works.

Because of his connections through the Royal Society, Harris had the immense advantage of being able to draw on the resources of the greatest scholars of the day. His work is one of the first examples of an editor drawing on the knowledge of experts and, as such, Harris can be credited with the innovation of the modern system of inviting contributions from established specialists.

A second edition of the *Lexicon Technicum* was issued between 1708 and 1710, when it was also expanded to two volumes, and a third and a fourth edition appeared at intervals of about ten years apart. The final edition (the fifth) was published in 1736, 17 years after the death of the compiler, and this appeared under the imprint of J. Walthoe, London. In 1744, a folio supplement, prepared by a "Society of Gentlemen" was issued.

The *Lexicon Technicum,* despite its Latin title, was thoroughly English, and emphasized the practical and scientific subjects of the time at the expense of the humanities. On the other hand, however, it was distinguished for its excellent plates, line drawings and diagrams and for its provision of bibliographies for several of the more important scientific subjects.

• Reference:
Collison.

LIBRARY OF ESSENTIAL KNOWLEDGE; the practical self educator, including "Webster's Comprehensive Encyclopedic Dictionary" and all its supplementary parts. Chicago: H. Ross, 1942. 1700p. 26cm. Editor in Chief: Franklin Julius Meine (b.1896).

Neither an encyclopedia nor a dictionary, but a haphazard collection of tables and text, without any discernible system of arrangement, and without an index. Although the work contains quite a lot of useful information, practical as well as general, its poor arrangement makes any information difficult to locate.

This work, or parts of it, have also been published as *Webster's Columbia Encyclopedic Dictionary* (1940), *Webster's Comprehensive Encyclopedic Dictionary* (1941) and *Webster's Encyclopedic Dictionary* (1941). Another edition of the *Library of Essential Knowledge* was issued in 1954, but with 600 fewer pages, simultaneously with the *Consolidated Webster Compre-*

hensive Encyclopedic Dictionary and the *Consolidated Webster Encyclo-pedic Dictionary*.

LIBRARY OF GENERAL KNOWLEDGE; embracing history, biography, astronomy, architecture, natural history, poetry, tales, etc., and about 120 useful receipts. Embellished by over 200 engravings. Cincinnati: J. A. & U. P. James, 1850. 248p. 25cm.

Not an encyclopedia, but a small handbook of miscellaneous information and irrelevant reading material, accompanied by some practical "how-to do-it" type of information.

LIBRARY OF KNOWLEDGE; multum in parvo; a compact, com-prehensive storehouse of general knowledge, treating history, geography, bi-ography, literature, economics, civics, art, science, discovery and invention, embracing over 16,000 subjects. Chicago: American Surveys Inc., 1936. 8v. 27cm. Editor: Paul Ingebrikt Neergaard (b.1884).

The only recorded copyright for this work in the Library of Congress catalog gives a publishing date of 1936, but it was certainly being dis-tributed much earlier than this in 1929 in a four-volume edition, with an additional fifth volume providing a loose-leaf extension service, the expan-sion to eight volumes coming later.

It was an extremely poor work and badly out-of-date by 1932. It appears to be a direct reprint from the plates of the old *Bufton's Universal Cyclo-paedia* (1919) with virtually no revision.

LIBRARY OF NATIONAL INFORMATION AND POPU-LAR KNOWLEDGE. London: Ward, Lock, 1884–1887. 9v. 22cm.

Between 1859 and 1891, the old, established firm of Ward, Lock were quite active in the publication of encyclopedias, beginning with the *Family Cyclopaedia* in 1859, followed by *Beeton's Encyclopaedia of Universal In-formation* in 1879, the *Universal Instructor* in 1880, and eventually the above work.

With the exception of the work by Beeton, no editors or compilers are listed, but it is not beyond the bounds of possibility that the *Library of National Information* is a re-issue or an adaptation of the earlier works.

LIBRARY OF ORIGINAL SOURCES. New York and Chicago: University Research Extension, 1907. 10v. 26cm. Editor in Chief: Oliver Joseph Thatcher (b.1857).

An anthology of general and specific sources of information on a wide variety of subjects, rather than actual information on given topics, arranged topically and chronologically, with an index in the tenth volume.

According to the collation this was an editor's edition, limited to 1,000 numbered and registered copies. Another edition was issued in 1915, with the additional sub-titling, "ideas that have influenced civilization".

LIBRARY OF UNIVERSAL KNOWLEDGE; a reprint of the last (1880) edition of "Chambers's Encyclopaedia", with copious additions by American editors. New York: American Book Exchange and S. W. Green's Sons, 1880–1881. 15v. 24cm.

As clearly stated in the sub-titling, this very useful and important work was a reprint, but with additions, of the ten-volume British encyclopedia, "Chambers's Encyclopaedia, an authoritative work which had gained wide acceptance as one of the foremost encyclopedias in the English language.

Of greater interest, however, is that the *Library of Universal Knowledge* provided the basic material from which the *International Cyclopaedia* was compiled and published by Dodd, Mead in 1898. This, in turn, was thoroughly revised and substantially enlarged to become the famous *New International Encyclopedia,* published between 1902–1904, one of the finest encyclopedias ever published, and still valuable as an authoritative source of reference because of the vast amount of accurate information it contained in its more than 80,000 subject entries.

LINCOLN LIBRARY OF ESSENTIAL INFORMATION; an up-to-date manual for daily reference, for self-instruction, and for general culture. Buffalo, N.Y.: Frontier Press Co., 1924. 2054p. 25cm. Compiler: Michael J. Kinsella (d.1928).

The *Lincoln Library* ranks along with the differently arranged **Columbia Encyclopedia** as one of the two best one-volume reference handbooks in the English language.

The work is arranged by subject, contains more than 3 million words, and is virtually an amalgamation of 12 separate books into one, linked by a very comprehensive index of more than 20,000 entries. Despite its one-, or alternative two-volume format, it contains more information than several multi-volume encyclopedias.

Since its inception, the *Lincoln Library* has been published regularly at intervals of two years, the edition of 1966 being the 27th in the series. Originally in a one-volume format only, the work has, since 1928, been available in a two-volume format also, the index in this edition being repeated in each volume.

The *Lincoln Library* is not, however, the first work of its type to be published by the Frontier Press. Before the first edition in 1924, they had also published a smaller but similar work entitled the *Standard Dictionary of Facts,* first published in 1908 and not discontinued until 1927. The *Lincoln Library* was not a revision, adaptation or enlargement of the earlier work, but the material assembled for the smaller handbook certainly provided the base from which the larger edition was launched.

It is not without significance that the *Standard Dictionary of Facts* was edited for several years by Henry Woldmar Ruoff (1867–1935), who also edited two very similar works at about the same period, the *Century Book of Facts* (1902), and the *Volume Library* (now *Cowles Comprehensive Encyclopedia*) in 1911.

- **References:**
Subscription Books Bulletin, January 1930, October 1937.
Booklist and Subscription Books Bulletin, January 1, 1962.

LITTLE & IVES ILLUSTRATED READY REFERENCE ENCYCLOPEDIA; for home and school use. New York: J. J. Little & Ives Co., 1961. 20v. 26cm. Editor in Chief: Franklin Dunham (b.1892).

According to the publishers, this was a completely new work when first published in 1961, and was designed primarily as a low cost reference work for family use, to be sold through supermarkets and similar outlets on the "book-a-week" plan.

It would appear, however, despite some improvements and revisions, that the work is derived from two earlier titles, published by Little & Ives, edited by Dunham, and published in 1956. Like the title under discussion, these were also designed for sale through supermarkets at a low cost, as the *New Pictorial Encyclopedia of the World*, and the *Illustrated Encyclopedia of the World*. Except for the addition of a two-volume atlas and gazetteer to the former title, the works were identical.

The firm of Little & Ives ran into financial difficulties in 1965, and further editions of the *Little & Ives Illustrated Ready Reference Encyclopedia* and other works were suspended indefinitely.

LITTLE CYCLOPAEDIA OF COMMON THINGS; with numerous illustrations. Second edition. London: Kegan Paul, Trench & Co., 1882. 660p. 24cm. Editor: Sir George William Cox (1827–1902).

According to the only traceable record, the 1882 edition of this small work is the second, from which it has to be assumed that a first edition had appeared, possibly under another title, about 1880. A third edition is recorded as having been published in 1884, and a twelfth, probably the last, in 1906, then published under the imprint of Swan Sonnenschein, and it was evidently a popular work.

The editor, Sir George Cox had, about 1860, been associated with the much larger *Dictionary of Science, Literature and Art*, edited by W. T. Brande, and first published in 1842, but there is no apparent connection between the two works.

LLOYD'S ENCYCLOPAEDIC DICTIONARY *see* **ENCYCLOPAEDIC DICTIONARY**

THE LONDON ENCYCLOPAEDIA; or, universal dictionary of science, art, literature and practical mechanics . . . by the original editor of the "Encyclopaedia Metropolitana", assisted by professional and other gentlemen. London: T. Tegg, 1829. 22v. 22cm. Editor: Thomas Curtis.

In the first half of the nineteenth century (and ever since), quite a number of relatively unimportant encyclopedias were appearing in both Britain and the United States to meet the growing demand for reasonably priced reference works, and the *London Encyclopaedia* was but one of these.

Its chief, if not its only, claim to fame lies in the fact that portions of it were edited by Thomas Curtis, the original editor of the excellent but ill-fated *Encyclopaedia Metropolitana*. In actual fact, the contribution of Curtis to the more famous work was quite small, only six of the original 59 parts being issued under his editorial direction.

LOOSELEAF ENCYCLOPEDIA *see* LIBRARY OF KNOWL-EDGE

LOW'S POCKET ENCYCLOPAEDIA *see* POCKET ENCY-CLOPAEDIA

MACMILLAN EVERYMAN'S ENCYCLOPEDIA. 4th edition. New York: Macmillan Co., 1959. 12v. 22cm. Editor: Ernest Franklin Bozman (b.1895).

Except for the title page and binding, this work is an identical reprint of the fourth edition of *Everyman's Encyclopaedia*, published in London by J. M. Dent in 1958. By arrangement with the Macmillan Co., the set was marketed in the United States under the Macmillan imprint, with that company's name preceding the original title.

Although now out of print, this is one of the finest "small" encyclopedias of modern times. It would probably not appeal as a family set to American users, both because of its emphasis on things British and the employment of a not readily understood system of abbreviations as a measure of economy. For public and academic libraries, however, this fine 9 million word small encyclopedia represented excellent value as a source of scholarly and highly accurate information to supplement the standard American reference works.

The *Everyman's Encyclopaedia* has a long and distinguished history, the first edition in 1913 being a complete revision and re-writing of the excellent *English Cyclopaedia* of 1854–1862 (frequently referred to as *Knight's Cyclopaedia*) which was itself modelled on the popular *Penny Cyclopaedia* of 1833–1843.

• Reference:
Booklist and Subscription Books Bulletin, July 15, 1959.

MAUNDER'S TREASURY OF KNOWLEDGE AND LI-BRARY OF REFERENCE. 2nd edition. London: Samuel Maunder, 1830. 2v. 17cm. Compiler: Samuel Maunder (1785–1849).

A small, but quite useful work published in two parts, but frequently bound as one volume. Part 1 comprised a dictionary of the English language, and Part 2 contained a miscellaneous collection of general information. The work was probably reprinted several times before the death of Maunder in 1849, but it was not until 1873 that a new edition was issued.

The revision of this work was begun by Bernard Bolingbroke Woodward who, however, died in 1869, before completing his revision, and it was carried through to completion by two of his assistants, John Morris and William Hughes (1817–1876).

The work was evidently popular in the United States also, and a so-called "third" edition was published in New York by the firm of Conner & Cooke in 1833, stereotyped, with some improvements, from the London edition, and another American edition followed in 1850 under the imprint of C. C. Childs. The name of Maunder was not included in these reprints, however, and the work was simply entitled the *Treasury of Knowledge and Library of Reference.*

MEE'S CHILDREN'S ENCYCLOPAEDIA see CHILDREN'S ENCYCLOPAEDIA

MERIT STUDENTS ENCYCLOPEDIA. New York: Crowell-Collier Educational Corporation, 1967. 20v. Editor in Chief: Bernard S. Cayne. Editorial Director: William D. Halsey.

An entirely new and originally researched encyclopedia for elementary and junior high school students, by the publishers of the highly reputable adult *Collier's Encyclopedia.* The work is geared to the school curricula of the United States, but it is international in scope, and pays special attention to advanced instruction in the sciences.

Reputed to have cost more than $7,000,000 to produce and taken more than seven years to prepare. More than 15,000 illustrations (many in color) accompany its 9 million words and 12,000 pages.

MODERN ACHIEVEMENT. New York: University Society, 1904. 10v. 24cm. Editor in Chief: Edward Everett Hale (1822–1909).

A topically arranged anthology of general knowledge, each volume dealing with a specific subject area and complete within itself.

Hale is not known to be connected with any other encyclopedic work, but the University Society were quite active in the field, although their encyclopedic publications were almost invariably of a sub-standard quality.

MODERN AMERICAN ENCYCLOPEDIA; progressively planned. Chicago: Modern American Corporation, 1934. 8v. 24cm. Editorial Director: Calvin Rogers Fisk (b.1896).

The history of this work is rather complicated. It can be traced back with certainty to 1900, when a two-volume work entitled the *Students Cyclopaedia* was both edited and published by Chandler Belden Beach (1839–1928), and also issued under the imprint of J. M. Howard, afterwards the Howard-Severance Co. In 1902, this was republished, again in two volumes, as the *Students Reference Work*, and a reprint followed in 1903. By 1909, however, the publishing rights had been acquired by F. E. Compton & Co., and they, after revising and expanding the work to four volumes, re-titled it the *New Students Reference Work*, and under the Compton imprint, further editions were issued in 1911, 1912, 1913, 1919 and 1920, by which time the set had been expanded to seven volumes.

At about this time, however, Compton was engaged in the compilation of their completely new *Compton's Pictured Encyclopedia* and, before this was published in 1922, they transferred the publishing rights pertaining to the *New Students Reference Work* to the firm of S. L. Weedon & Co., Cleveland, and under the Weedon imprint, further editions were issued in 1925, 1928 and 1930. By then, however, Weedon were themselves engaged in the compilation of a new junior encyclopedia, and in 1933 the Modern American Corp. purchased the original plates from Weedon and reissued the work as the *Modern American Encyclopedia* in 1934.

By this time much of the material was obsolete, and the 1934 issue was very much below the acceptable norm. Apparently the Modern American Corp. resorted to some questionable tactics in the selling of the work, and in 1939, the Federal Trade Commission dealt with complaints against the work (Docket#3503).

Although Fisk is named as the editorial director of the 1934, 1935 and 1936 issues of the work, his actual contribution appears to have been the lending of his name for prestige and sales purposes. During the three years of issue of the *Modern American Encyclopedia*, Fisk was also the editorial director of the *New Standard Encyclopedia*, but apart from a probable common ownership, the works are otherwise unrelated.

• Reference:
Subscription Books Bulletin, April 1934.

MODERN CHILDREN'S LIBRARY OF KNOWLEDGE.
London: New Educational Press (Odhams), 1957. 6v. 25cm.

A broadly classified set with an encyclopedic index in the final volume, Books 1–5 dealing with nature, geography, history, science, invention, arts and pastimes. Additional material is provided in the form of questions, "how-to-do-it" projects etc., while stories and other literary features are included in Book 6, along with the index.

Designed for younger readers, the work is quite well produced and provides enjoyable browsing material, but is of less value as a reference for specific information.

A work with an identical title, but now in eight volumes, has been published by the Grolier Society, London, since 1963, with Leslie Wolff and Geoffrey Spencer as editors.

• References:
Library Association Record, October 1961.
Walford, A. J. Guide to Reference Material (suppl.)

MODERN CONCISE ENCYCLOPEDIA; a library of world knowledge, containing over 1400 illustrations and 64 maps made expressly for this work. New York: Unicorn Press, 1940. 15v. 22cm. Editor: Alexander Hopkins McDannald (1877–1948).

This is the supermarket edition, in 15 thin volumes, of a work which first appeared in a one-volume format in 1933 as the *Modern Encyclopedia*, with further editions in 1935, 1936 and 1937. In the latter year, the work was quite considerably revised and expanded and published as the *Concise Encyclopedia*, in eight relatively thin volumes, and the present work is a revision of this.

Originally, the work was compiled by the staff of the *Encyclopedia Americana* (McDannald was at that time the editor of the larger work), but the revisions for the 1940 edition were implemented by William H. Hendelson. Of the 15 volumes comprising the 1940 reprint, only 12 actually contained the encyclopedic material of the earlier titles, two others being devoted to a chronological history of the world, with the last volume containing a rather poor index.

In its earlier days, this work was quite useful, but by 1940 much of the material had become badly dated. In 1943, it reverted to its original one-volume format as the *New Modern Encyclopedia*, and went through several printings until its demise in 1949.

• Reference:

Subscription Books Bulletin, January 1942.

THE MODERN CYCLOPAEDIA . . . a new edition revised and extended. London: Gresham Publishing Co., 1906–1907. 8v. 24cm. Editor: Charles Annandale (1843–1915).

The history of this work goes back to at least 1841, when an eight-volume work entitled the *Popular Encyclopaedia* appeared under the imprint of Blackie & Son, Glasgow. Aptly named, the set went through several printings up to 1893, Annandale having succeeded to the editorship in 1882. In 1901, under the Gresham imprint, the work was re-issued as the *New Popular Encyclopaedia*. Annandale also edited, in 1889–1890, *Blackie's Modern Cyclopedia of Universal Information*, which bears striking similarities to the *Modern Cyclopedia*. Blackie's publication was also issued in the United States as the *New Cabinet Cyclopaedia* in 1891, which later became the *New National Cyclopaedia and Treasury*.

Annandale, who is probably better known for his compilation of dictionaries, was associated with several other encyclopedic works published in the United States up to 1913, but it is doubtful if any of these were original, all probably stemming from the earlier *Popular Encyclopaedia*.

THE MODERN ENCYCLOPAEDIA (Burrowes); or, general dictionary of arts, sciences and literature. London: Richards & Co., 1816–1820. 11v. 23cm. Editor: Amyas Deane Burrowes.

A rather poor work which failed to compete with the larger more authoritative works of the time. Neither Burrowes, nor Richards are connected with any other encyclopedic works, and no further editions of the *Modern Encyclopaedia* are recorded.

THE MODERN ENCYCLOPAEDIA (Gorell); illustrated. London: Odhams Press, 1961. 8v. 23cm. Advisory Editor: Lord Gorell (Ronald Gorell Barnes Gorell, b.1884).

This rather small work, which was still in print in 1966, appears to be the same or similar to the *Odhams Encyclopaedia* published in 1953, of which Lord Gorell was also the advisory editor.

Odhams have published a considerable number of encyclopedic works of varying size since 1932 or even earlier, and this work is probably derived from one or more of the earlier titles.

THE MODERN ENCYCLOPAEDIA (Hammerton); an abridged version of the "Harmsworth Universal Encyclopaedia". London: Amalgamated Press, 1933. 1024p. 24cm. Editor: Sir John Alexander Hammerton (1871–1949).

As clearly stated in the subtitling, this is a one-volume condensation of the useful multi-volume *Harmsworth's Universal Encyclopaedia*, published between 1920 and 1923 by the same company. It is probably derived also from the *Concise Universal Encyclopaedia*, a larger one-volume desk encyclopedia published in 1930 and also edited by Hammerton, as was *Cassell's Modern Encyclopaedia* which, except for the imprint, was identical to the *Modern Encyclopaedia*.

In 1939, with an additional 31 pages of maps, the work was re-issued as the *Modern Encyclopaedia and World Atlas*.

MODERN ENCYCLOPEDIA (McDannald); a new library of world knowledge, complete in one volume. New York: W. H. Wise & Co., 1933. 1327p. 23cm. Editor in Chief: Alexander Hopkins McDannald (1877–1948).

In its day a very useful one-volume desk encyclopedia containing some 22,000 brief items of information. Originally the work was compiled by the editorial staff of the *Encyclopedia Americana*, which was also edited by McDannald, but this much smaller work is by no means an abridgement or condensation. Useful for quick reference, it proved very popular during the Depression years, meeting the needs of its time, and running through several printings between 1933 and 1937. A cheap edition also appeared under the imprint of Grosset & Dunlap in 1936.

The merit of the work declined in later years, especially when it changed title and format in 1937 and was published in a supermarket edition of eight volumes as the *Concise Encyclopedia*. This was followed by an edition under the imprint of the Unicorn Press in no less than 15 volumes (some 100 pages to each volume) in 1940 as the *Modern Concise Encyclopedia*.

Finally, in 1943, reverting to its original one-volume format, Wise published a completely revised edition, again as the *Modern Encyclopedia*, under the editorship of Frank Webster Price (b.1901). Further editions followed in 1946 and 1947, when it was again revised and expanded. The last edition appeared in 1949, since when this once useful work has been out of print.

• Reference:
Subscription Books Bulletin, January 1934.

MODERN ENCYCLOPEDIA (Saalfield). Akron: Saalfield Publishing Co., 1912. 2v.

No copyrights appear to have been issued for this small work, nor could copies be traced for examination. The Saalfield Publishing Co. had earlier issued the *Werner Universal Encyclopedia* in 1899, and it is possible that the *Modern Encyclopedia* is derived either from this or from one of the other encyclopedias issued under the Werner imprint (also of Akron) between 1897 and 1909, when Saalfield apparently acquired Werner.

Both companies were concerned with pirated reprints of the ninth edition of the *Encyclopaedia Britannica*, and it is also possible that this work was designed as a supplement to the reprints.

MODERN ENCYCLOPAEDIA FOR CHILDREN; a companion to school work and out of school interests, etc. London and Glasgow: Collins & Sons, 1933. 756p. 25cm. Editors: John Redgwick Crossland (b.1892) and John Maxey Parrish.

A small one-volume miscellany of simply presented information for children. It was published simultaneously in 1933, under the imprint of the Odhams Press, as the *Wonder Encyclopaedia for Children*.

In 1934, a two-volume version was issued by British Books as the *Golden Encyclopaedia for Children*, while in the United States it was also published under a slightly different title in 1935 as the *Modern Encyclopedia for Young People*. The work was re-issued in 1940 as the *Modern Illustrated Encyclopedia*, but in 1965 re-appeared under its original title again under the imprint of Odhams Press.

MODERN ILLUSTRATED ENCYCLOPAEDIA. London and Glasgow: Collins Clear Type Press, 1940. 756p. 25cm. Editors: John Redgwick Crossland (b.1892) and John Maxey Parrish.

An identical reprint of the *Modern Encyclopaedia for Children* and the *Wonder Encyclopaedia for Children*, both issued in 1933, and the two-volume *Golden Encyclopaedia for Children* published under a different imprint in 1934. It was subsequently re-issued in 1965 as the *Modern Encyclopaedia for Children*.

MODERN LIBRARY OF KNOWLEDGE. New York: The Abbey Book Co., Inc., 1940. 15v. 24cm. Editor: Silas Edgar Farquhar (1887–1948).

A poor work, designed mainly for sale through supermarkets and apparently published once only. No clear indication of its origins could be gleaned either from the work itself or from any other source, but it may well have been derived from the nondescript *Library of Knowledge,* an eight-volume set last published in 1937, which was itself based on the old *Bufton's Universal Cyclopaedia.* Bibliographies, but not particularly well compiled, are included at the end of most volumes.

The editor, Farquhar, was previously associated with the *World Book Encyclopedia* and subsequently edited the *Grolier Encyclopedia,* but there is certainly no connection with either work insofar as content is concerned.

MODERN MARVELS ENCYCLOPEDIA *see* STANDARD ENCYCLOPEDIA

MODERN STANDARD ENCYCLOPAEDIA. London and Glasgow: Collins, 1938. 448p. 25cm. Editor: John Redgwick Crossland (b.1892).

A very small, simply presented one-volume work for children, probably derived from the *New Standard Encyclopaedia,* first published in 1932, and other one-volume handbooks edited by Crossland.

MODERN UNIVERSAL ENCYCLOPEDIA; a reference book of universal knowledge, with illustrations and pronunciation, compiled with the assistance of a large corps of specialists and experts. New York and Chicago: Fidelity Publishing House, 1910. 624p. 21cm. Editors: Charles Higgins, Charles Annandale (1843–1915), R. Archer Johnson and H. D. Lovett.

Although Annandale's name is associated with this small work, it is apparent that it appears there for prestige purposes only, as this inferior small work is in no way connected with the much more important multi-volume works published under his editorship.

The *Modern Universal Encyclopedia* is quite certainly an abridged or adapted version of *Webster's Universal Encyclopedia,* edited by Charles Higgins and published in 1909 by the De Bower-Chapline Co. under both this and two other titles simultaneously. In 1913, the work was re-issued in a slightly larger format as the *Home and Office Reference Book of Facts.*

MODERN UNIVERSITY ENCYCLOPEDIA; with extensive illustrations, world atlas, sports supplement and chronological tables. London: Educational Book Co., 1957. 1200p. 22cm. Editors: George F. Maine and J. B. Foreman.

A small one-volume work with a somewhat pretentious title, containing a miscellany of interesting general information. Under the imprint of Collins, it was also issued as the *New Age Encyclopaedia, World Atlas and Sports Supplement* in 1957 and again in 1963.

NATIONAL CYCLOPAEDIA OF USEFUL KNOWL-
EDGE. London: Charles Knight, 1847–1851. 12v. 22cm.

This work is probably derived from the *Penny Cyclopaedia* of the Society
for the Diffusion of Useful Knowledge, published in London between 1833
and 1843 in either 27- or 14-volume editions. It is also related directly to
the *English Cyclopaedia*, published subsequently in 1854–1862, and the
much smaller *Imperial Cyclopaedia*, published between 1850–1853, all of
which were published under the imprint of Charles Knight.

A second edition of the *National Cyclopaedia* appeared between 1856
and 1859, enlarged to 13 volumes, but this appeared under the imprint
of George Routledge. Subsequently, ownership of the work was acquired
by the firm of W. Mackenzie, who published a new edition in 1867 as
the *National Encyclopaedia*.

• Reference:
Collison.

THE NATIONAL ENCYCLOPAEDIA (Brabner); a dictionary
of universal knowledge, by writers of eminence in literature, science and art.
London: W. Mackenzie, 1867–1868. 13v. 24cm. Editor: J. H. F. Brabner.

Owing its origins to the popular *Penny Cyclopaedia* published by the
Society for the Diffusion of Useful Knowledge between 1833 and 1843,
the *National Encyclopaedia* of 1867 is a revised edition of the *National
Cyclopaedia of Useful Knowledge*, published by Charles Knight between
1847 and 1851, and by George Routledge between 1856–1859.

Mackenzie's edition increased the size of the work to 14 volumes, the
last of which was a world atlas. Another edition was issued in 1875, and
a revised edition, which became the last, between 1884 and 1888.

THE NATIONAL ENCYCLOPEDIA (Colange); a compendium
of universal information, with the pronunciation of every term and proper
name. Illustrated with 746 wood engravings. New York and Philadelphia:
National Encyclopedia Publishing Co., 1873. 960p. 26cm. Compiler: Leo de
Colange (b.1819).

Evidently a re-issue or adaptation of *Zell's Popular Encyclopedia*, a two-
volume work compiled by Colange and first published in 1870. There is
strong evidence that it was also issued in London, also in 1873, as the
Peoples Encyclopaedia, the sub-titling being identical.

Subsequently, the work was re-issued in 1878 as the *Universal Encyclopedia* and in 1899 as the *School Encyclopedia*, although all the titles appeared under different imprints.

NATIONAL ENCYCLOPEDIA (Suzallo). New York: P. F. Collier
& Co., 1932. 11v. 27cm. Editor in Chief: Henry Suzallo (1875–1933) Editorial Director: William Waite Beardsley (b.1885).

Although the firm of Collier had been actively engaged in the publication of encyclopedias since 1898, their *National Encyclopedia* of 1932 was an entirely new work, and not a revision of their *Collier's New Encyclopedia*, which had enjoyed a successful run from 1902 to 1929, although the editorial staff for both works was much the same.

The *National Encyclopedia* was designed for popular adult use, providing brief and readily comprehensible information on a wide range of subjects. With a supplementary year book and a loose leaf revision service (the eleventh volume), Collier published the work annually until 1950. The publishing rights were then acquired by Educational Enterprises, a Washington-based publisher, who re-issued the work in 1960, but with so little revision as to make it basically the same printing as in 1950. In fact, the edition of 1960 was "edited" by Henry Suzallo, who had died twenty-seven years previously. Revisions have been implemented since then, but the work, which was originally a very useful one, has deteriorated considerably and can no longer be considered as an authoritative source of information.

Collier's Encyclopedia, first published in 1949, replaced the *National Encyclopedia* as the major product of the firm, but the works are not related in any other manner.

• Reference:
Subscription Books Bulletin, January 1933.

NATIONAL ENCYCLOPEDIA FOR THE HOME, SCHOOL AND LIBRARY. Chicago: National Encyclopedia Co., 1923. 10v. 24cm. Editorial Director: Harold Melvin Stanford (b.1875).

Published once only under this title, the work is an identical reprint of the 1922 edition of the *Standard Reference Work*, published by the Standard Education Society. This work originated in 1910 as *Aiton's Encyclopedia*, changing its title to the *Standard Reference Work* in 1912.

It is not clear whether the new title was intended to be permanent, but as it clearly clashed with a similarly named work published by Collier in 1932, the work reverted to its original title of the *Standard Reference Work* in later years.

In 1930 it changed title once again to the *New Standard Encyclopedia*, under which title it is still being published by the Standard Education Society. For a short period the work was published in Canada as the *Consolidated Encyclopedia* for distribution in other English-speaking countries.

NATIONAL ENCYCLOPEDIA OF REFERENCE; authoritative, practical, complete; an American library embracing science, sociology, philosophy, history, fine arts, languages, religion, law, literature, useful arts and the many thousands of subjects into which they branch. Compiled with the assistance of a large body of the most eminent authorities in the various departments. New York and Philadelphia: Standard Bookbinding Co., 1912. 9v.

23cm. Editors: Thomas Francis Furey (b.1852), Charles Annandale (1843–1915), Walter Hart Blumenthal (b.1883).

This work has been published under so many different titles and under so many different imprints, that its actual origins are obscure.

Evidently, however, it is a re-issue of the *New and Complete Universal Self Pronouncing Encyclopedia* (1905) and the *New Cosmopolitan Encyclopedia* (1906), as both Annandale and Blumenthal are associated with these titles. Annandale's name, however, must have been used in a rather loose context, as he is listed as the editor or joint editor of at least eight earlier works, the first to appear in the United States under his name being the *New Cabinet Cyclopaedia* first published in 1891, which was the American revision of *Blackie's Modern Cyclopaedia of Universal Information,* published in Glasgow between 1889 and 1890.

The *National Encyclopedia of Reference* or variations or adaptations from it have been published in the United States as the *New National Cyclopaedia* (1899), *XX Century Cyclopaedia* (1901) and the *New Twentieth Century Cyclopaedia* (1903).

NELSON COMPLETE ENCYCLOPEDIA. London and New York: Thomas Nelson & Sons, 1937. 24v. 25cm. Editor in Chief: John Huston Finley (1863–1940). Canadian Editor: Sir Robert Falconer. European Editor: Sir Henry John Newbolt (1862–1938).

This is a reprint, with revisions to October 1, 1937, of the much older *Nelson's Perpetual Looseleaf Encyclopedia,* published in 12 volumes between 1917 and 1926. The 1937 edition, however, omitted the index and colored illustrations of the loose-leaf edition and was encased in a cheaper binding. Both titles are directly derived from the original *Nelson's Encyclopaedia,* first published in 1906.

In 1940, both works were re-issued as *Nelson's Encyclopedia: Unabridged,* and *Nelson's New Looseleaf Encyclopedia,* in 15 and 12 volumes respectively, the former appearing under the imprint of Columbia Educational Books, a subsidiary of the Consolidated Book Publishers, and the latter under the imprint of Thomas Nelson & Sons.

The work is reputed to have provided the background material for two other quite different works, the *Home University Encyclopedia* (1937) and the *American Peoples Encyclopedia* (1948), but, whereas the *Home University Encyclopedia* is an inferior work, the *American Peoples* is a work of stature, and it seems odd that two works, so widely divergent in quality, could emanate from a common source.

• Reference:
Subscription Books Bulletin, April 1938.

NELSON'S ENCYCLOPAEDIA (Colby); everybody's book of reference . . . profusely illustrated. New York: Thomas Nelson & Sons. 1906–1907. 12v. 25cm. Editor in Chief: Frank Moore Colby (1865–1925). British Editor: George Sandeman.

In its day, this was one of the most popular encyclopedias which could be purchased at a reasonable cost, and enjoyed substantial sales both in Britain and the United States for several years.

Nelson's Encyclopaedia is the American edition of the British *Harmsworth Encyclopaedia*, re-edited for use in the United States by Frank Moore Colby, one of the editors of the excellent *New International Encyclopedia*. In 1907, a variation, sub-titled the "Perpetual Loose-leaf edition", was made available, in which the publishers issued subscribers with about five hundred sheets of revised material each year, which were intended to update the subject matter by insertion between the loose unpaged volumes.

A reprint of the main work was issued in London in 1911 and again in 1913, but these were updated by *Nelson's Encyclopaedia Year Book*. Subsequently, in 1917, the work was re-issued as *Nelson's Perpetual Looseleaf Encyclopedia*, with further printings in 1920 and 1926, when an index volume was also made available.

Meanwhile, in Britain, another edition was published in 1920 as the *New Age Encyclopaedia*. It was not until 1937, however, that the work was again revised, when it was published in a 24-volume edition as the *Nelson Complete Encyclopedia*, but this in turn was succeeded by *Nelson's Encyclopedia: Unabridged* and *Nelson's New Looseleaf Encyclopedia*, both of which were issued in 1940.

The *Nelson's Encyclopaedia* and its various editions have been out of print for several years, but it is of interest to note that the good *American Peoples Encyclopedia* was based on the most recent editions of the work, as also was the *World Wide Illustrated Encyclopedia* (later the *Home University Encyclopedia*). However, this latter work was so badly edited that it does not fairly represent its connection with the Nelson reference works.

NELSON'S ENCYCLOPAEDIA (Gee). London and New York: Thomas Nelson & Sons, 1951. 743p. 22cm. Compiler: Herbert Leslie Gee (b.1901).

Although the title is the same, this small one-volume work is totally unrelated to the multi-volume work first published under the Nelson imprint in 1905 and not finally discontinued until 1940.

The present title has gone through several printings since first issued in 1951 and was still in print in 1966. It is too small a work, however, than to be other than a useful desk encyclopedia providing very brief and limited information.

NELSON'S ENCYCLOPEDIA: UNABRIDGED. Chicago: Columbia Educational Books Inc., 1940. 15v. 24cm. Editor in Chief: Franklin Julius Meine (b.1896). Former Editors: John Huston Finley (1863–1940), Sir Robert A. Falconer and Sir Henry J. Newbolt (1862–1938).

This is the last known edition of the once very popular *Nelson's Encyclopaedia*, first published in 1906, and the *Nelson's Perpetual Looseleaf Encyclopedia*, which was revised and reprinted as the *Nelson Complete En-*

cyclopedia in 1937. This final edition was apparently designed to be sold through drug stores and food supermarkets at about $1.00 per volume. Each volume was in two parts, which meant a total outlay of $30.00 to subscribers.

At one time a very good work indeed, the set had suffered badly through inadequate editing and, as a result, it had deteriorated badly in quality. It is of interest to note, however, that Meine, the editor of the last edition, later directed the compilation of the very good *American Peoples Encyclopedia*, first published in 1948, which drew extensively on the background material in *Nelson's Encyclopaedia*.

- Reference:
Subscription Books Bulletin, April 1943; October 1943.

NELSON'S NEW LOOSELEAF ENCYCLOPEDIA. New York: Thomas Nelson & Sons, 1940. 12v. 26cm. Editor in Chief: John Huston Finley (1863–1940). Canadian Editor: Sir Robert Alexander Falconer (b.1867). European Editor: Sir Henry John Newbolt (1862–1938).

The final printing of *Nelson's Perpetual Looseleaf Encyclopedia*, first published in 1907, revised in the editions of 1917 to 1920 through the last recorded edition in 1926, and then re-issued in 1937 as the *Nelson Complete Encyclopedia*. The work, basically, is that of the *Nelson's Encyclopaedia* of 1905. The work was also issued in 1940 by Columbia Educational Books as the *Nelson Encyclopedia: Unabridged*, with Franklin J. Meine as editor in chief, although this also listed Finley, Falconer and Newbolt as former editors. The *World Wide Illustrated Encyclopedia* (now the *Home University Encyclopedia*) is reputed to be derived from the 1932 printing of the looseleaf edition of *Nelson's Encyclopaedia*, but was so poorly re-edited that it is not representative of the more accurate quality of the larger work.

- Reference:
Subscription Books Bulletin, April 1941.

NELSON'S PERPETUAL LOOSELEAF ENCYCLOPEDIA; an international work of reference, complete in twelve volumes, with 7,000 illustrations. New York and London: Thomas Nelson & Sons, 1917. 12v. 26cm. Editor in Chief: John Huston Finley (1863–1940). Canadian Editor: Sir William Peterson (1856–1921). European Editor: Sir Edward Parrott (1863–1921).

A thorough revision of the original *Nelson's Encyclopaedia* first published in 1905, and of which a "Perpetual Looseleaf" edition was issued in 1907. A second edition of the revised work was published in 1920 (and also as the *New Age Encyclopaedia* in Britain) and an index volume was made available in 1926.

It was not until 1937 that the work was again revised and it was then re-published as the *Nelson Complete Encyclopedia*, and this was followed in 1940 with two further changes in title, but under different imprints, as the

Nelson's New Looseleaf Encyclopedia and the *Nelson Encyclopedia: Un-abridged.*

The work was popular and useful for many years, containing, as it did, some 70,000 brief entries on a wide variety of topics. The idea of loose-leaf inserts, though not a novel idea, never really caught on and the practice was eventually abandoned.

• Reference:

Subscription Books Bulletin, April 1930.

NEW AGE ENCYCLOPAEDIA. London and New York: Thomas Nelson & Sons, 1920–1921. 10v. 16cm. Editor: Sir Edward Parrott (1863–1921).

A very small pocket-sized work, almost certainly condensed from *Nelson's Perpetual Looseleaf Encyclopedia,* first published in 1917, of which Sir Edward Parrott was listed as the European editor, and itself derived from the popular *Nelson's Encyclopaedia* of 1906, published in Britain, at the same time, as the *Harmsworth Encyclopaedia.*

NEW AGE ENCYCLOPAEDIA, WORLD ATLAS AND SPORTS SUPPLEMENT. New edition. London: Collins, 1957. 1200p. 21cm. Editors: George F. Maine and J. B. Foreman.

A one-volume miscellany of general information for general use. Issued in an identical format as the *Modern University Encyclopedia.* A reprint was issued in 1963.

NEW AMERICAN COMPREHENSIVE ENCYCLOPEDIA; a complete encyclopedia of the arts, sciences, history, biography, geography and general literature. New York: J. A. Hill & Co., Akron: Werner Co., 1906. 5v. 28cm.

An identical reprint of Volumes 1–5 of the *Anglo-American Encyclopedia and Dictionary,* first published in 1902 in 12 volumes, the last seven of which comprised a dictionary of the English language.

Both are believed to be identical to the five-volume supplement to the *Encyclopaedia Britannica* published by Werner in 1900, which was reprinted in 1901, 1903, 1904 and 1905. The 1906 edition of the *Anglo-American Encyclopedia and Dictionary* was also published by J. A. Hill.

NEW AMERICAN CYCLOPAEDIA; a popular dictionary of general knowledge. New York: D. Appleton & Co., 1858–1863. 16v. 25cm. Editors: George Ripley (1802–1880) and Charles Anderson Dana (1819–1897).

One of the most important encyclopedias ever published in the United States and, although long since out of print, still valuable for its historical information. More than 300 specialists are reputed to have collaborated in the compilation of the work. Dana was a well-known journalist and editor of the now defunct *New York Sun,* but he is perhaps best remembered for his famous reply to a child's letter, "Is There a Santa Claus?".

The work was supplemented by the excellent *American Annual Cyclopaedia* from 1862 to 1875. The work was so successful that a second edition, under the same editorial direction was issued between 1873 and 1876, but this was re-titled the *American Cyclopaedia,* and this was updated by the re-titled supplement, *Appleton's Annual Cyclopaedia,* from 1876–1903. A final edition of the work was published in 1883 and 1884, and this edition incorporated supplements at the end of each volume.

In addition to the updating annual supplements, two fine analytical indexes were published, one in 1878 and a second in 1884.

NEW AMERICAN ENCYCLOPEDIA (Hendelson). Washington, D.C.: Publishers Company, 1963. 12v. 24cm. Editor: William H. Hendelson (b.1904).

Not to be confused with the much smaller *New American Encyclopedia* published prior to 1963 by the same company's Books Inc., who later transferred the title to this larger work, the *New American Encyclopedia* is, in actual fact, a continuation of the *World Scope Encyclopedia,* a work which was acquired by the company in 1963.

The history of the work reaches back more than sixty years when a work entitled the *Teacher's and Pupil's Cyclopaedia,* in four volumes, was published in 1902, although there is some evidence that it was in existence even earlier than this. This, in turn, became the *New Teacher's and Pupil's Cyclopaedia* in 1910, when it was expanded to five volumes, and it continued under this title until 1927. Between 1923 and 1927, however, it was also issued, in a ten-volume edition, as the *International Reference Work.* All of these titles were issued under the imprint of the Holst Publishing Co., and the editor in chief was one Bernhart Paul Holst.

The practice of issuing the work under different titles had, by the mid-twenties, contravened the regulations of the Federal Trade Commission, who in 1927, issued a "Cease and Desist" order (Docket #1331) against the International Publishing Co. As a result, the two titles were discontinued and when the work re-appeared in 1928, it was under the title of the *Progressive Reference Library,* under which title it continued until 1939, when the owner and editor, Bernhart Holst, died. In between 1939 and 1945 ownership of the work was acquired by a New York publisher, who re-issued what was virtually the same work in 1945 as the *World Scope Encyclopedia,* and the first edition still listed Holst as editor, although by now the actual editor was Hendelson, whose name was to appear on all the subsequent editions.

Under Hendelson's direction, the work was drastically revised and improved considerably over the earlier editions. Unfortunately, while the work itself improved, the sales tactics of the publisher did not. While the *World Scope Encyclopedia* was being sold on a subscription basis at a quite high cost, two virtually identical works were being issued simultaneously for sale through supermarkets as the *New World Family Encyclopedia* and the

Standard International Encyclopedia, both of which were first published in 1953, and were discontinued in 1957. The only material difference between the three titles was that the supermarket editions were in 20 thinner volumes.

In about 1962 and 1963, the World Scope publishers ran into financial difficulties and, eventually, in 1963 all rights were acquired by the present publishers, who promptly re-named the work the *New American Encyclopedia*. In 1964, the history of this rather poor work was complicated still further by the issuance of the same work under two further titles, the *World University Encyclopedia*, which is designed to be sold through department stores, and the *World Educator Encyclopedia*, which is retailed on a subscription basis by a Florida distributor. The present work is, of course, far removed from the original compilation of 1902, but it is truly remarkable that, despite its mediocre quality, it has not only survived the many changes of title, but is actually flourishing.

NEW AMERICAN ENCYCLOPEDIA (Taylor); a concise and comprehensive reference work especially planned, compiled and written for school, college, office and home use; with special articles and departmental supervision by a corps of educators, writers and specialists in the United States and Europe. New York and Boston: Books Inc., 1938. 1496p. 23cm. Editor in Chief: Charles Ralph Taylor (b.1877).

A small and poorly produced work designed primarily as a premium offer in supermarkets, etc. The basic material is probably derived from the *World Wide Illustrated Encyclopedia*, published by the same company in 1937 and also edited by Taylor. The work was available in either a single-volume format or in four- and eight-volume editions, and its quality can be measured by the fact that there is at least one known instance of it being offered at 50¢ per volume when purchased with 48 cans of dog food!

Reprints, apparently with little or no revision, have appeared over a number of years, and the encyclopedic material was also reproduced in other sub-standard works, such as the *Encyclopedic Library of Knowledge* (1944) and *Webster's Unified Dictionary and Encyclopedia* (1953). In 1963, the title of *New American Encyclopedia* was transferred to a quite different encyclopedia owned by the same publishers, and the original *New American* was re-published in 1963 as the *American Family Encyclopedia*, in an eight-volume edition.

• References:
Subscription Books Bulletin, July 1940; April 1950.

NEW AMERICANIZED ENCYCLOPAEDIA BRITANNICA *see* ENCYCLOPAEDIA BRITANNICA

NEW AND COMPLETE AMERICAN ENCYCLOPAEDIA *see* ENCYCLOPAEDIA PERTHENSIS

NEW AND COMPLETE UNIVERSAL SELF PRO-
NOUNCING ENCYCLOPEDIA, for home, school and office; a
compendium of information and instruction on all subjects. Chicago and
Philadelphia: International Press, 1905. 8v. 20cm. Editors: Charles Annan-
dale (1843–1915), Ainsworth Rand Spofford (1825–1908), Isaac Thorne
Johnson, Walter Hart Blumenthal (b.1883).

Charles Annandale was a well-known British educator, who is first connected with the editing of encyclopedic reference works with the 1882
edition of the old *Popular Encyclopaedia,* published at that time by Blackie
& Son. In 1889–1890, this same company published *Blackie's Modern Cyclopaedia of Universal Information,* also edited by Annandale.

This work was exported to the United States, revised by Spofford, and
published by Gebbie & Co. in 1891–1892 as the *New Cabinet Cyclopaedia
and Treasury of Knowledge.* In 1899, at Toledo, this was re-issued by Brown.
Eager & Hull as the *New National Cyclopaedia and Treasury.* Gebbie re-
entered the scene in 1901 and issued the work, under yet another title,
as the *XX Century Cyclopaedia,* and this was followed, in 1903, under
E. R. Dumont, New York, imprint by the *New Twentieth Century Cyclopaedia,* but which now included a four-volume dictionary.

This, in turn, became the *New and Complete Universal Self Pronouncing
Encyclopedia* in 1905. In 1906, it was again re-titled the *New Cosmopolitan
Encyclopedia* and then, finally, in 1912, still listing Annandale as the editor,
it made its terminal appearance as the *National Encyclopedia of Reference.*

NEW BOOK OF KNOWLEDGE (Hammerton); a pictorial treasury
of reading and reference for young and old. With 8000 illustrations. London:
Waverley Book Co., 1938. 10v. (4882p.) 22cm. Editor: Sir John Alexander
Hammerton (1871–1949).

The first edition of this useful work appeared in 1922, and has been
issued under a variety of titles since then, such as *Cassell's Book of Knowledge, Waverley Book of Knowledge,* and the *Hammerton Book of Knowledge.*

In 1938, with Hammerton as editor, the work was issued as the *New
Book of Knowledge* and a further edition was published in 1953. The set
was then substantially revised, and in 1959, with Gordon Stowell as editor,
the work was re-issued in a so-called sixth edition as the *Book of Knowledge,*
under the imprint of the Waverley Book Co.

Although the titles are identical, this work is not related in content to the
American *Book of Knowledge* (1912) and the *New Book of Knowledge*
(1966) both of which are issued under the imprint of Grolier Inc.

• References:
Library Association Record, October 1961.

NEW BOOK OF KNOWLEDGE (Shapp). New York: Grolier Inc.,
1966. 20v. Editor: Martha G. Shapp.

An entirely new work published by Grolier Inc. in 1966, and which promises to become an exceptionally fine addition to the range of top quality encyclopedias in the United States. In 20 volumes, on the unit letter system of arrangement, each volume contains all the entries for one or more letters of the alphabet, and each also contains its own section of the general and fact entry index.

Although the title is identical, this work is no way related with the British *New Book of Knowledge,* which is a much older publication, nor is it related, except for common ownership, with the *Book of Knowledge,* a topically arranged encyclopedia for children which has been published by Grolier since 1912.

The editor, Martha G. Shapp, is a well-known educator with a wide experience in the compilation of encyclopedias. The overall direction of the work falls under Dr. Lowell A. Martin, Editorial Director of all Grolier reference works, and formerly Dean of the Library School at Rutgers University.

- Reference
Booklist and Subscription Book Bulletin, December 15, 1967.

NEW CABINET CYCLOPAEDIA AND TREASURY OF KNOWLEDGE; a handy book of reference on all subjects and for all readers. With about 2,000 pictorial illustrations, a compete atlas of 64 colored maps and 100 maps in the text. The articles relating to America revised and edited by Ainsworth Rand Spofford. Philadelphia: Gebbie & Co., 1891–1892. 8v. 20cm. Editors: Charles Annandale (1843–1915) and Ainsworth Rand Spofford (1825–1908).

An American reprint of the British *Blackie's Modern Cyclopaedia of Universal Information* (1889–1890), but with the articles pertaining to America revised and edited by Spofford.

The work was subsequently continued in the United States as the *New National Cyclopaedia* in 1899, the *XX Century Cyclopaedia* in 1901, the *New Twentieth Century Cyclopaedia and Dictionary* in 1903, the *New and Complete Universal Self Pronouncing Encyclopedia* in 1905, the *New Cosmopolitan Encyclopedia* in 1906 and finally the *National Encyclopedia of Reference* in 1912.

NEW CAXTON ENCYCLOPEDIA. London: Caxton Publishing Co., 1966. 18v. 24cm. Editor: Bernard A. Workman.

This is, in fact, a reprint, with some revisions of *Purnell's New English Encyclopaedia,* which was originally published in 216 weekly parts. The original work was exceptionally well illustrated in profuse color, and the information contained therein was accurate and, generally, sufficiently full to provide good subject coverage. There was, however, a noticeable trend toward subjects of Italian interest, and, indeed, many of the illustrations were of Italian origin.

NEW CENTURY BOOK OF FACTS; a handbook of ready reference. Chicago and Springfield (Mass.): King-Richardson Co. 1909. 1117p. 25cm. Editor in Chief: Carroll Davidson Wright (1840–1909).

A considerably enlarged and re-titled edition of the *Century Book of Facts*, first published by the King-Richardson Co. in 1902 under the editorship of Henry Woldmar Ruoff, further editions of which were issued in 1905, 1906, and 1908. King-Richardson continued to publish the *New Century Book of Facts* until 1926, when the rights were acquired by the Continental Publishing Co. of Wheeling, West Virginia. This firm continued with the work until 1964 when it was acquired by a New York publisher, who is reported to be preparing a completely revised edition.

Arranged in 15 departments, this work is very similar in size and arrangement to the *Lincoln Library of Essential Information* and *Cowles Comprehensive Encyclopedia* (formerly the *Volume Library*) and it is interesting to note that the latter title was also edited at one time by Ruoff, who was also responsible for the compilation of the *Standard Dictionary of Facts*, a work which preceded the *Lincoln Library*.

Another similar work, the *Universal Manual of Ready Reference*, was published by King-Richardson in 1904, and this, also edited by Ruoff, was probably identical to the original *Century Book of Facts*.

• References:

Subscription Books Bulletin, January 1930.
Booklist and Subscription Books Bulletin, December 1, 1956.

NEW CENTURY CYCLOPEDIA OF UNIVERSAL KNOWLEDGE; containing concise and exhaustive articles upon science, arts and mechanics . . . all the latest discoveries and inventions. Philadelphia: National Publishing Co., 1902. 624p. 25cm.

A nondescript one-volume miscellany of general and practical information first published as the *Standard Cyclopedia* in 1897. Adaptations or abridgements of the original compilation subsequently appeared as the peculiarly named *X-Rays of Intellectual Light* (1899), the *Standard American Book of Knowledge* (1900), the *World's Book of Knowledge* (1901), the *20th Century Cyclopedia of Universal Knowledge* (1901), the *American Educator and Library of Knowledge* (1902), the *American Home Educator and Book of Universal Knowledge* (1903) and the *Standard Library of Knowledge* (1904).

The compiler of the original work was Henry Davenport Northrop (1836–1909), but his name does not appear on most of the later editions.

NEW CENTURY REFERENCE LIBRARY of the world's most important knowledge. Philadelphia: National Press Association, 1907. 8v. 20cm. Editor in Chief: Charles Leonard Stuart (b.1868).

Only volumes 1–6 of this work contain encyclopedic material, the remaining two volumes comprising a dictionary of the English language.

Basically, the work is a re-issue of the five-volume *Crown Encyclopedia,* published in 1903 by the Christian Herald. In 1905, however, the work was being sold also as the *Continental Encyclopedia,* in eight volumes by the Success Co., which also included a two-volume dictionary.

NEW CHAMPLIN CYCLOPEDIA FOR YOUNG FOLKS. New York: H. Holt & Co., 1924. 6v. (also in 12v.) 23cm. Original Compiler: John Denison Champlin (1834–1915). Editor: Lincoln MacVeagh (b.1890).

Not really an encyclopedia, although classified as such for sales purposes. The work was actually comprised of six separate books on general subjects— Common Things—Games and Sports—Literature and Art—Natural History —Persons and Places—all of which were originally written by Champlin and published as individual titles between 1883 and 1905, and formed a series bearing the general title *Young Folks' Cyclopaedia of* . . .

The 1924 printing merely re-assembled the independent volumes into one collection and could, in fact, be purchased singly from one company, but only as a subscription set from another. The amount of revision implemented was small, and the same printing of 1924 was still being retailed in 1937.

In 1946, however, with more extensive revisions, the work was re-titled the *Champlin Encyclopedia* and vended as a 12-volume set by Consolidated Book Publishers. Further editions were issued in 1947 and 1950, but the work was discontinued shortly afterwards.

• Reference:
Subscription Books Bulletin, January 1937.

NEW COMPLETE CONDENSED ENCYCLOPEDIA . . . this new edition, which includes more than 2,500 new articles, has been revised to date and compared with the latest authorities; illustrated with over 3,000 engravings and maps, all of which were made especially for this work. New York: P. F. Collier & Son, 1909. 1703p. 29cm. Editor: William Henry Chandler (1841–1906).

This large one-volume encyclopedia is evidently a re-issue of the three-volume *Chandler's Encyclopedia,* published by Collier in 1898 and which, of course, was also edited by Chandler. The size of the work would indicate that it must have been designed primarily for brief reference, although it apparently never achieved a notable degree of popularity or acceptance.

NEW CONCISE ILLUSTRATED ENCYCLOPEDIA (World's Home Reference Library). Cleveland and New York: World Publishing Company, 1943.

A small one-volume work which contained a considerable amount of brief information, it was originally published in the United States as *Facts* in 1934, although this was in itself undoubtedly an adaptation of the British *Routledge's Universal Encyclopaedia,* also published in 1934.

In 1938, the work was re-issued in a one-volume format as the *New Concise Pictorial Encyclopedia*, under the imprint of Doubleday, Doran & Co. Acquired by the World Publishing Co. shortly thereafter, it was again issued in a one-volume format as the *Comprehensive Pictorial Encyclopedia* in 1942 and the present title in 1943.

It was finally published in 1951, once again in a four-volume format, as the *World Home Reference Encyclopedia*, under the imprint of the Consolidated Book Publishers. By then, however, the work had become badly dated and lacked authenticity, and no further editions have been issued.

NEW CONCISE PICTORIAL ENCYCLOPEDIA. New revised edition, complete in one volume. New York: Doubleday, Doran & Co., 1938. 1271p. 21cm. Editor in Chief: Nella Braddy Henney (b.1894); British Editor: Lawrence H. Dawson. European Editor: Richard Friedenthal (b.1896).

A one-volume revised edition of *Facts: The New Concise Pictorial Encyclopedia*, first published in a four-volume set in 1934, and apparently adapted from the British one-volume *Routledge's Universal Encyclopaedia*, also published in 1934. Originally a quite useful desk encyclopedia providing brief and accurate information on a wide variety of topics, the work deteriorated through lack of revision in later years.

Shortly after the edition of 1938, the rights were acquired by the World Publishing Co., who re-issued it, again in a one-volume format, as the *Comprehensive Pictorial Encyclopedia* in 1942 and as the *New Concise Illustrated Encyclopedia* in 1943.

The original plates were subsequently used by the Consolidated Book Publishers to issue the *World Home Reference Encyclopedia* in 1951, in its original four-volume format.

• Reference:
Subscription Books Bulletin, January 1939.

NEW COSMOPOLITAN ENCYCLOPEDIA; for home, school and office; a compendium of information and instruction on all subjects. Chicago and St. Louis: Thompson Publishing Co., 1906. 8v. 20cm. Editors: Charles Annandale (1843–1915), Isaac Thorne Johnson, Walter Hart Blumenthal (b.1883).

One of the many re-issues in the United States of *Blackie's Modern Cyclopaedia of Universal Information*, edited by Annandale and published in London in 1889. The work was imported to America and reprinted there (with revisions) as the *New Cabinet Cyclopaedia and Treasury of Knowledge* by Gebbie & Son.

In 1899, it was re-issued as the *New National Cyclopaedia and Treasury*, followed in 1901 by the *XX Century Cyclopaedia*, in 1903, by the *New Twentieth Century Cyclopaedia*, in 1905, as the *New and Complete Universal Self Pronouncing Encyclopedia*, and finally, in 1912, as the *National Encyclopedia of Reference*.

THE NEW CYCLOPAEDIA; or, universal dictionary of arts and sciences . . . biography, geography and history. London: Longman Hurst, 1802–1820. 44v. 28cm. Editor: Abraham Rees (1743–1825).

This very large and scholarly British encyclopedia was planned, edited, and largely written by Abraham Rees, who had previously done fine work on the 1753 and the 1786 editions of the famous *Cyclopaedia* originally compiled by Ephraim Chambers. For this work he had been elected a Fellow of the Royal Society and the Linnean Society, which enabled him to obtain the services of the outstanding scholars of the day for his new encyclopedia.

The first part of Rees' *Cyclopaedia* was issued in January 1802, and the work was eventually completed in 44 large quarto volumes (each comprising two parts) in 1820. Four of the volumes contained collections of well engraved and practical plates, arranged alphabetically by subject, while a fifth comprised a world atlas.

To some extent, the work was based on the *Cyclopaedia* of Chambers, with Rees re-writing most of the articles, but the work was original in many respects and very comprehensive for its time. Surprisingly, however, despite its merits, it was not revived after the death of Rees in 1825.

- Reference:
Collison.

THE NEW ENCYCLOPAEDIA. London and Edinburgh: T. C. and E. C. Jack, 1913. 1626p. 22cm. Editor: Herbert Charles O'Neill (b.1879).

A small, but quite useful one-volume collection of general and practical information. The publishers also issued, at the same time, the more comprehensive and popular *Jack's Reference Book*.

NEW ENGLISH ENCYCLOPEDIA *see* PURNELL'S NEW ENGLISH ENCYCLOPAEDIA

NEW FUNK & WAGNALLS ENCYCLOPEDIA, prepared by an editorial staff of experts. (De luxe edition.) New York: Unicorn Press, 1949–1950. 36v. 22cm. Editor: Joseph Laffan Morse (b.1902).

Containing some 50,000 articles in more than 8 million words, this very useful medium-sized encyclopedia was directly derived from the *Funk & Wagnalls New Standard Encyclopedia of Universal Knowledge,* edited by Frank Vizetelly and published from 1931 to 1949. This latter work was a surprisingly comprehensive encyclopedia which contained some material from the authoritative *New International Encyclopedia,* which had been acquired by Funk & Wagnalls in 1931.

A further edition of the *New Funk & Wagnalls Encyclopedia* was published in 1952, but in 1954, the size of the work was drastically reduced to 25 volumes and the title changed to the *Universal Standard Encyclopedia.* In 1959, the title was again changed to *Funk & Wagnalls Standard Reference Encyclopedia,* under which title it is still extant.

A one-volume work, based on the *Universal Standard Encyclopedia*, was published in 1959 as *Funk & Wagnalls Standard Encyclopedia of Modern Knowledge*.

• Reference:
Subscription Books Bulletin, January 1952.

NEW GEM ENCYCLOPEDIA. London and Glasgow: Collins, 1935 512p. Editors: John Redgwick Crossland (b.1892) and John Maxey Parrish.

One of several small encyclopedias for children compiled by Crossland and Parrish for Collins. The work was re-issued in 1938 as the *Encyclopedia of Modern Knowledge*.

NEW GENERAL ENCYCLOPEDIA. Toronto: General Press Distributors, 1935. 10v. 24cm.

This is the title under which the *American Educator* was being vended in Canada in the 1930's. Previously, since 1919, it had been sold there as the *Dominion Educator*, but this title was changed to the above to avoid the implication that the work was basically Canadian.

NEW GOLDEN ENCYCLOPEDIA. Revised edition. New York: Golden Press, 1963. 155p. 31cm. Original Compiler: Dorothy Agnes Bennett (b.1909). Revision Editor: Jane Werner Watson (b.1915).

A very brief and simple work for preschoolers, with large type and lavish color illustrations. The work had previously been issued as the *Golden Encyclopedia* in 1946.

NEW GRESHAM ENCYCLOPAEDIA. London: Gresham Publishing Co., 1921–1924. 12v. 22cm. Editors: Angelo Solomon Rappoport (b.1871), Richard Ferrer Patterson (b.1888), John Dougall.

A completely new work when first published, although the Gresham Publishing Co. had earlier issued the *New Popular Encyclopaedia* (1901) and the *Modern Cyclopaedia* (1906–1907).

In 1927, this quite useful family work was re-issued in a considerably abridged edition as the *Compact Encyclopaedia*, with Patterson and Dougall as editors, but this work was little more than half the size of its predecessor. The publishers, however, preferred to describe the reprint as "compressed" rather than abridged.

• Reference:
Collison.

NEW HUMAN INTEREST LIBRARY. Chicago: Midland Press, 1928. 6v. 24cm. Editor: Silas Edgar Farquhar (1887–1948).

An anthology of general information, topically arranged, rather than a direct reference encyclopedia, each volume dealing with a large general subject area, with an additional seventh volume containing a course of study, a reader's guide and brief bibliographies. The work was not new, having been previously published since 1914 as the *Human Interest Library*.

Under the imprint of the Midland Press, further editions were issued in 1933, 1935 and 1937. In 1938 the work was acquired by Books Inc., a New York subsidiary of the Publishers Co., who are still retailing the work in much the same format and apparently with little textual revision. Silas Farquhar was still being listed as editor of the work as late as 1952, although he had in fact severed his connection with the publishers about 1930.

• References:

Subscription Books Bulletin, July 1930; January 1939; July 1953.

NEW IDEA SELF INSTRUCTOR; a home book of knowledge. Chicago and Philadelphia: Monarch Book Co., 1904. 702p. 24cm. Editor in Chief: Ferdinand Ellsworth Cary (b.1848). Assistant Editors: Austin Norman Palmer (1859–1927), Morton McCormac and Edward J. Dahms.

A one-volume miscellany of general and practical information of very poor quality. It was also issued simultaneously in 1904 in an identical format as the *Complete Library of Universal Knowledge*.

Many years later it was revived and re-issued in an enlarged and revised edition as the *Knowledge Book* (1915), the *Knowledge Library* (1918) and finally the *New Knowledge Library* (1919). The three latter titles were published under the imprint of G. A. Millikan, Ohio.

NEW ILLUSTRATED UNIVERSAL REFERENCE BOOK. London: Odhams Press, 1933. 1280p.

One of several one-volume miscellanies published by Odhams Press, especially during the 1930's, and reprinted in 1949 in a condensed version of 768 pages. The work is very similar to the *New Standard Encyclopaedia and World Atlas* (1932), *Universal Knowledge A–Z* (1938) and the *Great Encyclopaedia of Universal Knowledge* (1948).

NEW IMPERIAL ENCYCLOPEDIA AND DICTIONARY; a library of universal knowledge and an unabridged dictionary of the English alphabet under one alphabet, compiled with the assistance of a large corps of trained cyclopedists. San Francisco: Pacific Newspaper Union, 1906, 40v. 21cm. Editor in Chief: Richard Gleason Greene (1829–1914).

This rather large work is surely descended from the *Columbian Cyclopaedia* which, according to an entry in the American Catalogue (1895–1900), was published by Funk & Wagnalls in 1899 in a set of 39 similarly sized volumes, and which was also edited by Richard Gleason Greene.

Evidently, this earlier work, married to a dictionary, provided the material for the publication in 1903, of the *Imperial Encyclopedia and Dictionary*, published jointly by H. G. Allen, of New York, and the Gilbert Publishing Co. of Chicago. This, in turn, was re-issued in an identical 40-volume format as the *New Imperial Encyclopedia and Dictionary* in 1906. Subsequently the work was re-issued as the *United Editors Encyclopedia and Dictionary* in 1909, again in 40 volumes, but this was followed in 1911, by the 30-volume *United Editors Perpetual Encyclopedia.*

The sub-titling on all of the titles from the *Imperial* of 1903 to the *Perpetual* of 1911 is virtually identical, and there is no question that these are all one and the same work. As no copy of the *Colombian Cyclopaedia* could be found for examination, however, it can only be surmised from the scant evidence available that this earlier work was the direct ancestor of the later titles.

NEW INTERNATIONAL ENCYCLOPEDIA. New York: Dodd, Mead & Co., 1902–1904. 17v. 26cm. Editors: Harry Thurston Peck (1856–1914), Daniel Coit Gilman (1831–1908), Frank Moore Colby (1865–1925).

One of the most outstanding general encyclopedias ever published in the English language, the *New International Encyclopedia* was first issued under this title in 1902, publication being completed in 1904. This massive and brilliant encyclopedia contained more than 80,000 articles and, in its hey-day, excelled even the *Encyclopaedia Britannica,* the *Encyclopedia Americana* and *Chambers's Encyclopaedia,* as well as other major works of the early twentieth century. It is still, even in mid-century, invaluable for its historical articles and portrayal of the times.

The word "New" in the title is perhaps a little misleading, as the new work was in fact a thorough revision of the *International Cyclopaedia,* a 15-volume set published in 1898 by Dodd, Mead, and also edited by H. Thurston Peck. Of greater interest is that the 1898 work was itself based on the older *Library of Universal Knowledge,* a 15-volume work first published in 1880 under the imprint of S. W. Green & Son, which was itself a reprint of the 1880 edition of the major British encyclopedia, *Chambers's Encyclopaedia.* There is thus a direct relationship between *Chambers's* and the *New International,* despite the massive revisions which had been implemented in the *International Cyclopaedia* of 1898, and the still greater revisions effected for the 1902–1904 *New International Encyclopedia.*

The acceptance of the new edition was immediate and popular, and a reprint was necessary again in 1904, and this was followed by further issues in 1905, 1907 (when it was corrected and expanded to 20 volumes), 1909 and 1911. At this stage another thorough revision was implemented and a new second edition was published in a 23-volume set between 1914 and 1917. With both Gilman and Peck now dead, the new edition was edited by Colby, with the assistance of Talcott Williams (1849–1928), who introduced some interesting innovations, particularly the inclusion of maps mounted on inserts, which enabled subscribers to replace them as new maps were issued. Another striking feature was the provision of really excellent bibliographies, where references were given both to translations and the original titles of foreign works.

With the First World War interrupting the further progress of this splendid work of reference, a further edition did not appear until 1923, but this was largely a reprint, the only significant revision being for a history of the war, which was contained in Volume 24, previously containing a reading and study guide only. In the same year a popular edition, on thinner paper, enabling the compression of two volumes into one, was made available. In 1925 a two-volume supplement was issued to update the now ten year-old text of the main work and, in 1927, a complete reprint, incorporating the supplement, was issued in 25 volumes. This was followed by a further two-volume supplement in 1930, and in the same year the main work was reprinted once again, which was the last to appear under the Dodd, Mead imprint.

In 1931 the publishing rights were acquired by the Funk & Wagnalls Co., but it was not until 1935 that an issue appeared under their imprint, which included an updating supplement by Herbert Treadwell Wade (b.1872). This proved to be the last printing of this once great and still historically important work. However, when the work was acquired by Funk & Wagnalls in 1931, they did incorporate some of the material into their new, popular and quite excellent *Funk & Wagnalls New Standard Encyclopedia of Universal Knowledge* which, for several years, was available only as a premium to subscribers to the now defunct *Literary Digest.* The currently published *Funk & Wagnalls Standard Reference Encyclopedia* is a direct descendant of this latter work.

A most valuable supplement to the *New International Encyclopedia* was the annual *New International Yearbook* (still one of the best yearbooks currently available) published from 1908 to 1931 by Dodd, Mead and since 1932 by Funk & Wagnalls. From 1907 to his death in 1925 the yearbook was edited by Frank Moore Colby, and from 1925 to 1936 by Herbert Treadwell Wade. Thereafter it was edited by Frank Horace Vizetelly, who also edited the *Funk & Wagnalls New Standard Encyclopedia.*

• References:
Collison.
Subscription Books Bulletin, October 1941.

NEW KNOWLEDGE *see* KNOWLEDGE

NEW KNOWLEDGE LIBRARY; science, invention, discovery, progress . . . supplemented by a series of review questions for students. Marietta [Ohio]: G. A. Millikan Co., 1919. 928p. 24cm. Editors: Emory Adams Allen (b.1853), Ferdinand Ellsworth Cary (b.1848), Thomas Herbert Russell (b.1862).

The final issue of a one-volume miscellany of general and practical knowledge, first issued in 1904 as the *Complete Library of Universal Knowledge* and also as the *New Idea Self Instructor,* and subsequently as the *Knowledge Book* in 1915 and the *Knowledge Library* in 1918. This final edition, however, was expanded from the previous issue by about 150 pages.

NEW MASTERS PICTORIAL ENCYCLOPEDIA. Chicago: Walton Educational Plan, c.1955. 8v.

A very shabby work with an equally obscure history. It was known to be sold through food stores in 1955, but it was, in all probability, a reprint of some earlier work.

No copyrights appear to have been issued, but in 1965 it was still being retailed in both a cheap paperback and a hardcover edition by the Publishers Co., although this is evidently the same edition as first recorded in 1955.

NEW MODERN ENCYCLOPEDIA; a library of world knowledge: a complete revision, with comprehensive World War II references. New York: W. H. Wise & Co., 1943. 1176p. 22cm. Editor in Chief: Alexander Hopkins McDannald (1877–1948). General Editor: Frank Webster Price (b.1901).

A smaller desk encyclopedia which was based on an earlier work entitled the *Modern Encyclopedia,* edited by Alexander Hopkins McDannald, the editor of the *Encyclopedia Americana,* whose editorial staff compiled the smaller work.

Wise published the *Modern Encyclopedia* from 1933 to 1937 and in the latter year also issued it in expanded eight-volume edition as the *Concise Encyclopedia,* primarily for sale through supermarkets. In 1940, by arrangement with the Unicorn Press, it was re-issued in 15 very thin volumes as the *Modern Concise Encyclopedia.*

During the ten years of its existence little actual revision had been implemented and the many errors which crept in rendered the later editions much less useful than the original. Further editions of the *New Modern Encyclopedia* were issued in 1946, 1947 (when it was expanded to 1494 pages) and 1949, which proved to be the terminal issue.

• References:
Subscription Books Bulletin, October 1943; January 1952.

NEW NATIONAL CYCLOPAEDIA AND TREASURY; a handy book of ready reference for schools. Toledo [Ohio]: Brown, Eager & Hull, 1899. 8v. 21cm. Editors: Ainsworth Rand Spofford (1825–1908) *articles relating to America,* Charles Annandale (1843–1915) *articles relating to Europe.*

A re-issue of the *New Cabinet Cyclopaedia and Treasury of Knowledge* (1891–1892), which was the American edition of *Blackie's Modern Cyclopaedia of Universal Information,* published in London in 1889. The only significant difference between the two earlier works was the revision and editing of the articles pertaining to America.

Subsequently the work was re-issued, with little change, as the *XX Century Cyclopaedia* (1901), the *New Twentieth Century Cyclopaedia* and *Dictionary* (1903), the *New and Complete Universal Self Pronouncing En-*

cyclopedia (1905); the *New Cosmopolitan Encyclopedia* (1906) and the *National Encyclopedia of Reference* (1912).

NEW OUTLINE OF KNOWLEDGE. Philadelphia: Progressive Publishing Co., 1936. 20v. 21cm. Original Editor: James Albert Richards (b.1890). General Editor: Uttley Edwin Crane (b.1883).

A topically arranged discussion of various general subjects by modern authors. With a style of presentation more adult than juvenile, an illogical arrangement, no index or table of contents, although a reader's guide was provided in the final volume, the work was of little value.

What was virtually the same work had been compiled and published by J. A. Richards in 1924 as the *Outline of Knowledge,* and although the name of the original compiler was still associated with this new edition, his name was retained for prestige purposes only, and any revisions implemented were the work of Uttley Crane.

• Reference:
Subscription Books Bulletin, April 1938.

NEW PEOPLES CYCLOPEDIA OF UNIVERSAL KNOWLEDGE; with numerous appendixes invaluable for reference in all departments of industrial life, containing also 3,500 illustrations and 300 maps and charts, the latter delineating every portion of the known world, the work thus including a complete and indexed atlas of the globe. New York: Eaton & Mains, 1903. 8v. 29cm. Original Editor: William Harrison De Puy (1821–1901). Editors: Alpheus S. Packard, Dudley Buck, Thomas Sargent Parry.

A revised edition of the *Peoples Cyclopedia of Universal Knowledge,* the fourth edition of which was published in 1883.

As De Puy, the original editor, was dead before the appearance of this edition, what little revision had been implemented must have been carried out by the publisher's own editorial staff. De Puy is also listed as the editor of another work published in 1908, the *World Wide Encyclopedia and Gazetteer,* and it is probable that this is yet another re-issue of the *Peoples Cyclopedia of Universal Knowledge.*

De Puy is also associated with at least one of the pirated reprints of the ninth edition of the *Encyclopaedia Britannica.*

NEW PICTORIAL ENCYCLOPEDIA OF THE WORLD. New York: Pictorial Encyclopedia Corp., 1954. 18v. 23cm. Editor in Chief: Franklin Dunham (b.1892).

A poorly produced collection of thin volumes containing a limited amount of general information, designed to be sold through food stores. In 1956, the work was re-issued as the *Illustrated Encyclopedia of the Modern World,* a two-volume atlas and gazetteer expanding the set to 20 volumes.

Dunham later edited a very similar work, the *Little & Ives Illustrated*

Ready Reference Encyclopedia, which was probably derived from these two earlier works.

The illustrative material was taken from the Bettman Archives and International News Photos.

• Reference:
Subscription Books Bulletin, July 1955.

NEW POPULAR EDUCATOR. London: Amalgamated Press, 1933–1934. 2v. (1456p.) 25cm. Editor: Sir John Alexander Hammerton (1871–1949).

A popular manual of self-instruction and miscellany of general knowledge. It is evidently a re-issue of the one-volume *Concise Universal Encyclopaedia* (1931), which was itself abridged from the multi-volume *Harmsworth's Universal Encyclopaedia* (1920).

THE NEW POPULAR ENCYCLOPAEDIA; a new and revised edition of the "Popular Encyclopaedia". With a supplement in every volume, and plates. London and Glasgow: Gresham Publishing Co., 1901. 14v. 22cm. Editor: Charles Annandale (1843–1915).

With an editorial supplement in each volume, this was a new and revised edition of the *Popular Encyclopaedia,* first published in 1841 by Blackie & Son in a seven-volume format. Further editions of the original work were issued in 1849, 1862 and 1877, all of which were edited by Alexander Whitelaw. With the 1882 edition, however, the editorial direction of the work was supervised by Charles Annandale, and in 1890–1893, this was revised again and expanded to fourteen volumes, also under the Blackie imprint.

At the same time, Blackie was also publishing *Blackie's Modern Cyclopaedia of Universal Information,* which first appeared in 1889–1890 in an eight-volume set. This was also edited by Annandale, and shortly afterwards, the work was exported to the United States, where it was reprinted under a variety of titles, beginning with the *New Cabinet Cyclopaedia and Treasury of Knowledge* in 1891–1892, edited jointly by Annandale and Spofford, who revised the American articles.

Meanwhile, in Britain, another edition of *Blackie's Modern Cyclopaedia* was issued in 1896–1897. Ownership of the Blackie reference sets was then acquired by the Gresham Publishing Co., who re-issued the original work as the *New Popular Encyclopaedia* in 1901. It again changed title in the issue of 1906–1907, when it became the *Modern Cyclopaedia of Universal Information.*

Annandale is listed as editor of no less than 14 encyclopedias, most of which were published in the United States, but his actual output is probably limited to only two or three of these, his name being used only for prestige and sales purposes in most cases.

NEW PRACTICAL REFERENCE LIBRARY. Chicago and New York: Dixon, Hanson & Co., 1907. 5v. 24cm. Editor in Chief: Charles Herbert Sylvester. Associate Editor: William Francis Rocheleau. Assistant Editors: Kenneth L. Pray, Anna McCaleb, Helga M. Leburg, Albertus V. Smith.

The history of this work is pertinent both because of its origins and its subsequent development. Despite its title it was not a "new" work, but the continuation of an encyclopedia which had first been published in 1901, simultaneously under two titles, as *Hill's Practical Encyclopedia* (under the imprint of the Chicago Book Co.) and as the *School Library Encyclopedia* (under the imprint of the Caxton Co.). In 1902, in an identical format, and with Rocheleau as an associate editor, it was re-titled *Hill's Practical Reference Library of General Knowledge,* and this edition appeared under the imprint of Dixon and Hanson, as did the revised reprints of 1904 and 1905. Thomas Edie Hill (1832–1915), the original compiler, was apparently not connected with the work after the 1905 edition. His name was omitted from the title when Dixon and Hanson re-issued the work in 1907 as the *New Practical Reference Library,* in which year the work was also expanded to five volumes.

Another edition followed in 1911 under the imprint of Dixon, Hanson and Bellows, but when the 1912 edition was published, Dixon's name was not included in the imprint, and he was then engaged on a quite different work which was to be published in 1913. Under the Hanson-Bellows imprint, further editions of the *New Practical Reference Library* followed in 1913, 1914, and 1915, but an important change is noted in 1917, when the work appeared under the imprint of the Hanson-Roach-Fowler Co.

This is of particular interest, as this same company was also the original publisher of the *World Book* and, in fact, both works were published under the identical imprint in 1917–1918. The *World Book,* however, was an entirely new work and not derived from the original works of Hill, and its only relationship to the *New Practical Reference Library* was a short period of common ownership and a sharing of what may have been basically the same editorial staff.

The last edition of the *New Practical* appeared in 1918, and it was then acquired from Hanson-Roach-Fowler by the Ralph Durham Co., who revised and re-issued the work as the *American Educator* in 1919. It has been published under this title ever since, with the exception that the word "Encyclopedia" was added to the title in 1932, when it also came under new ownership.

NEW ROYAL CYCLOPAEDIA AND ENCYCLOPAE-DIA; or, complete, modern and universal dictionary of arts and sciences . . . in three large elegant volumes . . . on an entire new and improved plan. London: Alex. Hogg, 1788. 3v. 43cm. Editor in Chief: George Selby Howard. Assistant Editors: John Bettesworth, Henry Boswell and Felix Stonehouse.

This work is unusual in that it is the only recorded instance of a work styling itself both as a "cyclopaedia" and an "encyclopaedia", but without explaining the difference, if any, between the two terms. It is also unusual in its exceptionally large format, although the term "elegant" is hardly applicable.

Despite its grandiose title and flamboyant claims, it is nothing more than an extensive and vulgar plagiarization of the authoritative *Cyclopaedia* of Ephraim Chambers, published some sixty years previously, and recently revised (1778–1788) by Abraham Rees.

• Reference:
Collison.

NEW STANDARD ENCYCLOPAEDIA AND WORLD ATLAS. London: Odhams Press, 1932. 1352p. 22cm. Editors: John Maxey Parrish, John Redgwick Crossland (b.1892) and A. W. Holland.

A small one-volume miscellany of information, similar in content to several other one-volume works compiled by Parrish and Crossland in later years, most, if not all of which are abridgements of the present work.

NEW STANDARD ENCYCLOPEDIA (Colledge); compiled with the assistance of more than 200 experts and specialists in every department of human knowledge. New York: University Society Inc., 1906. 12v. 26cm. Editors: William A. Colledge (1859–1927), Nathan Haskell Dole (1852–1935), George Jotham Hagar (1847–1921).

Although the titles are identical, this is not the same work as the *New Standard Encyclopedia* which has been published by the Standard Education Society since 1930.

The work published by the University Society in 1906 is evidently original, as neither the publishers nor the editors were connected with earlier works. It was re-issued in 1907–1908, 1911 and 1916, together with separate booklets on courses in home reading and self-study.

In 1909, with Hagar as editor, and under the imprint of the Hamilton Book Co., it was also issued as the *Practical Home Encyclopedia*, but in eight volumes instead of twelve. In the same format, it was also issued in 1912 as the *Standard American Encyclopedia*, this title appearing under the imprint of the Wheeler Publishing Co.

Once again under the imprint of the University Society, another edition of the *Standard American Encyclopedia* appeared in 1916. In 1937, the title was revived, but it is doubtful if the work is the same.

NEW STANDARD ENCYCLOPEDIA (Stanford); systematized information, clear, concise, correct, complete. Chicago: Standard Encyclopedia Corporation, 1930. 10v. 24cm. Editor in Chief: Harold Melvin Stanford (b.1875).

This work stems directly from the five-volume *Aiton's Encyclopedia*, first published in 1910 under the imprint of Welles Bros. In 1912, with Stanford as editor, the work was expanded to six volumes and re-titled the *Standard Reference Work*, this appearing under the imprint of the Interstate Publishing Co., an assoicate of Welles Bros. Further editions of the *Standard Reference Work* were issued in 1913, 1915, 1917 (when it was expanded to seven volumes), and 1922, when the Standard Education Society published an edition in ten volumes.

In 1923 it again changed title to the *National Encyclopedia for the Home, School, and Library*, but reverted back to the title of *Standard Reference Work* in 1927.

In 1930, the title was changed once again to the *New Standard Encyclopedia*, and it has appeared under that title ever since, although it was, for a short period, sold in Canada during the pre-war years as the *Consolidated Encyclopedia*.

Editions of the *New Standard Encyclopedia* have been published regularly since 1930 and it is currently maintained under a policy of continuous annual revision. The edition of 1966 completed a massive program of revision spread over a period of 12 years and is vastly improved over the earlier editions.

Stanford ceased to be the editor of the work about 1950 and he was succeeded by Calvin Rogers Fisk who directed the editorial work until 1964, when he was succeeded by the present editor, Douglas Downey.

In no way connected with a work of the same title published from 1906 to 1917, the present *New Standard Encyclopedia* has improved steadily over the past decade and is now one of the more popular smaller family encyclopedias available.

• References:

Subscription Books Bulletin, January 1931; April 1934; April 1940; July 1951. Booklist and Subscription Books Bulletin, May 15, 1960.

NEW STUDENTS REFERENCE WORK; for teachers, students and families. Chicago: F. E. Compton & Co., 1909. 4v. 25cm. Editor: Chandler Belden Beach (1839–1928). Associate Editor: Frank Morton McMurray (1862–1936).

Descended from the *Students Cyclopaedia*, a two-volume work compiled and edited by Chandler Beach and published by the J. M. Howard Co. in 1900. In 1902 and 1903 this was re-issued by both Beach and the Howard-Severance Co. as the *Students Reference Work*. F. E. Compton took over control of the set shortly afterwards, and in a completely revised and expanded edition of four volumes, they re-titled the work the *New Students Reference Work*, first published in 1909.

This was followed in 1911 by another edition, to which was added a fifth volume containing reading material entitled the "How and Why Program," a feature which continued to be a part of the set for many years afterwards. Compton published further editions in 1912, 1913 and 1919, but in the 1920 edition, the set was expanded again, comprising seven volumes in all, the last of which continued to be the "How and Why Program".

Compton's were at this time engaged in the compilation of an entirely new work, *Compton's Pictured Encyclopedia*, which was to replace the *New Students Reference Work* as their major product. As a result, the older set was acquired by the firm of S. L. Weedon, Cleveland, who reissued the work in eight volumes (seven encyclopedic and the "How and Why Library") in 1925, and followed this with further editions in 1928 and 1930. Weedon, however, were also engaged in the compilation of a new work at this time, *Weedon's Modern Encyclopedia*, which was to be published in 1931 and which afterwards became the *Britannica Junior Encyclopaedia*. Weedon, in their turn, sold the publishing rights for the *New Students Reference Work* to the L. J. Bullard Co., also operating out of Cleveland.

The work was never published under the Bullard imprint, but it did re-appear in 1934 as the *Modern American Encyclopedia*, under the editorial direction of Calvin Rogers Fisk, who was simultaneously editing the *New Standard Encyclopedia*, but in fact the 1934 printing was little changed from the last 1930 edition. Further issues were released in 1934 and 1936, but the poor quality of the work by that time had rendered the encyclopedic material virtually obsolete, and no further printings were issued.

• References:

Subscription Books Bulletin, October 1930; July 1932.

NEW TEACHER'S AND PUPIL'S CYCLOPAEDIA; a reference library of history, geography, biography, literature, economics, civics, arts, sciences, discoveries and inventions. Chicago and Boone: Holst Publishing Co., 1910. 5v. (3600p.) 26cm. Editor in Chief: Bernhart Paul Holst (1861–1939). Associate Editor: Ruric Neval Roark (1859–1909).

This is a re-issue of the four-volume work first published in 1902 (possibly earlier) as the *Teacher's and Pupil's Cyclopaedia*, further editions of which were published in 1905, 1906, and 1907, when it was expanded to five volumes. In 1906 a two-volume abridgement was also published as *Encyclopaedic Current Reference*. From 1910 to 1927, the work was published as the *New Teacher's and Pupil's Cyclopaedia*, expanding to six volumes in 1913, seven volumes in 1915, and eight volumes in 1927, but the last two volumes in each case were comprised of a "Practical Home and School Methods" section. However, while the work was being published under this title, it had also been issued in 1911 as the *Practical American Encyclopedia* (in two volumes), and in the same year, an abridged edition (described as five volumes in one) was issued as the *Unrivalled Encyclopedia*, both of which appeared under the imprint of W. B. Conkey, who was in fact the printer of Holst's works.

Beginning with 1923, the work was also issued as the *International Reference Work*, and from then until 1927, the two titles, although identical in content, were sold simultaneously as ostensibly different works. As a result, a "Cease and Desist" order was issued against the publishers by the Federal Trade Commission in 1927 (Docket #1331).

Some idea of the poor quality of the work can be gauged from the listing (in 1927) of Ruric Nevel Roark as an associate editor, although he had died in 1909.

Holst, as editor and publisher, then merged the two titles under that of the *Progressive Reference Library,* which was published in a ten-volume edition in 1928, and regularly thereafter until 1939, when Holst died. In 1945, the rights were acquired by a New York distributor who immediately re-issued the work as the *World Scope Encyclopedia,* in 12 volumes, and this was published annually thereafter, with quite substantial revisions, until 1963. What improvements had been effected, however, were spoilt by the practice of the publishers in issuing the same work under different titles. In 1953, the identical work was published, for supermarket consumption, as the *New World Family Encyclopedia* and the *Standard International Encyclopedia,* both in 20 thinner volumes.

In 1963, the publishing rights were acquired by the Publishers Co., Washington, D.C., who immediately re-titled the set the *New American Encyclopedia,* and published it also as the *World University Encyclopedia,* and, by arrangement with a Florida distributor, as the *World Educator Encyclopedia.* Thus, from its initial copyright in 1902, to the issuance of the same basic work under three different titles in 1964, this work has appeared under no less than 13 different titles.

NEW TWENTIETH CENTURY CYCLOPAEDIA AND DICTIONARY; biography, history, art, science, dictionary and gazetteer of the world. (Grand siècle edition.) Chicago and New York: E. R. Du Mont, 1903. 12v. 23cm. Editors: Charles Annandale (1843–1915), Ainsworth Rand Spofford (1825–1908), John W. Leonard (b.1849), C. M. Stevens (b.1861).

With the addition of a two-volume dictionary of prominent living Americans, and a two-volume dictionary of the English language, this is an exact re-issue of the *XX Century Cyclopaedia,* an eight-volume set published in 1899, which was itself a reprint of the eight-volume *New Cabinet Cyclopaedia and Treasury of Knowledge,* published in Philadelphia by Gebbie & Son in 1891–1892.

The origin of the work can be traced with some certainty much further back in time to 1841, when a British work entitled the *Popular Encyclopaedia* was published in London, of which Annandale became the editor in 1882. What was basically the same work was then issued by Blackie & Son as *Blackie's Modern Cyclopaedia of Universal Information* in 1889, again with Annandale as editor, and this was re-issued in 1901 as the *New Popular Encyclopaedia* and finally, in 1906, as the *Modern Cyclopaedia of Universal Information.*

Meanwhile, back in 1890, the work had been imported to America, and with Spofford revising those articles of particular interest to American users, it was first published there as the *New Cabinet Cyclopaedia and*

Treasury of Knowledge, over a period of two years, between 1891–1892. After the edition of 1903, it was re-issued as the *New and Complete Universal Self Pronouncing Encyclopedia* in 1905, the *New Cosmopolitan Encyclopedia* in 1906, and finally, in 1912, as the *National Encyclopedia of Reference.*

NEW UNIVERSAL ENCYCLOPAEDIA (a revised edition of "Harmsworth's Universal Encyclopaedia"). London: Educational Book Co., 1951. 10v. (8712p.) 22cm. Editor: Sir John Alexander Hammerton (1871–1949).

As is clearly stated in the sub-titling, this work is a revised edition of *Harmsworth's Universal Encyclopaedia,* a very popular and useful work first published between 1920–1923 by the Amalgamated Press, and which had been reprinted from time to time with revised impressions. This work, however, showed some quite substantial revisions, and another edition was issued by the same publisher in 1959. Hammerton was still being listed as editor of this, although he had died ten years previously.

The work is directly related to some contemporary American sets, in that in 1931, *Doubleday's Encyclopedia* was also an adaptation of *Harmsworth's Universal Encyclopaedia.* In 1944 *Doubleday's* was retitled the *Grolier Encyclopedia,* which ceased publication in 1964, although some of the material was contained in the *Unified Encyclopedia,* published from 1960–1965.

NEW UNIVERSAL ENCYCLOPEDIA (Appleton's); a new work of reference based on the best authorities and systematically arranged for use in home and school. New York: Foster, Temin & Oliver, 1930. 10v. 24cm. Editorial Board: Arthur Elmore Bostwick (1860–1942), Elmer Ellsworth Brown (b.1861), Gerald Van Casteel (b.1860), Marcus Benjamin (1857–1932), George Jotham Hagar (1847–1921).

The claim of the publishers that this is "a new work of reference" is not borne out by the facts, as this shoddy production was nothing more than a reprint from the original plates of the once quite useful *Appleton's New Practical Cyclopedia,* a six-volume work published from 1910 to 1920.

No editors as such are listed for the work, but the title page contains a list of members of a so-called Editorial Advisory Board, four of whom had been associated with the editing of the original Appleton work, but at least one of them, protested the use of his name without permission, while yet another, Hagar, had been dead since 1921.

The work was so aged and so badly produced as to be virtually a swindle. Fortunately, no further editions were thrust upon the unsuspecting public.

• Reference:
Subscription Books Bulletin, October 1931.

NEW UNIVERSAL HANDBOOK OF NECESSARY INFORMATION; for home, school, shop and office, practically arranged for ready reference, compiled with the assistance of a large corps of experts, and including a dictionary on a new plan. Philadelphia: Universal Book and Bible House, 1920. 1046p. 19cm. Editors: William Henry Johnston (b.1875), William Dodge Lewis (b.1870), Edgar Arthur Singer (b.1873).

A small one-volume handbook of useful general and practical everyday information, allied to a dictionary of the English language. Sometimes known simply as the *Universal Handbook*, the work proved popular, although it lacked authority, and further editions were published at regular intervals until 1937.

The same company issued a very similar work in 1930, entitled *Winston's Universal Reference Library*, which is evidently an adaptation of this work.

NEW UNIVERSITIES ENCYCLOPEDIA. New York: Outlook Company Book Department, c.1928. 5v.

A search for copies of this work failed to produce a set or part of it for examination, and the only record of its existence is a brief entry in the United States Catalog of 1928, which did not provide sufficient bibliographical data to determine its origin.

NEW WONDER BOOK CYCLOPEDIA OF WORLD KNOWLEDGE; the thrilling stories of twentieth century industry, science, nature, transportation, communication and other marvels of the world. Prepared and edited by the National Lexicographic Board. Philadelphia: International Press (John C. Winston Co.), 1954. 12v. 22cm.

A poorly produced work, designed for sale through chain and food stores in an inexpensive and flimsy edition. Badly organized and with a very limited subject coverage, the work could be regarded as encyclopedic only in the very broadest of terms, despite its alphabetical arrangement. The contents comprised only 325 long story-form articles, supplemented by a limited index of ten thousand entries.

The National Lexicographic Board, with Albert H. Horehead as editor and chairman, also compiled the *Illustrated Encyclopedia of Knowledge* in 1954, but the two works, although similar in parts, are quite different.

• Reference:
Subscription Books Bulletin, July 1955.

NEW WONDER WORLD; a library of knowledge. Chicago: G. L. Shuman Co., 1932. 11v. 26cm. Editor in Chief: James Ralph McGaughy (b.1888).

A thorough revision and re-titling of a work which was published by the same company from 1914 to 1927 as *Our Wonder World*. Arranged by subject, the work was designed to meet the needs of children through high school. As a source of ready reference it was limited in usefulness, but was a much improved set for enticing younger readers to browse through.

The eleventh volume of the set contained an index and a home and school study guide. Further editions were published at regular intervals until 1943, and copyrights were issued annually thereafter, until the last edition to appear under the Shuman imprint in 1955.

The rights to the work were then acquired by the Parents Magazine Educational Press, and they, in 1959 and 1960, issued revised editions in ten volumes under the slightly different title of the *New Wonder World Encyclopedia,* but in 1962 this was changed to the *New Wonder World Cultural Library* and finally, in 1964, it became simply the *Cultural Library.*

• References:

Subscription Books Bulletin, April 1932; January 1939; October 1947; July 1953.

NEW WONDER WORLD CULTURAL LIBRARY. New York: Parents Magazine Educational Press, 1962. 10v. 26cm. Editor in Chief: George Dinsmore Stoddard (b.1897).

A topically arranged work for children, readable and attractive. First published as *Our Wonder World* from 1914 to 1927. Changed title to the *New Wonder World* in 1932. Then acquired by Parents Magazine Educational Press, thoroughly revised and re-issued as the *New Wonder World Encyclopedia* in a new and better arrangement. Subsequently, in 1964, the words "New Wonder World" were omitted from the title and the work is now known simply as the *Cultural Library.*

NEW WONDER WORLD ENCYCLOPAEDIA. London: Collins, 1965.

A smaller one-volume and inexpensive work for children, previously issued in 1935 as the *Wonder World of Knowledge.*

NEW WONDER WORLD ENCYCLOPEDIA. New York: Parents Magazine Educational Press, 1959. 10v. 26cm. Editor in Chief: George Dinsmore Stoddard (b.1897).

A completely revised edition of a work first published in 1914 as *Our Wonder World,* and continued under that title until 1927. In 1932 the work was re-titled the *New Wonder World,* and was published by G. L. Shuman under this title until 1955 when the rights were acquired by the present publisher.

The 1959 edition reduced the set from eleven to ten volumes, and the index formerly included in the last volume was re-arranged and distributed throughout the ten volumes of text. Containing some 2½ million words, 4,000 illustrations, and the same number of pages, with over 25,000 index entries, the work was accepted by most authorities as an attractive, readable and useful set for children to browse through. Because of its topical arrangement, however, it was not suitable for ready reference.

• Reference:
Booklist and Subscription Books Bulletin, April 15, 1960.

NEW WORLD ENCYCLOPEDIA; a library of reference, superbly and profusely illustrated with hundreds of subjects in full color, monotone and text cuts, with a valuable appendix of often sought for facts in almost every department of human knowledge, a chronological history of the world showing the most important events in history from the earliest times, and a most comprehensive narrative of the Great War. Compiled with the assistance of many associate editors, special contributors, and United States and Canadian government officials. New York: Christian Herald, 1919. 6v. 20cm. Editor in Chief: George Jotham Hagar (1847–1921).

This work has an astonishing history. Based on the evidence available it is almost certainly descended from a work entitled the *Crown Encyclopedia*, published by the Christian Herald in 1903, which was edited by Charles L. Stuart. This was followed in 1905 by the *Continental Encyclopedia*, but enlarged by the addition of a two-volume dictionary. This in turn was followed in 1907 by the *New Century Reference Library*, and in 1909 by the *Current Cyclopedia of Reference*. All of these earlier titles were edited either solely or jointly by Charles L. Stuart, and some of them had also appeared under different imprints as the *Twentieth Century Encyclopedia* (1901–1907) and the *Imperial Reference Library* (1901–1910).

In 1911, Stuart was again the editor, but now jointly with Hagar, of *Everybody's Cyclopedia*, and this was re-issued by the same publisher in 1914 as the *People's Cyclopedia*. From thereon, Stuart's name is omitted, but the sub-titling of the *New World Encyclopedia* is almost identical to that of the *Peoples Cyclopedia*, and the two works are unquestionably related.

In 1918, however, the work had been issued under the slightly different title of the *New World Wide Cyclopedia* (a title which was to be revived in 1927), and, in 1919, it was also issued as the *World Wide Cyclopedia*. Hagar's name then disappears from the scene, but crops up again in 1929, when he is listed as the original compiler of the *Times Encyclopedia and Gazetteer*, but the actual editor of this work was Francis Joseph Reynolds (1867–1937) who also edited the 1928 edition of the *New World Wide Cyclopedia*. Still earlier, he was responsible for *Adair's New Encyclopedia* (1923), which was almost certainly a re-issue of the several earlier titles.

In 1930, the work developed still further and was issued in a ten-volume edition as the *Twentieth Century Encyclopedia* (a title first used by the same publisher in 1901) and further editions of this appeared in 1932 and 1934. Reynolds' link with this work was eventually terminated with the re-issue, in the year of his death, of the *World's Popular Encyclopedia*, in 1937.

Further editions of this were published in 1940 and 1942, in 12 volumes, although neither Reynolds nor Hagar were associated with the last editions.

NEW WORLD FAMILY ENCYCLOPEDIA. Unabridged. De luxe edition. New York: Standard International Library, 1953. 20v. 23cm. Editor in Chief: William H. Hendelson (b.1904).

Comprised of 20 quite thin volumes, this work was vended through food stores on the "book-a-week" plan, but it is purely and simply an inexpensive reprint of the much more expensive 12-volume *World Scope Encyclopedia*, which was first published in 1945, and which terminated under that title in 1964.

At the same time (1953) the same work was issued as the *Standard International Encyclopedia*, which was also reprinted in 1956–1957. All three works are directly descended from the four-volume *Teacher's and Pupil's Cyclopaedia* (1902–1907); the *New Teacher's and Pupil's Cyclopaedia* (1910–1927); the *International Reference Work* (1923–1927); and the *Progressive Reference Library* (1928–1939). Subsequently, in 1964, the *World Scope Encyclopedia* was acquired by the Publishers Co., Washington, D.C., who re-issued it simultaneously as the *New American Encyclopedia* and the *World University Encyclopedia*, and, by arrangement with a Miami distributor, as the *World Educator Encyclopedia*.

NEW WORLD LIBRARY. London: Caxton Publishing Co., 1964. 13v. 25cm.

Encyclopedic in character, but by no means a new work, the *New World Library* is a compilation of three works previously published by Caxton.

Four of its thirteen volumes were derived from Stuart Miall's *World of the Children* (1948), six from the *Caxton Encyclopaedia* (1960), which was re-issued as the *Caxton World of Knowledge* in 1961, and three from the *World of Science* (1959) also compiled by Stuart Miall.

Mediocre in quality and awkwardly arranged, the work was inadequate for reference use, although sold at an extremely high price.

THE NEW WORLD WIDE CYCLOPEDIA; a complete library of reference, superbly and profusely illustrated with hundreds of subjects in full color, monotone and text cuts, with a valuable appendix of often sought for facts in almost every department of human knowledge, a chronological history of the world, the most comprehensive narrative of the world war briefly noted day by day. Compiled with the assistance of many associate editors, special contributors and United States and Canadian government officials. New York: Syndicate Publishing Co., 1918. 6v. 20cm. Editor in Chief: George Jotham Hagar (1847–1921).

A detailed history of this work is given under the *New World Encyclopedia*, under which title it had been issued in 1919. It was also re-issued in 1919 as the *World Wide Cyclopedia*.

In 1928, under the imprint of the Consolidated Book Publishers, it was re-issued in an eight-volume edition. This particular reprint was the subject of an investigation by the Federal Trade Commission who, in 1930 (Docket

#1538) ordered the publishers to cease and desist from selling the work under more than one name or title. Despite this edict, the work was re-issued in 1929 as the *Times Encyclopedia and Gazetteer*, as the *Twentieth Century Encyclopedia* from 1930 to 1934, and finally, from 1937 to 1942 as the *World's Popular Encyclopedia*.

NEW YORK POST WORLD WIDE ILLUSTRATED EN-CYCLOPEDIA *see* WORLD WIDE ILLUSTRATED EN-CYCLOPEDIA

NEWNES EVERYTHING WITHIN; a library of information for the home, with plates. London: George Newnes, 1933. 1207p. 22cm. Editor: Arthur Courland Marshall.

In its day a quite useful small one-volume compendium of general and practical information. It appears to have been issued simultaneously as *Newnes Golden Treasury*. A work entitled the *Children's Everything Within* (1939) is evidently an abridgement of the earlier work.

NEWNES FAMILY ENCYCLOPAEDIA. London: George Newnes Ltd. (Oxford: Buckingham Press), 1966. 4v.

This is one of several encyclopedic publications which have been issued by the old established firm of George Newnes over a period of years, including the much more famous *Chambers's Encyclopaedia*.

It would seem, however, that the *Newnes Family Encyclopaedia*, far from being a new work is simply a re-titling and compression into four volumes of the older *Newnes Popular Encyclopaedia*, which was published in eight volumes in 1960 and in a series of 38 weekly parts in 1963. In size, the works are practically identical; 3,000 pages, 2 million words, and 2,500 illustrations. As with most of the lesser British encyclopedias, revision is implemented at infrequent intervals, and the 1966 edition examined showed little change from the 1960 edition, and, as a result, much of the text was badly dated.

Of interest is that the Buckingham Press, which was the subscription books division of George Newnes, was acquired by the Pergamon Group of Companies in 1966. This acquisition brought into new ownership both the *Newnes Family Encyclopaedia* and the *Chambers's Encyclopaedia*. In 1967, Pergamon expanded their interests still further by acquiring the Caxton Publishing Co. and the encyclopedic works owned by them. This makes Pergamon the largest single encyclopedia publishing group in the United Kingdom, and on a par with some of the more prominent American publishers of reference works.

NEWNES GOLDEN TREASURY; a library of good reading and general knowledge for every home, with plates. London: George Newnes, 1933. 1192p. 22cm. Editor: Arthur Courland Marshall.

Evidently a reprint, with some minor changes, of *Newnes Everything Within,* also published in 1933.

NEWNES PICTORIAL KNOWLEDGE; an educational treasury and children's dictionary. London: Home Library Book Co. (George Newnes Ltd.), 1932. 7v. (2688p.) Editor: H. A. Pollock.

A topically arranged work for older children, but with a rather sketchy subject coverage. Another edition is recorded as having been issued in 1954, when the set was expanded to ten volumes, with Reginald Heber Poole and Peter Finch as general editors. This edition added two volumes of miscellaneous information and a fact index volume to the original seven.

In 1960, the work was revised and re-issued, again in ten volumes, with Peter Finch as editor, assisted by Walter Shepherd and Cedric Dover.

• Reference:
Subscription Books Bulletin, July 1934.

NEWNES POPULAR ENCYCLOPAEDIA; an authoritative survey of universal knowledge, compiled in the editorial offices of "Chambers's Encyclopaedia", under the general editorship of the managing editor. London: George Newnes Ltd., 1963. Editor: Margaret D. Law.

This work was first published in an eight-volume edition of 3,040 pages in 1960, but beginning in October of 1963, it was also issued in a series of 38 weekly parts.

The work, being compiled by the same editorial staff, bears a resemblance to the much more comprehensive *Chambers's Encyclopaedia,* and the information contained in this smaller work has the same stamp of accuracy and authority as has always been found in the larger work.

NORTH AMERICAN REFERENCE BOOK *see* SOURCE BOOK

THE NUTTALL ENCYCLOPAEDIA; being a concise and comprehensive dictionary of general knowledge, consisting of over 16,000 terse and original articles on nearly all subjects discussed in larger encyclopaedias, and especially dealing with such as come under the categories of history, biography, geography, literature, philosophy, religion, science and art. London and New York: Frederick Warne, 1900. 700p. 20cm. Originator: P. Austin Nuttall. Editor: James Wood.

A small one-volume useful work, more akin to a dictionary than an encyclopedia, which has been popular in Britain for more than half-a-century. Editions have been recorded in 1920, 1930, 1938 and 1956 (by which time it had been expanded to 718 pages), and it was still being retailed in 1966. The editors of the 1930 edition were G. Elgie Christ and A. L. Haydon. The 1938 edition was edited by Lawrence Hawkins Dawson (who had

earlier edited the more comprehensive *Routledge's Universal Encyclopaedia*).
The last recorded edition in 1956 was edited by C. M. Prior.

According to the title page of the 1900 edition, the work was originated
by P. Austin Nuttall, but no earlier work could be found recorded under
his name.

O DHAMS ENCYCLOPAEDIA: illustrated. London: Odhams
Press, 1953. 960p. 22cm. General Advisory Editor: Lord Gorell (Ronald Gorell
Barnes Gorell, b.1884).

A small but popular inexpensive one-volume compendium of general information, and just one of many similar works published by Odhams Press,
although Lord Gorell is associated with only one later work, the *Modern
Encyclopaedia,* an eight-volume work published in 1961.

ODHAMS ENCYCLOPAEDIA FOR CHILDREN. London:
Odhams, 1961. Editors: J. A. Lauwerys, R. L. James and Brian Vesey-Fitzgerald.

A small and inexpensive one-volume work for children, also published
in 1961 as *Odhams Wonder World of Knowledge.*

ODHAMS WONDER WORLD OF KNOWLEDGE. London:
Odhams, 1961. Editors: J. A. Lauwerys, R. L. James and Brian Vesey-Fitzgerald.

A small one-volume work for children also issued as *Odhams Encyclopaedia for Children.*

OGILVIE'S ENCYCLOPAEDIA OF USEFUL INFORMA-
TION, and atlas of the world. London: G. W. Ogilvie, 1891. 653p. 26cm.
Compiler: G. W. Ogilvie.

A small and rather poorly produced one-volume work, with a limited
subject coverage. Published once only, it was compiled, edited and published by Ogilvie.

OUR WONDER WORLD; a library of knowledge. Chicago and Boston: G. L. Shuman & Co., 1914. 10v. 26cm.

A topically arranged work, containing fictional as well as factual information, designed for children to browse through rather than for direct
reference. No editors are listed for the original edition, but in the fifteenth
printing of the work in 1926, by which time the set had been expanded to
eleven volumes (Volume 11 being a school and study guide), Howard
Bristol Grose (b.1879) was named as editor.

In 1932, still under the Shuman imprint, a considerably revised edition
appeared as the *New Wonder World,* and further editions of this were issued

at regular intervals until 1943, and then annually until 1955. Beginning with the 1943 edition, the work was edited by James Ralph McGaughy (b.1888). Shortly after the 1955 edition, the publishing rights were acquired by the Parents Magazine Educational Press. After an extensive revision under the editorship of George Dinsmore Stoddard (b.1897), the work was re-issued in ten volumes as the *New Wonder World Encyclopedia,* and a second edition under this title was published in 1960, but in 1962 the title was altered yet again to the *New Wonder World Cultural Library.*

Beginning with the 1964 edition, the words "New Wonder World" were omitted from the title, and the work is currently known simply as the *Cultural Library.*

OUR WONDERFUL WORLD; the young people's encyclopedic anthology. Editorial Board, Leonard Davidow and others. Chicago: Spencer Press, 1955–1957. 18v. 27cm. Editor in Chief: Herbert Spencer Zim (b.1909).

A splendid but rather unusual work, of which the first eight volumes were issued in 1955, six more in 1956, and the remaining four in 1957. Originally, the work was available only through the Sears, Roebuck chain of department stores and that firm's mail order catalog (see also the *American Peoples Encyclopedia*).

The work is unusual in that it was designed not as an encyclopedia as such, but for general informational reading, and it was comprised in the main of brief excerpts from hundreds of books, magazines, pamphlets etc., all of which were carefully chosen for their accuracy and authority, and these were supplemented by commissioned articles to fill in the gaps where already published material was not available. The arrangement of the work is "thematic", or topical, under 30 themes, the informative material being based on the Shores-Rudman study of the reading interests and informational needs of children.

A second edition was published by the Spencer Press in 1960, but the rights to this work (and the *American Peoples Encyclopedia*) were acquired by Grolier Inc. shortly afterwards. The work is now published under their imprint under a policy of continuous revision.

• Reference:
Subscription Books Bulletin, September 1, 1958.

THE OUTLINE OF KNOWLEDGE. New York: J. A. Richards Inc. 1924. 20v. 19cm. Editor: James Albert Richards (b.1890).

A rather poor work, topically arranged, containing discussions by various authors on a variety of subjects. The arrangement was haphazard and the lack of an index and a table of contents nullified any merits it might have had. A "Reader's Guide" was contained in the final volume, arranging subjects for self-study, but this was also rather poorly compiled.

At about this time Richards was engaged in the compilation of a new work, which he afterwards published in 1933 as the *Richards Cyclopedic* and he announced in 1931 that the *Outline of Knowledge* was being discontinued. Apparently, however, the original plates were sold to a Philadelphia publisher, who re-issued the work in 1936 as the *New Outline of Knowledge*. The amount of revision was insignificant and the work was substantially the same as the original edition of 1924, although the cost had risen by almost 300%.

OXFORD ENCYCLOPAEDIA; or, dictionary of arts, sciences and general literature. Illustrated with nearly 200 elegant engravings. Printed at Oxford by Bartlett and Hinton for T. Kelly, London, 1828. 6v. 28cm. Editors: W. Harris, J. A. Stewart, C. Butler, and J. H. Hinton.

Despite its title, the only connection this small work appears to have had with the famous university town is that it was printed there. At about this time, the vogue appears to have been to name the different British encyclopedias after the towns in which they originated, e.g., the *London Encyclopaedia*, the *Edinburgh Encyclopaedia*, etc.

Neither the editors nor the publishers have been recorded as connected with any other encyclopedic work. It does not appear to have survived beyond the original printing, although a supplement of 860 pages was issued in 1831.

OXFORD JUNIOR ENCYCLOPAEDIA. London: Oxford University Press, 1948–1954. 13v. 26cm. General Editors: Laura E. Salt, Geoffrey Boumphrey.

A systematically arranged encyclopedia for older children, each of the first 12 volumes dealing with a specific subject area and, being alphabetically arranged, each volume was to all intents and purposes, a subject encyclopedia. The thirteenth volume comprised a quick ready-reference and general index to the other twelve volumes.

One of the best of the British junior encyclopedias, it has a rather more adult approach than the title implies. The articles, mostly of a moderate length, are well written and authoritative. A striking feature of the work is its illustrative material.

The second, and current, edition of the *Oxford Junior Encyclopaedia* appeared in 1964.

Although the work was sold in its own right for several years in the United States, it lacked appeal there because of its British orientation, and, as a result, an arrangement was entered into with the firm of Little & Ives to revise and adapt the work for American use as the *American Oxford Encyclopedia for Home and School*. The first volume of this was issued in late 1964 and was quite well done. Shortly thereafter, however, the American publisher encountered financial difficulties, with the result that the publication of further volumes was suspended indefinitely, and the likelihood of their continuation now seems remote.

PANNELL'S REFERENCE BOOK FOR HOME AND OFFICE. London: Granville Press, 1905. 984p. 22cm.

No editors are recorded for this quite useful one-volume compendium of general and practical information, but it appears to be identical to *Everybody's Everyday Reference Book for Home and Office,* also issued by the Granville Press in 1905.

The publishing rights were then acquired by the Edinburgh firm of T. C. & E. C. Jack, who re-issued a revised and enlarged edition in 1908 as *Jack's Reference Book for Home and Office,* under which title it enjoyed a popular and relatively long life for this type of work until a terminal edition in 1936.

PANTOLOGIA; a new encyclopaedia comprehending a complete series of essays, treatises and systems, alphabetically arranged; with a general dictionary of arts, sciences and words . . . illustrated with . . . engravings, those on natural history being from original drawings by Edwards and others. London: G. Kearsley, 1813. 12v. 25cm. Editors: John Mason Good (1764–1827), Olinthus Gilbert Gregory (1774–1841), Newton Bosworth (d.1848).

The compilation of this work was commenced by Newton Bosworth in 1802, under the proprietorship of the London bookseller and publisher, George Kearsley, and he was assisted by the well-known theologian and mathematician, Olinthus Gilbert Gregory.

A very curious situation arose at this time, however, which is described in Gregory's *Memoirs of the Life, Writings and Character, Literary, Professional and Religious, of the late John Mason Good, M.D.,* . . . (London, Fisher, 1828). According to Gregory, a competing bookseller tried to anticipate the publication of the *Pantologia* by commencing the publication of a new cyclopedia, of which Dr. George Gregory (no relation to Olinthus) was named as editor and, as a result, Kearsley and the editors sought a new arrangement for their work. John Mason Good, who had recently published his "Song of Songs" through Kearsley, enjoyed a high reputation for erudition, and seemed admirably qualified to co-operate in the new enterprise. According to Gregory, Good himself approached the proprietor, but it seems more likely that it was Good who was approached in the first instance. In any event, Good did then undertake to compile a quite extensive portion of the work and supplied his contribution with a considerable versatility of talent. Good's name was placed first on the title page, despite his protests, quite obviously to differentiate the *Pantologia* from the *Dictionary of Arts and Sciences,* of which Dr. George Gregory was the nominal editor.

In 1802, in the same year in which the compilation of the *Pantologia* commenced, Kearsley had published the ten-volume *English Encyclopaedia.* The sub-titling of this work, "a collection of treatises and a dictionary of terms illustrative of the arts and sciences" is not dissimilar to that of the

Pantologia and it is by no means improbable that this may well have provided the basic material from which the later work was assembled.

• Reference:
Collison.

PEALE'S POPULAR EDUCATOR AND CYCLOPEDIA OF REFERENCE; historical, biographical and statistical. Embracing the most improved and simple methods of self instruction in book-keeping, penmanship, commercial law, etc., together with laws and forms used in every department of social and business life. Prepared under the direction of the publishers by a specialist in each department. Illustrated with original drawings, colored maps and diagrams. Chicago and St. Louis: R. S. Peale & Co., 1883. 702p. 27cm. Editorial Director: Richard S. Peale.

Not an encyclopedia in the usual sense, but a handbook of practical information designed for self instruction and guidance in everyday life. In actual fact, Peale had condensed some 52 books into one volume, which provided a wide subject coverage in briefer form.

The work apparently enjoyed a moderate success and further editions were issued in 1884 and 1885, but in 1886, under the title of the *Home Library of Useful Knowledge,* it was re-issued by the Home Library Association, after which it went out of print.

Peale's contribution to the work was relatively minimal, and he is better known for his publication of a pirated reprint of the ninth edition of the *Encyclopaedia Britannica* and the 1902 edition of the *Encyclopedia Americana.*

PEARS CYCLOPAEDIA; twenty-two complete works of reference in one handy volume of over 1,000 pages. Isleworth: A. & F. Pears Ltd., 1897. 1,000p. 18cm. Compiler: Thomas J. Barratt.

It is no exaggeration to say that this is by far the most popular one-volume encyclopedia ever published in Britain. Its origin was particularly unusual in that the publishers were well-known soap manufacturers, and had no real connection with the publishing industry, and it was only in 1961 that they transferred the publishing rights to a British publisher, Pelham Books, who are also producing the junior version of the work, *Junior Pears Cyclopaedia.*

Pears Cyclopaedia is an extraordinarily useful little work which has been published annually since 1897, and in that time it has gained and retained a large public in Britain, although it is only in recent years that it has been generally available in North America. The arrangement of the work is by subject, supplemented by a very comprehensive index, and it contains an astonishing amount of general and practical information within its small compass.

PEARSON'S EVERYTHING WITHIN; a library of up to date and authoritative information on every aspect of home and family life. London:

C. A. Pearson, 1957. 659p. 19cm. Editor: Francis Addington Symonds (b.1893).

A small one-volume work very similar to the *Everything Within* published by George Newnes, but much less comprehensive than *Pears Cyclopaedia*. The 1957 edition is a revision of an earlier issue of the work, but the exact date of origin is not ascertainable from the information available.

THE PENGUIN ENCYCLOPAEDIA. London: Penguin Books, 1965. Editor: Sir John Summersale.

A very useful, compact but fairly comprehensive desk reference work, and one of the very few encyclopedias published in paperback form. In size, compactness and accuracy, it compares favorably with the *Columbia-Viking Desk Encyclopedia*, which has also been published recently in a paperback format.

PENNY CYCLOPAEDIA; of the Society for the Diffusion of Useful Knowledge. London: Charles Knight, 1833–1843. 27v. in 14v. 30cm. Editor: George Long (1800–1879).

Despite its name, this very useful and popular work of its time was issued at 9d. per part or 7/6d. per each cloth bound volume. Originally it was issued in 27 thinner volumes, but a larger edition was afterwards made available, which compressed two volumes into one. In 1851, and again in 1858, one-volume supplements were issued, which brought the total number of volumes up to 29, and in the year 1860, these were reprinted by a publisher named Sangster, in an edition of 16 volumes (or 27 volumes in 16).

Meanwhile, between 1854 and 1862, Knight was publishing, in parts, his *English Cyclopaedia* in 22 volumes, which was modelled on the *Penny Cyclopaedia*. More directly descended from the original work, however, was the two-volume *Imperial Cyclopaedia*, which was based on the *Penny Cyclopaedia*, and also edited by Long, but the contents of this smaller work appear to have been confined to subjects pertinent to the British Empire.

Directly derived from the *Penny Cyclopaedia* was Knight's *National Cyclopaedia of Useful Knowledge*, published in 12 volumes between 1847 and 1851. Due to the heavy excise duty on paper at that time, Knight suffered severe financial losses on his enterprises, and when the *National Cyclopaedia* was re-issued between 1856–1859, it appeared under the imprint of George Routledge, in alternative seven- or thirteen-volume editions. Subsequently, in 1867–1868, it was re-issued in 13 volumes (with a fourteenth as an atlas) as the *National Encyclopaedia* under the imprint of W. Mackenzie, and with J. H. F. Brabner as editor. Mackenzie published further editions in 1875 and 1884–1888.

Finally, in 1913–1914, under the editorship of Andrew Boyle, and the imprint of J. M. Dent, the original works were thoroughly revised and re-written and published as the highly authoritative and popular *Everyman Encyclopaedia* in a 12-volume edition. A second edition of this excellent small encyclopedia was published by Dent in 1931–1932, a third in 1939–

1950 and a fourth in 1958, the latter also being vended in the United States as the *Macmillan Everyman's Encylopedia*. A fifth edition appeared in 1967.

In 1934, an edition was published in Canada as the *Cambridge Encyclopaedia*, but, except for some external changes, this was identical to the second edition of *Everyman's* in 1931–1932.

• Reference:
Collison.

PEOPLE'S CYCLOPEDIA; a complete library of reference containing the exact knowledge of the world condensed to the plainest terms consistent with accuracy and clearness, with a valuable appendix of often sought for facts in almost every department of human knowledge, and a chronological history of the world . . . superbly and profusely illustrated by hundreds of subjects in full color, monotone and text cuts, besides a series of agricultural charts prepared from the latest government data. Prepared by more than 200 of the most eminent editors, educators, scholars, scientists, inventors, explorers, etc. New York: Syndicate Publishing Co., 1914. 5v. 19cm. Editors in Chief: Charles Leonard Stuart (b.1868), George Jotham Hagar (1847–1921).

In 1903, Charles Stuart was the editor, and the Christian Herald Co. were the publishers, of the *Crown Encyclopedia and Gazetteer*, a five-volume work containing some 60,000 brief entries. This was re-issued in 1905, by the Success Co., as the *Continental Encyclopedia*, in eight volumes, the last two of which contained a general dictionary.

In 1907, under the imprint of the National Press Association, another eight-volume edition was issued as the *New Century Reference Library*, and this was followed, in 1909, under the imprint of the Syndicate Publishing Co., by the *Current Cyclopedia of Reference*. In 1911, reverting to its original five-volume format, the Syndicate Co. published the work as *Everybody's Cyclopedia*, in which Hagar's name appeared for the first time.

Stuart was not listed as an editor of the work after 1914, but Hagar continued as editor, and further issues appeared in 1918 as the *New World Wide Cyclopedia* and in 1919 as the *World Wide Cyclopedia* and the *New World Encyclopedia*. Significantly, in 1928, the work was re-issued under the title of the *New World Wide Cyclopedia*, listing Hagar (who had died in 1921) and Francis Joseph Reynolds (1867–1937) as joint editors.

Reynolds had, in 1923, been editor of *Adair's New Encyclopedia*, a five-volume set also issued by the Syndicate Publishing Co., which was almost certainly a reprint of the 1919 editions of this many-titled work. In 1929, again under the editorship of Hagar and Reynolds, the work was re-issued in eight volumes as the *Times Encyclopedia and Gazetteer*, but this was re-titled the *Twentieth Century Encyclopedia* in 1930 and 1934, although only Reynolds was now listed as the editor.

The complicated history of this poor work seems to have terminated with the appearance of the *World's Popular Encyclopedia*, issues of which were released in 1937, 1940 and 1942, although Reynolds (who had died in 1937) is not listed as the editor in the two latter editions.

PEOPLES CYCLOPEDIA OF UNIVERSAL KNOWL-EDGE; brought down to the year 1882 . . . illustrated with numerous colored maps, etc. 4th edition. New York: Phillips & Hunt, 1883. 3v. (2092p.) Editor: William Harrison De Puy (1821–1901).

According to the collation, this 1883 edition is the fourth of the *Peoples Cyclopedia of Universal Knowledge,* but no record could be traced of earlier editions under this title or under the names of the editor and publisher.

Its subsequent history is more easily ascertained, however. In 1903, in an eight-volume edition, revised and enlarged, it was re-issued as the *New Peoples Cyclopedia of Universal Knowledge,* with De Puy, although recently deceased, as editor. In 1908, again with De Puy as editor, it re-appeared in a 12-volume edition as the *World Wide Encyclopedia and Gazetteer,* under the imprint of the Christian Herald Co.

THE PEOPLES ENCYCLOPAEDIA; a compendium of universal information. London: Encyclopaedia Publishing Co., 1873. 980p. 22cm. Compiler: Leo de Colange (b.1819).

This one-volume work is probably derived from *Zell's Popular Encyclopedia,* a two-volume work published in Philadelphia in 1870, also compiled by Colange. It appears to be identical, also, to the one-volume *National Encyclopedia,* also published in 1873, and it is most likely that the *Peoples Encyclopaedia* is the British edition of this.

The American edition re-appeared in 1878 as the *Universal Encyclopedia* and then, finally, as the *School Encyclopedia* in 1899.

PERPETUAL LOOSE-LEAF PICTURED ENCYCLOPE-DIA *see* SOURCE BOOK

PICTURED KNOWLEDGE; visual instruction practically applied for the home and school. Chicago: Compton-Johnson Co., 1916. 2v. 25cm (1056p.) Editor in Chief: Calvin Noyes Kendall (1858–1921). Associate Editor: Mrs. Eleanor Stackhouse Atkinson (1863–1942).

The Compton-Johnson Co. was evidently a subsidiary of F. E. Compton & Co., and at least one of the editors of this work, Mrs. Atkinson, was directly concerned with the *New Students Reference Library,* at that time F. E. Compton's main product. This is significant, as both the *New Students Reference Work* and *Pictured Knowledge* were acquired by other publishers when Compton's issued their major *Compton's Pictured Encyclopedia* in 1922, and it is not unlikely that both works, one for the text and the other for its illustrative material, were drawn on in compiling their new work.

Be that as it may, *Pictured Knowledge* was, as its name correctly implies, a collection of pictures arranged by subject, with the text relegated to a minor place. It was evidently quite successful, and further editions were issued in 1917 and 1919, when it was expanded to five volumes. Some time thereafter, it was acquired by the Marshall-Hughes Co. of Kansas City who re-issued it in 1927 in a ten-volume edition, but in 1935, it was again reduced to a five-volume format. Further editions, in eight volumes, with Garry Cleveland Myers (b.1884) as editor, were published in 1937 and 1939.

It was not until seventeen years later, in 1956, that the title re-appeared, when an edition in 14 volumes (3584 pages) was issued by Little & Ives, under the editorship of Franklin Dunham, who had edited the *New Pictorial Encyclopedia of the World* for the same company in 1954.

• References:
Subscription Books Bulletin, July 1930; January 1939.

POCKET ENCYCLOPAEDIA; a compendium of general knowledge for ready reference. London: Sampson, Low, 1888. 1206p. 22cm.

A quite useful one-volume work containing a great deal of concise information on a wide variety of subjects. The work was also published in a reduced format as *Low's Pocket Encyclopaedia.*

POCKET LIBRARY OF THE WORLD'S ESSENTIAL KNOWLEDGE. New York and London: Funk & Wagnalls Co., 1929. 10v. 17cm. Editor in Chief: Henry Cook Hathaway.

Regrettably little is known of this work, the only recorded entry for which is to be found in the British Museum catalogue. In all probability, the work is a condensation of the multi-volume works published by Funk & Wagnalls in the United States in previous years, although Hathaway is not known to be connected with any of these.

POPULAR COMPENDIUM OF USEFUL INFORMATION . . . and handy dictionary of common things. Philadelphia: 1901. 606p. 25cm. Editor in Chief: Charles Smith Morris (1833–1922).

This mediocre, one-volume work is almost certainly a reprint, with some omissions, of the *Twentieth Century Cyclopedia of Practical Information,* edited by Morris and published by the John Winston Co. of Philadelphia also in 1901. It is certainly identical, in all respects, to the *World Encyclopedia,* also published in Philadelphia in 1901.

In 1902, it was re-issued under two further titles, the *Golden Treasury of Useful Information* and the curiously titled *World's Best Knowledge and How to Use It.*

An abridgement was also published in 1902 as the *Home Cyclopedia of Necessary Knowledge,* which was re-issued in 1905 as the *Home Educator in Necessary Knowledge* and in 1907 as *Everybody's Encyclopedia for Everyday Reference.*

With some additional material, including an atlas, the work seems to have made a final appearance in 1909 as the *Cyclopedia, Dictionary and Atlas of the World.*

THE POPULAR ENCYCLOPAEDIA; or, Conversations Lexicon, being a general dictionary of arts, sciences, literature, biography, history, ethics and political economy. With dissertations on the rise and progress of literature by Sir D. K. Sandford; on the progress of science by T. Thomson, and on the progress of the fine arts by A. Cunningham. Glasgow: Blackie & Son, 1841. 7v. 22cm. Editor: Alexander Whitelaw.

A work with an interesting history on both sides of the Atlantic. In its day, it was a very popular work and ran through several editions, in 1849–1850, 1862, and 1877, all under the editorship of Whitelaw. In 1882, however, Charles Annandale (1843–1915), a well-known educationalist, became the editor, and under his direction the edition of 1890–1893 was expanded to 14 volumes. But Annandale, in 1889–1890, had also edited, for the same publisher, *Blackie's Modern Cyclopedia of Universal Information,* an eight-volume work which evidently stems directly from the *Popular Encyclopaedia.*

Blackie's, in turn, was exported to the United States, where it was published in Philadelphia by Gebbie & Sons as the *New Cabinet Cyclopaedia and Treasury of Knowledge* (1891–1892), which Ainsworth Rand Spofford (1825–1908) adapted for American use. This was continued in 1899 by the *New National Cyclopaedia,* in 1901 by the *XX Century Cyclopaedia,* in 1903 by the *New Twentieth Century Cyclopaedia and Dictionary,* in 1905 by the *New and Complete Universal Self Pronouncing Encyclopedia,* in 1906 by the *New Cosmopolitan Encyclopedia* and finally, in 1912, by the *National Encyclopedia of Reference.*

Meanwhile, in Britain, the Gresham Publishing Co. had acquired the publishing rights to the works issued under the imprint of Blackie, and in 1901, with Annandale as editor, they re-issued the original work as the *New Popular Encyclopaedia,* again in 14 volumes. Five years later, in 1906–1907, this was re-issued in an eight-volume edition as the *Modern Cyclopaedia of Universal Information,* which ties it directly to the work issued by Blackie in 1889.

Many years later, Gresham published the *New Gresham Encyclopaedia* (1921), but apart from common ownership, there is no connection with the earlier works.

PRACTICAL AMERICAN ENCYCLOPEDIA; a universal reference library in the arts, sciences and literature, with nearly 1,000 illustrations. Chicago and New York: W. B. Conkey Co., 1911. 2v. (4584p.) 22cm. Editor in Chief: Bernhart Paul Holst (1861–1939). Associate Editor: Ruric Neval Roark (1859–1909).

This work appears to be an identical reprint of the *New Teacher's and Pupil's Cyclopaedia,* a five-volume work also edited and published by Holst It is clearly related also to the one-volume *Unrivalled Encyclopedia,* also published in 1911, by the W. B. Conkey Co., and edited by Holst, although the latter contains only 2,576 pages, and is described as being five volumes in one.

All three titles are directly derived from the *Teacher's and Pupil's Cyclopaedia*, edited and published by Holst in a four-volume edition in 1902, but believed to have been in existence in 1895 in a three-volume edition. Both the *Practical American Encyclopedia* and the *Unrivalled Encyclopedia* appeared once only under the imprint of W. B. Conkey (actually the printer of the Holst publications), but the works were continued under the Holst imprint for almost half-a-century afterwards.

As the *New Teacher's and Pupil's Cyclopaedia*, it was published at regular intervals from 1910 to 1927, although for four years of the same period (1923–1927) it was also issued as the *International Reference Work*, a practice which brought forth a "Cease and Desist" order (Docket #1331) against the International Publishing Co. from the Federal Trade Commission. As a result the work was re-vamped, and, from 1928 to 1939, it was published only as the *Progressive Reference Library*. Holst, who had "edited" and published all these titles, died in 1939, and no further editions were published during the Second World War, but, by 1945, the original plates had been acquired by a New York publisher (The Universal Educational Guild Inc.) and it was re-issued in 1945, with little change, even citing Holst as the editor, as the *World Scope Encyclopedia*.

From 1946 to 1964, it was edited by William H. Hendelson (b.1904), who revised it so thoroughly as to be unrecognizable from the editions of twenty years before. But despite the very considerable improvement which was implemented by Hendelson, the publishers reverted to the questionable practice of issuing the same work under different names, and in 1953, it was issued as the *New World Family Encyclopedia*, and in both 1953 and 1957, as the *Standard International Encyclopedia*. Both of these editions were in 20 thinner volumes as against the 12 of the *World Scope*, and they were intended for supermarket distribution. In content, however, they were substantially the same, but the two supermarket editions were so cheap in comparison to the subscription-vended *World Scope*, that it was apparent that the latter was grossly overpriced.

In 1963, due to financial stress, the World Scope Publishers went into liquidation, and the publishing rights were acquired by the Washington firm of the Publishers Co., who re-issued the work in 1964 under no less than three different titles, at a wide variety in cost, as the *New American Encyclopedia*, the *World University Encyclopedia*, and, by arrangement with a Miami distributor, as the *World Educator Encyclopedia*.

PRACTICAL ENCYCLOPAEDIA FOR CHILDREN. London: Odhams Press, 1944. 320p. 24cm.

A small, topically arranged, simply written one-volume work for younger children, probably abridged from the *Wonder Encyclopaedia for Children*, published by the same company in 1933.

PRACTICAL HOME ENCYCLOPEDIA; a dictionary of universal knowledge. New York: Hamilton Book Company, 1909. 8v. 24cm. Editor in Chief: George Jotham Hagar (1847–1921).

A re-issue of the *Standard American Encyclopedia*, originally edited by John Clark Ridpath (1840–1900) and published in 1899 by the Standard American Publishing Co. In 1906, with Hagar listed as a joint editor, it was re-titled and re-issued as the *New Standard Encyclopedia*, under the imprint of the University Society, further editions being issued in 1907–1908, 1908 and 1911. In 1912, an edition was published under the imprint of the Wheeler Publishing Co., again as the *Standard American Encyclopedia*, and a final edition, expanded to 12 volumes, was published in 1916 by the University Society.

The title of *New Standard Encyclopedia* was adopted by a quite different work in 1930, and the title of *Standard American Encyclopedia* was also revived in 1937, although this latter may very well have derived from the earlier editions.

The extent to which Hagar contributed to the work is questionable, as he was also employed, in 1910, as an editor for the entirely different *Appleton's Practical Encyclopedia*, and, from 1911 onwards, with several other apparently unrelated works.

PRACTICAL KNOWLEDGE FOR ALL; comprising easy courses in literature, language, history, geography, the arts and sciences, written by experts and arranged for home study, with plates. London: Fleetway House, 1934. 6v. 22cm. Editor: Sir John Alexander Hammerton (1871–1949).

Although this work contained quite a fair quantity of general information, and although classed as an encyclopedia, it can only be considered one in the very broadest sense.

The volumes comprised a series of courses of an elementary nature on a fairly broad base for home study and self-instruction, but lacking an index, it was virtually valueless as a source of reference.

In common with similar works in the 1930's, it could be acquired by subscribing for a prescribed period to one of the British national daily newspapers.

PROGRESSIVE REFERENCE LIBRARY; a new edition with extensive revisions, constituting a consolidation of the publications formerly on the market as the "International Reference Work" and the "New Teacher's and Pupil's Cyclopaedia"; a library of history, geography, biography, biology, literature, economics, civics, arts, sciences, discoveries, inventions, explorations, commerce, etc., and a cyclopaedia of general and recent information. Boone and Chicago: Holst Publishing Co., 1928. 10v. 25cm. Editor in Chief: Bernhart Paul Holst (1861–1939).

As correctly stated by the publisher, this work is a consolidation (although re-titling would be even more accurate) of the *International Reference Work*, published by Holst from 1923 to 1927, and the *New Teacher's and Pupil's Cyclopaedia,* also edited and published by Holst, which appeared between 1910 and 1927. What it omits to mention, however, is that the consolidation resulted from an order of the Federal Trade Commission against the International Publishing Co. to cease and desist from selling the same work under more than one title. It also conveniently omits to mention that the text, although revised and enlarged to some extent, is substantially the same as the *Teacher's and Pupil's Cyclopaedia,* a four-volume work published by Holst in 1902 (although believed to have been in existence in 1895), which had also appeared under at least two other titles, as the *Unrivalled Encyclopedia,* and the *Practical American Encyclopedia,* both published in 1911 under the imprint of the W. B. Conkey Co., who were the actual printers of these earlier editions.

The history of the work subsequent to 1928 was relatively respectable, despite its mediocre quality, and further editions were issued in 1935, when the previous titles were no longer mentioned, and 1939, in which year Holst died.

It was not revived until 1945, when the publishing rights were acquired by a New York enterprise, who re-issued what was substantially the 1939 edition (listing Holst as the editor) as the *World Scope Encyclopedia.* Thereafter the work was extensively revised by William H. Hendelson as the editor in chief, and was in fact improved quite considerably, although never to the extent where it could seriously compete with the more established and accepted works in the same price range. The improvement in the contents of the work was marred, however, by the practice of issuing the work under more than one title.

In 1953, a cheap edition in 20 volumes, designed for sales through food stores, was issued both as the *New World Family Encyclopedia* and the *Standard International Encyclopedia,* and these were produced so much more cheaply than the *World Scope Encyclopedia,* that a reflection was thrown on the true worth of the latter or basic work. The *World Scope Encyclopedia* ceased publication rather abruptly in 1964, when the then publishers encountered financial difficulties.

Subsequently the publishing rights were acquired by the Publishers Co. of Washington, D.C., who immediately re-issued the same work under no less than three different titles (at a considerable variation in cost) as the *New American Encyclopedia,* the *World University Encyclopedia,* and the *World Educator Encyclopedia,* all of which have appeared in successive editions since.

• Reference:

Subscription Books Bulletin, April 1932.

PURNELL'S NEW ENGLISH ENCYCLOPAEDIA. London: Purnell & Sons, 1966. 12v. 25cm. Editor in Chief: Bernard A. Workman.

This is an alphabetically arranged encyclopedia which is being published in 216 weekly parts, the first issue of which appeared in January, 1966. When completed, the work will be in 12 goodly-sized volumes, two of which will comprise a dictionary which, with the encyclopedic material, is included in each weekly part.

An examination of the first few issues indicates a high quality of production, and the illustrative material, most of which is in clear and accurate color, is surprisingly good, as also is the paper and the typography.

The idea of issuing an encyclopedia in weekly parts is not new, of course, but the many improvements in printing techniques which have evolved in recent years enable a much higher quality work than was possible when such works as *Harmsworth's Universal Encyclopaedia* was issued in parts almost half a century previously.

Although the work is printed in Britain, Purnell's holds the copyright jointly with the Instituto Geografico de Agostini and there is a noticeable leaning towards subjects of Italian interest and a great deal of Italian illustrative material in the work.

The work is also being published as a complete encyclopedia by the Caxton Publishing Co. as the *New Caxton Encyclopedia*, beginning in 1966.

READY REFERENCE; the universal cyclopaedia, containing everything that everybody wants to know. London: Griffith, Farran & Co., 1890. 812p. 22cm. Compiler: William Ralston Balch (b.1852).

The sub-titling of this small work is indicative of its quality. No work of such small content could hope to "contain everything that everybody wants to know", not even in 1890. A revised edition was published in 1894.

RICHARDS CYCLOPEDIA. New York: J. A. Richards Inc., 1933. 12v. 25cm. Editors: Ernest Hunter Wright (b.1882), Mary Heritage Wright. Managing Editor: James Albert Richards (b.1890).

Described as being 24 volumes in 12, the last two of which contained an index and a bibliography, this is a topically arranged work with a distinctly juvenile approach, quite well compiled, with good bibliographies, and of use as a browsing supplement to an alphabetically arranged encyclopedia.

Prior to the compilation of this work, Richards had published a work similar in style and arrangement (but deficient in quality) under the title of the *Outline of Knowledge* (1924), and there can be little doubt that to some extent at least, the new work was derived from this earlier compilation. On the publication of *Richards Cyclopedia,* the older *Outline of Knowledge* was discontinued and the original plates sold to another publisher, who re-issued it in 1936 as the *New Outline of Knowledge.*

A second edition of *Richards Cyclopedia* was published in 1937, but with the edition of 1939, the title of the work was changed to *Richards Topical Encyclopedia,* and it was re-arranged and expanded to 15 volumes.

Some time afterwards, about 1945, it was acquired by the firm of

Grolier Incorporated, who published it annually from 1949 until it was eventually discontinued in 1962. Just prior to its discontinuance, however, most of the material had been incorporated into a work known as the *Unified Encyclopedia*, a 30-volume work first published in 1960, which merged the topical articles from *Richards Topical Encyclopedia* with the alphabetical entries from the *Grolier Encylopedia* into one alphabetical sequence.

• Reference:

Subscription Books Bulletin, July 1934.

RICHARDS TOPICAL ENCYCLOPEDIA. New York: J. A. Richards Inc., 1939. 15v. 25cm. Editors: Ernest Hunter Wright (b.1882), Mary Heritage Wright. Managing Editor: James Albert Richards (b.1890).

A re-titled, re-arranged and enlarged edition of the 12-volume *Richards Cyclopedia*, published under the same imprint from 1933 to 1937. It enjoyed considerable success and popularity for several years, but, towards the end of the 1950's, its usefulness declined and it was eventually discontinued in 1962, although most of the material had previously been incorporated into the *Unified Encyclopedia*, a 30-volume work published by H. S. Stuttman & Co. from 1960 to 1964.

This work merged (or unified) the entries from the topically arranged *Richards Topical Encyclopedia* with the alphabetically arranged *Grolier Encyclopedia* into one complete alphabetical sequence, an unusual but unsuccessful concept.

Richards Topical Encyclopedia had been acquired by Grolier Incorporated about 1945, and editions were published annually by them from 1949 together with an updating supplement, the *Richards Yearbook* which, unlike the main work, was arranged alphabetically.

• References:

Subscription Books Bulletin, January 1940; October 1950.
Booklist and Subscription Books Bulletin, January 1, 1957.

ROUTLEDGE'S EVERYMAN'S CYCLOPAEDIA; of biography, history, geography, general information, law, spelling, abbreviations, synonyms, pseudonyms, etc. London: G. Routledge. New York: E. P. Dutton, 1910. 650p. 20cm. Editor: Arnold Villiers.

A fairly useful and popular, small, one-volume compendium of general and practical and miscellaneous information. There is no connection between this small work and the much more comprehensive and scholarly *Everyman's Encyclopaedia*.

Curiously, Routledge had in 1847 published the *National Cyclopaedia*, which was a re-issue of the popular *Penny Cyclopaedia*, which, in turn was thoroughly revised and rewritten to become the 1913 *Everyman Encyclopaedia*. Another curious relationship is that E. P. Dutton distributed both works in the United States.

ROUTLEDGE'S UNIVERSAL ENCYCLOPAEDIA; an entirely new reference book on an original plan, containing 31,200 entries, 800,-000 words, 3,100 illustrations, 160 statistical diagrams and colored maps. London: G. Routledge & Sons, 1934. 1176p. 21cm. Editor in Chief: Lawrence Hawkins Dawson (b.1880).

A remarkably well compiled one-volume desk encyclopedia containing a substantial amount of brief information on a wide range of subjects, which sold widely in Britain for several years.

It is believed to have been adapted for American consumption as *Facts: The New Concise Pictorial Encyclopedia,* in an enlarged four-volume format, published by Doubleday, Doran & Co. in 1934, with Dawson listed as the British editor of that work.

In 1938, *Facts* was published in a one-volume edition comprising 1,271 pages, which made it remarkably uniform in size with *Routledge's Universal Encyclopaedia.* In later years, *Facts* was re-issued as the *Comprehensive Pictorial Encyclopedia* (1942) and as the *World Home Reference Encyclopedia* (1951). In each instance, Dawson was listed as the British editor.

SCHOOL ENCYCLOPEDIA, THE; a summary of universal knowledge, with pronunciation of every subject title; for teachers, pupils and families. Syracuse: W. Gill, 1899. 991p. 22cm. Compiler: Leo de Colange (b.1819).

Apparently the terminal printing of a work which had first been published as the *National Encyclopedia* (1873), the *Peoples Encyclopaedia* (1873) and the *Universal Encyclopedia* (1878).

All of these works were compiled by Colange, and, with the exception of the *Peoples Encyclopaedia,* all were published in Philadelphia, although under different imprints. The work is almost certainly derived from *Zell's Popular Encyclopedia,* a two-volume work compiled by Colange in 1870.

THE SCHOOL LIBRARY ENCYCLOPEDIA; embracing history, geography, discovery, invention, biography, arts, sciences and literature, prepared especially for use in the public schools of America; with "Guideposts"—a reading index. Chicago: Caxton Co., 1901. 4v. 23cm. Editor: L. Brent Vaughan (b.1873).

The history of this work is important in that it throws light on the origin and development of two of the most popular home and school encyclopedias of the present time.

The *School Library Encyclopedia* is in itself an exact reprint of *Hill's Practical Encyclopedia,* also issued in 1901, but under the imprint of the Chicago Book Co. This latter title is named after the originator, Thomas Edie Hill (1832–1915) although this work, and the *School Library Encyclo-*

pedia were actually edited by L. Brent Vaughan. In 1902, the work was issued simultaneously under three different titles and under three different imprints as (1) *The School Library Encyclopedia,* (2) *Hill's Practical Encyclopedia* and (3) *Hill's Practical Reference Library of General Knowledge.* Of these, only the latter title, which was published under the imprint of Dixon & Hanson, continued in existence after 1902, and under the Dixon & Hanson imprint, further editions were issued in 1904 and 1905. But, by this time, it should be noted, neither Hill nor Vaughan were connected with the work, and what revisions were implemented were done by William Francis Rocheleau.

In 1907, still under the imprint of Dixon & Hanson, the work was revised and expanded to five volumes, and with Charles Herbert Sylvester as editor in chief, and William Francis Rocheleau as associate editor, it was re-issued as the *New Practical Reference Library.* This was followed by another edition in 1911, in which the imprint was changed to read the Dixon-Hanson-Bellows Co., but in the edition of 1912, Dixon's name was no longer associated with the work, and it would appear also that Rocheleau was not connected with any editorial direction. What had in fact happened was that Dixon had broken away to compile an encyclopedia of his own, and Rocheleau went with him as his editor in chief.

Not long afterwards, in 1913, Dixon published his *Home and School Reference Work,* with Rocheleau as editor. The 1912 edition of the *New Practical Reference Library* expanded the set to 12 volumes, and it was undoubtedly very popular, as yet another edition appeared in 1913, but in this edition, Rocheleau had been replaced as associate editor by Ellsworth Decatur Foster (1869–1936), a particularly significant change, as Foster was to figure prominently in the subsequent development of the work.

Further editions of the *New Practical Reference Library,* with little change, were issued in 1914 and 1915 under the imprint of the Hanson-Bellows Co., but the 1917 and 1918 editions revealed a most significant change of ownership, as the imprint for both of these editions reads the Hanson-Roach-Fowler Co., and clearly, both Dixon and Bellows were not connected with these specific editions. Of particular interest is that, in 1917 and 1918, the Hanson-Roach-Fowler Co. published not only the *New Practical Reference Library,* but also the new and highly successful *World Book,* and there can be little doubt that, although the *World Book* was a completely new and carefully planned independent publication, some of the original material had been adapted from the earlier work. Indeed, some of it was taken verbatim, which is not altogether surprising, as Foster was at that time on the editorial staff of both works.

In 1919, however, the *World Book* (afterwards the *World Book Encyclopedia*) was acquired by the W. F. Quarrie Co., and ever since then has gone from strength to strength to become perhaps the most popular family and school encyclopedia in the world. It was not, despite a common origin, a direct continuation of the *New Practical Reference Library,* but an entirely new work which had drawn to some extent on the basic material assembled for the earlier title, and this is clearly evinced by the fact that the rights to the *New Practical Reference Library* were acquired by the Ralph Durham Co., who, with Ellsworth Decatur Foster as editor in chief, re-issued it in a revised and expanded set of eight volumes as the *American Educator* (afterwards the *American Educator Encyclopedia*) in 1919.

It is interesting to note that Bellows, who had been connected with earlier editions of the *New Practical Reference Library*, came back into the picture with the 1926 edition of the *American Educator*, which was issued under the imprint of the Bellows-Durham Co.

Quite obviously, today's *American Educator Encyclopedia* is a direct, albeit much changed, descendant of the original *School Library Encyclopedia* and the other two titles published in 1901, and the continuation of these, the *New Practical Reference Library*. On the other hand, the *World Book Encyclopedia*, although it borrowed originally from these earlier works, owes very much less and was, to all intents and purposes, an entirely new concept when it was first published in 1917.

SOURCE BOOK; an international encyclopedic authority written from the new world viewpoint, prepared by over 200 authorities in the fields of literature, art and science. Chicago: Perpetual Encyclopedia Corp., 1924. 10v. 24cm. Editor: William Francis Rocheleau.

A very poor work, indeed, despite its pretentious claims, and one which was frequently investigated by the Federal Trade Commission.

The history of the work begins in 1913, when it was first published as the six-volume *Home and School Reference Work*, with Rocheleau as editor in chief. One of the publishers, H. M. Dixon, had previously been associated with *Hill's Practical Reference Library* (as also had been Rocheleau in an editorial capacity), and both had clearly dissociated themselves from that work prior to 1913 in order to publish their new compilation, which was obviously intended to compete with the products of their former partners. A further edition of the *Home and School Reference Work*, expanded to seven volumes, the last of which was a "Methods of Study" guide, was issued in 1915, under the imprint of the Dixon-Rucker Co.

About 1922, Dixon-Rucker sold all rights in the work to the Perpetual Encyclopedia Corp., who continued selling the remaining stocks until 1923. They then revised the work, expanding it to ten volumes (seven encyclopedic, three methods of study), and published it in 1924 under its new title of the *Source Book*, a title which was clearly designed to make it competitive to the best-selling *World Book* of the period. But a very confused situation arose through the contracts made with a number of distributors and jobbers, who sold the set, under their own imprints as the *Home and School Reference Work*, the *American Reference Library*, and the *North American Reference Book*, and probably other titles also, although none of these are recorded as having been copyrighted.

This thoroughly mixed up vending of the same work under different titles continued for a number of years until about 1929, when the Perpetual Encyclopedia Corp. was ordered by the Federal Trade Commission to cease and desist from selling under any other name than *Source Book* (Docket #1371), and apparently this order was observed, as from then until its terminal edition in 1936, the *Source Book* was sold on a relatively respectable basis, editions being copyrighted in 1930 (Rocheleau no longer being listed as editor), 1932, and 1935 when the Source Research Council was listed as publisher.

• Reference:
Subscription Books Bulletin, January 1931.

STANDARD AMERICAN BOOK OF KNOWLEDGE; containing concise special articles of research upon all the latest topics of science, art, mechanics, education, history and travel . . . the whole forming a complete guide and self instructor on scientific, commercial, historical, artistic and all other subjects . . . embellished with 400 fine engravings. Philadelphia: National Publishing Co., 1900. 846p. 26cm. Compiler: Henry Davenport Northrop (1836–1909).

An expanded edition of a mediocre one-volume work which was first issued in 1897 (by the same publisher) as the *Standard Cyclopedia,* which was re-issued in 1899 as the extraordinarily titled *X-Rays of Intellectual Light.* Either in whole or in part, it was afterwards re-issued as the *20th Century Cyclopedia of Universal Knowledge* (1901), the *World's Book of Knowledge* (1901), the *New Century Cyclopedia of Universal Knowledge* (1902) and the *American Home Educator and Book of Universal Knowledge* (1903). It may well have appeared under other unrecorded titles also.

STANDARD AMERICAN ENCYCLOPEDIA; a dictionary of universal knowledge. New York and San Francisco: Wheeler Publishing Co., 1912. 8v. 24cm. Editor in Chief: George Jotham Hagar (1847–1921). Associate Editors: Samuel Walker Beyer (1865–1931), Amos P. Brown (1864–1917).

This work is identical in all respects to the eight-volume *Practical Home Encyclopedia,* published in 1909 by the Hamilton Book Co., and this was evidently derived from the *New Standard Encyclopedia,* a 12-volume set published by the University Society in 1906, of which Hagar was one of the editors. It is unlikely that even this edition was original and the work is, in all probability, derived from the *Standard American Encyclopedia of Arts,* etc., published by the Standard American Publishing Co. in 1899. The University Society, who had published the 1906 *New Standard Encyclopedia* was subsequently concerned with a new edition of the *Standard American Encyclopedia,* published in 1916, once again in a 12-volume format. But from 1916 until 1937, the work seemed to have been suspended and no further editions under any of the earlier titles could be traced.

However, in 1937, a work with the same title and a very similar subtitling ("a library of universal knowledge") was published by the Standard

American Corporation of Chicago. This was in 15 volumes and was evidently a very poorly edited revision of the much older work. The principal method of selling the work was as a premium with a number of American daily newspapers, which is indicative of its poor quality, despite the naming of Walter Miller (b.1864) as the new editor in chief. By 1939, the work, now expanded to 20 volumes, had been acquired by the Consolidated Book Publishers, also of Chicago, and it was sold by them for home use, although little revision had been implemented. Some improvements were, however, noted in the 1940 and 1941 editions, the last edition being published under the editorship of Franklin Julius Meine (b.1896).

In 1942, under the imprint of the International Reader's League, the work was re-vamped and re-issued in a 10-volume edition (described as being 20 volumes in 10) entitled the *International's World Reference Encyclopedia*, again under the editorship of Meine, but listing Miller also as a former editor. This was evidently only an interim edition, as it was re-issued in 1945, under the imprint of the Encyclopedia Library Inc., as the *Universal World Reference Encyclopedia*, although in fact the copyright was still owned by the Consolidated Book Publishers, under whose imprint the work has appeared regularly since. At the present time it is published in a 16-volume edition, which bears little resemblance to its ancestors of more than half a century ago.

• References:
Subscription Books Bulletin, April 1937; January 1938.

STANDARD AMERICAN ENCYCLOPEDIA; of arts, sciences, history, biography, geography, statistics and general knowledge . . . prepared with the assistance of a large corps of editors and over 100 writers on special subjects. New York: Standard American Publishing Co., 1899. 8v. 29cm. Editor: John Clark Ridpath (1840–1900).

In its shortened form, the title of this work is identical to an eight-volume set published in 1912 by the Wheeler Publishing Co. of New York, and also with the edition published in 1937 under the imprint of the Standard American Corporation. Based on the evidence available, it seems certain that the *Standard American Encyclopedia* of 1899 was reprinted in 1906 as the *New Standard Encyclopedia*, and the *Practical Home Encyclopedia* in 1909, but the original title was used for the editions of 1912 and 1916.

There is a long gap between then and the revival of the title in 1937, when it was offered as a premium with several daily newspapers. In 1942 the work was re-titled the *International's World Reference Encyclopedia*, but this was changed in 1945 to the *Universal World Reference Encyclopedia*, under which title it was extant in 1966.

STANDARD CYCLOPEDIA; being a complete treasury of information for everyday use . . . the whole forming a complete guide and self instructor on scientific, commercial and all other subjects. Philadelphia: National Publishing Co., 1897. 708p. 26cm. Compiler: Henry Davenport Northrop (1836–1909).

A sub-standard one-volume compendium of miscellaneous information, its mediocrity being clearly indicated by the publisher's practice of issuing the same work, in whole or in part under a wide variety of titles, such as the curiously named *X-Rays of Intellectual Light* (1899), the *Standard American Book of Knowledge* (1900), the *World's Book of Knowledge* (1901), the *20th Century Cyclopedia of Universal Knowledge* (1901), the *American Educator and Library of Knowledge* (1902), the *New Century Cyclopedia of Universal Knowledge* (1902), the *American Home Educator and Book of Universal Knowledge* (1903) and the *Standard Library of Knowledge* (1904).

Northrop is not always acknowledged as the compiler, but there is no doubt that all of these titles derive from a common origin.

STANDARD DICTIONARY OF FACTS; history, language, literature, biography, geography, travel, art, government, politics, industry, invention, commerce, science, education, natural history, statistics and miscellany. Buffalo: Frontier Press, 1908. 844p. 25cm. Editor: Henry Woldmar Ruoff (1867–1935).

For almost twenty years, this compact and well compiled one-volume handbook of reference was one of the most popular works available. The original publishers, the Frontier Press, are today far more renowned for their *Lincoln Library of Essential Information,* and it is not generally realized that this was preceded by the *Standard Dictionary of Facts,* a smaller work, to be sure, but there can be little doubt that the experience gained through the publication of the older work played a material part in the compilation of the *Lincoln Library.* For a short period, 1924–1927, the works were marketed as rivals, but the tremendous success of the larger work eventually caused the demise of the *Standard Dictionary.*

The original work was compiled by Henry Woldmar Ruoff, but his connection with the work was apparently rather short, and his name was certainly not mentioned when the *Standard Dictionary* was extensively revised and enlarged in 1917. It is interesting to note, however, that Ruoff had earlier, between 1902 and 1908, edited the original *Century Book of Facts,* a one-volume work very similar in content and arrangement to the works of the Frontier Press. From 1911, Ruoff also edited the *Volume Library,* another one-volume work similar in style and arrangement to all the other works with which he was associated.

The last edition of the *Standard Dictionary of Facts* was issued in 1927, under the editorship of John W. Taylor, by which time it had increased in size to 974 pages. Undoubtedly, it would have remained in print for many years longer had it not been for the success of the *Lincoln Library,* which is today one of two recommended one-volume encyclopedias.

THE STANDARD ENCYCLOPEDIA. Glasgow: Literary Press, 1937. 316p. 22cm. Editors: John Maxey Parrish and John Redgwick Crossland (b.1892).

A small and insignificant work for children. In 1935 it had been published in an identical format as the *Laurel and Gold Encyclopedia* and the *Clear Type Encyclopaedia*. These, and other works by the same editors, evidently stem from the larger *New Standard Encyclopaedia and World Atlas* of 1932.

STANDARD ILLUSTRATED BOOK OF FACTS; a comprehensive survey of the world's knowledge and progress, with an historical, scientific, statistical, geographical and literary appendix. New York: Syndicate Publishing Co., 1912. 1150p. 20cm. Editor in Chief: Harry Thurston Peck (1856–1914). Associate Editor: Robert Campbell McCombie Auld (b.1857).

Harry Thurston Peck was the brilliant and respected editor of the *International Cyclopaedia* (1898) and its even more famous successor, the *New International Encyclopedia* (1902). It is all the more surprising, under these circumstances, to find his name designated as the editor in chief of a relatively insignificant one-volume work, especially one which appeared under the imprint of a company which was notorious for its marketing of several spurious works.

STANDARD INTERNATIONAL ENCYCLOPEDIA: de luxe edition. New York: Standard International Library, 1953. 20v. 23cm. Editor in Chief: William H. Hendelson (b.1904).

This work is identical in content to two other works published simultaneously as the *World Scope Encyclopedia* (1945–1964) and the *New World Family Encyclopedia* (1953). Both the *Standard International* and the *New World Family* encyclopedias were designed for sale through food stores, and differed from each other only in that the *Standard International* contained an additional two volumes of Hammond world maps. The difference in cost between all three titles was very much more marked, the *World Scope Encyclopedia* being marketed on a subscription basis at more than double the cost of the supermarket editions.

The history of the work is a long and sorry one. Its origin can be traced back to the *Teacher's and Pupil's Cyclopaedia*, a four-volume work edited and copyrighted by Bernhart Paul Holst from 1902 to 1907. In 1910, this was retitled the *New Teacher's and Pupil's Cyclopaedia*, and it continued under this title until 1927, although, in the interim, editions had been published in 1911 both as the *Unrivalled Encyclopedia* and the *Practical American Encyclopedia*, and also, from 1923 to 1927, as the *International Reference Work*.

As a result of investigations by the Federal Trade Commission against the International Publishing Co., the work was, from 1928 to 1939, published only as the *Progressive Reference Library*. This apparently ceased publication in 1939 on the death of Holst, but it was revived in 1945 as the *World Scope Encyclopedia*. This latter title had a long run until 1964, when the publishing rights were acquired by a Washington publisher, who re-issued it under three different titles as the *New American Encyclopedia*, the *World University Encyclopedia* and the *World Educator Encyclopedia*. A second edition of the *Standard International Encyclopedia* was published in 1956, when a two-volume index was also made available.

• References:
Subscription Books Bulletin, October 1953; April 1955.

STANDARD LIBRARY OF KNOWLEDGE AND UNI-VERSAL EDUCATOR; for home study, compiled from the writings of such eminent authorities as Edison, Marconi, Santos-Dumont, Franklin . . . and many other renowned discoverers and inventors. Philadelphia: National Publishing Co., 1904. 606p. 25cm.

No editor is given for this one-volume miscellany, but it is believed to be adapted from the similarly-sized *Standard Cyclopedia*, edited by Henry Northrop (1839–1909), and issued under the same imprint in 1897.

Thereafter, the work, either in whole or in part, was issued under several different titles between 1899 and 1904.

STANDARD REFERENCE WORK; for the home, school and library. Chicago: Interstate Publishing Co., 1912. 6v. 25cm. Chief Editor: Harold Melvin Stanford (b.1875).

This is a revision and extension of the five-volume work published in 1910 as *Aiton's Encyclopedia*. A second edition of the *Standard Reference Work* was issued in 1913 under the imprint of Welles Brothers, who had also issued *Aiton's* in 1910. Reprints were issued in 1915 and 1917 (when it was expanded to seven volumes, the last of which was a reading and study guide). In 1922 the work was expanded to ten volumes (the last two comprising the study guide), but now under the imprint of the Standard Education Society. It was this edition which became the subject of an investigation by the Federal Trade Commission, as a result of which a "Cease and Desist" order was issued against the publishers (for misrepresentation) in 1923 (Docket #994). Probably, as a result of the order, a change of title was made in 1923, when the work was re-issued as the *National Encyclopedia for the Home, School and Library*, but when the work reappeared in 1927, it had reverted to its original title of the *Standard Reference Work*. This proved to be the terminal edition under this title.

With Stanford still as editor, the work was re-issued in a new format in 1930 as the *New Standard Encyclopedia*, in ten volumes, and under the imprint of the Standard Encyclopedia Corp.

Since then it has been published regularly by the Standard Education Society under this title, and over the years has progressed from a poor work to one of fair quality, and especially, with the edition of 1966, which was the result of a twelve-year revision program.

STOKES COMPLETE ONE VOLUME ENCYCLOPEDIA. New York: F. A. Stokes Co., 1914. 1626p.

The only record of this work ever having been in existence is a brief entry in the United States Catalog for 1912–1917, but the bibliographical data provided was inadequate for any further identification. Since no copy of the work could be traced for examination, a detailed description and history cannot be provided.

STUDENTS CYCLOPAEDIA; a ready reference library for school and home, embracing history, biography, geography, discovery, invention, arts, sciences, literature. Chicago and Philadelphia: J. M. Howard & Co., 1900. 2v. 23cm. Editor: Chandler Belden Beach (1839–1928).

Although the first recorded copyright date for this work is dated 1900, it is believed that it may well have been in existence many years earlier and, according to one authority, an edition was published in 1893. The earlier issues of the work may have had some merit, but its subsequent history shows a steady and quite rapid deterioration of the original material.

In 1902, under the imprint of C. B. Beach & Co., it was re-issued as the *Students Reference Work*, but when another edition was issued in 1903, the imprint was that of the Howard-Severance Co. The work was apparently vended with little change from the 1903 edition until 1909, when, in an expanded edition of four volumes, it was issued under the imprint of F. E. Compton as the *New Students Reference Work*. Compton published further editions in 1911 (expanded to five volumes to include the "How and Why Program"), 1912, 1913, 1919, and 1920, by which time it had increased in size to seven volumes.

At this time, Compton's were preparing their new major work, *Compton's Pictured Encyclopedia*, and the publishing rights to the *New Students Reference Work* were acquired by the firm of S. L. Weedon & Co., who re-issued the set in an eight-volume edition (including the "How and Why Program" in two volumes) in 1925, 1928 and 1930. Weedon were themselves engaged in the compilation of a new work at this time, and the publishing rights were sold to the L. J. Bullard Co.

Subsequently, in 1934, the work, with practically no revision, was re-issued as the *Modern American Encyclopedia*, under the nominal editorship of Calvin Rogers Fisk (who was simultaneously editing the *New Standard Encyclopedia*), and further editions were issued under the imprint of the Modern American Corp. in 1935 and 1936.

The work had by this time become so dated as to be valueless, and the publishers were investigated by the Federal Trade Commission. "Cease and Desist" orders were brought in 1938 against the Midwest Publishing Co. (Docket #2893) and against the Modern American Co. (Docket #3503) in 1939 for improperly selling the work.

STUDENT'S ENCYCLOPAEDIA OF UNIVERSAL KNOWLEDGE; containing articles by eminent specialists. London: Hodder & Stoughton, 1883. 6v. 27cm. Editor: John Merry Ross (1833–1883).

This is a re-issue of the six-volume *Globe Encyclopaedia of Universal Information*, published by T. C. & E. C. Jack in 1876–1881, with apparently no revision in the main contents. Some years later, between 1890–1893, the work was re-issued by Virtue & Co. under yet another title, as the *Illustrated Globe Encyclopaedia*. This latter edition still cited Ross as the editor although he had then been dead for seven years.

In itself, the work, in any of its editions, was of little merit, its major claim to respectability resting in the fact that it was edited by Ross, a Scottish educationalist who had assisted in the compilation and editing of the first edition of the highly authoritative *Chambers's Encyclopaedia* (1860–1868), a factor which doubtless played no small part in the compilation of the *Globe Encyclopaedia* in 1876.

• Reference:
Collison.

STUDENTS REFERENCE WORK; a cyclopaedia for teachers, students and families. New York and Chicago: C. B. Beach & Co., 1902. 2v. 25cm. Editor: Chandler Belden Beach (1839–1928). Associate Editor: Graeme Mercer Adam (1839–1912).

A re-issue of the *Students Cyclopaedia* first copyrighted in 1900, but believed to have been in existence as early as 1893. A second edition of the *Students Reference Work* was issued in 1903, but the publishing rights were then acquired by the F. E. Compton Co., who revised and enlarged the work to four volumes and published it in 1909 as the *New Students Reference Work*. Further editions were issued under the Compton imprint at regular intervals up to 1920, by which time the set had been expanded to seven volumes, two of which, however, contained additional reading material entitled the "How and Why Program".

Soon afterwards the publishing rights were acquired by the S. L. Weedon Co., who re-issued it in an expanded eight-volume format in 1925, 1928 and 1930. In turn, Weedon passed the publication rights on to the Modern Encyclopedia Corp., of Chicago, who re-published the work, little changed from the earlier editions, as the *Modern American Encyclopedia*, in 1934, 1935 and 1936, but, as the result of "Cease and Desist" orders (Dockets #2893 and #3503) against the Midwest Publishing Co. and the Modern American Corp. from the Federal Trade Commission for false and deceptive selling practices, no further editions were issued after 1936.

TEACH YOURSELF CONCISE ENCYCLOPAEDIA OF GENERAL KNOWLEDGE. London: English Universities Press, 1956. 535p. 18cm. Editor: Stanley Graham Brade-Birks. Associate Editor: Frank Higenbottam.

A handy, little desk encyclopedia providing brief but accurate information on a wide variety of topics. A second edition was published in 1957 and a third in 1963. A useful feature of the work is a thirty-two-page section providing sources of further information and a list of reference books.

The English Universities Press had earlier, from 1938 to 1949, issued a very similar one-volume work, but smaller (362 pages), entitled the *Book of General Knowledge,* and the present title is most probably an expansion and adaptation of the earlier work.

TEACHER'S AND PUPIL'S CYCLOPAEDIA; a popular dictionary of geography, biography, history, literature, economics, civics, arts, sciences, discoveries and inventions. Boone and Chicago: Holst Publishing Co., 1902–1904. 4v. 26cm. Editor in Chief: Bernhart Paul Holst (1861–1939). Special Contributors: Ruric Neval Roark (1859–1909), James Mickleborough Greenwood (1836–1914), Gustavus Richard Glenn (b.1848), John L. Stevens.

This is the first recorded edition of a work which is believed to have been in existence in 1895 in a three-volume format, but which, since 1902, has been published under an incredible number of titles, several of them simultaneously, right up to the present time. An extraordinary feat unequalled by any other work of a sub-standard quality.

According to an inquiry by the Federal Trade Commission in 1927 (Docket #1331) against the International Publishing Co., the work was in fact first published in 1895 in a three-volume edition, although the existence of this could not be verified in the usual bibliographical sources. Its subsequent history is, however, as clear as it is unsatisfactory.

Under its original title, further editions were issued in 1905, 1906 and 1907, when it was expanded to five volumes. In 1906, a two-volume work entitled *Encyclopaedic Current Reference* was also published by Holst, with an identical list of editors and contributors. The next development came in 1910, when the work, apparently little changed, was re-issued as the *New Teacher's and Pupil's Cyclopaedia.* Further editions of this were issued in 1913 (when it was expanded to six volumes), 1915 and 1927, by which time it had expanded to eight volumes, the latter two of which comprised a "Practical Home and School Methods". Some idea of the quality of the work can be gleaned from the listing, as late as 1927, of Ruric Neval Roark as a special contributor. Roark had in fact died in 1909!

Meanwhile, in 1911, two other titles, edited by Holst (and Roark) were issued under the imprint of the W. B. Conkey Co., who were in fact the printers of most of the Holst publications. The first of these was the two-volume *Practical American Encyclopedia,* the second the "five volumes in one" *Unrivalled Encyclopedia,* but both were quite clearly derived from the same material as in the original *Teacher's and Pupil's Cyclopaedia.*

However, it was between 1923 and 1927 that the practice of issuing the same work under different titles fell under the eagle eye of the Federal Trade Commission who, in 1927, issued a "Cease and Desist" order against the International Publishing Co. and their agents, in which they were directed not to sell the *New Teacher's and Pupil's Cyclopaedia* simultaneously as the *International Reference Work* (a ten-volume version) which had been copyrighted as an ostensibly different work in 1923 and 1927.

This edict certainly produced results, as, in 1928, the works were re-titled the *Progressive Reference Library*, a ten-volume work which stated clearly in its sub-titling that it was a consolidation of the two previous titles.

Under its new mantle, the work assumed an aura of respectability for at least ten years, as no records are extant of its issuance from 1928 to 1939 under any other title. Further editions of the *Progressive Reference Library* were issued in 1935 and 1939, by which time it was increased in size to 11 volumes.

Holst, who had edited and published all of the aforementioned titles, died in 1939 and so, apparently, did the publishing company which he headed. The work itself, however, did not, and it was, between 1939 and 1945, acquired by the Universal Educational Guild of New York, who re-issued it (with Holst still cited as editor) in a ten-volume edition in 1945 as the *World Scope Encyclopedia*.

In actual fact, William H. Hendelson had been appointed as the new editor, and under his direction, revisions were implemented from 1946 onwards which resulted in quite improved editions in the later 1940's and early 1950's. From 1946 until 1964, when the title and publication rights were acquired by a Washington publisher, the *World Scope Encyclopedia* was issued annually, but despite the improvements, it never offered serious competition to the more established works.

The rash of titles with which the work had been afflicted was by no means over, however, and in 1953 it was issued simultaneously through food stores in inexpensive editions as the *New World Family Encyclopedia* and the *Standard International Encyclopedia*, the latter being reprinted again in 1957. In late 1963, the World Scope Publishers apparently ran into financial difficulty, as a result of which the publishing rights were acquired by the Publishers Co., of Washington, D.C., who were actively engaged in the marketing of several other encyclopedic works, all of which were of a sub-standard quality.

During 1964, this company outdid its predecessors by re-issuing the work simultaneously under no less than three different titles, which differed substantially in cost but not at all in content or quality. These were the *New American Encyclopedia*, a set which was sold on a subscription basis, the *World University Encyclopedia*, a set which was vended through department stores at little more than half the cost, and the *World Educator Encyclopedia*, another set sold on subscription, but under the imprint of a Florida distributor, but which was in fact produced by the Publishers Co.

Thus, since 1902 (or earlier), this work, although admittedly much changed over the years, has appeared under no less than 13 known titles, three of which are being sold at the present time.

TIMES ENCYCLOPEDIA AND GAZETTEER; superbly and profusely illustrated with hundreds of subjects in full color, monotone and text cuts, augmented by a fine collection of colored maps of the principal countries, and a valuable appendix of often sought for facts in almost every department of human knowledge, including a chronological history of the world, and a most comprehensive narrative of the world war briefly noted day by day. Chicago: Times Sales Co., 1929. 8v. 21cm. Editor in Chief: Francis Joseph Reynolds (1867–1937). Original Compiler: George Jotham Hagar (1847–1921).

Despite the title which (perhaps intentionally) might imply a relationship, this work has no connection whatsoever with the *New York Times* or the London *Times*. It is in fact a very poor work with a sordid history, being sold both before and afterwards under a wide variety of titles.

It evidently originated with *Everybody's Cyclopedia,* published in 1911 by the Syndicate Publishing Co., a work which was edited jointly by Hagar and Charles Leonard Stuart, but, and this is by no means improbable, this work may have been based on the *Crown Encyclopedia and Gazetteer,* a five-volume work edited by Stuart and published by the Christian Herald in 1903. This was re-issued in 1905 as the *Continental Encyclopedia,* in 1907 as the *New Century Reference Library,* and in 1909 as the *Current Cyclopedia of Reference,* all of which were edited by Stuart, and there is only a short gap between this last title and the appearance of the *Everybody's Cyclopedia* in 1911.

Certainly, however, the *People's Cyclopedia,* edited by Stuart and Hagar in 1914, was a continuation of *Everybody's.* This was the last work with which Stuart was connected, but Hagar went on to edit the similarly-sized *New World Wide Cyclopedia* in 1918, which was re-issued in 1919 as the *New World Encyclopedia* and as the *World Wide Cyclopedia.* Quite a gap in time occurs before we again find Hagar's name associated with an encyclopedic work, but it does appear in the 1928 edition of the *New World Wide Encyclopedia,* although he had in fact been dead some eight years. This edition must have been edited in actuality by Reynolds, who had earlier, in 1923, been cited as the editor in chief of *Adair's New Encyclopedia* which, significantly, was also published by the Syndicate Publishing Co., and it is highly probable that this was in fact a re-issue of the earlier titles. There is some evidence also that the work was also issued between 1912 and 1928 as *Every American's Encyclopedia,* but this could not be verified from the evidence available.

After 1929, some considerable revision seems to have been implemented and in 1930, again under the editorship of Reynolds, and again under the imprint of the Syndicate Publishing Co., a ten-volume edition was published as the *Twentieth Century Encyclopedia,* with reprints in 1932 and 1934. This very poor work evidently came to an overdue end with the issuance of the *World's Popular Encyclopedia,* which the Syndicate Publishing Co. issued in 1937, 1940 and 1942. Reynolds is listed as the editor of the 1937 edition, but his name is omitted from the two latter editions, quite correctly, as he had died in 1937.

• Reference:
Subscription Books Bulletin, July 1930.

TREASURY OF KNOWLEDGE AND LIBRARY OF REFERENCE. 3rd edition. New York: Conner & Cooke, 1833. 2v. 17cm. Compiler: Samuel Maunder (1785–1849).

Apparently a reprint of the 1830 London edition of *Maunder's Treasury of Knowledge and Library of Reference*. Volume 1 of the work comprised a general dictionary, with Volume 2 containing a compendium of miscellaneous information. A new and revised edition was published by the New York firm of C. C. Childs in 1850.

XX CENTURY CYCLOPAEDIA AND ATLAS; biography, history, art, science, and gazetteer of the world. New York and Philadelphia: Gebbie & Co., 1901. 8v. 21cm. Editors: Charles Annandale (1843–1915), Ainsworth Rand Spofford (1825–1908).

A revised reprint of the work first published in the United States as the *New Cabinet Cyclopaedia and Treasury of Knowledge* (1891–1892), which was an enlarged adaptation of the British *Blackie's Modern Cyclopaedia of Universal Information* (1889–1890) edited by Annandale. Spofford's contribution was to revise the articles relating to America.

In 1899, the work was re-issued as the *New National Cyclopaedia and Treasury*. Subsequently the work was re-issued as the *New Twentieth Century Cyclopaedia* (1903), the *New and Complete Universal Self Pronouncing Encyclopedia* (1905), the *New Cosmopolitan Encyclopedia* (1906) and finally, in 1912, as the *National Encyclopedia of Reference*.

TWENTIETH CENTURY CYCLOPEDIA OF PRACTICAL INFORMATION . . . and encyclopedic dictionary of common things. Compiled with the assistance of a staff of specialists and distinguished authorities. Philadelphia and Chicago: John C. Winston Co., 1901. 848 p. 25cm. Editor: Charles Smith Morris (1833–1922).

A small one-volume compendium of miscellaneous information. In whole or in part it was also issued as the *Popular Compendium of Useful Information* (1901), the *World Encyclopedia* (1901), the *Handy Cyclopedia of Common Things* (1901), the *Golden Treasury of Useful Information* (1902), the *World's Best Knowledge* (1902), *Home Cyclopedia of Necessary Knowledge* (1902), *Home Educator in Necessary Knowledge* (1905), *Everybody's Encyclopedia for Everyday Reference* (1907) and the *Cyclopedia, Dictionary and Atlas of the World* (1909).

Morris also edited several multi-volumed works, beginning with the *Universal Cyclopaedia and Dictionary* in 1898, and it is probable that the one-volume works issued under his editorship are derived from the same basic material.

20th CENTURY CYCLOPEDIA OF UNIVERSAL KNOWLEDGE; containing concise and exhaustive articles upon sci-

ence, arts and mechanics . . . all the latest discoveries and inventions . . .
being a complete treasury of knowledge on scientific, historical, artistic and
all important subjects. Philadelphia: National Publishing Co., 1901. 624p.
25cm. Compiler: Henry Davenport Northrop (1836–1909).

Yet another of the many nondescript one-volume handbooks of general
information which abounded at the turn of the century. This work is
derived directly from the *Standard Cyclopedia*, compiled by Northrop and
published by the same company in 1897.

With or without additional material, the work has also been published
as the curiously named *X-Rays of Intellectual Light* (1899), *Standard American Book of Knowledge* (1900), *World's Book of Knowledge* (1901),
American Educator and Library of Knowledge (1902), *New Century Cyclopedia of Universal Knowledge* (1902), *American Home Educator and Book
of Universal Knowledge* (1903), and the *Standard Library of Knowledge*
(1904), all of which were issued under the imprint of the National Publishing Co., although Northrop was not always acknowledged as the editor.

TWENTIETH CENTURY ENCYCLOPAEDIA (Morris); a
library of universal knowledge. Philadelphia: Syndicate Publishing Co., 1901.
6v. 25cm. Editor: Charles Smith Morris (1833–1922).

In 1898 Charles Smith Morris edited the six-volume *Universal Cyclopaedia
and Dictionary* for the National Book Concern of Chicago, and this was
re-issued, in 1899, by L. F. Smith of St. Louis, as the *International Library
of Reference*. In 1900, under the imprint of the Dictionary and Cyclopedia
Co., the same work was re-issued as the *Universal Reference Library*, although this latter edition was expanded to eight volumes to include an
atlas. This, in turn, became the present work, which was re-issued in 1907.
It is interesting to note that the sub-titling of this edition is identical to
the differently titled 1899 and 1900 printings. Simultaneously, from 1901
to 1910, the Syndicate Publishing Co. marketed an identical set as the *Imperial Reference Library*.

Morris, who is credited with the editorship of all the above titles, also
edited, in 1909, the *Current Cyclopedia of Reference*, jointly with Charles
Leonard Stuart, and in the same year, jointly with Ainsworth Rand Spofford, the *Winston's Encyclopedia*, and it would appear that these works
are in all likelihood related to each other in parts. The Syndicate Publishing Co., which became the World Syndicate Publishing Co. sometime in
the 1920's, revived the title of *Twentieth Century Encyclopedia* in the
1930's, but, apart from common ownership, the works appear to be only
indirectly related.

TWENTIETH CENTURY ENCYCLOPEDIA (Reynolds);
. . . showing the most important events in history, science, literature, etc.
Cleveland: World Library Guild, 1930. 10v. 24cm. Editor in Chief: Francis
Joseph Reynolds (1867–1937).

This is the same title which had been used thirty years previously by the same owners, but the two works do not appear related, although the editors of the earlier editions did have close connections. To a large extent, this work was merely a reprint of a work published by the same company (Syndicate Publishing Co.) in 1903 as the *Crown Encyclopedia and Gazetteer,* in 1905 as the *Continental Encyclopedia,* in 1907 as the *New Century Reference Library,* in 1909 as the *Current Cyclopedia of Reference,* in 1911 and 1912 as *Everybody's Cyclopedia,* and in 1914 as the *People's Cyclopedia.* All of these were edited by Charles Leonard Stuart (b.1868), but the latter two were edited jointly with George Jotham Hagar (1847–1921). It is of interest to note that the *Current Cyclopedia of Reference* (1909) was edited jointly with Charles Smith Morris (1833–1922), who had edited the 1901 edition of the *Twentieth Century Encyclopaedia.*

In 1918, under the editorship of Hagar, the work was re-issued as the *New World Wide Cyclopedia,* and in 1919, both as the *New World Encyclopedia* and the *World Wide Cyclopedia.* In 1923, under the editorship of Reynolds, the Syndicate Publishing Co. published *Adair's New Encyclopedia,* which was almost certainly a continuation of the earlier titles. A gap exists from then until 1928, when the work was again published as the *New World Wide Encyclopedia,* but now under the imprint of the Consolidated Book Publishers, and this was followed in 1929 by *Times Encyclopedia and Gazetteer,* which listed Hagar as the compiler, although he had by then been dead for almost ten years.

This, in turn, was continued as the *Twentieth Century Encyclopedia* in 1930, with further editions in 1932 and 1934. The publishers revised and re-issued the work under yet another title as the *World's Popular Encyclopedia* in 1937, again with Reynolds as the editor in chief. Two further editions of this terminal title appeared in 1940 and 1942, but Reynolds, who had died in 1937, was not cited as the editor.

• References:
Subscription Books Bulletin, July 1932; April 1935.

TWENTIETH CENTURY HOUSEHOLD LIBRARY . . .
comprising a complete encyclopedia of useful information. Philadelphia: A. J. Holman & Co., 1903. 600p. 32cm.

A relatively small, despite its large format, anonymously edited one-volume compendium of miscellaneous practical information, plus a minimal amount of more general knowledge. Further editions were issued in 1908 and 1909.

UNIFIED ENCYCLOPEDIA: A modern reference library of unified knowledge for the parent, student and young reader because it represents and reprints the "Grolier Encyclopedia" unified with reading units from

"Richards Topical Encyclopedia". New York: Unified Encyclopedia Press, 1960. 30v. 26cm. Editorial Board: Ellen Veronica McLoughlin (b.1893) and others.

This rather large work is unusual in that it represents a merging under one alphabetical arrangement of two quite different works; the alphabetically-arranged *Grolier Encyclopedia,* which went out of print in 1964, and the topically-arranged *Richard Topical Encyclopedia,* which also went out of print in 1964. The project was an ambitious one, but it was doomed to failure through being based on two works which, although once quite useful, had declined in authority and popularity during the 1950's, and in fact, after further editions of the *Unified Encyclopedia* had been issued in 1961, 1962, 1963 and 1964, the publishers announced its discontinuance in 1965.

The listing of Ellen Veronica McLoughlin as the chief member of the Editorial Board is questionable. She had been connected with *Richards Topical Encyclopedia* and with other Grolier productions, but it is highly unlikely that she played any material part in the shaping of the *Unified Encyclopedia.*

The history of the work can be traced back to 1920 to the publication of *Harmsworth's Universal Encyclopaedia* in London. In 1931, this work was adapted for American use and issued as *Doubleday's Encyclopedia.* This, in turn, became the *Grolier Encyclopedia* about 1944. *Richards Topical Encyclopedia* is of more recent vintage, being first published in 1933 as *Richards Cyclopedia,* although this was in itself quite probably based to some extent on the *Outline of Knowledge,* a similarly arranged work issued by the same company in 1924.

UNITED EDITORS ENCYCLOPEDIA AND DICTION-ARY; a library of universal knowledge and an unabridged dictionary of the English language. New York: United Editors Association, 1909. 40v. 21cm.

The history of this work is open to some doubt, and can only be surmised on the evidence available in the usual sources. As far as can be ascertained, it almost certainly begins with the publication in 1899 of a 39-volume work entitled the *Columbian Cyclopaedia,* which appeared under the imprint of the Funk & Wagnalls Co. No copy of this earlier title could be found for examination, but the listing in the American Catalogue of 1895–1900 indicates that it was edited by Richard Gleason Greene (1829–1914), but as Greene was seventy years old at the time, it is probable that even this work had a pre-existence.

That the works are related is verified by the listing of Greene as editor of the *Imperial Encyclopedia and Dictionary,* a 40-volume set published in 1903, which was continued in 1906 as the *New Imperial Encyclopedia and Dictionary.* The sub-titling of the *United Editors Encyclopedia and Dictionary* is identical to that of the *New Imperial,* and there can be no doubt that the two works are the same, although Greene is not mentioned in either instance.

In 1911, the United Editors Association re-issued the work in 30 larger volumes as the *United Editors Perpetual Encyclopedia,* but in this edition, the managing editor is cited as George Rines (b.1860), who, at the same time, was associated with the *Encyclopedia Americana,* a rather puzzling relationship, especially as the sub-titling of a later edition of that work is the same as that used in 1909 for the title under discussion. The dictionary part of the work was probably the *New American Encyclopedic Dictionary* compiled by Edward Thomas Roe (b.1847).

UNITED EDITORS PERPETUAL ENCYCLOPEDIA; a library of universal knowledge combined with an unabridged dictionary of the English language. Compiled with the assistance of more than 500 of the most eminent scholars and specialists. New York and Chicago: United Editors Association, 1911. 30v. 22cm. Managing Editor: George Edwin Rines (b.1860).

This is quite clearly a continuation of the *United Editors Encyclopedia and Dictionary* (1909), which was itself a reprint of the *New Imperial Encyclopedia and Dictionary* (1906) and the *Imperial Encyclopedia and Dictionary* (1903), edited by Richard Gleason Greene (1829–1914).

The several titles are evidently derived from the *Columbian Cyclopaedia,* a 39-volume work edited by Greene and published by Funk & Wagnalls in 1899.

UNIVERSAL CYCLOPAEDIA; a new edition, prepared by a large corps of editors, assisted by eminent European and American specialists. Illustrated with maps, plans, colored plates and engravings. New York: D. Appleton & Co., 1900. 12v. 28cm. Editor in Chief: Charles Kendall Adams (1835–1902).

One of the best American encyclopedias of its time, the *Universal Cyclopaedia* is a thoroughly revised edition of the work first published between 1876 and 1878, in four volumes, as *Johnson's New Universal Cyclopaedia,* under the editorship of Frederick Augustus Porter Barnard (1809–1889) and Arnold Henry Guyot (1807–1884). The original edition, and a reprint in 1884 (in optional four- or eight-volume formats) were issued under the imprint of Alvin J. Johnson & Co.

Under the editorial direction of Adams, the work was then revised and re-issued as *Johnson's Universal Cyclopaedia* (1893–1897) but before the publication of this was completed the publishing rights were acquired by Appleton, with the unusual result that five of the eight volumes bear the Appleton imprint, with the others bearing the Johnson imprint. It was this edition, revised by Adams and expanded to 12 volumes which was published as the *Universal Cyclopaedia* in 1900, further editions of which appeared in 1901, 1903 and 1905. *Appleton's New Practical Cyclopedia* (1920), which was re-issued in 1930 as the *New Universal Encyclopedia* was probably derived from the same background material.

• Reference:
Collison.

UNIVERSAL CYCLOPAEDIA AND DICTIONARY; comprising a general encyclopedia of literature, history, art, science, invention and discovery; a pronouncing dictionary of the English language; a gazetteer of the world; a comprehensive dictionary of universal biography, etc. Chicago: National Book Concern, 1898. 6v. 30cm. Editor: Charles Smith Morris (1833–1922).

A rather nondescript work and the first of a series of titles under which the same basic material was published over a number of years. In 1899, it was re-issued as the *International Library of Reference,* and in 1900 as the *Universal Reference Library.* From 1901 to 1910 it was issued both as the *Imperial Reference Library* and the *Twentieth Century Encyclopaedia.*

All were ostensibly edited by Charles Morris who, with Charles Stuart, also edited the *Current Cyclopedia of Reference* in 1909, and, with Ainsworth Rand Spofford (1825–1908), *Winston's Encyclopedia,* also in 1909.

UNIVERSAL DICTIONARY OF ARTS AND SCIENCES. London, c.1770. (Never published.) Compiler: Oliver Goldsmith (1728–1774).

A work which was contemplated and planned, but never actually compiled or published. When Oliver Goldsmith died in 1774, among his posthumous papers was discovered a draft prospectus for an encyclopedia which he intended to be the British equivalent of the French *Encyclopédie* of Diderot.

The evidence available suggests that the work could well have formed an important contribution to British encyclopedia publishing, as Goldsmith evidently planned to include comprehensive and scholarly articles from such specialists as Dr. Samuel Johnson, Sir Joshua Reynolds, Sir William Jones, Adam Smith, Gibbon and Fox.

THE UNIVERSAL ENCYCLOPEDIA; a compendium of general information, embracing agriculture, anatomy, architecture, archaeology, astronomy, banking &c. Philadelphia: W. T. Amies, 1878. 983p. 24cm. Compiler: Leo de Colange (b.1819).

Despite its grandiloquent title, a small and limited work of reference. It was probably derived from the two-volume *Zell's Popular Encyclopedia,* also compiled by Colange, and published in 1870.

In its one-volume format, it was certainly preceded by the *National Encyclopedia* (in the United States) and the *Peoples Encyclopaedia* (in Britain), both of which were issued in 1873. It was finally re-issued by another publisher in 1899 as the *School Encyclopedia.*

UNIVERSAL HANDBOOK *see* NEW UNIVERSAL HANDBOOK

UNIVERSAL, HISTORICAL, GEOGRAPHICAL, CHRON-
OLOGICAL AND CLASSICAL DICTIONARY. London, 1703.
Preceding the *Lexicon Technicum* of John Harris by only a few months,
this is the first known instance of an alphabetically arranged reference
work in the English language. Compiled by an unknown editor or compiler, the work is, however, much inferior to the work of Harris.

AN UNIVERSAL HISTORY OF ARTS AND SCIENCES.
London, 1745. 2v. Compiler: Denis de Coëtlogon.
A curious work, which treated the general knowledge of the time under
main headings arranged alphabetically; a method which was to be imitated
to some extent with greater effect in the nineteenth-century editions of
the *Encyclopaedia Britannica*.

• Reference:
Collison.

UNIVERSAL INSTRUCTOR, or, "Self Culture For All"; fully
and accurately illustrated. London: Ward, Lock; New York: W. H. Stelle,
1880–1884. 3v. 25cm.
Not a general reference encyclopedia, but a series of courses of self-
study and instruction. A fairly comprehensive 47-page index in Volume 3
made it of some use as a source of direct ready reference. A second edition was published in 1890.

UNIVERSAL KNOWLEDGE; a dictionary and encyclopedia of
arts and sciences, history and biography, law, literature, religions, nations,
races, customs and institutions. New York: Universal Knowledge Founda-
tion Inc., 1927. 12v. 26cm. Editors: Edward Aloysius Pace (b.1861), Conde
Benoit Pallen (1858–1929), Bishop Thomas Joseph Shahan (1857–1932),
James Joseph Walsh (1865–1942), John J. Wynne (b.1859).
Although this useful and well compiled work contained a considerable
amount of general information, it was basically a Catholic encyclopedia,
representing the views of the Roman Catholic Church on religious and
social subjects. It was wider in range, but much less comprehensive than
the large and authoritative *Catholic Encyclopedia*.
Publication of the work was scheduled to appear at the rate of about
three volumes each year, with completion intended about 1931, but no
further editions are recorded.

• Reference:
Subscription Books Bulletin, April 1931.

UNIVERSAL KNOWLEDGE A-Z; a new encyclopaedia of general knowledge. London: Odhams Press, 1938. 1144p. 22cm.

A fairly comprehensive compendium of miscellaneous information in brief form for quick desk reference. It was re-issued in 1948 as the *Great Encyclopaedia of Universal Knowledge*.

UNIVERSAL MANUAL OF READY REFERENCE; antiquities, history, geography, biography, government, law, politics, industry, invention, science, religion, literature, art, education and miscellany. Springfield and Chicago: King-Richardson Co., 1904. 741p. 24cm. Compiler: Henry Woldmar Ruoff (1867–1935).

This one-volume handbook is so similar to the *Century Book of Facts* (1902–1908), also compiled by Ruoff and published by the King-Richardson Co., there can be little doubt that, give or take some omissions or additions, the two works are the same. Ruoff's contribution to this type of one-volume topically arranged handbook is considerable. He also edited the *Standard Dictionary of Facts* (1908) and the *Volume Library* (1911).

It is not without significance that the original *Century Book of Facts* is still in existence today as the *New Century Book of Facts*, as also is the *Volume Library* (recently re-titled the *Cowles Comprehensive Encyclopedia—The Volume Library*). The successful *Standard Dictionary of Facts* which Ruoff edited in 1908 was a predecessor of the present day *Lincoln Library of Essential Information*, the most successful work of this type.

UNIVERSAL REFERENCE LIBRARY; comprising a general encyclopedia of literature, history, art, science, invention and discovery; a pronouncing dictionary of the English language, etc. With nearly 4,000 illustrations. Compiled with the assistance of more than 200 specialists in the various departments. New York and Chicago: Dictionary & Encyclopedia Co., 1900. 8v. 27cm. Editor in Chief: Charles Smith Morris (1833–1922). Assistant Editors: Fredric A. Lucas and John F. Hurst.

A reprint, with some modifications and the inclusion of an atlas, of the six-volume *Universal Cyclopaedia and Dictionary*, published in 1898, which was succeeded in 1899 by the *International Library of Reference*. All three titles appeared under the editorship of Morris, but under different publishing imprints, although the copyright was undoubtedly the property of the Syndicate Publishing Co., who re-issued the work in 1901 as the *Twentieth Century Encyclopaedia*, the sub-titling of which is identical to the earlier works. From 1901 to 1910, the Syndicate Co. issued the work simultaneously as the *Imperial Reference Library*.

The same publishers, in 1909, issued an eight-volume work entitled the *Current Cyclopedia of Reference*, edited jointly by Morris and Charles Leonard Stuart. Additionally, Morris, in 1909, was also cited as the joint editor, with Ainsworth Rand Spofford (1825–1908) of the *Winston's En-*

cyclopedia, another eight-volume work, but published under the imprint of the John C. Winston Co.

UNIVERSAL STANDARD ENCYCLOPEDIA; an abridgement of the "New Funk & Wagnalls Encyclopedia". New York: Unicorn Publishers, 1954. 25v. 22cm. Editor in Chief: Joseph Laffan Morse (b.1902).

As correctly stated in the sub-titling, this is an abridgement of the useful *New Funk & Wagnalls Encyclopedia*, a 36–volume work also published by the Unicorn Press in 1949–1950. This, in turn, was based on the excellent *Funk & Wagnalls New Standard Encyclopedia of Universal Knowledge* (sometimes referred to simply as the *Standard Encyclopedia*), a work in 25 small volumes prepared under the editorship of Francis Horace Vizetelly (1864–1938), and published by Funk & Wagnalls from 1931 to 1937, and the Unicorn Press in 1942 and 1943.

The origin of the work is interesting, as much of the material was abstracted from the large and authoritative *New International Encyclopedia*, which had been acquired by Funk & Wagnalls in 1930.

Subsequently, the *Universal Standard Encyclopedia* was issued in a further edition in 1957–1958, but in 1959, it was re-titled the *Funk & Wagnalls Standard Reference Encyclopedia*, under the imprint of the Standard Reference Works Publishing Co., and again under the editorial direction of Morse. This useful work is still being published under the last title.

Based as it was upon an authoritative source, this work has always been a useful smaller encyclopedia, and is one of the very few works sold through food stores and other retail outlets which has won official recognition and commendation. In some 6 million words, and approximately 30,000 articles, it provides a considerable amount of brief factual information at a very low cost of about $50.00, although naturally, at this price, such desirable features as bibliographies, colored illustrations, etc., have been omitted.

• References:

Subscription Books Bulletin, October 1955.
Booklist and Subscription Books Bulletin, June 15, 1957.

UNIVERSAL WORLD REFERENCE ENCYCLOPEDIA. Chicago: Consolidated Book Publishers, 1945. 10v. 23cm. Editor in Chief: Franklin Julius Meine (b.1896). Associate Editors: Harold L. Hitchens, Mary Frances McKenna.

Described as being 20 volumes in 10, the last of which contained a multi-pictured dictionary, this is a reprint of the *International's World Reference Encyclopedia*, a 10-volume work published in 1942 by the International Reader's League and Publishers Periodical Service. Although the imprint on the two works differs, the actual publishers were the Consolidated Book Publishers, the copyright being held by a subsidiary, Columbia Educational Books.

Both titles were, however, preceded by the *Standard American Encyclopedia*, a 15-volume work issued by the Standard American Corp. in

1937, and by the Consolidated Book Publishers from 1939 to 1941. A poor work, it would appear that the 1937 edition is a revived issue of the same title first issued in 1912 by the Wheeler Publishing Co.

Since 1945, the *Universal World Reference Encyclopedia* has been published at regular intervals, usually under the imprint of the Consolidated Book Publishers, but occasionally, as in 1951, under the imprint of a distributor such as the Publishers Guild, New York.

Meine apparently ceased to edit the work about 1948 (he was at that time editor in chief of the much more authoritative *American Peoples Encyclopedia*) and, from 1949 to 1955, the actual editor was Mary Frances McKenna. Since 1958, the editor in chief has been Virginia Sarah Thatcher (b.1917), who also edited the *Golden Home and High School Encyclopedia* for Simon & Schuster (Golden Press) in 1961.

The present day *Universal World Reference Encyclopedia* is a substantially improved 16-volume family encyclopedia, containing a great deal of useful information, although inferior to similar works in the same price range.

• References:

Subscription Books Bulletin, July 1946; July 1956.
Booklist and Subscription Books Bulletin, April 1, 1965.

UNIVERSITY ENCYCLOPEDIA OF TWENTIETH CEN-TURY KNOWLEDGE. New York: P. F. Collier & Son, 1902. 10v. 24cm. Editor: Henry Mitchell McCracken (1840–1918).

Little information could be gathered about this work, and it was apparently published once only. It is, however, in all probability, an abridgement, adaptation or actual reprint of *Collier's New Encyclopedia*, a 16-volume work issued by the same publisher at the same time, for which no editors were listed.

UNIVERSITY ILLUSTRATED ENCYCLOPEDIA; with special articles and departmental supervision by 462 leading editors, educators and specialists in the United States and Europe. Revised edition. New York: Publishers Guild Inc., 1938. 15v. 22cm. Editor in Chief: Charles Ralph Talor (b.1877). Advisory Editor: Carl Clinton Van Doren (1885–1950).

An identical reprint of the *New York Post World Wide Illustrated Encyclopedia*, a 15-volume work published in 1937 by Books Inc., which had previously been published as the *New York Post World Wide Illustrated Encyclopedia* in 1935. The work is reputed to be based to some extent on *Nelson's New Looseleaf Encyclopedia* (1940), but the difference in quality between these two works is very marked.

In 1941, the title of the work was changed to the *Home University Encyclopedia*, and it is still being published at the present time by Books Inc., a subsidiary of the Publishers Co., Washington, D.C., although it is little changed from the original edition of almost thirty years ago.

• Reference:
Subscription Books Bulletin, July 1939.

UNIVERSITY OF KNOWLEDGE. Chicago: University of Knowledge Inc. (Consolidated Book Publishers), 1937–1938. 24v. Editor: Glenn Frank.

This large work is not actually an encyclopedia, but a topically arranged compendium of miscellaneous information, each volume dealing with a broad subject area. Although some of the material was good, it was too inefficiently arranged to make facile use of the set possible. Works of this nature must be indexed for maximum usefulness, but this most essential feature was lacking in the *University of Knowledge*.

• Reference:
Subscription Books Bulletin, July 1938.

UNRIVALLED ENCYCLOPEDIA. Chicago: W. B. Conkey Co., 1911. 5v. in 1v. (2576p.) Editor in Chief: Bernhart Paul Holst (1861–1939).

This work is almost certainly a reprint of the *Teacher's and Pupil's Cyclopaedia*, a four-volume work edited and published by Holst in 1902, and re-issued as a five-volume set in 1905, 1906 and 1907. This was re-issued in 1910 as the *New Teacher's and Pupil's Cyclopaedia*, under which title it continued until 1927, although, between the years 1923 and 1927, it was issued simultaneously as the *International Reference Work*. From 1928 to 1939, it was continued as the *Progressive Reference Library*, but after the death of Holst in 1939, the publishing rights were acquired by a group of New York and Washington publishers who, since 1945, have issued the same basic work as the *World Scope Encyclopedia* (1945–1963), the *New World Family Encyclopedia* (1953), the *Standard International Encyclopedia* (1953–1957), and, since 1964, as the *New American Encyclopedia*, the *World University Encyclopedia* and the *World Educator Encyclopedia*.

Conkey was evidently the printer of the earlier Holst publications, and the copyright both to the *Unrivalled Encyclopedia* and the *Practical American Encyclopedia*, also published in 1911 under the Conkey imprint, was held by the Holst Publishing Co.

VOLUME LIBRARY, THE; a concise, graded repository of practical and cultural knowledge designed for both instruction and reference. Chicago: W. E. Richardson Co., 1911. 678p. 30cm. Editor in Chief: Henry Woldmar Ruoff (1867–1935).

In size and arrangement, this work is so similar to the *Century Book of Facts* (1902–1908)—afterwards the *New Century Book of Facts*—and the *Universal Manual of Ready Reference* (1904), that a common origin is almost certain, a supposition supported by the fact that Ruoff edited or compiled all three titles, and all were published by either the W. E. Richardson Co. or the King-Richardson Co. Ruoff also, in 1908, edited the *Standard Dictionary of Facts*, another very similar work which preceded the remarkably well compiled *Lincoln Library of Essential Information* (1924). The works, however, continued in existence as separate entities and both the *Volume Library* and the original *Century Book of Facts* are still in print at the time of writing.

As the *Volume Library*, further editions of the work were issued in 1912 and 1913 (under the imprint of R. E. Trosper), by which time it had expanded to 976 pages. In 1922, a so-called eleventh edition was published under the imprint of the Educators' Association, who published regular editions thereafter until the late 1950's, by which time it had multiplied almost four times in size to over 2,400 pages.

In 1963, the publishing rights were acquired by Cowles Communications Inc., who re-issued a thoroughly revised and greatly improved edition in the same year as *Cowles Comprehensive Encyclopedia—The Volume Library*. Little is known of Henry Ruoff, but his original compilations have certainly stood up to the test of time.

- **References:**
  Subscription Books Bulletin, January 1930; April 1934; July 1939; July 1945; October 1953.
  Booklist and Subscription Books Bulletin, September 1, 1959.

WARD LOCK'S UNIVERSAL INSTRUCTOR *see* UNIVERSAL INSTRUCTOR

WAVERLEY BOOK OF KNOWLEDGE *see* BOOK OF KNOWLEDGE (British)

THE WAVERLEY ENCYCLOPAEDIA . . . with plates. London: Waverley Book Co., 1953. 1072p. 22cm. Editor: Gordon Stowell.

A small one-volume compendium of miscellaneous information, probably derived from the 1936 edition of the *Children's Home Educator and Treasury of Knowledge*.

WAVERLEY ENCYCLOPAEDIA OF GENERAL INFORMATION. London: Waverley Book Co., 1930. 10v. 22cm. Editor: Sir John Alexander Hammerton (1871–1949).

Probably, a re-issue of the *Waverley New Era Encyclopaedia*, published by the same company in 1920. Sir John Hammerton also edited the nine-volume *Harmsworth's Universal Encyclopaedia* in 1920, the five-volume *Encyclopaedia of Modern Knowledge* in 1936, the ten-volume *New Book of*

Knowledge in 1938, and the ten-volume *New Universal Encyclopaedia* in 1951. The Waverley Book Co., whose titles were acquired by the Grolier Society in 1963, was also the publisher of the *Book of Knowledge* in 1959.

It is likely that these various titles are related to each other, and, in some cases, may be reprints of one another.

WAVERLEY NEW ERA ENCYCLOPAEDIA, with colored plates, etc. London: Waverley Book Co., 1920. 6v. 22cm.

The first work to be registered under the imprint of this company, it was probably continued, in 1930, as the *Waverley Encyclopedia of General Information*. It is probably related to several other works published by the same company and other works edited by Sir John Hammerton.

WEBSTER'S COLUMBIA ENCYCLOPEDIC DICTION-ARY; a library of essential knowledge. Chicago: Columbia Educational Books, Inc., 1940. 1400p. Editor in Chief: Franklin Julius Meine (b.1896).

A one-volume compendium of quite useful information, but so badly arranged as to be virtually useless for quick reference.

In whole or in part it has also been published as *Webster's Comprehensive Encyclopedic Dictionary* and *Webster's Encyclopedic Dictionary*, both in 1941, as the *Library of Essential Knowledge* in 1942, and, since 1954, as the *Consolidated Webster Comprehensive Encyclopedic Dictionary* and the *Consolidated Webster Encyclopedic Dictionary*.

The "comprehensive" editions contain additional material but, apart from this, the works are identical.

WEBSTER'S COMPREHENSIVE ENCYCLOPEDIC DIC-TIONARY; a library of essential knowledge. Chicago: Columbia Educational Books, 1941. 1600p. 26cm. Editor in Chief: Franklin Julius Meine (b.1896).

Except for an additional 200 pages of miscellaneous material, this is identical to the *Webster's Columbia Encyclopedic Dictionary* (1940) and *Webster's Encyclopedic Dictionary* (1941). With an additional 100 pages it was re-issued in 1942 as the *Library of Essential Knowledge*. Since 1954 it has been issued as the *Consolidated Webster Comprehensive Encyclopedic Dictionary*.

WEBSTER'S ENCYCLOPEDIC DICTIONARY; a library of essential knowledge. Chicago: Columbia Educational Books, Inc., 1941. 1400p. 26cm. Editor in Chief: Franklin Julius Meine (b.1896).

An identical reprint of *Webster's Columbia Encyclopedic Dictionary* (1940).

This same work has appeared under several other titles: *Webster's Comprehensive Encyclopedic Dictionary* (1941), *Library of Essential Knowledge* (1942), *Consolidated Webster Comprehensive Encyclopedic Dictionary*

(1954), and the *Consolidated Webster Encyclopedic Dictionary* (1954).
The "comprehensive" editions contain additional material but, apart from
this, the works are identical.

• Reference:
Subscription Books Bulletin, January 1941.

WEBSTER'S UNIFIED DICTIONARY AND ENCYCLO-
PEDIA; a concise and comprehensive reference work, completely new
and up-to-date, planned and written by modern educators and lexicographers
to serve the essential requirements of school, college, office and self education at home. New York: H. S. Stuttman & Co. Inc., 1953. 2400p. 29cm.
Editor: Lewis Mulford Adams.

Far from being "completely new and up-to-date", this work was an arrangement under one alphabet, of the dictionary entries from *Webster's
New American Dictionary*, and the encyclopedic entries from the *New
American Encyclopedia*, first published in 1938. Both of the basic works
were of very poor quality and the merging of the two under one title
only compounded their inferiority.

Further editions of the unified one-volume edition were published in
1958, 1959 and 1961, since when it has gone out of print. In 1955, however, it was also published, in 14 thin volumes, under the inverted title
of *Webster's Unified Encyclopedia and Dictionary*, an edition which was
designed for sale through food stores on the book-a-week plan. Similarly,
in 1961, it was issued in a one-volume looseleaf edition as *Webster's Encyclopedic Dictionary of the English Language*. Action was brought against
the printer, George McKibbin & Sons and others (Docket #7245) by the
Federal Trade Commission for false and deceptive advertising and failure to
disclose that large parts of the work were reprints.

The encyclopedic material was issued simultaneously as the *New American Encyclopedia* from 1938 to 1963, and since 1964 it has been available
as the *American Family Encyclopedia*.

WEBSTER'S UNIVERSAL ENCYCLOPEDIA . . . compiled
with the assistance of a large corps of specialists and experts. Chicago: De
Bower-Chapline Co., 1909. 1367p. 28cm. Editor: Charles Higgins.

A one-volume compendium of encyclopedic information and dictionary
definitions, published simultaneously by the same company in an identical
format as the *La Salle Extension University Encyclopedia* and the *Everybody's Encyclopedia*.

Higgins afterwards edited the *Modern Universal Encyclopedia* (1910)
and the *Home and Office Reference Book of Facts* (1913), two smaller
works which were probably derived from the three earlier titles.

WEEDON'S MODERN ENCYCLOPEDIA. Cleveland: S. L.
Weedon Co., 1931–1932. 8v. 26cm. Editor in Chief: Garry Cleveland Myers
(b.1884).

About 1925, the S. L. Weedon Co. commenced the compilation of an entirely new, alphabetically arranged work for children, designed to compete with the highly successful *World Book* and *Compton's Pictured Encyclopedia* in the same age range. Prior to the publication of this new work, however, they had been publishing the *New Students Reference Work,* an eight-volume work which they had acquired from the F. E. Compton Co. about 1922, and there is little doubt that the new *Weedon's Modern Encyclopedia* was based on this work to some degree.

Weedon's Modern Encyclopedia was, however, a much better work than the earlier publication, and was an attractive and well written set, which included a good fact index. The work was so good, it interested the editors of the *Encyclopaedia Britannica,* who immediately purchased the publishing rights from Weedon, thoroughly revised and expanded it, and re-issued it in 1934 as the *Britannica Junior,* in 12 volumes, under which title this good work is still being published.

By a curious twist of fate, the F. E. Compton Co., who, about 1922, had sold the rights in the *New Students Reference Work* to Weedon, were themselves acquired by the Encyclopaedia Britannica Inc., in 1964.

• Reference:
Subscription Books Bulletin, October 1932.

WERNER ENCYCLOPEDIA; a standard work of reference in art, literature, science, history, geography, commerce, biography, discovery and invention . . . with new supplemental matter added to each volume, coverin the very latest information on all important subjects. Akron: The Werner Co., 1909. 25v. 28cm.

This is believed to be the last American reprinting of the ninth edition of the *Encyclopaedia Britannica.*

In 1908, in an agreement between Encyclopaedia Britannica Inc., and the Werner Co., the publishers of the *Britannica* paid to Werner the sum of $60,000 in settlement of Werner's discontinued use of their title but, after that date, Werner could continue to sell its edition printed from any of the plates then in existence, provided that different title pages and prefaces were prepared. It seems evident from the foregoing that Werner did in fact comply with the agreement by reprinting the work as the *Werner Encyclopedia,* adding supplementary material to each volume to bring it up to date.

It is believed that the work was also published in London as the *Anglo-American Encyclopedia* in 1911, in 50 volumes, under the imprint of the Anglo-American Encyclopedia Co., the sub-titling of the two works being absolutely identical.

WERNER'S UNIVERSAL ENCYCLOPEDIA. Akron: Saalfield Publishing Company, 1899. 12v.

The only recorded entry which could be found for this work is in the

United States Catalog for 1912, and no copies could be traced for physical examination.

Both Saalfield and the Werner Co. were actively concerned in pirated reprintings of the ninth edition of the *Encyclopaedia Britannica* between 1895 and 1904, and it is not at all unlikely that this work, published in the same year that the ninth edition was completed, is a compression of that august work from 24 volumes into 12, as Poole similarly did in 1891. On the other hand, it may have formed a 12-volume supplement to the main work.

WHITAKER'S ALMANACK. London: J. Whitaker & Sons, 1868. Compiler: Joseph Whitaker (1820–1895).

An outstanding example of a one-volume compendium of encyclopedic information, published annually under a system of continuous revision. The work can be described as encyclopedic in only a general sense, however, as it is more accurately a yearbook of statistical and other pertinent information, arranged by subject and comprehensively indexed. As an updating supplement to any encyclopedia, British or American, it is almost indispensable.

Similar American publications are the *World Almanac* (1868 to date) and the *Information Please Almanac,* which commenced publication in 1947.

WINSTON'S CUMULATIVE LOOSE LEAF ENCYCLO-PEDIA; a comprehensive reference book. Compiled with the assistance of a corps of contributors . . . illustrated with colored plates, maps, drawings and photographs. Philadelphia and Chicago: John C. Winston Co., 1912. 10v. 23cm. Editor in Chief: Charles Smith Morris (1833–1922).

The origin of this work is open to some doubt, and it is improbable that it was original in 1912. It was most certainly based upon, if not an actual continuation of, *Winston's Encyclopedia,* an eight-volume work published in 1909 under the joint editorship of Charles Morris and Ainsworth Rand Spofford (1825–1908). Morris had, prior to this, edited several other works, basically the same; the *Universal Cyclopaedia and Dictionary* in six volumes (1898); the *International Library of Reference,* also in six volumes (1899); the *Universal Reference Library* (1900); the *Twentieth Century Encyclopaedia,* again in six volumes, from 1901 to 1907; the *Imperial Reference Library,* from 1901 to 1910, and finally, the *Current Cyclopedia of Reference,* an eight-volume set published in 1909. Spofford, on the other hand, had been associated with the *New Cabinet Cyclopaedia* (1891–1899); the *New National Cyclopaedia* (1899); the *XX Century Cyclopaedia* (1901); the *New Twentieth Century Cyclopaedia* (note the similarity of titles) in 1903, and the *New and Complete Universal Self Pronouncing Encyclopedia* (1905). The similarity, not only of the works, but of the titles also, with which both men were connected, strongly suggests that the present work is but a development of one or more of these earlier titles.

One of the few encyclopedias to employ the method of keeping an encyclopedia up-to-date by the insertion of loose leaf supplements, *Winston's Cumulative Loose Leaf Encyclopedia* remained in existence under its original name for an unusual length of time, running through several editions and printings up to 1942.

After the death of Morris in 1922, the work was edited by Thomas Edward Finegan (b.1866) until 1933, and from 1934 until its demise in 1950, William Dodge Lewis (b.1870) was cited as editor. The publishing rights to the work were apparently sold by Winston in 1942, and when the work was re-issued in the same year, and again in 1943, it was re-titled the *Encyclopedia Library*. It made its final appearance as the *American International Encyclopedia* in 1950.

• Reference:
Subscription Books Bulletin, October 1932.

WINSTON'S ENCYCLOPEDIA; a compendium of information and instruction on all subjects for home, school and office . . . with nearly 1,000 illustrations. Philadelphia and Chicago: John C. Winston Co., 1909. 8v. 20cm. Editors: Charles Smith Morris (1833–1922), Ainsworth Rand Spofford (1825–1908).

Although ostensibly a new work, this is probably derived or developed from several other multi-volume works edited by either Morris or Spofford between 1891 and 1905.

The work was subsequently continued as *Winston's Cumulative Loose Leaf Encyclopedia* from 1912 to 1942, in which latter year it was re-titled the *Encyclopedia Library* under the imprint of a New York publisher who had acquired the rights to the work. It made its terminal appearance as the *American International Encyclopedia* in 1950.

WINSTON'S UNIVERSAL REFERENCE LIBRARY . . . with 3,000 illustrations and an atlas of the world. Philadelphia and Chicago: Universal Book and Bible House, 1930. 1500p. 23cm. Editors: William Dodge Lewis (b.1870), Henry Seidel Canby, Thomas Kite Brown.

A one-volume collection of dictionary and encyclopedic material, probably a revised and expanded edition of the *New Universal Handbook of Necessary Information*, published, between 1920 and 1957, by the same company and also edited by Lewis. The entries in the work are so brief that it is more like a dictionary than an encyclopedia.

WONDER BOOK ENCYCLOPAEDIA. London: Ward, Lock, 1956. 448p. 26cm. Editor: Gerald E. Speck.

A small and simple work for children. In whole, or in part, or with additional material, it was re-issued in 1959 as the *Junior Pictorial Encyclopedia* and in 1965 as the *Encyclopaedia of Modern Knowledge*.

WONDER ENCYCLOPAEDIA FOR CHILDREN. London: Odhams Press, 1933. 756p. 22cm. Editors: John Redgwick Crossland (b.1892) and John Maxey Parrish.

A small work for children, subsequently published as the *Golden Encyclopaedia for Children* (1934), the *Modern Illustrated Encyclopaedia* (1940) and the *Practical Encyclopaedia for Children* (1944). This work, and several other one-volume compendiums by the same editors, are probably derived from their *New Standard Encyclopaedia* of 1932.

WONDER WORLD ENCYCLOPAEDIA. London and Glasgow: Collins, 1936. 520p. 22cm. Editors: John Redgwick Crossland (b.1892) and John Maxey Parrish.

Between them, these two editors are responsible for a considerable number of one-volume encyclopedias for children, beginning with the *New Standard Encyclopaedia* in 1932.

The present work, which was re-issued in 1947 by Virtue & Co., is probably abridged or adapted from the earlier title, and appears to be identical to the *Encyclopaedia of General Knowledge* (1938).

WONDER WORLD OF KNOWLEDGE. London and Glasgow: Collins Clear Type Press, 1935–1937. 8v. 27cm. Editors: John Redgwick Crossland (b.1892) and John Maxey Parrish.

A topically arranged work for children, developed and expanded from the one-volume *New Standard Encyclopaedia and World Atlas,* compiled by the same editors in 1932.

WONDERLAND OF KNOWLEDGE (British); an up to date illustrated encyclopedia. London: Odhams Press, 1933–1934. 12v. (6144p.) 22cm. Editor: Ernest Ogan.

Believed to be a re-issue of the *Book of Knowledge,* published under a number of imprints as *Cassell's Book of Knowledge,* the *Hammerton Book of Knowledge,* the *Waverley Book of Knowledge,* etc., at approximately the same time. It may have been re-issued as the *Modern Children's Library of Knowledge* in 1957.

WONDERLAND OF KNOWLEDGE (American); a new pictorial encyclopedia. Chicago: Publishers Productions Inc., 1937. 15v. 24cm. Editor in Chief: Lorimer Victor Cavins (b.1880). Associate Editors: Bertha Maude White (b.1881), Roderick M. Grant. Managing Editor: Paul Randall.

In size, this work is very similar indeed to the British *Wonderland of Knowledge,* a 12-volume set published in London in 1933, but there is no known connection between the two, although it was by no means uncommon to see the same works published in both countries under different titles.

The American *Wonderland of Knowledge* is an alphabetically arranged, simply presented, encyclopedia for children, compiled by the same editorial staff as for the companion *American Educator Encyclopedia*. The last three volumes of the original issue (discontinued in 1950) contained additional material on "Hobbies", "Our Continent", and a "Reading and Study Guide".

Harry Orrin Gillet edited the work from 1948 to about 1955, since when it has been edited under the direction of Everett Edgar Sentman. Both men also edited the *American Educator Encyclopedia,* a more advanced work, which the *Wonderland of Knowledge* was designed to supplement.

- **References:**

Subscription Books Bulletin, July 1939; April 1948; July 1953.

WORLD ALMANAC AND BOOK OF FACTS. New York: New York World Pub. Co., 1868.

The American equivalent of *Whitaker's Almanack,* this compact one-volume work contains an astonishing amount of useful and current information. Except for a period of ten years between 1876 and 1885, it has been published annually.

Available in an inexpensive paperback binding, it is a most useful work, either in its own right, or as an updating supplement to any encyclopedia.

THE WORLD BOOK; organized knowledge in story and picture, compiled with the assistance of 150 distinguished scientists, educators, artists and leaders of thought in the United States and Canada. Chicago and New York: Hanson-Roach-Fowler Co. (World Book Inc.), 1917–1918. 8v. (6600p.) 25cm. Editor in Chief: Michael Vincent O'Shea (1866–1932). General Editor: Ellsworth Decatur Foster (1869–1936). Editor for Canada: George Herbert Locke (1870–1937).

Although there had been, for years, some works designed for home and school use, no serious attempt had ever been made to compile an encyclopedia specifically for children. The original publishers of the *World Book,* recognizing this need, carefully planned and prepared to meet this with their completely new *World Book.* Towards this end they engaged the services of Michael Vincent O'Shea, Professor of Education at the University of Wisconsin, and one of the leading educational theorists of the time. Under his able direction the new work took shape and the first volume was published on January 24, 1917. Within the year, all eight volumes of the first edition had been published, although, in fact, the publishers had originally intended to publish it in only five volumes with 5,000 pages and 5,000 illustrations.

The concept of the new work from the very start was to incorporate a great deal of illustrative material to supplement the highly accurate and carefully graded text. That this concept was valid was evinced by the immediate acceptance of *World Book* by educators and librarians, and a new edition was called for even before the first edition had been completely published and, in 1918, again under the imprint of Hanson-Roach-Fowler, a new edition, expanded to ten volumes, was issued. Shortly after this, the publishing rights were acquired by the publishing firm of W. F. Quarrie & Co., a farseeing firm who guided the development of the work for the next twenty-five years.

Under the Quarrie imprint, new printings, with substantial revisions, were issued in 1919, 1921, 1922, 1923, 1925, 1926, 1927 and 1928 (which was called the tenth edition). Although the work was maintained under a policy of continuous revision to ensure its accuracy, no appreciable increase in size had taken place, but it was becoming clear by the mid-1920's that a major revision and expansion was unavoidable. This was implemented in the completely new edition of 1929–1930, when the set was expanded to 13 volumes, which contained over 9,000 pages. With this edition also, the word "Encyclopedia" was added to the title, and the sub-titling was changed to read: "Modern, Pictorial, Comprehensive". Reputed to have cost more than a million dollars, the new edition was even more successful than the original and marked a real milestone in the development of the work.

On a sadder note, this was to be O'Shea's last major achievement. Since 1917 he had been the editor in chief of *World Book* and it was a fitting tribute to him that he concluded his career (he died in 1932) with this substantial contribution to American education. Other notable features of the new 1929–1930 edition were (a) the introduction of a volume devoted to "Reading Courses and Study Units" and (b) the successful change over from a separate index to innumerable cross references in the text, a feature which is still one of the more remarkable features of the work.

O'Shea edited another edition in 1931, but when a new edition appeared in 1933, the chief editor was cited as Silas Edgar Farquhar. Another important change in this edition was the re-arrangement of the work by the unit-letter system, whereby each volume contained all the entries for one or more letters of the alphabet. This increased the number of volumes to 19, although there was no appreciable increase in content. Yet another important introduction in the 1933 edition was a provision of a bibliography of books for further reading, which was contained at the end of the text, in the eighteenth volume. The nineteenth volume continued as the well compiled "Reading and Study Guide".

Since 1933 the *World Book Encyclopedia* has been published annually without interruption, even through the war years and through a number of major editorial changes. Silas Farquhar (1887–1948) remained as editor for most of the 1930's, although by 1940 he was listed as editor of the *Modern Library of Knowledge* and in 1944 as the editor of the *Grolier Encyclopedia*, works totally unrelated to the *World Book*. Certainly, from 1941, or perhaps a few years earlier, the work was being edited by John Morris Jones (1896–1962), a Welsh-born educator, whose contribution was to be as important and significant as that of O'Shea many years previously.

Yet another important change took place in 1945, when the publishing rights to the *World Book Encyclopedia* were acquired by the Field Enterprises Educational Corporation, a subsidiary of the gigantic Marshall Field organization, with headquarters at Chicago. With Jones now at the editorial helm, a massive revision of the encyclopedia was implemented in 1947, when all 19 volumes were completely rebuilt and remodelled throughout. Every existing article was revised and newly written or, in many instances, completely rewritten, and the entire subject content was reviewed, revised and expanded to include thousands of additional subjects. He also completely remodelled the typography and the layout, and an important feature was the tremendous increase in the number of illustrations to more than 18,000, many of which were in color. At the same time the number of pages increased to more than 10,000. Under the leadership of Jones, until his death in 1962, further improvements were effected with almost every edition, and at least one particular feature was the introduction, in 1948, of graded bibliographies under major and important topics, in which the titles were divided into works suitable for younger and older readers, replacing the former list of books which was contained in the eighteenth volume. In 1950, Rand McNally commenced making a special series of maps for the *World Book Encyclopedia*, a series which has since become famous as the "Cosmo" series in the Rand McNally range. It was not until ten years later, in 1960, that Jones and his editorial staff implemented yet another major revision of the work, when the set was expanded to 20 volumes (the twentieth volume continuing as the now familiar "Reading and Study Guide") with an increasing use of color illustrations. By this time the work had almost doubled in size (11,600 pages) from the original edition, and the number of illustrations had more than doubled to more than 21,000, with a very substantial increase in the use of color.

The importance which the publishers themselves attach to keeping the *World Book Encyclopedia* up to date can be gauged from the fact that they are reputed to spend more than a million dollars each year in revising the material to keep the work abreast of current developments, and it is claimed that more than 5,000 pages are revised, in part at least, with each annual printing. Since 1960 no significant changes have occurred except that, in 1964, the "Reading and Study Guide" was omitted from the twentieth volume (although still available separately) to make more space available, while the volume containing all the entries for the letter "C" was split into two volumes because of its increased size. The only other major change has been the complete rewriting of all 50 articles relating to each of the individual states of the Union, which was implemented in the 1965 edition.

After the death of John Morris Jones in 1962, the encyclopedia was edited by David C. Whitney, but his stay was relatively short and in 1964 he accepted an appointment as editor in chief of the adult *Encyclopedia Americana*. Whitney was succeeded by Robert O. Zeleny, Executive Editor and Vice-President of the company, who is the current editor in chief, and who shares the responsibility with William Henry Nault, the Executive Director of Research.

The *World Book Encyclopedia* is also the first and, at present, the only general encyclopedia to be published in special editions for the blind and the partially sighted. In 1961, on a non-profit basis, a Braille edition was published in 145 volumes, and in 1964, a large type edition in 30 volumes was published for the benefit of the partially sighted and those with special reading problems.

In 1961, Field Enterprises also set up an editorial and sales office in Britain with the object of preparing an international edition for use in English-speaking countries other than those in North America. The international edition was compiled under the direction of Gilbert C. E. Smith, with the assistance of Patrick M. O'Brien, and was first published in January of 1966. Smaller than its American counterpart, it is comprised of 12 volumes of general material and two additional volumes devoted to the different English-speaking countries in which it is sold. The concept of an international edition of the *World Book Encyclopedia* was not new, however, and had been preceded in 1936–1937 by the *World Book: British Empire Edition*, published in London in 10 volumes by the New Era Publishing Co., with Harold Shelton as general editor, and Lord Gorell as advisory editor, a purely nominal position.

Since 1922, the *World Book* has been supplemented by an annual publication of outstanding quality. From 1922 to 1940, this was known as the *World Book LooseLeaf Annual*, but the title was changed to the *World Book Encyclopedia Annual* in 1941, and it continued as that until 1961. Since 1962 it has been published as the *World Book Year Book*, each issue containing an index to the events of the preceding ten years.

While it must be emphasized that, in itself, the *World Book* was an entirely new work when it was first published, it is of interest to note that some of the original editorial staff, and the original publishers, were directly concerned with earlier works. These began with the four-volume *Hill's Practical Encyclopedia*, published by the Chicago Book Co. in 1901, and issued simultaneously as the *School Library Encyclopedia* by the Caxton Book Co. In 1902, both titles were changed to *Hill's Practical Reference Library*, which was published under the imprint of Dixon & Hanson, who issued further editions in 1904 and 1905. In 1907, the work was expanded to five volumes and re-titled the *New Practical Reference Library*, which again appeared under the imprint of Dixon & Hanson, but in the edition of 1911, the publishers were increased by the addition of Bellows to the imprint, which now read the Dixon-Hanson-Bellows Co.

At about this time, however, Dixon broke away to publish a new encyclopedia of his own compilation (the very poor *Source Book*) and when the edition of 1912 was published, the imprint was that of the Hanson-Bellows Co., who published further editions in 1914 and 1915. Of interest at this point also is that Ellsworth Decatur Foster was cited as an associate editor from 1913 onwards.

It is in 1917 that the most significant relationship is evident. Both the *New Practical Reference Library* (5 volumes, 3,800 pages) and the *World Book* (8 volumes, 6,600 pages) for that year, and again in 1918, appeared under the imprint of the Hanson-Roach-Fowler Co., and Foster is named as one of the principal editors of both works. It might be argued from this that the two works are closely related, but this is not borne out by the facts.

Michael Vincent O'Shea, for example, had nothing to do with the earlier works, and the *World Book* was largely his creation. Quite clearly, however, as the works were competitors for a short period, it is not at all surprising that an economical use was made of the same basic editorial staff for each work, and thus, to a minimal extent, there may have been superficial resemblances. This is evinced by the fact that, in 1919, the *New Practical Reference Library* was completely remodelled to become the *American Educator*, after being acquired by the Ralph Durham Co. *World Book*, on the other hand, was acquired by the W. F. Quarrie Co., so that, from 1919 onwards, the two works had no relation to each other.

The *World Book* has, of course, gone from strength to strength to become the best-selling encyclopedia in the world, both in terms of quantity and quality. The original work of Hill in 1901 is still with us as the *American Educator Encyclopedia*, but this has remained a relatively small work, quite a useful encyclopedia in its own right, and still with a faint resemblance to the more comprehensive *World Book*.

• References:

Collison.

Subscription Books Bulletin, January 1930; January 1935; April 1938; January 1940; October 1943; October 1947; January 1953.

Booklist and Subscription Books Bulletin, June 15, 1959; November 1, 1963.

THE WORLD EDUCATOR ENCYCLOPEDIA. Miami, Florida: International Book Distributors, 1964. 12v. 24cm. Editor in Chief: William H. Hendelson (b.1904).

Except for the imprint and outward appearance, this set is identical to the *New American Encyclopedia* and the *World University Encyclopedia*, both of which were published in 1964 and annually since. Although Hendelson is cited as the editor of this and the other titles, he had in fact dissociated himself from the work in 1963. He had, however, edited the immediate predecessor of these titles, the *World Scope Encycopedia* from 1945 to its terminal edition in 1963.

The origin of the *World Educator Encyclopedia* can be traced with certainty back to 1902 (and possibly earlier) when Bernhart Paul Holst (1861–1939) edited and published the four-volume *Teacher's and Pupil's Cyclopaedia*, which was re-issued as the *New Teacher's and Pupil's Cyclopaedia* from 1910 to 1927, and published simultaneously from 1923 to 1927 as the *International Reference Work*. Previously, it had also been issued in a different format in 1911 as the *Practical American Encyclopedia* and as the *Unrivalled Encyclopedia*.

In 1928, as the result of a "Cease and Desist" (Docket #1331) order against the International Publishing Co. from the Federal Trade Commission, it was re-titled the *Progressive Reference Library*, and was published as such until 1939. In 1945, under new ownership, it was re-issued as the *World Scope Encyclopedia*, with further editions annually until 1963.

In 1953 it was also issued as the *New World Family Encyclopedia,* and in 1953 and again in 1957, it was issued in a supermarket edition as the *Standard International Encyclopedia.*

THE WORLD ENCYCLOPEDIA; a library of ready reference . . . and handy dictionary of common things. Philadelphia: World Bible House, 1901. 606p. 24cm. Editor in Chief: Charles Smith Morris (1833–1922). Assistant Editors: Edward C. Mills, Robert Samuel Collins, Henry Haines Albertson.

A small and nondescript work, it was also published in 1901 as the *Popular Compendium of Useful Information* and, with additional material, as the *Twentieth Century Cyclopedia of Practical Information.* In 1902 it was re-issued in an identical format as the *Golden Treasury of Useful Information* and the oddly termed *World's Best Knowledge and How to Use It.* In abridged forms, and also with additional material, it was also published as the *Handy Cyclopedia of Common Things* (1901), the *Home Cyclopedia of Necessary Knowledge* (1902) the *Home Educator in Necessary Knowledge* (1905), *Everybody's Encyclopedia for Everyday Reference* (1907) and the *Cyclopedia, Dictionary and Atlas* (1909).

WORLD HOME REFERENCE ENCYCLOPEDIA. Chicago Consolidated Book Publishers, 1951. 4v. (1262p.) 26cm. Editor in Chief: Eugene M. Fisher. British Editor: Lawrence H. Dawson (b.1880). European Editor: Richard Friedenthal (b.1896).

This is the last issuance of a once quite useful compendium of brief factual information on some 30,000 subjects. It was first published in the United States as *Facts—the New Concise Pictorial Encyclopedia,* in a four-volume format in 1934 by Doubleday, Doran & Co., but this was almost certainly adapted from the British work, published in London in 1934 as *Routledge's Universal Encyclopaedia,* indicated by the fact that Lawrence H. Dawson, who is listed as the "British" editor of *Facts* and all its subsequent editions, was the editor in chief of the British encyclopedia.

The work was republished by Doubleday in 1938 in a one-volume format as the *New Concise Pictorial Encyclopedia,* and further editions under both this title and as *Facts* were issued in 1939 and 1941. In 1942 the publishing rights were acquired by the World Publishing Co., and it was re-issued by them in 1942 and 1943 as both the *Comprehensive Pictorial Encyclopedia* and the *New Concise Illustrated Encyclopedia.*

The work had, by this time, deteriorated badly through lack of revision and its re-issuance in 1951 as the *World Home Reference Encyclopedia* showed little or no change from the earlier editions.

• Reference:
Subscription Books Bulletin, October 1952.

WORLD OF THE CHILDREN. London: Caxton Publishing Co., 1948. 4v. Editor: Stuart Miall.

A topically-arranged work for children, quite well printed in large clear type, but limited in subject coverage and inadequately indexed. A second edition was published in 1957. The Caxton Publishing Co. afterwards issued the *Caxton Encyclopaedia* in 1960 and an identical reprint in 1961 as the *Caxton World of Knowledge*.

• Reference:
Library Association Record, October 1961.

WORLD SCOPE ENCYCLOPEDIA; the new universal encyclopedia of the world. New York: Readers League of America—Universal Educational Guild, 1945. 20v. in 10v. 24cm. Editor in Chief: Bernhart Paul Holst (1861–1939). Associate Editors: Daniel W. Morehouse (b.1876), O. C. Kreinheder, Alexander Dervisse.

This was a re-issue, virtually unchanged, of the ten-volume *Progressive Reference Library*, last published in 1939, edited and published by Holst, who had died in the same year. In actual fact, a new editor had been appointed, William H. Hendelson (b.1904), but his name was not to appear until the editions of 1946 and later. The first 17 volumes of the 1945 edition of the *World Scope Encyclopedia* were encyclopedic, the eighteenth contained a miscellany, and the last two contained *Webster's New Illustrated Dictionary*. At this time the work was very poor indeed, as had been its many predecessors, but in later years, under the editorship of Hendelson, it improved considerably, although never to the extent where it offered serious competition to similar home and school encyclopedias.

A quite extensive revision program led to a marked change in 1946, when the two-volume dictionary was omitted, and the encyclopedic material expanded to 12 volumes. The work was now appearing under the imprint of the Universal Educational Guild, but, oddly, Holst's name was carried as editor in this edition and the edition of 1947, and it was not until 1948 that Hendelson's name appeared alone as the editor in chief.

From 1948 onwards, editions were published annually, and a steady improvement in quality was effected. In 1959 the publishers changed their imprint to the World Scope Encyclopedia Corp., and this was altered slightly again in 1962 to the World Scope Publishers. The improvements which had been made in the set from 1948 and after were offset by the issuance in 1953 of the same work under two different titles—the 18-volume *New World Family Encyclopedia* and the 20-volume *Standard International Encyclopedia*, the latter differing only in that it included a two-volume atlas.

The *Standard International Encyclopedia* was re-issued in 1957 with a two-volume index. Both of these reprints were intended for sale through food stores but the enormous difference in cost reflected poorly on the much more expensive *World Scope Encyclopedia*, and the reputation of the publishers was further diminished by an order from the Federal Trade Commission in 1954 (Docket #5938), in which they were admonished for deceptive selling practices.

The *World Scope Encyclopedia* as such came to an end in 1963, when the publishers ran into financial difficulties. As a result, the work was acquired by a Washington-based firm, who confused the issue still further when they re-published the work in 1964 and afterwards as the *New American Encyclopedia*, the *World University Encyclopedia*, and by arrangement with a Florida distributor, the *World Educator Encyclopedia*.

The history of the work can be traced back with certainty to at least 1902, and perhaps even earlier to 1895. It began with the issuance in 1902 of the *Teacher's and Pupil's Cyclopaedia*, a four-volume work edited and published by Bernhart Holst, which, according to one source, was in existence in 1895 in a three-volume format. This was followed in 1910 by the *New Teacher's and Pupil's Cyclopaedia*, which continued until 1927, although it was also issued in 1911 as the *Unrivalled Encyclopedia* and the *Practical American Encyclopedia*, and from 1923 to 1927 as the *International Reference Work*. In 1928, it was retitled the *Progressive Reference Library*.

• References:
Subscription Books Bulletin, July 1947; October 1948; July 1956.

WORLD UNIVERSITY ENCYCLOPEDIA; an illustrated treasury of knowledge. Unabridged. De luxe edition. Washington, D.C.: Publishers Company Inc., 1964. 12v. 24cm. Editor in Chief: William H. Hendelson (b.1904).

An identical reprint of the *New American Encyclopedia* (1964) published by the same company, and identical also to the *World Educator Encyclopedia* (1964) published under the imprint of International Book Distributors, Miami, Florida. All three titles are a continuation of the *World Scope Encyclopedia*, first published in 1945 and discontinued in 1963. The same work has also been published as the *New World Family Encyclopedia* (1953) and the *Standard International Encyclopedia* (1953–1957).

Prior to 1945, the work had originated in 1902 as the *Teacher's and Pupil's Cyclopaedia*, which was re-titled the *New Teacher's and Pupil's Cyclopaedia* in 1910, and the *Progressive Reference Library* (1928–1939). In 1911 the same basic work was published as the *Unrivalled Encyclopedia* and the *Practical American Encyclopedia*, and, from 1923 to 1927, as the *International Reference Work*.

WORLD WIDE CYCLOPEDIA; a complete library of reference, superbly and profusely illustrated with hundreds of subjects in full color, monotone and text cuts, with a valuable appendix of often sought for facts in almost every department of human knowledge; a chronological history of the world . . . the most comprehensive narrative of the world war, briefly noted day by day. Edited with the assistance of many associate editors, special contributors and United States and Canadian Government officials. New York:

Syndicate Company, Inc., 1919. 6v. 20cm. Editor in Chief: George Jotham Hagar (1847–1921).

A most inferior work, despite its extravagant claims, which probably derived from a work published in 1903 as the *Crown Encyclopedia and Gazetteer,* a five-volume set which appeared under the imprint of Christian Herald, and edited by Charles Leonard Stuart (b.1868). This, with the addition of a two-volume dictionary, was re-issued in 1905 as the *Continental Encyclopedia,* by the Success Co. of New York and this, in turn, was re-issued in an identical format by the National Press Association in 1907 as the *New Century Reference Library.* Stuart then edited, jointly with Charles Morris, the *Current Cyclopedia of Reference,* which was published in eight volumes by the Syndicate Co., and then, in 1911, the same publisher issued the five-volume *Everybody's Cyclopedia,* jointly edited by Stuart and Hagar, and this was re-issued in 1914 as the *People's Cyclopedia.* In 1918 and 1919, the Syndicate Co., increasing the set to six volumes, re-issued the same work under three different titles as the *New World Wide Cyclopedia,* the *New World Encyclopedia* and the *World Wide Cyclopedia.*

Hagar died in 1921 and the editing of future editions was entrusted to Francis Joseph Reynolds (1867–1937), and under his direction a work entitled *Adair's New Encyclopedia* was published in five volumes in 1923 by the World Syndicate Co., and although no acknowledgement is made, this was evidently a re-issue of the earlier titles. It was not until 1928 that the work re-appeared in eight volumes as the *New World Wide Encyclopedia,* in which both Reynolds and Hagar were listed as editors. This was followed in 1929 by the *Times Encyclopedia and Gazetteer,* and this, more accurately, listed Hagar as the original compiler, with Reynolds as editor in chief.

These rapid changes of title were clearly designed to promote the sales of the work on the pretense of it being a new publication. Between 1930 and 1934 it was published as the *Twentieth Century Encyclopedia,* although Hagar was no longer being listed either as a compiler or an editor. Finally, just before the death of Reynolds in 1937, the work was published as the *World's Popular Encyclopedia* (by the World Syndicate Co.), and further editions were issued in 1940 and 1942.

WORLD WIDE ENCYCLOPEDIA. Washington, D.C.: Publishers Company, Inc., 1967. 10v.

An inferior, cheaply produced work available in both hard cover and paperback through mail order houses and containing 20,000 entries, 3,200 pages and 2 million words. It is unlikely that it is related to any of the similarly-titled encyclopedias.

WORLD WIDE ENCYCLOPEDIA AND GAZETTEER; compiled and revised to date from the leading encyclopedias of the world. A dictionary of arts, sciences and literature, to which is added biographies of living subjects. One hundred colored maps and numerous illustrations.

New York: Christian Herald, 1908. 12v. 24cm. Editor: William Harrison De Puy (1821–1901).

As this work was published several years after the death of its editor, it is obviously not a new publication and is believed to be a reprint of the *New Peoples Cyclopedia of Universal Knowledge,* published by Eaton & Mains in 1903 in an eight-volume format, which was also edited by De Puy originally. This, in turn, is clearly descended from the *Peoples Cyclopedia of Universal Knowledge,* a three-volume work published in 1883 by Phillips & Hunt, again edited by De Puy.

WORLD WIDE ILLUSTRATED ENCYCLOPEDIA; with special articles and departmental supervision by 462 leading editors, educators and specialists in the United States and Europe. Revised edition. New York and Boston: Books Inc., 1937. 15v. 24cm. Editor: Charles Ralph Taylor (b.1877). Advisory Editor: Carl Clinton Van Doren (1885–1950).

In 1935 the old *New York Post* published this encyclopedia as an inducement to obtain subscribers, and it was originally known as the *New York Post World Wide Illustrated Encyclopedia,* which was in two volumes (4,892 pages). Supposed to have been based on the 1930 edition of *Nelson's Perpetual Looseleaf Encyclopaedia,* but if so, the editing must have been extremely poor, as there is a wide variation in quality between the two works.

Shortly after its issuance by the *New York Post,* it was acquired by the present publishers, who re-issued it in 1938 as the *University Illustrated Encyclopedia.* In 1941, it was re-arranged into 15 volumes and published as the *Home University Encyclopedia* under the imprint of the University Society Inc., although it was virtually unchanged from the earlier edition.

No bibliographical references could be traced of further editions until 1961 (although it was certainly being sold through the 1940's and 1950's), when it re-appeared in a new 12-volume format under the imprint of Books Inc., with Sherman Day Wakefield (b.1894) as joint editor, and another copyright was registered in 1962. The work is reported to be under revision, but at the time of writing it was being offered at a ridiculously low cost, although probably commensurate with its quality, in regular and de luxe bindings, by the Publishers Co.

WORLD'S BEST KNOWLEDGE AND HOW TO USE IT . . . and handy dictionary of common things. Philadelphia, 1902. 606p. 25cm. Editor in Chief: Charles Smith Morris (1833–1922). Assistant Editors: E. C. Mills, R. S. Collins, H. H. Albertson.

An odd little work with an odd title, it was first published in 1901 as the *Popular Compendium of Useful Information,* and as the *World Encyclopedia,* and under the present title and as the *Golden Treasury of Useful Information* in 1902.

With additional material or in an abridged form it has also been issued as the *Twentieth Century Cyclopedia of Practical Information* (1901), the

Handy Cyclopedia of Common Things (1901), the *Home Cyclopedia of Necessary Knowledge* (1902), the *Home Educator in Necessary Knowledge* (1905), the *Everybody's Encyclopedia for Everyday Reference* (1907) and the *Cyclopedia, Dictionary and Atlas* (1909).

WORLD'S BOOK OF KNOWLEDGE AND UNIVERSAL EDUCATOR; containing concise and exhaustive articles upon science, arts and mechanics . . . all the latest discoveries and inventions. Philadelphia: National Publishing Co., 1901. 688p. 25cm.

A nondescript one-volume work, this is substantially a reprint of the *Standard Cyclopedia*, compiled by Henry Davenport Northrop and issued by the National Publishing Co. in 1897.

Subsequently, in whole or in part, and frequently omitting Northrop as the compiler, it was re-issued as the *X-Rays of Intellectual Light* (1899), the *Standard American Book of Knowledge* (1900), the *20th Century Cyclopedia* (1901), *American Educator and Library of Knowledge* (1902), the *New Century Cyclopedia of Universal Knowledge* (1902), the *American Home Educator and Book of Universal Knowledge* (1903) and the *Standard Library of Knowledge* (1904).

WORLD'S POPULAR ENCYCLOPEDIA; a modern compilation of essential facts gathered from all branches of the world's knowledge. Cleveland and New York: World Syndicate Publishing Co., 1937. 10v. 21cm. Editor in Chief: Francis Joseph Reynolds (1867–1937).

An inferior work which, far from being a "modern compilation", was based upon a work first published in 1903 as the *Crown Encyclopedia and Gazetteer*, which was succeeded in 1905 by the *Continental Encyclopedia* and in 1907 by the *New Century Reference Library*. All of these earlier titles were edited by Charles Leonard Stuart and he, jointly with Charles Smith Morris (1833–1922) edited the *Current Cyclopedia of Reference* for the Syndicate Co. in 1909, and the same company re-issued the work in 1911 as *Everybody's Cyclopedia*. In 1914, this was re-titled the *People's Cyclopedia*. Both works were edited jointly by Stuart and George Jotham Hagar (1847–1921).

In 1918 and 1919, the Syndicate Publishing Co. republished the set as the *New World Wide Cyclopedia* and the *World Wide Cyclopedia*, with an identical reprint appearing under the imprint of the Christian Herald as the *New World Encyclopedia*. The work is then believed to have been re-issued in 1923 as *Adair's New Encyclopedia*, edited by Reynolds and published by the Syndicate Publishing Co. In 1928, the title of the *New World Wide Cyclopedia* was used again, but now under the imprint of the Consolidated Book Publishers, a Chicago-based firm. The following year saw yet another change of title when the work was issued as the *Times Encyclopedia and Gazetteer*, and it is indicative of the quality of the work that Hagar was still being listed as the original editor or compiler, although he had died several years previously.

In 1930, 1932 and 1934, the World Syndicate Publishing Co. re-issued the same basic work in an expanded ten-volume format as the *Twentieth Century Encyclopedia,* under the editorship of Reynolds. Finally, in 1937, the work was published as the *World's Popular Encyclopedia,* followed by further printings in 1940 and 1942.

• Reference:
Subscription Books Bulletin, April 1937.

X-RAYS OF INTELLECTUAL LIGHT AND UNIVER-SAL KNOWLEDGE; being a complete treasury of information for everyday use . . . with 350 fine engravings. Philadelphia: National Publishing Co., 1899. 708p. 26cm. Compiler: Henry Davenport Northrop (1836–1909).

Distinguished only by the oddity of its title, this small work had previously been issued as the *Standard Cyclopedia* in 1897. It was subsequently issued, in whole or in part, and sometimes with additional material, under several titles, culminating with the *Standard Library of Knowledge* in 1904.

YOUNG FOLK'S CYCLOPAEDIA *see* CHAMPLIN CY-CLOPEDIA FOR YOUNG FOLKS

YOUNGER CHILDREN'S ENCYCLOPAEDIA. London: Odhams Press, 1956. 384p. 25cm. Advisory Editors: J. C. Hill, M. G. Rawlins, W. G. Moore.

A small and simple topically-arranged compendium of miscellaneous information for very young children.

ZELL'S POPULAR ENCYCLOPEDIA; a universal dictionary of English language, science, literature and art. Illustrated by over 2,000 wood cuts. Philadelphia: T. E. Zell, 1870–1871. 2v. 31cm. Compiler: Leo de Colange (b.1819).

Named after the publisher, this small, but quite useful work, was reprinted in 1875 in editions of two, three, four and five volumes. Colange afterwards edited four smaller works, all of which were probably derived or abridged from the original compilation. These were: the *National Encyclopedia*

(1873), the *Peoples Encyclopedia* (1873), the *Universal Encyclopedia* (1878) and the *School Encyclopedia* (1899).

All were printed and published in the United States, with the exception of the *Peoples Encyclopedia*, which was published in London and was apparently the same as the *National Encyclopedia*.

I

Index OF ORIGINATORS, COMPILERS, EDITORS, ASSISTANT EDITORS, PRINCIPAL CONTRIBUTORS, ETC., AND THE ENCYCLOPEDIC WORKS WITH WHICH THEY WERE ASSOCIATED.

• •

ABBOTT, Leonard Dalton (b.1878)
Research Editor: *Handy Encyclopedia of Useful Information* (1946–1947)

ABELES, Elvin A.
Editor: *National Encyclopedia* (1961–)

ABRAMS, Alfred Willis (b.1866)
Director of Visual Instruction: *Pictured Knowledge* (1915)

ADAM, Graeme Mercer (1839–1912)
Associate Editor: *Students Reference Work* (1902–1903)

ADAMS, Charles Kendall (1835–1902)
Editor in Chief: *Johnson's Universal Cyclopaedia* (1893–1897)
Editor in Chief: *Universal Cyclopaedia* (1900–1905)

ADAMS, Lewis Mulford
Editor: *Webster's Unified Encyclopedia and Dictionary* (1953–1961)
Managing Editor: *American Family Encyclopedia* (1963–)

AITCHISON, Alexander
Editor: *Encyclopaedia Perthensis* (1806–1816)

AITON, George Briggs (b.1856)
Originator and Editor: *Aiton's Encyclopedia* (1910)

ALBERTSON, H. H.
Assistant Editor: *Popular Compendium of Useful Information* (1901)
Assistant Editor: *World Encyclopedia* (1901)
Assistant Editor: *Golden Treasury of Useful Information* (1902)
Assistant Editor: *World's Best Knowledge and How to Use It* (1902)
Assistant Editor: *Everybody's Encyclopedia for Everyday Reference* (1907)

ALLEN, Emory Adams (b.1853)
Joint Editor: *Knowledge Book* (1915)
Joint Editor: *Knowledge Library* (1918)
Joint Editor: *New Knowledge Library* (1919)

ALWEIS, Frank
Editor: *The Complete Reference Handbook* (1964–)

ANNANDALE, Charles (1843–1915)
Editor: *The Popular Encyclopaedia* (1882–1893)
Editor: *Blackie's Modern Cyclopaedia of Universal Information* (1889–1897)
Editor: *New Cabinet Cyclopaedia and Treasury of Knowledge* (1891–1899)

Joint Editor: *New National Cyclopaedia and Treasury* (1899)

Editor: *New Popular Encyclopaedia* (1901)

Joint Editor: *XX Century Cyclopaedia and Atlas* (1901)

Joint Editor: *New Twentieth Century Cyclopaedia and Dictionary* (1903)

Joint Editor: *New and Complete Universal Self Pronouncing Encyclopedia* (1905)

Editor: *The Modern Cyclopaedia* (1906–1907)

Joint Editor: *New Cosmopolitan Encyclopedia* (1906)

Joint Editor: *Modern Universal Encyclopedia* (1910)

Joint Editor: *National Encyclopedia of Reference* (1912)

Joint Editor: *Home and Office Reference Book of Facts* (1913)

ANSLEY, Clarke Fisher (1869–1939)
Editor in Chief: *Columbia Encyclopedia* (1935–1939)

ARMITAGE, John
Editor: *Children's Britannica* (1960–   )
London Editor: *Encyclopaedia Britannica* (1960–   )

ASHMORE, Harry S.
Editor in Chief: *Britannica Junior Encyclopaedia* (1961–1964)
Editor in Chief: *Encyclopaedia Britannica* (1961–1964)

ATKINS, M. G. de St. V.
Editor: *Chambers's Encyclopaedia* (1966–   )
Editor: *Newnes Popular Encyclopaedia* (1966–   )

ATKINSON, Mrs. Eleanor Stackhouse (1863–1942)
Editor: *How and Why Library* (1913–1942)
Associate Editor: *Pictured Knowledge* (1916–1935)

AULD, Robert Campbell McCombie (b.1857)
Associate Editor: *Standard Illustrated Book of Facts* (1912)

BAIRD, Spencer Fullerton (1823–1887)
Editor: *Iconographic Encyclopaedia of Science, Literature and Art* (1851)

BAKER, L. Mary
Editor: *Pears Cyclopaedia* (1953–   )

BAKER, Richard S.
Contributor: *Children's Pictorial Encyclopedia* (1948)

BALCH, William Ralston (b.1852)
Compiler: *Ready Reference* (1890–1894)

BARNARD, Frederick Augustus Porter (1809–1889)
Editor in Chief: *Johnson's New Universal Cyclopaedia* (1876–1884)

BARRATT, Herbert Charles
General Editor: *Pears Cyclopaedic* (c.1929)

BARRATT, Thomas J.
Compiler: *Pears Cyclopaedia* (1897–   )

BARRY, Charles Patrick (b.1902)
Editor in Chief: *Collier's Encyclopedia* (1949–1951)

BATEMAN, Oliver W.
Joint Editor: *American Home Library* (1930–1953)

BAYNES, Thomas Spencer (1823–1887)
Editor: *Encyclopaedia Britannica. 9th ed.* (1875–1889)

BEACH, Chandler Belden (1839–1928)
Editor: *Students Cyclopaedia* (1900)
Editor: *Students Reference Work* (1902–1903)
Editor: *New Students Reference Work* (1909–1930)

BEACH, Frederick Converse (1848–1918)
Editor: *Encyclopedia Americana* (1902–1906)
Joint Editor: *Americana* (1907–1912)

BEARDSLEY, William Waite (b.1885)
Editorial Director: *National Encyclopedia* (1932–1950)
Editor: *Collier's Encyclopedia Yearbook* (1939–1950)

BEETON, Samuel Orchart (1831–1877)
Compiler: *Beeton's Encyclopaedia of Universal Information* (1879–1881)

BELL, Andrew (1726–1809)
Joint Originator: *Encyclopaedia Britannica* (1771–1809)

BELL, Hill McClelland (1860–1927)
Associate Editor: *International Reference Work* (1923)

BELL, Raymond Martin

Editor: *New Century Book of Facts* (1955–)

BENJAMIN, Marcus (1857–1932)
Joint Editor: *Appleton's New Practical Cyclopedia* (1910–1920)
Member, Editorial Board: *New Universal Encyclopedia* (1930)

BENNETT, Dorothy Agnes (b.1909)
Original Compiler: *The Golden Encyclopedia* (1946)
Original Compiler: *New Golden Encyclopedia* (1963)

BETTESWORTH, John
Assistant Editor: *New Royal Cyclopaedia and Encyclopaedia* (1788)

BEVANS, Margaret (b.1917)
Editor in Chief: *Golden Treasury of Knowledge* (1961–)

BEYER, Samuel Walker (1865–1931)
Associate Editor: *Standard American Encyclopedia* (1912–1916)

BIRCH, Thomas (1705–1766)
Compiler: *A General Dictionary, Historical and Critical* (1734–1741)

BLISHEN, Edward
Editor: *Junior Pears Encyclopaedia* (1961–)

BLUM, Harold J.
Executive Editor: *Illustrated World Encyclopedia* (1963–)

BLUMENTHAL, Walter Hart (b.1883)
Joint Editor: *New and Complete Universal Self Pronouncing Encyclopedia* (1905)
Joint Editor: *New Cosmopolitan Encyclopedia* (1906)
Joint Editor: *National Encyclopedia of Reference* (1912)

BOAG, Walter Rainsford
Advisory Editor: *Standard American Encyclopedia* (1937–1941)

BOSTWICK, Arthur Elmore (1860–1942)
Joint Editor: *Appleton's New Practical Cyclopedia* (1910–1920)
Member, Editorial Board: *New Universal Encyclopedia* (1930)
Editor: *Doubleday's Encyclopedia* (1931–1943)

BOSWELL, Henry

Assistant Editor: *New Royal Cyclopaedia and Encyclopaedia* (1788)

BOSWORTH, Newton (d.1848)
Joint Editor: *Pantologia* (1813)

BOTHAMLEY, C. H.
Assistant Editor: *Cassell's Concise Cyclopaedia* (1883–1899)

BOUMPHREY, Geoffrey
Joint Editor: *Oxford Junior Encyclopaedia* (1948–1954)

BOWMAN, Peter
Editor: *New Century Book of Facts* (1963–)

BOYLE, Andrew
Editor: *The Everyman Encyclopaedia* (1913–1914)

BOZMAN, Ernest Franklin (b.1895)
Editor: *Everyman's Encyclopaedia* (1958)
Editor: *Macmillan Everyman's Encyclopedia* (1959)

BRABNER, J. H. F.
Editor: *The National Encyclopaedia* (1867–1888)

BRADDY, Nella *see* HENNEY, Mrs. Nella Braddy

BRADE-BIRKS, Stanley Graham
Editor: *Teach Yourself Concise Encyclopaedia of General Knowledge* (1956–1963)

BRADFORD, Thomas Gamaliel (1802–1887)
Assistant Editor: *Encyclopaedia Americana:* Vols. 5–13 (1829–1849)

BRANDE, William Thomas (1788–1866)
Joint Editor: Supplements to the 4th, 5th and 6th editions of the *Encyclopaedia Britannica* (1824)
Editor: *Dictionary of Science, Literature and Art* (1842–1875)

BRENTON, Daniel G.
Joint Editor: *International Library of Reference* (1899)

BREWSTER, Sir David (1781–1868)
Editor: *Edinburgh Encyclopaedia* (1830)

BRIDGEWATER, William
Editor in Chief: *Columbia Encyclopedia* (1950–)
Editor in Chief: *Columbia-Viking Desk Encyclopedia* (1953–)

BRONNER, Milton
American Editor: *The Everyman Encyclopaedia* (1931–1932)

BROWN, Amos Peaslee (1864–1917)
Associate Editor: *Standard American Encyclopedia* (1912–1916)
BROWN, Elmer Ellsworth (1861–1934)
Member, Editorial Board: *New Universal Encyclopedia* (1930)
BROWN, Thomas Kite
Joint Editor: *Winston's Universal Reference Library* (1930)
BRUBACHER, Abram Royer (1870–1939)
Advisory Editor: *The Volume Library* (1922–1931)
BUCJNAKK, G. K.
Managing Editor: *The World Book: British Empire Edition* (1936–1937)
BUCK, Dudley
Joint Editor: *New Peoples Cyclopedia of Universal Knowledge* (1903)
BUCKLEY, Edmund
Joint Editor: *The Current Encyclopedia* (1901–1902)
BUEL, James William (1849–1920)
Joint Editor: *Encyclopaedic Dictionary of American Reference* (1901)
BUFTON, James D. (b.1884)
Publisher and Managing Editor: *Bufton's Universal Cyclopaedia* (1919)
BUONGIORNO, Nunzia A.
Managing Editor: *Grolier Encyclopedia* (1954–1955)
BURPEE, Lawrence Johnstone (b.1873)
Advisory Editor: *Grolier Encyclopedia* (1944–   )
BURROWES, Amyas Deane
Editor: *The Modern Encyclopaedia* (1816–1820)
BUTLER, C.
Joint Editor: *Oxford Encyclopaedia* (1828–1831)

CAMPBELL-COPELAND, Thomas
Assistant Editor: *Encyclopedia Americana* (1902–1906)
CANBY, Henry Seidel
Joint Editor: *Winston's Universal Reference Library* (1930)
CARPENTER, Benjamin Franklin (b.1908)
Joint Editor: *Universal World Reference Encyclopedia* (1949–1951)
CARTER, M. D.

Editor: *Junior World Encyclopaedia* (1960–   )
CARY, Ferdinand Ellsworth (b.1848)
Editor in Chief. *Complete Library of Universal Knowledge* (1904)
Editor in Chief: *New Idea Self Instructor* (1904)
Joint Editor: *The Knowledge Book* (1915)
Joint Editor: *The Knowledge Library* (1918)
Joint Editor: *New Knowledge Library* (1919)
CAUVIN, Joseph
Assistant Editor: *Dictionary of Science, Literature and Art* (1842–1852)
CAVINS, Lorimer Victor (b.1880)
Editor in Chief: *American Educator Encyclopedia* (1937–1946)
Editor in Chief: *Wonderland of Knowledge* (1937–1946)
CAYNE, Bernard S.
Editor in Chief: *Merit Students Encyclopedia* (1967–   )
CHAMBERS, Ephraim (c.1680–1740)
Compiler: *Cyclopaedia* (1728–1791) (Posthumous)
CHAMBERS, Robert (1802–1871)
Joint Editor: *Chambers's Information for the People* (1857–1880)
Joint Founder: *Chambers's Encyclopaedia* (1860–1868)
CHAMBERS, William (1800–1883)
Joint Editor: *Chambers's Information for the People* (1857–1880)
Joint Founder: *Chambers's Encyclopaedia* (1860–1868)
CHAMPLIN, John Denison (1834–1915)
Original Compiler: *New Champlin Cyclopedia for Young Folks* (1924)
Original Compiler: *Champlin Encyclopedia* (1946–1950)
CHANCELLOR, John
Editor: *Knowledge* (1961–1965)
CHANDLER, William Henry (1841–1906)
Editor: *Chandler's Encyclopedia* (1898)
Editor: *New Complete Condensed Encyclopedia* (1909)
CHISHOLM, Hugh (1866–1924)
Joint Editor: *Encyclopaedia Britannica. 10th ed.* (1902–1903)

Editor: *Encyclopaedia Britannica*. 11th ed. (1910–1911)

Editor: *Britannica Year Book* (1913–1924)

Editor: *Encyclopaedia Britannica*. 12th ed. (1922)

Editor: *Encyclopaedia Britannica*. 13th ed. (1926)

CHOUINARD, Carroll
Editor in Chief: *American Peoples Encyclopedia* (1960)

CHRIST, G. Elgie
Joint Editor: *Nuttall Encyclopaedia* (1930)

CHURCHILL, Allen Leon (b.1873)
Joint Editor: *New International Yearbook* (1908–1917)

CLARK, Samuel
Joint Editor: *The Complete Dictionary of Arts and Sciences* (1764–1766)

CLARKEM, W. E.
Assistant Editor: *Cassell's Concise Cyclopaedia* (1883–1899)

CLOWES, Sir William Laird (1856–1905)
Compiler: *Cassell's Miniature Cyclopaedia* (1888–1898)

COËTLOGON, Dennis de
Compiler: *Universal History of Arts and Sciences* (1745)

COLANGE, Leo de (b.1819)
Compiler: *Zell's Popular Encyclopedia* (1870–1871)
Compiler: *The National Encyclopedia* (1873)
Compiler: *The Peoples Encyclopaedia* (1873)
Compiler: *Universal Encyclopedia* (1878)
Compiler: *The National Encyclopedia* (1899)

COLBY, Frank Moore (1865–1925)
Joint Editor: *New International Encyclopedia* (1902–1935)
Joint Editor: *Nelson's Encyclopaedia* (1906–1907)
Editor: *New International Yearbook* (1907–1924)

COLERIDGE, Samuel Taylor (1772–1834)
Planner: *Encyclopaedia Metropolitana* (1817–1858)

COLLEDGE, William A. (1859–1927)

Joint Editor: *New Standard Encyclopedia* (1906–1916)

Editor: *Bufton's Universal Cyclopaedia* (1919)

COLLINS, R. S.
Assistant Editor: *Popular Compendium of Useful Information* (1901)
Assistant Editor: *The World Encyclopedia* (1901)
Assistant Editor: *Golden Treasury of Useful Information* (1902)
Assistant Editor: *World's Best Knowledge and How to Use It* (1902)
Assistant Editor: *Everybody's Encyclopedia for Everyday Reference* (1907)

CONANT, T. J.
Compiler: Index to *American Cyclopaedia* (1878–1884)

COPELAND, Lewis
Editor: *Handy Encyclopedia of Useful Information* (1946–1947)
Joint Editor: *Austin's New Encyclopedia of Usable Information* (1948)
Joint Editor: *Everyday Reference Library* (1951–)

CORNISH, George A.
Editor in Chief: *Encyclopedia International* (1963–1964)
Editor in Chief: *Encyclopedia Americana* (1965–)

COUCH, William Terry (b.1901)
Editor in Chief: *Collier's Encyclopedia* (1951–1960)
Editor in Chief: *American Oxford Encyclopedia for Home and School* (1965)

COX, Sir George William (1827–1902)
Assistant Editor: *Dictionary of Science, Literature and Art* (1866–1875)
Editor: *Little Cyclopaedia of Common Things* (1882–1906)

COX, Warren Earle (b.1895)
Art Editor: *Encyclopaedia Brittanica*. 14th ed. (1929–1936)

CRANE, Uttley Edwin (b.1883)
General Editor: *New Outline of Knowledge* (1936)

CROKER, Temple Henry (1730–c.1790)
Joint Editor: *The Complete Dictionary of Arts and Sciences* (1764–1766)

CROSSLAND, John Redgwick (b.1892)
Joint Editor: *New Standard Encyclopaedia and World Atlas* (1932)

Joint Editor: *Concise Encyclopaedia* (1933)

Joint Editor: *Modern Encyclopaedia for Children* (1933–1948)

Joint Editor: *Wonder Encyclopaedia for Children* (1933)

Joint Editor: *Golden Encyclopaedia for Children* (1934)

Joint Editor: *Clear Type Encyclopaedia* (1935)

Joint Editor: *Laurel and Gold Encyclopedia* (1935)

Joint Editor: *New Gem Encyclopedia* (1935)

Joint Editor: *Wonder World of Knowledge* (1935–1937)

Joint Editor: *Wonder World Encyclopaedia* (1936–1947)

Joint Editor: *Standard Encyclopedia* (1937)

Joint Editor: *Encyclopedia of General Knowledge* (1938)

Joint Editor: *Modern Marvels Encyclopedia* (1938)

Editor: *Modern Standard Encyclopaedia* (1938)

Joint Editor: *Modern Illustrated Encyclopaedia* (1940)

CROUCH, Warwick Wyatt
Revision Editor: *The Concise Pocket Encyclopaedia* (1925)

CUNNINGHAM, A.
Contributor: *The Popular Encyclopaedia* (1841–1893)

CURTIS, Thomas
Editor: *Encyclopaedia Metropolitana* (1817)
Editor: *The London Encyclopaedia* (1829)

DAHMS, Edward J.
Assistant Editor: *Complete Library of Universal Knowledge* (1904)
Assistant Editor: *New Idea Self Instructor* (1904)

DANA, Charles Anderson (1819–1897)
Joint Editor: *New American Cyclopaedia* (1858–1863)
Joint Editor: *The American Cyclopaedia* (1873–1884)

DAWSON, Lawrence Hawkins (b.1880)
British Editor: *Facts* (1934–1941)

Editor in Chief: *Routledge's Universal Encyclopaedia* (1934)

British Editor: *New Concise Pictorial Encyclopedia* (1938)

Editor: *The Nuttall Encyclopaedia* (1938)

British Editor: *The Comprehensive Pictorial Encyclopedia* (1942–1943)

British Editor: *World Home Reference Encyclopedia* (1951)

DE PUY, William Harrison (1821–1901)
Editor: *Peoples Cyclopedia of Universal Knowledge* (1883)
Assistant Editor: *New Americanized Encyclopaedia Britannica* (1896)
Original Editor: *New Peoples Cyclopedic of Universal Knowledge* (1903)
Editor (Posthumous): *World Wide Encyclopedia and Gazetteer* (1908)

DE WIT, Cornelius Hugh (b.1905)
Illustrator: *The Golden Encyclopedia* (1946)
Illustrator: *New Golden Encyclopedia* (1963)

DELL, W. R.
Managing Editor: *Britannica Junior* (1962–   )

DENNY, A.
Assistant Editor: *Cassell's Concise Cyclopaedia* (1883–1899)

DERVISSE, Alexander
Associate Editor: *World Scope Encyclopedia* (1945–1947)

DICKINSON, Asa Don (b.1876)
Managing Editor: *Doubleday's Encyclopedia* (1931–1943)

DIEMER, George Willis (b.1885)
Joint Editor: *The How and Why Library* (Volumes 4–5) (1934–   )

DIXON, M. Vibart
Managing Editor: *Chambers's Encyclopaedia* (1963–1965)
Managing Editor: *Newnes Popular Encyclopaedia* (1963–1965)

DODGE, John V.
Executive Editor: *Britannica Junior Encyclopaedia* (1960–   )
Executive Editor: *Encyclopaedia Britannica* (1960–   )

DOHERTY, Robert H.
Co-ordinating Editor: *The Complete Reference Handbook* (1964–   )

DOLE, Nathan Haskell (1852–1935)

Assistant Editor: *Encyclopedia Americana* (1902–1906)

Joint Editor: *New Standard Encyclopedia* (1906–1916)

DORING, Paul

Research Editor: *Handy Encyclopedia of Useful Information* (1946–1947)

DOUGALL, John

Joint Editor: *New Gresham Encyclopaedia* (1921–1924)

Joint Editor: *The Compact Encyclopaedia* (1927)

DOVER, Cedric

Associate Editor: *Newnes Pictorial Knowledge* (1960–   )

DOWNEY, Douglas W.

Editor: *New Standard Encyclopedia* (1963–   )

DUDLEY, Lavinia Pratt

Editor in Chief: *Encyclopedia Americana* (1948–1963)

DUNHAM, Franklin (b.1892)

Editor in Chief: *New Pictorial Encyclopedia of the World* (1954)

Editor in Chief: *Illustrated Encyclopedia of the Modern World* (1956)

Editor in Chief: *Pictured Knowledge* (1956–1957)

Editor in Chief: *Little & Ives Illustrated Ready Reference Encyclopedia* (1961–   )

ELLIOTT, Dorothy O.

Associate Editor: *Consolidated Webster Comprehensive Encyclopedic Dictionary* (1954)

ERSKINE, John

Introduction: *Facts* (1934–1941)

Introduction: *New Concise Pictorial Encyclopedia* (1938)

Introduction: *The Comprehensive Pictorial Encyclopedia* (1942–1943)

Introduction: *World Home Reference Encyclopedia* (1951)

EVERETT, Marshall (*pseud.*) *see* NEIL, Henry

EXLEY, Thomas

Joint Editor: *The Imperial Encyclopaedia* (1812)

FALCONER, Sir Robert Alexander (1867–1943)

Canadian Editor: *Nelson's Perpetual Looseleaf Encyclopedia* (1926)

Canadian Editor: *Nelson Complete Encyclopedia* (1937)

Former Editor: *Nelson's Encyclopedia: Unabridged* (1940)

Canadian Editor: *Nelson's New Looseleaf Encyclopedia* (1940)

FALLOWS, Samuel *bp.* (1835–1922)

Joint Editor: *The Current Encyclopedia* (1901–1902)

Joint Editor: *Human Interest Library* (1914–1922)

FARQUHAR, Silas Edgar (1887–1948)

Managing Editor: *Human Interest Library* (1925–1926)

Editor: *New Human Interest Library* (1928–1930)

Managing Editor: *The Volume Library* (1931–1932)

Revision Editor: *The World Book Encyclopedia* (1933–1937)

Managing Editor: *The World Book Encyclopedia* (1938–1940)

Editor: *Modern Library of Knowledge* (1940)

Editor: *Grolier Encyclopedia* (1944–1948)

FINCH, Peter

Editor: *Newnes Pictorial Knowledge* (1954–1960)

FINDLATER, Andrew (1810–1885)

Editor: *Chambers's Encyclopaedia* (1860–1878)

FINEGAN, Thomas Edward (b.1866)

Editor in Chief: *Winston's Cumulative Looseleaf Encyclopedia* (1922–1955)

FINLEY, John Huston (1863–1940)

Editor in Chief: *Nelson's Perpetual Looseleaf Encyclopedia* (1917–1926)

Editor in Chief: *Nelson Complete Encyclopedia* (1937–1940)

Former Editor: *Nelson's Encyclopedia: Unabridged* (1940)

Editor in Chief: *Nelson's New Looseleaf Encyclopedia* (1940)

FISHER, Eugene M.

Editor: *World Home Reference Encyclopedia* (1951)

FISK, Calvin Rogers (b.1896)

Editorial Director: *Modern American Encyclopedia* (1934–1936)

Editorial Director: *New Standard Encyclopedia* (1934–1964)

FORD, Charles Alfred
Editor in Chief: *Compton's Pictured Encyclopedia* (1962–1964)

FORD, Guy Stanton (b.1873)
Editor in Chief: *Compton's Pictured Encyclopedia* (1922–1964)

FOREMAN, J. B.
Joint Editor: *Modern University Encyclopedia* (1957)
Joint Editor: *New Age Encyclopaedia, World Atlas and Sports Supplement* (1957–1963)

FORKERT, Ella Wheeler
Associate Editor: *Standard American Encyclopedia* (1937–1941)

FOSTER, Ellsworth Decatur (1869–1936)
Associate Editor: *New Practical Reference Library* (1913–1918)
General Editor: *The World Book* (1917–1935)
Editor in Chief: *The American Educator* (1919–1936)
Editor in Chief: *Dominion Educator* (1919–1934)
Managing Editor: *The World Book* (1929–1935)

FOSTER, Mary Elizabeth (b.1892)
Bibliography Compiler: *The World Book* (1933)

FRANK, Glenn
Editor: *University of Knowledge* (1937–1938)

FRIEDENTHAL, Richard (b.1896)
European Editor: *Facts* (1934–1941)
European Editor: *New Concise Pictorial Encyclopedia* (1938)
European Editor: *The Comprehensive Pictorial Encyclopedia* (1942–43)
European Editor: *World Home Reference Encyclopedia* (1951)

FUREY, Francis Thomas (b.1852)
Joint Editor: *National Encyclopedia of Reference* (1912)

GARVIN, James Louis (1868–1947)
Editor: Volumes 29–32: *Encyclopaedia Britannica*. 13th ed. (1926)
Editor in Chief: *Encyclopaedia Britannica*. 14th ed. (1929–1935)

GEDDIE, William
Editor: *Chambers's Encyclopaedia* (1923–1935)

GEE, Herbert Leslie (b.1901)
Editor: *Nelson's Encyclopedia* (1951–1966)

GILBERT, Harry B.
Advisory Editor: *Children's Pictorial Encyclopedia* (1948)

GILLET, Harry Orrin (b.1879)
Editor: *The American Educator* (1946–1953)
Editor: *Wonderland of Knowledge* (1946–1953)

GILMAN, Daniel Coit (1831–1908)
Joint Editor: *New International Encyclopedia* (1902–1911)

GLEIG, George *bishop of Brechin* (1753–1840)
Editor: Volumes 13–18: *Encyclopaedia Britannica*. 3rd ed. (1797) and Supplement in two volumes (1801–1803)

GLENN, Gustavus Richard (b.1848)
Special Contributor: *Teacher's and Pupil's Cyclopaedia* (1902–1907)
Contributor: *Encyclopaedic Current Reference* (1906)

GOLDSMITH, Oliver (1728–1774)
Planner: *Universal Dictionary of Arts and Sciences* (1745)

GOOD, John Mason (1764–1827)
Joint Editor: *Pantologia* (1813)

GOODWIN, Karl Henry (b.1864)
Managing Editor: *The American Educator* (1934–   )

GORELL, Lord (Ronald Gorell Barnes Gorell, b.1884)
Advisory Editor: *The World Book—British Empire Edition* (1936–1937)
Advisory Editor: *Odhams Encyclopaedia* (1953)
Advisory Editor: *The Modern Encyclopaedia* (1961)

GRANT, Roderick M.
Associate Editor: *Wonderland of Knowledge* (1937)

GREENE, Richard Gleason (1829–1914)
Editor: *Columbian Cyclopaedia* (1899)
Editor: *New Imperial Encyclopedia and Dictionary* (1906)

GREENWOOD, James Mickleborough (1836–1914)

Contributor: *Teacher's and Pupil's Cyclopaedia* (1902–1907)

Contributor: *Encyclopaedic Current Reference* (1906)

GREGORY, George
Editor: *Dictionary of Arts and Sciences* (1806–1807)

GREGORY, Olinthus Gilbert (1774–1841)
Joint Editor: *Pantologia* (1813)

GROSE, Howard Bristol (b.1879)
Editor: *Our Wonder World* (1926–1927)

GUILLOT, René (b.1900)
Compiler: *Illustrated Encyclopedia* (1959)

GUYOT, Arnold Henry (1807–1884)
Editor in Chief: *Johnson's New Universal Cyclopaedia* (1876–1884)

HADLEY, A. T.
Joint Editor: *Encyclopaedia Britannica.* 10th ed. (1902–1903)

HAGAR, George Jotham (1847–1921)
Joint Editor: *New Standard Encyclopedia* (1906–1916)
Editor in Chief: *Practical Home Encyclopedia* (1909)
Joint Editor: *Appleton's New Practical Cyclopedia* (1910–1920)
Editor in Chief: *Everybody's Cyclopedia* (1911–1912)
Editor in Chief: *Standard American Encyclopedia* (1912–1916)
Editor in Chief: *People's Cyclopedia* (1914)
Editor in Chief: *New World Wide Cyclopedia* (1918–1928)
Editor in Chief: *New World Encyclopedia* (1919)
Editor in Chief: *World Wide Cyclopedia* (1919)
Original Compiler: *Times Encyclopedia and Gazeteer* (1929)
Member, Editorial Board: *New Universal Encyclopedia* (1930)

HALE, Edward Everett (1822–1909)
Editor in Chief: *Modern Achievement* (1904)

HALL-QUEST, Alfred L.
Associate Editor: *Collier's Encyclopedia* (1949–)

HALSEY, William D.

Editorial Director: *Collier's Encyclopedia* (1960–)

Editorial Director: *Merit Students Encyclopedia* (1967–)

HAMMERTON, Sir John Alexander (1871–1949)
Editor: *Harmsworth's Universal Encyclopaedia* (1920–1930)
Editor: *Concise Universal Encyclopaedia* (1930–1931)
Editor: *Waverley Encyclopaedia of General Information* (1930)
Foreign Editor: *Doubleday's Encyclopedia* (1931–1943)
Editor: *The Modern Encyclopaedia* (1933–1939)
Editor: *New Popular Educator* (1933–1934)
Editor: *Cassell's Modern Encyclopaedia* (1934)
Editor: *Practical Knowledge for All* (1934)
Editor: *Encyclopaedia of Modern Knowledge* (1936–1937)
Editor: *New Book of Knowledge* (1938)
Editor: *New Universal Encyclopaedia* (1951–1959)

HANLEY, Miles Lawrence
Consultant: *Collier's Encyclopedia* (1949–)

HARRINGTON, Rt. Rev. Msgr. John H.
Editor in Chief: *Catholic Encyclopedia for School and Home* (1965–)

HARRIS, John (1667?–1719)
Compiler: *Lexicon Technicum* (1704–1736)

HARRIS, W.
Joint Editor: *Oxford Encyclopaedia* (1828–1831)

HARTSHORNE, Henry (1823–1897)
Joint Editor: *Home Cyclopedia of Necessary Knowledge* (1902)
Joint Editor: *Home Educator in Necessary Knowledge* (1905)

HATHAWAY, Henry Cook
Editor in Chief: *Pocket Library of the World's Essential Knowledge* (1929)

HAYDON, A. L.
Joint Editor: *The Nuttall Encyclopaedia* (1930)

HAYWARD, Mrs. Margurite Lindquist

Managing Editor: *Hayward's Key to Knowledge* (1931)

HEATON, William
Editor: *Cassell's Concise Cyclopaedia* (1883–1899)

HECK, Johann Georg
Original Compiler: *Iconographic Encyclopaedia of Science, Literature and Art* (1851)

HENDELSON, William H. (b.1904)
Revision Editor: *Modern Concise Encyclopedia* (1940)
Revision Editor: *Facts* (1941)
Revision Editor: *The Comprehensive Pictorial Encyclopedia* (1942–1943)
Editor in Chief: *World Scope Encyclopedia* (1945–1964)
Editor in Chief: *New World Family Encylopedia* (1953)
Editor in Chief: *Standard International Encyclopedia* (1953–1957)
Editor in Chief: *New American Encyclopedia* (1963)
Editor in Chief: *The World Educator Encyclopedia* (1964)
Editor in Chief: *World University Encyclopedia* (1964)

HENNEY, Mrs. Nella Braddy (b.1894)
Associate Editor: *Doubleday's Encyclopedia* (1931–1943)
Editor in Chief: *Facts* (1934–1941)
Editor in Chief: *New Concise Pictorial Encyclopedia* (1938)
Editor in Chief: *Comprehensive Pictorial Encyclopedia* (1942–1943)

HETHERINGTON, John
Joint Editor: *Encyclopaedia of Modern Knowledge* (1965)

HIGENBOTTAM, Frank
Associate Editor: *Teach Yourself Concise Encyclopaedia of General Knowledge* (1956)

HIGGINS, Charles
Editor: *Everybody's Encyclopedia* (1909)
Editor: *La Salle Extension University Encyclopedia* (1909)
Editor: *Webster's Universal Encyclopedia* (1909)
Editor: *Modern Universal Encyclopedia* (1910)
Joint Editor: *Home and Office Reference Book of Facts* (1913)

HILL, J. C.
Advisory Editor: *Younger Children's Encyclopaedia* (1956)

HILL, Mrs. Janet McKenzie (1852–1933)
Joint Editor: *Home Cyclopedia of Necessary Knowledge* (1902)
Joint Editor: *Home Educator in Necessary Knowledge* (1905)

HILL, Thomas Edie (1832–1915)
Supervisor: *Hill's Practical Encyclopedia* (1901–1902)
Originator: *School Library Encyclopedia* (1901)
Editor: *Hill's Practical Reference Library of General Knowledge* (1902–1905)

HINTON, J. H.
Joint Editor: *Oxford Encyclopaedia* (1828–1831)

HIRSCH, Arthur Henry (b.1878)
Associate Editor: *The American Educator* (1944–)

HITCHENS, Harold Lee
Associate Editor: *Universal World Reference Encyclopedia* (1945)
Associate Editor: *Consolidated Webster Encyclopedic Dictionary* (1954)

HODGSON, James Goodwin (b.1892)
Bibliography Compiler: *The World Book* (1933)

HOLLAND, Arthur William
Joint Editor: *New Standard Encyclopaedia and World Atlas* (1932)
Editor: *Children's Home Educator and Treasury of Knowledge* (1936)

HOLMYARD, Eric John (b.1891)
Science Editor: *The Everyman Encyclopaedia* (1931–1932)
Assistant Editor: *Hutchinson's Pictorial Encyclopaedia* (1936–1937)

HOLST, Bernhart Paul (1861–1939)
Editor in Chief: *Teacher's and Pupil's Cyclopaedia* (1902–1907)
Editor in Chief: *Encyclopaedic Current Reference* (1906)
Editor in Chief: *New Teacher's and Pupil's Cyclopaedia* (1910–1927)
Editor in Chief: *Practical American Encyclopedia* (1911)
Editor in Chief: *Unrivalled Encyclopedia* (1911)
Editor in Chief: *International Reference Work* (1923–1927)

Editor in Chief: *Progressive Reference Library* (1928–1939)

Editor in Chief: *World Scope Encyclopedia* (1945–1947)

HOLST, Bertram P.

Associate Editor: *International Reference Work* (1923–1927)

HOOPER, Franklin Henry (1862–1940)

American Editor: *Encyclopaedia Britannica. 14th ed.* (1929–1940)

Editor: *Britannica Junior* (1934–1940)

HORSLEY, Edith M.

Revision Editor: *Hutchinson's Twentieth Century Encyclopaedia* (1952–1955)

Editor in Chief: *Hutchinson's New 20th Century Encyclopedia* (1965–   )

HOSKING, Arthur N.

Art Editor: *Collier's Encyclopedia* (1949–   )

HOWARD, George Selby

Editor: *New Royal Cyclopaedia and Encyclopaedia* (1788)

HUGHES, James Laughlin (1846–1935)

Editor: *Dominion Educator* (1919–1934)

Canadian Editor: *The American Educator* (1919–1935)

HUGHES, William (1817–1876)

Revision Editor: *Maunder's Treasury of Knowledge and Library of Reference* (1873)

HUMPHREY, Edward

Editor in Chief: *American Peoples Encyclopedia* (1962–   )

HUNTER, Robert (1824–1897)

Editor: *The Encyclopaedic Dictionary* (1879–1888)

HURST, John F.

Joint Editor: *International Library of Reference* (1899)

Assistant Editor: *Universal Reference Library* (1900)

Assistant Editor: *Imperial Reference Library* (1901–1910)

Assistant Editor: *Twentieth Century Encyclopaedia* (1901–1907)

HUTCHINSON, Walter (d.1950)

Editor: *Hutchinson's Pictorial Encyclopaedia* (1936–1937)

Editor: *Hutchinson's Twentieth Century Encyclopaedia* (1948–1955)

JACK, Edwin Chater

Publisher: *Jack's Reference Book for Home and Office* (1908–1929)

JACK, Thomas Chater

Publisher: *Jack's Reference Book for Home and Office* (1908–1929)

JAMES, R. L.

Joint Editor: *Odhams Encyclopaedia for Children* (1961)

Joint Editor: *Odhams Wonder World of Knowledge* (1961)

JAMESON, John Franklin (1859–1937)

Joint Editor: *Encyclopaedic Dictionary of American Reference* (1901)

JOHNSON, Alice A.

Joint Editor: *Home Cyclopedia of Necessary Knowledge* (1902)

Joint Editor: *Home Educator in Necessary Knowledge* (1905)

JOHNSON, Isaac Thorne

Joint Editor: *New and Complete Universal Self Pronouncing Encyclopedia* (1905)

Joint Editor: *New Cosmopolitan Encyclopedia* (1906)

JOHNSON, R. Archer

Joint Editor: *Modern Universal Encyclopedia* (1910)

JOHNSON, Rossiter (1840–1931)

Revision Editor: *Universal Cyclopaedia* (1900–1905)

JOHNSON, S.

Editor: *Encyclopedia for Boys and Girls* (1944)

JOHNSON, William Moore

Joint Editor: *The Imperial Encyclopaedia* (1812)

JOHNSON, Willis Fletcher (1857–1931)

Editor: New American Supplement to the *Encyclopaedia Britannica* (1904–1905)

JOHNSTON, William Henry (b.1875)

Joint Editor: *New Universal Handbook of Necessary Information* (1920–1937)

JONES, Greville

Joint Editor: Volumes 23–24—*Encyclopaedia Londinensis* (1810–1829)

JONES, John

Joint Editor: Volumes 1–22—*Encyclopaedia Londinensis* (1810–1829)

JONES, John Morris (1896–1962)

Managing Editor: *The World Book* (1940–1962)

JOYCE, Jeremiah (1763–1816)

Actual Editor: *A Dictionary of Arts and Sciences*

Actual Editor: *The British Encyclopaedia*

KASCH, Howard E.
Managing Editor: *Encyclopaedia Britannica* (1963–   )

KELLOGG, Day Otis (1796–1874)
Editor: New American Supplement to the *Encyclopaedia Britannica* (1900–1903)

KENDALL, Calvin Noyes (1858–1921)
Editor in Chief: *Pictured Knowledge* (1916–1921)

KIERAN, John
Editor: *Information Please Almanac* (1947)

KINSELLA, Michael J. (d.1928)
Founder: *Lincoln Library of Essential Information* (1924)

KLEEN, Henri F.
Managing Editor: *Nelson Complete Encyclopedia* (1937)

KNIGHT, Charles (1791–1873)
Originator: *The English Cyclopaedia* (1854–1870)

KOFFLER, Jacob
Revision Editor: *Nelson's Encyclopedia: Unabridged* (1940)

KONDO, Herbert
Managing Editor: *The Grolier Universal Encyclopedia* (1965–   )

KREINHEDER, O. C.
Associate Editor: *World Scope Encyclopedia* (1945–1947)

KRONBAUER, Anthony
Managing Editor: *Universal World Reference Encyclopedia* (1963–   )

KURTZ, Seymour
Joint Editor: *Columbia Encyclopedia*. 3rd ed. (1963)

LAING, Gordon Jennings (1896–1948)
Foreword: *Standard American Encyclopedia* (1937–1940)
Foreword: *International's World Reference Encyclopedia* (1942)
Chairman, Editorial Board: *American Educator Encyclopedia* (1946–1948)

LAMM, Lawrence W.
Joint Editor: *Austin's New Encyclopedia of Usable Information* (1948)
Joint Editor: *Everyday Reference Library* (1951–   )

LARDNER, Dionysius (1793–1859)
Editor: *The Cabinet Cyclopaedia* (1829–1849)

LAUWERYS, J. A.
Joint Editor: *Odhams Encyclopaedia for Children* (1961)
Joint Editor: *Odhams Wonder World of Knowledge* (1961)

LAW, Mrs. Margaret D.
Managing Editor: *Chambers's Encyclopaedia* (1943–1963)
Managing Editor: *Newnes Popular Encyclopaedia* (1960–1963)

LAWSON, Donald E.
Editor in Chief: *Compton's Pictured Encyclopedia* (1964–   )

LEBURG, Helga M.
Assistant Editor: *New Practical Reference Library* (1907–1918)

LEERBURGER Jr., Benedict A.
Managing Editor: *Cowles Comprehensive Encyclopedia—The Volume Library* (1963–   )

LEIBER, Fritz
Revision Editor: *Nelson's Encyclopedia: Unabridged* (1940)

LEISTER, B. M.
Designer: *International's World Reference Encyclopedia* (1942)

LEONARD, John William (b.1849)
Joint Editor: *New Twentieth Century Cyclopaedia and Dictionary* (1903)

LEONARD-STUART, Charles   *see* STUART, Charles Leonard

LEWIS, Chorlton Thomas (1834–1904)
Editor: *Harper's Book of Facts* (1895–1906)

LEWIS, William Dodge (b.1870)
Joint Editor: *New Universal Handbook of Necessary Information* (1920–1927)
Editor in Chief: *Winston's Cumulative Loose Leaf Encyclopedia* (1934–1942)
Editor in Chief: *Encyclopedia Library* (1942–1943)
Editor in Chief: *American International Encyclopedia* (1950)
Joint Editor: *Winston's Universal Reference Library* (1930)

LIEBER, Francis (1800–1872)
Editor: *Encyclopedia Americana* (1829–1849)

LINTON, Calvin D.

Consulting Editor: *The Complete Reference Handbook* (1964–   )

LITCHFIELD, Edward H.
Consulting Editor: *The Complete Reference Handbook* (1964–   )

LOCKE, George Herbert (1870–1937)
Canadian Editor: *The World Book* (1917–1937)

LONG, George (1800–1879)
Editor: *Penny Cyclopaedia* (1835–1858)
Editor: *The Imperial Cyclopaedia* (1850–1853)

LOVETT, H. D.
Joint Editor: *Modern Universal Encyclopedia* (1910)
Joint Editor: *Home and Office Reference Book of Facts* (1913)

LUCAS, Frederic A.
Assistant Editor: *Universal Reference Library* (1900)
Assistant Editor: *Imperial Reference Library* (1901–1910)
Assistant Editor: *Twentieth Century Encyclopaedia* (1901–1907)

McCALEB, Anna
Assistant Editor: *New Practical Reference Library* (1907–1918)

MacCORMAC, Morton
Assistant Editor: *Complete Library of Universal Knowledge* (1904)
Assistant Editor: *New Idea Self Instructor* (1904)

McCRACKEN, Henry Mitchell (1840–1918)
Editor: *University Encyclopedia of Twentieth Century Knowledge* (1902)

McDANNALD, Alexander Hopkins (1877–1948)
Editor in Chief: *Encyclopedia Americana* (1920–1948)
Editor in Chief: *Hayward's Key to Knowledge* (1931)
Editor in Chief: *Modern Encyclopedia* (1933–1937)
Editor in Chief: *The Concise Encyclopedia* (1937)
Editor in Chief: *Modern Concise Encyclopedia* (1940)
Editor in Chief: *New Modern Encyclopedia* (1943–1949)

McDONALD, Ethel M.

Associate Editor: *Library of Essential Knowledge* (1942–1954)

McDONNELL, John B.
Joint Editor: *Hayward's Key to Knowledge* (1931)

McDOWELL, Louis Irvine
Editor: *Book of Knowledge Annual* (1953–   )

MACFARQUHAR, Colin (1745–1793)
Joint Originator: *Encyclopaedia Britannica* (1771–1793)
Editor: Volumes 1–12: *Encyclopaedia Britannica*. 3rd ed. (1797)

McGAUGHY, James Ralph (b.1888)
Editor in Chief: *New Wonder World* (1932–1955)

McKENNA, Mary Frances
Associate Editor: *Universal World Reference Encyclopedia* (1945–1949)
Joint Editor: *Universal World Reference Encyclopedia* (1949–1954)
Editor in Chief: *Universal World Reference Encyclopedia* (1955–   )

MACLAREN, Charles (1782–1866)
Editor: *Encyclopaedia Britannica*. 6th ed. (1820–1823)

McLOUGHLIN, Ellen Veronica (b.1893)
Managing Editor: *The Book of Knowledge* (1941–1942)
Editor in Chief: *The Book of Knowledge* (1943–1959)
Editorial Director: *Grolier Encyclopedia* (1958–1960)
Member, Editorial Board: *Unified Encyclopedia* (1960–1965)

McMURRAY, Frank Morton (1862–1936)
Associate Editor: *New Students Reference Work* (1909–1930)

MacVEAGH, Lincoln (b.1890)
Editor: *New Champlin Cyclopedia for Young Folks* (1924)
Editor: *Champlin Encyclopedia*: Volumes 1–6 (1946–1950)

MAINE, George F.
Joint Editor: *Modern University Encyclopaedia* (1957)
Joint Editor: *New Age Encyclopaedia, World Atlas and Sports Supplement* (1957–1963)

MARSHALL, Arthur Courland
Editor: *Newnes Everything Within* (1933)

Editor: *Newnes Golden Treasury* (1933)
Compiler: *Children's Everything Within*
(1939)
MARTIN, Lowell Arthur
Editorial Director: *Grolier Incorporated*
(1965–   )
MARTIN, Ronald Russell (b.1891)
Editor: *Book of General Knowledge*
(1939–1949)
MARTIN, Tex
Joint Editor: *Universal World Reference*
Encyclopedia (1954–55)
MAUNDER, Samuel (1785–1849)
Compiler: *Maunder's Treasury of Knowl-*
edge and Library of Reference (1830–
1873)
Compiler: *Treasury of Knowledge and Li-*
brary of Reference (1833–1850)
MEE, Arthur (1875–1943)
Editor: *The Children's Encyclopaedia*
(1910–1935)
Joint Editor: *The Book of Knowledge*
(1912–1943)
Editor: *I See All* (1928–1930)
MEINE, Franklin Julius (b.1896)
Editor in Chief: *Nelson's Encyclopedia:*
Unabridged (1940)
Editor in Chief: *Webster's Columbia En-*
cyclopedic Dictionary (1940)
Editor in Chief: *Standard American En-*
cyclopedia (1941)
Editor in Chief: *Webster's Comprehensive*
Encyclopedic Dictionary (1941)
Editor in Chief: *Webster's Encyclopedic*
Dictionary (1941–1942)
Editor in Chief: *International's World*
Reference Encyclopedia (1942)
Editor in Chief: *Library of Essential*
Knowledge (1942–1954)
Editor in Chief: *Universal World Refer-*
ence Encyclopedia (1945–1947)
Editor in Chief: *American Peoples Ency-*
clopedia (1948–1956)
Editor in Chief: *Consolidated Webster*
Comprehensive Encyclopedic Diction-
ary (1954)
Editor in Chief: *Consolidated Webster*
Encyclopedic Dictionary (1954)
MIALL, Stuart
Editor: *World of the Children* (1948–
1957)
MILLAR, James (1762–1827)

Editor: *Encyclopaedia Britannica. 4th ed.*
(1810)
Editor: *Encyclopaedia Edinensis* (1816–
1827)
Editor: *Encyclopaedia Britannica. 5th ed.*
(1817)
MILLER, Frank Justus (1858–1938)
Assistant Editor: Volumes 6–15: *Standard*
American Encyclopedia (1937–1941)
MILLER, Walter (b.1864)
Editor in Chief: *Standard American En-*
cyclopedia (1937–1940)
Former Editor: *International's World Ref-*
erence Encyclopedia (1942)
Former Editor: *Universal World Reference*
Encyclopedia (1945–   )
MILLS, E. C.
Assistant Editor: *Popular Compendium of*
Useful Information (1901)
Assistant Editor: *The World Encyclopedia*
(1901)
Assistant Editor: *Golden Treasury of Use-*
ful Information (1902)
Assistant Editor: *World's Best Knowledge*
and How to Use It (1902)
Assistant Editor: *Everybody's Encyclope-*
dia for Everyday Reference (1907)
MITCHELL, Maurice B.
Editorial Director: *Encyclopaedia Britan-*
nica (1960–   )
MOORE, W. G.
Advisory Editor: *Younger Children's En-*
cyclopaedia (1956)
MOREHEAD, Albert H.
Chairman: National Lexicographic Board
(*q.v.*)
MOREHOUSE, Daniel Walter (b.1876)
Associate Editor: *International Reference*
Work (1927)
Associate Editor: *New Teacher's and Pu-*
pil's Cyclopaedia (1927)
Associate Editor: *World Scope Encyclo-*
pedia (1945–1947)
MORGAN, Forrest (b.1852)
Managing Editor: Volumes 1–7: *Ency-*
clopedia Americana (1903–1906)
MORRIS, Charles Smith (1833–1922)
Editor: *Universal Cyclopaedia and Dic-*
tionary (1898)
Joint Editor: *International Library of*
Reference (1899)

Editor in Chief: *Universal Reference Library* (1900)

Editor: *Handy Cyclopedia of Common Things and Biographical Dictionary* (1901)

Editor in Chief: *Imperial Reference Library* (1901–1910)

Editor in Chief: *Popular Compendium of Useful Information* (1901)

Editor: *Twentieth Century Cyclopedia of Practical Information* (1901)

Editor: *Twentieth Century Encyclopaedia* (1901–1907)

Editor in Chief: *The World Encyclopedia* (1901)

Editor in Chief: *Golden Treasury of Useful Information* (1902)

Joint Editor: *Home Cyclopedia of Necessary Knowledge* (1902)

Editor in Chief: *World's Best Knowledge and How to Use It* (1902)

Joint Editor: *Home Educator in Necessary Knowledge* (1905)

Editor in Chief: *Everybody's Encyclopedia for Everyday Reference* (1907)

Joint Editor: *Current Cyclopedia of Reference* (1909)

Editor: *Cyclopedia, Dictionary and Atlas of the World* (1909)

Joint Editor: *Winston's Encyclopedia* (1909)

Joint Editor: *Winston's Cumulative Loose Leaf Encyclopedia* (1912–1922)

MORRIS, John
Revision Editor: *Maunder's Treasury of Knowledge and Library of Reference* (1873)

MORRIS, William
Editor in Chief: *The Grolier Universal Encyclopedia* (1965–)

MORSE, Joseph Laffan (b.1902)
Editor in Chief: *New Funk and Wagnalls Encyclopedia* (1949–1952)
Editor in Chief: *Universal Standard Encyclopedia* (1954–1958)
Editor in Chief: *Funk and Wagnalls Standard Encyclopedia of Modern Knowledge* (1959)
Editor in Chief: *Funk & Wagnalls Standard Reference Encyclopedia* (1959–)

MOSSESSON, Gloria

Editor in Chief: *New American Encyclopedia* (1965–)

Editor in Chief: *The World Educator Encyclopedia* (1965–)

Editor in Chief: *World University Encyclopedia* (1965–)

MYERS, Garry Cleveland (b.1884)
Editor in Chief: *Weedon's Modern Encyclopedia* (1931–1934)
Editor in Chief: *Pictured Knowledge* (1937–1939)

NAPIER, Macvey (1776–1847)
Editor: Supplements to the 4th, 5th and 6th editions of the *Encyclopaedia Britannica* (1824)
Editor: *Encyclopaedia Britannica*. 7th ed. (1842)

NATIONAL LEXICOGRAPHIC BOARD
Compilers: *Illustrated Encyclopedia of Knowledge* (1954–1955)
Compilers: *New Wonder Book Cyclopedia of World Knowledge* (1954)
Compilers: *Illustrated Home Library Encyclopedia* (1955)
Compilers: *Illustrated World Encyclopedia* (1958–)

NAULT, William Henry
Executive Director of Research: *The World Book*

NEERGAARD, Paul Ingebrikt (b.1884)
Joint Editor: *Bufton's Universal Cyclopaedia* (1919–1935)
Editor: *Library of Knowledge* (1936)

NEIL, Henry (b.1863)
Compiler: *Everett's Encyclopedia of Useful Knowledge* (1905)
Compiler: *The Columbia Encyclopedia of Useful Knowledge* (1907)
Compiler: *American Home Encyclopedia of Useful Knowledge* (1908)

NEIL, Samuel (1825–1901)
Compiler: *The Home Teacher* (1886–1888)

NEWBOLT, Sir Henry John (1862–1938)
European Editor: *Nelson's Perpetual Looseleaf Encyclopedia* (1926)
European Editor: *Nelson Complete Encyclopedia* (1937)
Former Editor: *Nelson's Encyclopedia: Unabridged* (1940)

European Editor: *Nelson's New Looseleaf Encyclopedia* (1940)

NICHOLSON, William (1753–1815)
Compiler: *The British Encyclopaedia* (1809–1821)

NORTHROP, Henry Davenport (1836–1909)
Compiler: *Standard Cyclopedia* (1897)
Compiler: *X-Rays of Intellectual Light and Universal Knowledge* (1899)
Compiler: *Standard American Book of Knowledge* (1900)
Compiler: *20th Century Cyclopedia of Universal Knowledge* (1901)
Compiler: *American Home Educator and Book of Universal Knowledge* (1903)

NORWOOD, Cyril
Introduction: *The British Encyclopaedia* (1933)
Introduction: *Concise Encyclopaedia* (1933)

NUTTALL, P. Austin
Originator: *The Nuttall Encyclopaedia* (1900–1966)

O'BRIEN, Patrick M.
Assistant Managing Editor: *The World Book*—International Edition (1966–   )

OGAN, Ernest
Editor: *Wonderland of Knowledge* (1933–1934)

OGILVIE, G. W.
Compiler: *Ogilvie's Encyclopaedia of Useful Information* (1891)

O'NEILL, Herbert Charles (b.1879)
Editorial Compiler: *The New Encyclopaedia* (1913)

OSBORN, Loran David (b.1863)
Assistant Editor: *Home and School Reference Work* (1913–1915)

O'SHEA, Michael Vincent (1866–1932)
Editor in Chief: *The World Book* (1917–1932)

PACE, Edward Aloysius (b.1861)
Joint Editor: *Universal Knowledge* (1927–1931)

PACKARD, Alpheus S.
Joint Editor: *New Peoples Cyclopedia of Universal Knowledge* (1903)

PALLEN, Conde Benoit (1858–1929)

Joint Editor: *Universal Knowledge* (1927–1931)

PALMER, Austin Norman (1859–1927)
Assistant Editor: *Complete Library of Universal Knowledge* (1904)
Assistant Editor: *New Idea Self Instructor* (1904)

PARK, Clyde W.
Editor: *Lincoln Library of Essential Information*

PARKER, Bertha Morris
Editor: *Golden Book Encyclopedia* (1959–   )

PARRISH, John Maxey
Editor: *New Standard Encyclopaedia and World Atlas* (1932)
Joint Editor: *Concise Encyclopaedia* (1933)
Joint Editor: *Modern Encyclopaedia for Children* (1933–1948)
Joint Editor: *Wonder Encyclopaedia for Children* (1933)
Joint Editor: *Golden Encyclopaedia for Children* (1934)
Joint Editor: *The Clear Type Encyclopaedia* (1935)
Joint Editor: *Laurel and Gold Encyclopedia* (1935)
Joint Editor: *New Gem Encyclopedia* (1935)
Joint Editor: *Wonder World of Knowledge* (1935–1937)
Joint Editor: *Wonder World Encyclopaedia* (1936–1947)
Joint Editor: *The Standard Encyclopedia* (1937)
Joint Editor: *Encyclopedia of General Knowledge* (1938)
Joint Editor: *Modern Marvels Encyclopedia* (1938)
Joint Editor: *Modern Illustrated Encyclopaedia* (1940)

PARROTT, Sir Edward (1863–1921)
European Editor: *Nelson's Perpetual Looseleaf Encyclopedia* (1917–1920)
Editor: *New Age Encyclopaedia* (1920–1921)

PARRY, Thomas Sargent
Joint Editor: *New Peoples Cyclopedia of Universal Knowledge* (1903)

PARTINGTON, Charles Frederick (d.1857)

Compiler: *The British Cyclopaedia of Arts and Sciences* (1833–1838)

PATRICK, David (1844–1914)
Editor: *Chambers's Encyclopaedia* (1908–1933) (Posthumous)

PATTERSON, Richard Ferrer (b.1888)
Joint Editor: *New Gresham Encyclopaedia* (1921–1924)
Joint Editor: *The Compact Encyclopaedia* (1927)

PAYNE, Barrie
Revision Editor: *Nelson's Encyclopedia: Unabridged* (1940)

PEABODY, Selim Hobert (1829–1903)
Associate Editor: *International Cyclopaedia* (1898)

PEALE, Richard S.
Compiler: *Peale's Popular Educator and Cyclopedia of Reference* (1883–1885)
Compiler: *Home Library of Useful Knowledge* (1886–1887)

PECK, Harry Thurston (1856–1914)
Joint Editor: *International Cyclopaedia* (1898)
Joint Editor: *New International Encyclopedia* (1902–1911)
Editor in Chief: *Standard Illustrated Book of Facts* (1912)

PENGELLY, John Bradford (b.1880)
Associate Editor: *Standard American Encyclopedia* (1937–1941)

PERRY, Thomas Sargent
Assistant Editor: *New Peoples Cyclopedia of Universal Knowledge* (1903)

PETERSON, Sir William (1856–1921)
Canadian Editor: *Nelson's Perpetual Looseleaf Encyclopedia* (1917–1920)

PLAYFAIR, John
Joint Editor: Supplements to the 4th, 5th and 6th editions of the *Encyclopaedia Britannica* (1824)

POLLOCK, H. A.
Editor: *Newnes Pictorial Knowledge* (1932–)

POOLE, Reginald Heber
Joint Editor: *Newnes Pictorial Knowledge* (1954)

PRAY, Kenneth L.
Assistant Editor: *New Practical Reference Library* (1907–1918)

PREECE, Warren E.

Editor: *Encyclopaedia Britannica* (1964–)

PRICE, Frank Webster (b.1901)
General Editor: *New Modern Encyclopedia* (1943–1949)
Editorial Director: *Collier's Encyclopedia* (1949–1959)

PRIOR, C. M.
Editor: *The Nuttall Encyclopedia* (1956)

RAHTZ, Robert
Research Editor: *Handy Encyclopedia of Useful Information* (1946–1947)

RAMSAY, A.
Assistant Editor: *The English Cyclopaedia* (1854–1870)

RANDALL, Paul
Managing Editor: *Wonderland of Knowledge* (1937–)

RAPPOPORT, Angelo Solomon (b.1871)
Joint Editor: *New Gresham Encyclopaedia* (1921–1924)

RAWLINS, M. G.
Advisory Editor: *Younger Children's Encyclopaedia* (1956)

READ, A. J.
Assistant Editor: *Cassell's Concise Cyclopaedia* (1883–1899)

REES, Abraham (1743–1825)
Editor: *Cyclopaedia* (1778–1791)
Editor: *The New Cyclopaedia* (1802–1820)

REYNOLDS, Francis Joseph (1867–1937)
Editor in Chief: *Adair's New Encyclopedia* (1923)
Joint Editor: *New World Wide Cyclopedia* (1928)
Editor in Chief: *Times Encyclopedia and Gazetteer* (1929)
Editor in Chief: *Twentieth Century Encyclopedia* (1930–1934)
Editor in Chief: *World's Popular Encyclopedia* (1937–1942)

RICHARDS, James Albert (b.1890)
Editor: *Outline of Knowledge* (1924–1932)
Managing Editor: *Richards Cyclopedia* (1933–1937)
Original Editor: *New Outline of Knowledge* (1936)

Managing Editor: *Richards Topical Encyclopedia* (1939–1964)

RICHARDSON, Charles Francis (1851–1913)
Associate Editor: *International Cyclopaedia* (1898)

RICHARDSON, Lyon Norman (b.1898)
Advisory Editor: *The How and Why Library* (1948–1959)

RIDGWAY, Atheltsan
Editor: *Everyman's Encyclopaedia* (1931–1932)
Editor: *Cambridge Encyclopaedia* (1934)
Assistant Editor: *Hutchinson's Pictorial Encyclopaedia* (1936)
Editor: *Everyman's Encyclopaedia* (1949–1950)

RIDPATH, John Clark (1840–1900)
Editor: *Standard American Encyclopedia* (1899)

RINES, George Edwin (b.1860)
Editor: Volumes 8–16: *Encyclopedia Americana* (1903–1906)
Joint Editor: *Americana* (1907–1912)
Managing Editor: *United Editors Perpetual Encyclopedia* (1911)

RIPLEY, George (1802–1880)
Joint Editor: *New American Cyclopaedia* (1858–1863)
Joint Editor: *The American Cyclopaedia* (1873–1884)

ROARK, Ruric Neval (1859–1909)
Special Contributor: *Teacher's and Pupil's Cyclopaedia* (1902–1907)
Associate Editor: *Encyclopaedic Current Reference* (1906)
Associate Editor: *New Teacher's and Pupil's Cyclopaedia* (1910–1927)
Associate Editor: *Practical American Encyclopedia* (1911)
Associate Editor: *International Reference Work* (1923–1927)

ROBERTSON-SMITH, William
Joint Editor: *Encyclopaedia Britannica*. 9th ed. (1875–1889)

ROCHELEAU, William Francis
Revision Editor: *Hill's Practical Reference Library of General Knowledge* (1902–1905)
Associate Editor: *New Practical Reference Library* (1907–1912)

Editor in Chief: *Home and School Reference Work* (1913–1915)
Editor: *Source Book* (1924–1936)

ROE, Edward Thomas (b.1847)
Assistant Editor: *Encyclopedia Americana* (1902–1906)

ROLLINS, A. E.
Editor: *Compton's Pictured Newspaper* (1924–1928)

ROSE, Henry John (1800–1873)
Joint Editor: *Encyclopaedia Metropolitana* (1817–1858)

ROSE, Hugh James (1795–1838)
Joint Editor: *Encyclopaedia Metropolitana* (1817–1838)

ROSS, John Merry (1833–1883)
Editor: *Chambers's Encyclopaedia* (1860–1874)
Editor: *Globe Encyclopaedia of Universal Knowledge* (1876–1881)
Editor: *Student's Encyclopaedia of Universal Knowledge* (1883)
Editor: *Illustrated Globe Encyclopaedia* (1890–1893)

RUOFF, Henry Woldmar (1867–1935)
Compiler: *Century Book of Facts* (1902–1908)
Compiler: *Universal Manual of Ready Reference* (1904)
Editor: *Standard Dictionary of Facts* (1908–1916)
Editor: *The Volume Library* (1911–1912)
Editor: *Human Interest Library* (1914–1926)
Editor: *Circle of Knowledge* (1934)

RUSSELL, Thomas Herbert (b.1862)
Joint Editor: *The Knowledge Book* (1915)
Joint Editor: *The Knowledge Library* (1918)
Joint Editor: *New Knowledge Library* (1919)

SAINT CLAIR, Gordon (b.1885)
Art Director: *The World Book* (1929–)

SALT, Laura E.
General Editor: *Oxford Junior Encyclopaedia* (1948–)

SANDEMAN, George
Editor: *The Harmsworth Encyclopaedia* (1905–1906)

British Editor: *Nelson's Encyclopaedia* (1906–1907)

SANDFORD, Sir D. K.
Contributor: *The Popular Encyclopaedia* (1841–1893)

SCOTT, George Lewis (1708–1780)
Editor: Supplement to the *Cyclopaedia* (1753)

SCOTT, Walter Dill (b.1869)
Chairman: Editorial Board: *American Peoples Encyclopedia* (1948–1956)

SEGUIN, Jeanne
Editor: *The Boys and Girls Encyclopaedia* (1960)

SENTMAN, Everett Edgar (b.1913)
Editor in Chief: *The American Educator* (1955–   )
Editor in Chief: *Wonderland of Knowledge* (1955–   )

SHAHAN, Thomas Joseph, *bp.* (1857–1932)
Joint Editor: *Universal Knowledge* (1927–1931)

SHAPP, Martha Glauber
Editor: *New Book of Knowledge* (1966–   )

SHELTON, Harold
Editor: *The World Book*—British Empire Edition (1936–1937)

SHEPHERD, Walter
Associate Editor: *Newnes Pictorial Knowledge* (1960–   )

SHERMAN, Robert E.
Revision Editor: *Comprehensive Pictorial Encyclopedia* (1942–1943)

SHERWOOD, Elizabeth J.
Joint Editor: *Columbia Encyclopedia* (1950–1959)

SHORES, Louis
Library Consultant—Advisory Editor: *Collier's Encyclopedia* (1946–1959)
Editor in Chief: *Collier's Encyclopedia* (1960–   )

SINCLAIR, Robert
Joint Editor: *Oxford Junior Encyclopedia* (1948–   )

SINGER, Edgar Arthur (b.1873)
Joint Editor: *New Universal Handbook of Necessary Information* (1920–1937)

SMEDLEY, Edward (1788–1836)
Editor: *Encyclopaedia Metropolitana* (1817–1836)

SMELLIE, William (1740–1795)
Joint Originator and Editor: *Encyclopaedia Britannica*. 1st edition. (1771–1773)

SMITH, Alan H.
Executive Editor: *Encyclopedia Americana* (1964–   )

SMITH, Albertus V.
Assistant Editor: *New Practical Reference Library* (1907–1918)

SMITH, Gilbert C. E.
Managing Editor: *The World Book*—International Edition (1966–   )

SMITH, John J.
Executive Editor: *Encyclopedia Americana* (1964–   )

SPECK, Gerald E.
Editor: *Wonder Book Encyclopaedia* (1956)
Editor: *Junior Pictorial Encyclopaedia* (1959)
Joint Editor: *Encyclopaedia of Modern Knowledge* (1965)

SPOFFORD, Ainsworth Rand (1825–1908)
Revision Editor: *New Cabinet Cyclopaedia and Treasury of Knowledge* (1891–1899)
Joint Editor: *New National Cyclopaedia and Treasury* (1899)
Joint Editor: *XX Century Cyclopaedia and Atlas* (1901)
Joint Editor: *New Twentieth Century Cyclopaedia and Dictionary* (1903)
Joint Editor: *New and Complete Universal Self Pronouncing Encyclopaedia* (1905)
Joint Editor: *Winstons Encyclopedia* (1909)

STANFORD, Harold Melvin (b.1875)
Chief Editor: *Standard Reference Work* (1912–1927)
Editorial Director: *National Encyclopedia for the Home, School and Library* (1923)
Editor in Chief: *New Standard Encyclopedia* (1930–1933)

STEIN, Jess
Editor: *Basic Everyday Encyclopedia* (1954)

STEVENS, Charles McClellan (b.1861)
Joint Editor: *New Twentieth Century Cyclopaedia and Dictionary* (1903)

STEVENS, John L.
   Special Contributor: *Teacher's and Pu-*
   pil's Cyclopaedia (1902–1907)
   Contributor: *Encyclopaedic Current Ref-*
   erence (1906)
STEWART, Dugald
   Joint Editor: Supplements to the 4th, 5th
   and 6th editions of the *Encyclopaedia*
   Britannica (1824)
STEWART, J. A.
   Joint Editor: *Oxford Encyclopaedia*
   (1828–1831)
STODDARD, George Dinsmore (b.1897)
   Editor in Chief: *New Wonder World En-*
   cyclopedia (1959–1960)
   Editor in Chief: *New Wonder World Cul-*
   tural Library (1962–1964)
   Editor in Chief: *The Cultural Library*
   (1964–   )
STONEHOUSE, Felix
   Assistant Editor: *New Royal Cyclopaedia*
   and Encyclopaedia (1788)
STOWELL, Gordon
   Editor: *The Waverley Encyclopaedia*
   (1953)
   Editor: *The Book of Knowledge* (British)
   (1959–   )
STUART, Charles Leonard (b.1868)
   Editor: *Crown Encyclopedia and Ga-*
   zetteer (1903)
   Editor: *Continental Encyclopedia* (1905)
   Editor in Chief: *New Century Reference*
   Library (1907)
   Editor: *Current Cyclopedia of Reference*
   (1909)
   Editor in Chief: *Everybody's Cyclopedia*
   (1911–1912)
   Editor: *People's Cyclopedia* (1914)
STUART, D. T.
   Revision Editor: *Chambers's Condensed*
   Encyclopedia (1895)
SULTZER, Kenneth D.
   Managing Editor: *The Grolier Universal*
   Encyclopedia (1949)
SUMMERSALE, Sir John
   Editor: *The Penguin Encyclopaedia*
   (1965–   )
SUZALLO, Henry (1875–1933)
   Editor in Chief: *National Encyclopedia*
   (1932–1960) (Posthumous)
SYLVESTER, Charles Herbert

Editor in Chief: *New Practical Reference*
   Library (1907–1918)
SYMONDS, Francis Addington (b.1893)
   Editor: *Pearson's Everything Within*
   (1957)

TAYLOR, Charles Ralph (b.1877)
   Editor: *World Wide Illustrated Encyclo-*
   pedia (1935)
   Editor: *New American Encycloped a*
   (1938–1962)
   Editor: *University Illustrated Encyclop3-*
   dia (1938–1940)
   Editor: *Home University Encycloped a*
   (1941–   )
   Editor: *Encyclopedic Library of Knowl-*
   edge (1944)
   Editor in Chief: *American Family Ency-*
   clopedia (1963–   )
TAYLOR, John W.
   Editor: *Standard Dictionary of Facts*
   (1925–1927)
TEDFORD, John D.
   Executive Editor: *The Book of Knowledge*
   (1963–   )
THATCHER, Oliver Joseph (b.1857)
   Editor in Chief: *Library of Original*
   Sources (1907–1915)
THATCHER, Virginia Sarah (b.1917)
   Editor in Chief: *Universal World Refer-*
   ence Encyclopedia (1958–   )
   Editor in Chief: *Golden Home and H gh*
   School Encyclopedia (1961–   )
THOMPSON, Eunice W.
   Managing Editor: *The American Educctor*
   (1942–   )
THOMPSON, Holland (1873–1940)
   Joint Editor: *The Book of Knowledge*
   (1912–1940)
THOMSON, T.
   Contributor: *The Popular Encyclopaedia*
   (1841–1893)
THONE, J.
   Assistant Editor: *The English Cyclopaedia*
   (1854–1870)
TRAILL, T. S.
   Editor: *Encyclopaedia Britannica*. 8th ed.
   (1855–1860)
TYTLER, James (c.1747–1805)
   Editor: *Encyclopaedia Britannica*. 2nd ed.
   (1777–1784)

ULERY, Cloyce Benjamin (b.1889)
Joint Editor: *American Home Library* (1930–1953)
UNSTEAD, R. J.
Joint Editor: *Black's Children's Encyclopedia* (1961–)

VAN CASTEEL, Gerald (b.1860)
Joint Editor: *Appleton's New Practical Cyclopedia* (1910–1920)
Member: Editorial Board: *New Universal Encyclopedia* (1930)
VAN DOREN, Carl Clinton (1885–1950)
Advisory Editor: *World Wide Illustrated Encyclopedia* (1935)
Advisory Editor: *University Illustrated Encyclopedia* (1938–1940)
Advisory Editor: *Home University Encyclopedia* (1941–)
VAUGHAN, L. Brent (b.1873)
Editor: *Hill's Practical Encyclopedia* (1901–1902)
Editor: *The School Library Encyclopedia* (1901–1902)
Editor: *Hill's Practical Reference Library of General Knowledge* (1902–1905)
VESEY-FITZGERALD, Brian
Joint Editor: *Odhams Encyclopaedia for Children* (1961)
Joint Editor: *Odhams Wonder World of Knowledge* (1961)
VETHAKE, Henry (1792–1866)
Assistant Editor: *Encyclopedia Americana* (1829–1849)
VILLIERS, Arnold
Editor: *Routledge's Everyman's Cyclopaedia* (1910)
VIZETELLY, Francis Horace (1864–1938)
Editor: *Funk and Wagnall's New Standard Encyclopedia of Universal Knowledge* (1931–1943)
Editor: *New International Yearbook* (1936–1938)

WADE, Herbert Treadwell (b.1872)
Editor: Supplement (Volumes 24–25) to *New International Encyclopedia* (1935)
Editor: *New International Yearbook* (1924–1935)

WAKEFIELD, Sherman Day (b.1894)
Joint Editor: *Home University Encyclopedia* (1961–)
WALLACE, Sir Donald McKenzie
Joint Editor: *Encyclopaedia Britannica.* 10th ed. (1902–1903)
WALLACE, R.
Editor: *Cassell's Popular Educator* (1852–1910)
WALSH, James Joseph (1865–1942)
Joint Editor: *Universal Knowledge* (1927–1931)
WAPLES, Douglas (b.1893)
Revision Editor of Bibliographies: *The World Book* (1941)
WATSON, Jane Werner (b.1915)
Revision Editor: *New Golden Encyclopedia* (1963)
WEBSTER, Richard
Editor: *The Volume Library* (1939)
WHIPPLE, Chandler
Editor in Chief: *The Children's Encyclopedia* (1959)
WHITAKER, Joseph (1820–1895)
Compiler: *Whitaker's Almanack* (1868–1895)
WHITE, Bertha Maud (b.1881)
Literary Editor: *Home and School Reference Work* (1913–1915)
Associate Editor: *Wonderland of Knowledge* (1937–)
Assistant Editor: *The American Educator* (1941–)
WHITE, Henry Adelbert (b.1880)
Revision Editor: *New Century Book of Facts* (1927–1941)
WHITELAW, Alexander
Editor: *The Popular Encyclopaedia* (1841–1877)
WHITNEY, David C.
Managing Editor: *The World Book* (1962–1963)
Editor in Chief: *Encyclopedia Americana* (1964–1965)
WHITNEY, William Dwight (1827–1894)
Editor: *The Century Dictionary* (1889–1899)
Editor: *The Century Dictionary and Cyclopaedia* (1901–1911)
WICKS, Helen

Associate Editor: *Consolidated Webster Comprehensive Encyclopedic Dictionary* (1954)

WIGGLESWORTH, Edward (1804–1876)
Assistant Editor: *Encyclopedia Americana* (1829–1849)

WILGUS, Alva Curtis (b.1897)
Advisory Editor: *The Grolier Universal Encyclopedia* (1944–   )

WILKES, John (1727–1797)
Compiler: *Encyclopaedia Londinensis* (1810–1829)

WILLIAMS, Talcott (1849–1928)
Joint Editor: *New International Encyclopedia* (1914–1917)

WILLIAMS, Thomas
Co-editor: *The Complete Dictionary of Arts and Sciences* (1764–1766)

WILLIAMS, William Tom (b.1884)
Advisory Editor: *Children's Guide to Knowledge* (1949)

WILLSEY, Joseph H.
Compiler: *Harper's Book of Facts* (1895–1906)

WOOD, Florence Dorothy
Revision Editor: *The Champlin Encyclopedia, vs. 7–12* (1946–1950)

WOOD, Frances Elizabeth
Revision Editor: *The Champlin Encyclopedia vs. 1–6* (1946–1950)

WOOD, James
Editor: *The Nuttall Encyclopaedia* (1900–1920)

WOODWARD, Bernard Bolingbroke (1816–1869)
Revision Editor: *Maunder's Treasury of Knowledge and Library of Reference* (1873)

WORKMAN, Bernard A.

Editor: *New Caxton Encyclopedia* (1966–   )
Editor in Chief: *Purnell's New English Encyclopaedia* (1966–   )

WORTHY, William
Joint Editor: *Black's Children's Encyclopedia* (1961–   )

WRIGHT, Carroll Davidson (1840–1909)
Editor in Chief: *New Century Book of Facts* (1909–1926)

WRIGHT, Ernest Hunter (b.1882)
Joint Editor: *Richards Cyclopedia* (1933–1937)
Joint Editor: *Richards Topical Encyclopedia* (1939–1964)

WRIGHT, Mrs. Mary Heritage
Joint Editor: *Richards Cyclopedia* (1933–1937)
Joint Editor: *Richards Topical Encyclopedia* (1939–1964)
Advisory Editor: *Unified Encyclopedia* (1961–1964)

WYNNE, John Joseph (b.1859)
Joint Editor: *Universal Knowledge* (1927–1931)

YUST, Walter (b.1894)
Associate Editor: *Britannica Junior* (1934–1937)
Associate Editor: *Encyclopaedia Britannica* (1937–1938)
Editor: *Britannica Junior* (1938–1958)
Editor: *Encyclopaedia Britannica* (1939–1958)

ZELENY, Robert O.
Managing Editor: *The World Book* (1964–   )

ZIM, Herbert Spencer (b.1909)
Editor in Chief: *Our Wonderful World* (1955–   )

II

Index OF PUBLISHERS AND PRINCIPAL DISTRIBUTORS AND THE ENCYCLOPEDIC WORKS WHICH HAVE BEEN ISSUED UNDER THEIR IMPRINTS

●●●

ASPREY & CO., London
Concise Pocket Encyclopaedia (1925)
AVIL PRINTING CO., Philadelphia
Anglo-American Encyclopedia and Dictionary (1902)

J. BALFOUR, Edinburgh
Encyclopaedia Britannica. 2nd ed. (1777–1784)
A. S. BARNES & CO., New York
The Children's Encyclopedia (1959)
BARTLETT & HINTON, Oxford (*see also* T. Kelly)
Oxford Encyclopaedia (1828–1831)
C. B. BEACH & CO., Chicago and New York (*see also* Howard-Severance Co.)
Students Reference Work (1902)
BELFORD-CLARKE CO., Chicago
Americanized Encyclopaedia Britannica (1890)
BELL & MACFARQUHAR, Edinburgh and London
Encyclopaedia Britannica. 1st ed. (1771–1773)
Encyclopaedia Britannica. 2nd ed. (1777–1784)
Encyclopaedia Britannica. 3rd ed. (1797)
Encyclopaedia Britannica. 4th ed. (1810)
BELLOWS-DURHAM CO., Chicago (formerly Ralph Durham Co.)
American Educator (1926–1930)
BIBLE HOUSE, Chicago (*see also* Columbia House)
Everett's Encyclopedia of Useful Knowledge (1905)
ADAM & CHARLES BLACK, Edinburgh and London
Encyclopaedia Britannica. 7th ed. (1842)
Encyclopaedia Britannica. 8th ed. (1853–1860)
Encyclopaedia Britannica. 9th ed. (1875–1888)
Encyclopaedia Britannica. 10th ed. (1902–1903)
Black's Children's Encyclopedia (1961–)
BLACKIE & SON, Glasgow and London
The Popular Encyclopaedia (1841–1893)
Blackie's Modern Cyclopaedia of Universal Information (1889–1897)
WILLIAM BLACKWOOD, Edinburgh
Edinburgh Encyclopaedia (1830)
P. BLAKISTON CO., Philadelphia
Handy Encyclopedia of Useful Information (1946–1947)
BLUE RIBBON BOOKS, New York and Boston (*see also* Books Inc.) *World Wide Illustrated Encyclopedia* (1937)

BOBLEY PUBLISHING CORP., New York (afterwards Cove Industries)
Illustrated World Encyclopedia (1958–1965)
T. BONAR, Edinburgh
Encyclopaedia Britannica. 2v. suppl. to the 3rd ed. (1801–1803)
BOOKS INC., New York (a subsidiary of the Publishers Co.)
World Wide Illustrated Encyclopedia (1937)
New American Encyclopedia (1938–1963)
Home University Encyclopedia (1941–)
New Human Interest Library (1943–)
American Family Encyclopedia (1963–)
BRITISH BOOKS, London
Golden Encyclopaedia for Children (1934)
J. BROWN, Edinburgh
Encyclopaedia Perthensis (1816)
M. T. BROWN, Davenport, Iowa (*see also* A. J. Johnson & Sons)
Johnson's New Universal Cyclopaedia (1884)
BROWN, EAGER & HULL CO., Toledo
New National Cyclopaedia and Treasury (1899)
DAVID BRYCE & SON, Glasgow
Everyone's Cyclopaedia (1907)
BUFTON PUBLISHING CO., Kansas City, Mo.
Bufton's Universal Cyclopaedia (1919)
L. J. BULLARD CO., Cleveland, Ohio
How and Why Library (1934–1941)
How and Why Program (1948–1959)
A. L. BURT CO., New York
Chambers's Condensed Encyclopedia (1895)

CAMBRIDGE SOCIETY LTD., Montreal
Cambridge Encyclopaedia (1934)
CAMBRIDGE UNIVERSITY PRESS, Cambridge and London
Encyclopaedia Britannica. 11th ed. (1910–1911)
CAREY, LEA & BLANCHARD, Philadelphia (*see also* Lea & Blanchard)
Encyclopaedia Americana (1829–1833)
CASSELL & CO., London
Cassell's Concise Cyclopaedia (1883–1899)
Cassell's Miniature Cyclopaedia (1888–1898)
Cassell's Storehouse of General Information (1891–1894)
Cassell's Cabinet Cyclopaedia (1904)
Cassell's Encyclopaedia of General Information (1908)

Cassell's Modern Encyclopaedia (1934)
CASSELL, PETTER, GALPIN & CO., New York and London
Cassell's Popular Educator (1852–1910)
The Encyclopaedic Dictionary (1879–1888)
CAXTON CO., Chicago (*see also* Dixon & Hanson)
School Library Encyclopedia (1901–1902)
CAXTON PUBLISHING CO., London
World of the Children (1948–1957)
Caxton Encyclopaedia (1960–   )
Caxton World of Knowledge (1961–   )
New World Library (1964–   )
New Caxton Encyclopedia (1966–   )
THE CENTURY CO., New York
The Century Dictionary (1889–1899)
The Century Dictionary and Cyclopaedia (1901–1911)
WILLIAM & ROBERT CHAMBERS, Edinburgh and London
Chambers's Information for the People (1857–1880)
Chambers's Encyclopaedia (1860–1935)
CHICAGO BOOK CO., Chicago (*see also* Dixon & Hanson)
Hill's Practical Encyclopedia (1901–1902)
C. C. CHILDS, New York
Treasury of Knowledge and Library of Reference (1850–1876)
CHRISTIAN HERALD PUBLISHING CO., New York (*see also* the Syndicate Publishing Co.)
Crown Encyclopedia and Gazetteer (1903)
World Wide Encyclopedia and Gazetteer (1908)
New World Encyclopedia (1919)
P. F. COLLIER & SON, New York (afterwards the Crowell-Collier Educational Corp.)
Chandler's Encyclopedia (1898)
Collier's New Encyclopedia (1902–1929)
University Encyclopedia of Twentieth Century Knowledge (1902)
New Complete Condensed Encyclopedia (1909)
National Encyclopedia (1932–1950)
Columbia Encyclopedia. By arrangement. (1936)
Collier's Encyclopedia (1949–1951)
Merit Students Encyclopedia (1967–   )
WILLIAM COLLINS & SON, London and Glasgow (Collins Clear Type Press) (*see also* Odhams Press)
Concise Encyclopaedia (1933)

Modern Encyclopaedia for Children (1933–1948)
Clear Type Encyclopaedia (1935)
Laurel and Gold Encyclopedia (1935)
New Gem Encyclopedia (1935)
Wonder World of Knowledge (1935–1937)
International Encyclopedia and Dictionary (1936)
Wonder World Encyclopaedia (1936)
Encyclopedia of General Knowledge (1938)
Modern Marvels Encyclopaedia (1938)
Modern Standard Encyclopaedia (1938)
Modern Illustrated Encyclopaedia (1940)
New Age Encyclopaedia, World Atlas and Sports Supplement (1957–1963)
New Wonder World Encyclopaedia (1965)
COLUMBIA EDUCATIONAL BOOKS, INC. Chicago (*see also* Consolidated Book Publishers)
Nelson's Encyclopedia: Unabridged (1940)
Webster's Columbia Encyclopedic Dictionary (1940)
Webster's Comprehensive Encyclopedic Dictionary (1941)
Webster's Encyclopedic Dictionary (1941–1942)
Universal World Reference Encyclopedia (1945)
COLUMBIA HOUSE, Chicago (*see also* Bible House)
The Columbia Encyclopedia of Useful Knowledge (1907)
American Home Encyclopedia of Useful Knowledge (1908)
COLUMBIA UNIVERSITY PRESS, New York
Columbia Encyclopedia (1935–   )
F. E. COMPTON & CO., Chicago (a subsidiary of Encyclopaedia Britannica Inc., since 1963)
New Students Reference Work (1909–1920)
The How and Why Library (1913–1919)
Compton's Pictured Encyclopedia (1922–   )
COMPTON-JOHNSON CO., Chicago
Pictured Knowledge (1916–1919)
W. B. CONKEY CO., Chicago (printers to Holst Publishing Co.)
Practical American Encyclopedia (1911)
Unrivalled Encyclopedia (1911)
CONNER & COOKE, New York

Treasury of Knowledge and Library of Reference (1833)

CONSOLIDATED BOOK PUBLISHERS, Chicago (*see also* Columbia Educational Books Inc.)
New World Wide Cyclopedia (1928)
University of Knowledge (1937–1938)
Standard American Encyclopedia (1939–1941)
Library of Essential Knowledge (1942–1954)
Universal World Reference Encyclopedia (1945–   )
Champlin Encyclopedia (1946–1950)
World Home Reference Encyclopedia (1951)
Consolidated Webster Comprehensive Encyclopedic Dictionary (1954)
Consolidated Webster Encyclopedic Dictionary (1954)

CONSOLIDATED WORLD RESEARCH SOCIETY, Toronto and London
Consolidated Encyclopedia (1939–   )

ARNOLD CONSTABLE, Edinburgh
Encyclopaedia Britannica. 5th ed. (1817)
Encyclopaedia Britannica. 6th ed. (1823)
Supplements to the 4th, 5th and 6th editions of the Encyclopaedia Britannica (1824)

CONTINENTAL PUBLISHING CO., Wheeling, W. Va. and New York
New Century Book of Facts (1926–   )

COVE INDUSTRIES, New York (*formerly* the Bobley Publishing Corp.)
Illustrated World Encyclopedia (1966–   )

COWLES EDUCATIONAL BOOKS INC., New York
Cowles Comprehensive Encyclopedia—The Volume Library (1963–   )

CROWELL-COLLIER & MACMILLAN INC. (Crowell-Collier Educational Corp.)
Collier's Encyclopedia (1949–   )
Merit Students Encyclopedia (1967–   )

W. D. CUMMINGS, Pittsburgh (*see also* A. J. Johnson & Sons)
Johnson's New Universal Cyclopaedia (1876–1878)

J. & J. CUNDOE, London
The Imperial Encyclopaedia (1812)

CURRENT ENCYCLOPEDIA CO., Chicago
The Current Encyclopedia (1901)

DAILY EXPRESS PUBLICATIONS, London
Daily Express Encyclopaedia (1934)

DE BOWER-CHAPLINE CO., Chicago
Everybody's Encyclopedia (1909)
La Salle Extension University Encyclopedia (1909)
Webster's Universal Encyclopedia (1909)

J. M. DENT & CO., London
The Everyman Encyclopaedia (1913–1914)
Everyman's Encyclopaedia. 2nd ed. (1931–1932)
Everyman's Encyclopaedia. 3rd ed. (1950)
Everyman's Encyclopaedia. 4th ed. (1958)
Everyman's Encyclopaedia. 5th ed. (1967)

DICTIONARY & ENCYCLOPEDIA CO., New York and Chicago
Universal Reference Library (1900)

EDWARD & CHARLES DILLY, London
Encyclopaedia Britannica. Pirated reprint. (1771–1773)

DIXON & HANSON. Chicago, New York, Toledo (succeeded by Dixon-Hanson-Bellows Co.)
Hill's Practical Reference Library of General Knowledge (1902–1905)
New Pratcical Reference Library (1907)

DIXON-HANSON-BELLOWS CO., Chicago (succeeded by Hanson-Bellows Co.)
New Practical Reference Library (1911)

DIXON-RUCKER CO., Chicago
Home and School Reference Work (1913–1915)

THOMAS DOBSON, Philadelphia
Encyclopaedia (1798). *see Encyclopaedia Britannica. 3rd ed.*
Supplement to the Encyclopaedia Britannica. 3v. (1800–1803)

DODD, MEAD & CO., New York
International Cyclopaedia (1898)
New International Encyclopedia (1902–1930)

DOMINION EDUCATOR CO., Toronto (*see* United Educators Inc.)
Dominion Educator (1922–1935)

DOUBLEDAY & CO., New York
Information Please Almanac (1947)

DOUBLEDAY, DORAN & CO., New York
Doubleday's Encyclopedia (1931–1943)
Facts (1934–1941)
New Concise Pictorial Encyclopedia (1938)

E. R. DU MONT, Chicago and New York
New Twentieth Century Cyclopaedia and Dictionary (1903)

A. J. DUBOIS, Chicago
Handy Cyclopedia of Things Worth Knowing (1911)

RALPH DURHAM CO., Chicago (afterwards Bellows-Durham Co.)
The American Educator (1919–1925)
E. P. DUTTON & CO., New York (*see also* J. M. Dent & Co.)
Routledge's Everyman's Cyclopaedia (1910)
The Everyman Encyclopaedia (1913–1914)
Everyman's Encyclopaedia (2nd ed. 1931–1932)

EATON & MAINS, New York
New Peoples Cyclopedia of Universal Knowledge (1903)
EDUCATIONAL BOOK CO., New York (*see also* Amalgamated Press)
The Children's Encyclopaedia (1925–1953)
New Universal Encyclopaedia (1951–1959)
Modern University Encyclopaedia (1957)
EDUCATIONAL BOOK GUILD, New York (afterwards Bobley Publishing Corp. and Cove Industries Inc.)
Illustrated Home Library Encyclopedia (1955)
EDUCATIONAL ENTERPRISES, Washington, D. C.
National Encyclopedia (1951–   )
EDUCATORS ASSOCIATION, New York
The Volume Library (1922–1960)
ENCYCLOPAEDIA BRITANNICA CO. (INC.), Chicago, New York, London
Encyclopaedia Britannica. 11th ed. (1910–1911)
Encyclopaedia Britannica. 12th ed. (1922)
Encyclopaedia Britannica. 13th ed. (1926)
Encyclopaedia Britannica. 14th ed. (1929–   )
Britannica Junior (1934–   )
Children's Britannica (1960–1961)
ENCYCLOPAEDIA PUBLISHING CO., London
The People's Encyclopaedia (1873)
ENCYCLOPEDIA AMERICANA CORP., New York (*see also* Americana Corporation)
Encyclopedia Americana (1918–1924)
ENCYCLOPEDIA LIBRARY INC., New York (Distributors)
Encyclopedia Library (1942–1943)
Universal World Reference Encyclopedia (1945)
ENGLISH UNIVERSITIES PRESS, London

Book of General Knowledge (1938–1949)
Teach Yourself Concise Encyclopaedia of General Knowledge (1956–1963)
EXECUTIVES GUILD, Kansas City
Library of Knowledge (1937)
B. FELLOWES, London (*see also* F. & J. Rivington)
Encyclopaedia Metropolitana (1817–1821)
J. G. FERGUSON CO., Chicago
Everyday Reference Library (1951–   )
FIDELITY PUBLISHING HOUSE, New York and Chicago
Modern Universal Encyclopedia (1910)
FIELD ENTERPRISES EDUCATIONAL CORPORATION, Chicago (successors to the Quarrie Corp.)
World Book (1945–   )
FIFTH AVENUE LIBRARY SOCIETY, New York
Anglo-American Encyclopedia and Dictionary (1906)
FLEETWAY HOUSE, London (*see also* Amalgamated Press)
Practical Knowledge for All (1934)
FOSTER PUBLISHING CO., Philadelphia
Home Educator in Necessary Knowledge (1905)
FOSTER, TEMIN & OLIVER, New York
New Universal Encyclopedia (1930)
FRONTIER PRESS CO., Buffalo, N. Y.
Standard Dictionary of Facts (1908–1927)
Lincoln Library of Essential Information (1924–   )
FUNK & WAGNALLS CO., New York and London (*see also* Unicorn Press)
Columbian Cyclopaedia (1899)
Funk & Wagnalls Standard Encyclopedia of the World's Knowledge (1913)
Pocket Library of the World's Essential Knowledge (1929) (London)
Funk and Wagnalls New Standard Encyclopedia of Universal Knowledge (1931–1937)
New International Encyclopedia (1935)

R. GARRIGUE, New York
Iconographic Encyclopaedia of Science, Literature and Art (1851)
GEBBIE & CO., Philadelphia
New Cabinet Cyclopaedia and Treasury of Knowledge (1891–1899)
XX Century Cyclopaedia and Atlas (1901)
GENERAL PRESS DISTRIBUTORS, Toronto (*see also* United Educators)

New General Encyclopedia (1935–   )
J. L. GIBSON CO., Philadelphia
    Chambers's Information for the People
    (1858)
GILBERT PUBLISHING CO., Chicago (*see also* H. G. Allen & Co.)
    Imperial Encyclopedia and Dictionary
    (1903)
W. GILL, Syracuse
    The School Encyclopedia (1899)
GLOBE PUBLISHING CO., Philadelphia
    (*see also* Lippincott)
    Anglo-American Encyclopedia and Dictionary (1904)
GOLDEN PRESS, New York (*formerly* Simon & Schuster)
    Golden Home and High School Encyclopedia (1961–   )
    Golden Treasury of Knowledge (1961–   )
    New Golden Encyclopedia (1963–   )
GRANVILLE PRESS, London
    Everybody's Everyday Reference Book for Home and Office (1905)
    Pannell's Reference Book for Home and Office (1905–1906)
GRAY PUBLISHING CO., Chicago (*see also* Holst Publishing Co.)
    New Teacher's and Pupil's Cyclopaedia (1913)
S. W. GREEN'S SON, New York (*see also* American Book Exchange)
    Library of Universal Knowledge (1880–1881)
GRESHAM PUBLISHING CO., London and Glasgow
    New Popular Encyclopaedia (1901)
    The Modern Cyclopaedia (1906–1907)
    New Gresham Encyclopaedia (1921–1924)
    The Compact Encyclopaedia (1927)
J. J. GRIFFIN & CO., London
    Encyclopaedia Metropolitana. 2nd ed. (1845–1858)
GRIFFITH, FARRAN & CO., London
    Ready Reference (1890–1894)
GROLIER INC., New York (*see also* Grolier Society Ltd., Americana Corp., J. A. Richards Inc., Spencer Press)
    The Book of Knowledge (1912–1966)
    Grolier Encyclopedia (1944–1964)
    American Peoples Encyclopedia (1962–   )
    Our Wonderful World (1962–   )
    Encyclopedia International (1963–1964)
    The Grolier Universal Encyclopedia (1965–   )
    New Book of Knowledge (1966–   )

GROLIER SOCIETY LTD., London (*see also* Waverley Book Co., Educational Book Co., New Educational Press)
    Book of Knowledge. British (1962–   )
    Children's Encyclopaedia. Mee (1962–   )
    Modern Children's Library of Knowledge (1962–   )
GROSSET & DUNLAP, New York
    Modern Encyclopedia (1936)
    Illustrated Encyclopedia (1959)

HAMILTON BOOK CO., New York
    Practical Home Encyclopedia (1909)
HAMPDEN PUBLISHING CO., Springfield, Mass.
    Cyclopedia, Dictionary and Atlas of the World (1909)
HANSON-BELLOWS CO., Chicago (successors to Dixon, Hanson & Bellows: afterwards Hanson-Roach-Fowler Co.)
    New Practical Reference Library (1912–1915)
HANSON-ROACH-FOWLER CO., Chicago (formerly the Hanson-Bellows Co.)
    New Practical Reference Library (1917–1918)
    The World Book (1917–1918) (acquired by W. F. Quarrie Co.)
HARPER & BROTHERS, New York
    Dictionary of Science, Literature and Art (1844)
    Harper's Book of Facts (1895–1906)
GEORGE HARRAP LTD., London
    Columbia Encyclopedia. Distributors in Great Britain. (1935)
JOHN HARRIS, London
    Lexicon Technicum (1704)
HAWTHORN BOOKS, New York
    Hutchinson's New 20th Century Encyclopedia (1965–   )
JOHN A. HERTEL CO., Chicago
    Circle of Knowledge (1934)
J. A. HILL & CO., New York
    Anglo-American Encyclopedia and Dictionary (1906)
    New American Comprehensive Encyclopedia (1906)
HODDER & STOUGHTON, London
    Student's Encyclopaedia of Universal Knowledge (1883)
ALEX. HOGG, London
    New Royal Cyclopaedia and Encyclopaedia (1788)
A. J. HOLMAN & CO., Philadelphia
    Twentieth Century Household Library (1903)
HOLST PUBLISHING CO., Boone, Iowa

and Chicago (*see also* W. B. Conkey Co.)
Teacher's and Pupil's Cyclopaedia (1902–1907)
Encyclopaedic Current Reference (1906)
New Teacher's and Pupil's Cyclopaedia (1910–1927)
International Reference Work (1923–1927)
Progressive Reference Library (1928–1939)
H. HOLT & CO., New York
New Champlin Cyclopedia for Young Folks (1924)
HOME LIBRARY ASSOCIATION, Chicago (*see also* R. S. Peale & Co.)
Home Library of Useful Knowledge (1886–1887)
HOME LIBRARY BOOK CO., London (*see also* George Newnes Ltd.)
Newnes Pictorial Knowledge (1932)
J. M. HOWARD & CO., Chicago and Philadelphia (*see also* C. B. Beach & Co., Howard-Severance Co.)
Students Cyclopaedia (1900)
HOWARD-SEVERANCE CO., Chicago and Philadelphia (*see also* J. M. Howard Co., C. B. Beach & Co.)
Students Reference Work (1902)
HUBBARD BROS., Philadelphia
Encyclopaedia Britannica. Pirated (1884)
HUTCHINSON & CO., London
Hutchinson's Pictorial Encyclopaedia (1936–1937)
Hutchinson's 20th Century Encyclopedia (1948–1955)
Hutchinson's New Twentieth Century Encyclopaedia (1965–   )

INGRAM & LLOYD, Nashville, Tenn. (Distributors)
The British Encyclopaedia 3rd ed. (1819–1821)
W. INNYS, London
Cyclopaedia. 7th ed. (1751–1752)
INTERNATIONAL AMERICAN CO., Chicago
International American Encyclopedia (c.1943)
INTERNATIONAL BOOK DISTRIBUTORS, Miami (*see also* Publishers Co.)
World Educator Encyclopedia (1964–   )
INTERNATIONAL PRESS, Philadelphia and Chicago (*see also* John C. Winston Co., Publicity Publishing Co.)
New and Complete Universal Self Pronouncing Encyclopedia (1905)

New Wonder Book Cyclopedia of World Knowledge (1954)
INTERNATIONAL PUBLISHING CO., Philadelphia
Popular Compendium of Useful Information (1901)
Golden Treasury of Useful Information (1902)
INTERNATIONAL READER'S LEAGUE, New York (*see also* Publishers Periodical Service Bureau)
International's World Reference Encyclopedia (1942)
Encyclopedic Library of Knowledge (1944)
INTERNATIONAL UNIVERSITY SOCIETY, London and Nottingham
Golden Pathway to a Treasury of Knowledge (1931–1939)
INTERSTATE PUBLISHING CO., Chicago (*see also* Welles Bros.)
Golden Treasury of Useful Information (1902)
Standard Reference Work (1912)

T. C. & E. C. JACK, London and Edinburgh
Globe Encyclopaedia of Universal Information (1876–1881)
Jack's Reference Book for Home and Office (1908–1929)
The New Encyclopaedia (1913)
J. A. & U. P. JAMES, Cincinnati
Library of General Knowledge (1850)
ALVIN J. JOHNSON & SONS, New York
Johnson's New Universal Cyclopaedia (1876–1884)
Johnson's Universal Cyclopaedia (1893–1897) (*see also* Appleton)
JOHN JONES, Coventry
Complete Dictionary of Arts and Sciences (1764–1766)

GEORGE KEARSLEY, London
The English Encyclopaedia (1802)
Pantologia (1813)
KEGAN PAUL, TRENCH & CO., London
Little Cyclopaedia of Common Things (1882)
T. KELLY, London (*see also* Bartlett & Hinton)
Oxford Encyclopaedia (1828–1831)
KING-RICHARDSON CO., Chicago and Springfield, Mass. (*see also* W. E. Richardson Co.)
Century Book of Facts (1902–1908)
Universal Manual of Ready Reference (1904)

New Century Book of Facts (1909–1926)
JOHN & JAMES KNAPTON, London
　Cyclopaedia (1728)
　A General Dictionary (1734–1738)
CHARLES KNIGHT, London
　Penny Cyclopaedia (and supplements)
　　(1833–1858)
　National Cyclopaedia of Useful Knowl-
　　edge (1847–1851)
　The Imperial Cyclopaedia (1850–1853)
　English Cyclopaedia (1854–1870)

LEA & BLANCHARD, Philadelphia (see
　also Carey, Lea & Blanchard)
　Encyclopaedia Americana. Supplement.
　　(1847)
J. B. LIPPINCOTT CO., Philadelphia (see
　also W. & R. Chambers)
　Chambers's Encyclopaedia (1860–1880)
　Chambers's Information for the People
　　(1860–1880)
LITERARY PRESS, Glasgow (see also
　Wm. Collins & Son)
　The Standard Encyclopedia (1937)
J. J. LITTLE & IVES CO. INC., New York
　Illustrated Encyclopedia of the Modern
　　World (1956)
　Pictured Knowledge (1956–1957)
　Little & Ives Illustrated Ready Refer-
　　ence Encyclopedia (1961–　　)
　American Oxford Encyclopedia for Home
　　and School (1965–　　)
LONDON (Identity of publishers uncertain)
　Universal, Historical, Geographical and
　　Classical Dictionary (1703)
　Lexicon Technicum (1704–1736)
　A Dictionary of Arts and Sciences (1806–
　　1807)
　Encyclopaedia Londinensis (1810–1829)
　The Cabinet Cyclopaedia (1829–1849)
LONGMAN, BROWN, GREEN, London
　Dictionary of Science, Literature and Art
　　(1842–1875)
　Maunder's Treasury of Knowledge and
　　Library of Reference (1873)
LONGMAN, HURST, REES & ORME,
　London
　The New Cyclopaedia (1802–1820)
　British Encyclopaedia (1809)
JOHN LOW, New York
　New and Complete American Encyclo-
　　paedia (1805–1811)
LOW & MARSTON see SAMPSON, LOW
　& MARSTON

McGRAW-HILL & CO., New York

Catholic Encyclopedia for School and
　Home (1965–　　)
W. MACKENZIE, London and Glasgow
　The National Encyclopaedia (1867–1888)
　The Home Teacher (1886–1888)
MACMILLAN CO., New York
　Macmillan Everyman's Encyclopedia
　　(1959)
MARSHALL-HUGHES CO., Kansas City
　Pictured Knowledge (1927–1939)
SAMUEL MAUNDER, London
　Maunder's Treasury of Knowledge and
　　Library of Reference (1830)
MIDLAND PRESS, Chicago
　Human Interest Library (1914–1926)
　New Human Interest Library (1928–
　　1942)
D. MIDWINTER, London
　Cyclopaedia. 2nd ed. (1738)
G. A. MILLIKAN CO., Marietta (Ohio)
　The Knowledge Book (1915)
　The Knowledge Library (1918)
　New Knowledge Library (1919)
C. MITCHELL, Perth
　Encyclopaedia Perthensis (1796–1806)
MITCHELL, AMES & WHITE, Phila-
　delphia
　The British Encyclopaedia, 1st., 2nd & 3rd
　　editions (1816–1821)
MODERN AMERICAN CORP., Chicago
　Modern American Encyclopedia (1934–
　　1936)
MODERN RESEARCH SOCIETY, Chicago
　Current Encyclopedia (1901)
MODERN WORLD PRESS, London
　Everyday Knowledge (1936)
MONARCH PUBLISHING CO., Chicago
　(Monarch Book Co.)
　Complete Library of Universal Knowledge
　　(1904)
　New Idea Self Instructor (1904)

NATIONAL BOOK CONCERN, Chicago
　Universal Cyclopaedia and Dictionary
　　(1898)
NATIONAL ENCYCLOPEDIA CO., Chi-
　cago (see also Standard Education So-
　ciety Inc.)
　National Encyclopedia for the Home,
　　School and Library (1923)
NATIONAL ENCYCLOPEDIA PUBLISH-
　ING CO., Philadelphia
　The National Encyclopedia (1873)
NATIONAL PRESS ASSOCIATION, Phila-
　delphia
　New Century Reference Library (1907)

NATIONAL PUBLISHING CO., Philadelphia
Standard Cyclopedia (1897)
X-Rays of Intellectual Light and Universal Knowledge (1899)
Standard American Book of Knowledge (1900)
20th Century Cyclopedia of Universal Knowledge (1901)
World's Book of Knowledge and Universal Educator (1901)
American Educator and Library of Knowledge (1902)
New Century Cyclopedia of Universal Knowledge (1902)
American Home Educator and Book of Universal Knowledge (1903)
Standard Library of Knowledge and Universal Educator (1904)
Home and Office Reference Book of Facts (1913)
THOMAS NELSON & SONS, London and New York (*see also* Amalgamated Press)
The Harmsworth Encyclopaedia (1905–1906)
Nelson's Encyclopaedia (1906–1907)
Nelson's Perpetual Looseleaf Encyclopedia (1917–1926)
New Age Encyclopaedia (1920–1921)
Jack's Reference Book for Home and Office (1936)
Nelson Complete Encyclopedia (1937)
Nelson's New Looseleaf Encyclopedia (1940)
Nelson's Encyclopaedia. One-volume edition (1951)
NEW EDUCATIONAL PRESS, London (formerly a subsidiary of Odham's Press, now acquired by the Grolier Society)
Modern Children's Library of Knowledge (1957)
NEW ERA PUBLISHING CO., London
World Book: British Empire Edition (1936–1938)
NEW YORK WORLD PUB. CO., New York
World Almanac and Book of Facts (1868–)
GEORGE NEWNES LIMITED, London
Newnes Pictorial Knowledge (1932–1960)
Newnes Everything Within (1933)
Newnes Golden Treasury (1933)
Children's Everything Within (1939)
Chambers's Encyclopaedia (1950–)
Newnes Popular Encyclopaedia (1960–)

Newnes Family Encyclopaedia (1966–)

ODHAMS PRESS, London (*see also* Amalgamated Press, Wm. Collins & Sons, Waverley Book Co., New Educational Press, Grolier Society Ltd.)
New Standard Encyclopaedia and World Atlas (1932)
The British Encyclopaedia (1933)
New Illustrated Universal Reference Book (1933–1949)
Wonder Encyclopaedia for Children (1933)
Wonderland of Knowledge (1933–1934)
Universal Knowledge A–Z (1938)
Practical Encyclopaedia for Children (1944)
Great Encyclopaedia of Universal Knowledge (1948)
Children's Guide to Knowledge (1949)
Odhams Encyclopaedia (1953)
Children's Illustrated Encyclopaedia of General Knowledge (1954)
Young Children's Encyclopaedia (1956)
Boys and Girls Encyclopaedia (1960–)
The Modern Encyclopaedia (1961–)
Odhams Encyclopaedia for Children (1961–)
Odhams Wonder World of Knowledge (1961–)
Child's First Encyclopaedia (1964–)
Modern Encyclopaedia for Children (1965–)
G. W. OGILVIE, London
Ogilvie's Encyclopaedia of Useful Information (1891)
ORR & SMITH, London
British Cyclopaedia of Arts and Sciences (1833–1838)
OUTLOOK CO. BOOK DEPT., New York
New Universities Encyclopedia (c.1928)
OXFORD UNIVERSITY PRESS, London
Oxford Junior Encyclopaedia (1948–)
American Oxford Encyclopedia for Home and School (1964–)

PACIFIC NEWSPAPER UNION, San Francisco (*see also* United Editors Association)
New Imperial Encyclopedia and Dictionary (1906)
P. D. PALMER & CO., Toronto
Dominion Educator (1919–)
PARENTS MAGAZINE EDUCATIONAL PRESS (Parents Institute), New York
Children's Guide to Knowledge (1957)

New Wonder World Encyclopedia (1959–1960)

New Wonder World Cultural Library (1962–1964)

Columbia Encyclopedia (1963–) (special edition by arrangement)

Cultural Library (1965–)

PARKE, AUSTIN & LIPSCOMB, New York
Austin's New Encyclopedia of Usable Information (1948)

R. S. PEALE & CO., Chicago and St. Louis (*see also* Home Library Assn.)
Peale's Popular Educator and Cyclopedia of Reference (1883–1885)
American Revisions and Additions to the Encyclopaedia Britannica (1891)
Encyclopaedia Britannica. Pirated (1895)
Encyclopedia Americana (1902)

A. & F. PEARS LIMITED, Isleworth, England
Pears Cyclopaedia (1897–1961)

C. A. PEARSON, London
Pearson's Everything Within (1957–)

PELHAM BOOKS, London
Junior Pears Cyclopaedia (1961–)
Pears Cyclopaedia (1961–)

PENGUIN BOOKS, London
The Penguin Encyclopaedia (1965–)

PERIODICAL PUBLISHERS SERVICE BUREAU INC., New York (*see also* International Reader's League)
Encyclopedic Library of Knowledge (1944)

PERPETUAL ENCYCLOPEDIA CORPORATION, Chicago (*see also* Source Research Council)
Source Book (1924–1932)

PHILLIPS & HUNT, New York and San Francisco
Peoples Cyclopedia of Universal Knowledge (1883)

PHILOSOPHICAL LIBRARY INC., New York (*see also* Odhams Press)
Encyclopedia for Boys and Girls (1944)
Children's Illustrated Encyclopedia of General Knowledge (1957)

PICTORIAL ENCYCLOPEDIA CORP., New York
New Pictorial Encyclopedia of the World (1954)

PREMIUMWARES, Brooklyn, N.Y.
Illustrated Encyclopedia of Knowledge (1954–1955)

PROGRESSIVE PUBLISHING CO., Philadelphia
New Outline of Knowledge (1936)

PUBLICITY PUBLISHING CO., Chicago (*see also* International Press)
New and Complete Universal Self Pronouncing Encyclopedia (1905)

PUBLISHERS CO., Washington, D.C. (*see also* Books Inc.)
New Human Interest Library (1938–)
New Masters Pictorial Encyclopedia (c.1955)
New American Encyclopedia (1963–)
World Wide Encyclopedia and Gazetteer (1963–)
World Educator Encyclopedia (by arrangement, 1964–)
World University Encyclopedia (1964–)
World Wide Encyclopedia (1967)

PUBLISHERS GUILD INC., New York (*see also* Consolidated Book Publishers)
University Illustrated Encyclopedia (1933)
Universal World Reference Encyclopedia (1945)

PUBLISHERS PERIODICAL SERVICE BUREAU, New York (*see also* International Readers League)
International's World Reference Encyclopedia (1942)

PUBLISHER'S PRODUCTIONS INC., Chicago (associated with the United Educators Inc.)
Wonderland of Knowledge (1937–)

PURNELL & SONS, London (*see also* Caxton Publishing Co.)
Knowledge (1961–1965)
Purnell's New English Encyclopaedia (1966–)

W. F. QUARRIE & CO., Chicago (successors to Hanson-Roach-Fowler Co., afterwards the Quarrie Corp.)
World Book (1919–1937)

QUARRIE CORP., Chicago (succeeded by Field Enterprises Educational Corp.)
World Book (1938–1944)

RANDOM HOUSE INC., New York
Basic Everyday Encyclopedia (1954)

READERS LEAGUE OF AMERICA, New York (*see also* Universal Educational Guild)
World Scope Encyclopedia (1945)

RICHARDS & CO., London
The Modern Encyclopaedia (1816–1820)

J. A. RICHARDS INC., New York (a subsidiary of Grolier Inc.)

Outline of Knowledge (1924)
Richards Cyclopedia (1933–1937)
Richards Topical Encyclopedia (1939–1964)
W. E. RICHARDSON CO., Chicago (*see also* King-Richardson Co.)
The Volume Library (1911–1912)
RIVERSIDE PUBLISHING CO., Chicago
Encyclopaedia Britannica. Pirated (1905)
F. & J. RIVINGTON, London
Cyclopaedia (1786–1791)
Encyclopaedia Metropolitana (1822–1845)
H. ROSS, Chicago (*see also* Consolidated Book Publishers)
Library of Essential Knowledge (1942)
G. ROUTLEDGE LIMITED, London
National Cyclopaedia of Useful Knowledge (1856–1859)
Routledge's Everyman's Cyclopaedia (1910)
Routledge's Universal Encyclopaedia (1934)

SAALFIELD PUBLISHING CO., Akron, Ohio (*see also* Werner Co.)
Werner's Universal Encyclopedia (1899)
New Americanized Encyclopaedia Britannica (1904)
Modern Encyclopedia (1912)
SAMPSON, LOW & MARSTON, London
Pocket Encyclopaedia (1888) (*Low's Pocket Encyclopaedia*)
Junior World Encyclopaedia (1960–   )
SANGSTER, London
Penny Cyclopaedia (1860)
SCIENTIFIC AMERICAN COMPILING DEPARTMENT, New York (*see also* Americana Corp., Encyclopedia Americana Co.)
Encyclopedia Americana (1903–1906)
Americana (1907–1912)
CHARLES SCRIBNER'S SONS, New York
Encyclopaedia Britannica. 9th ed. (1878–1889) (Distributor)
A. F. SHELDEN & CO., Chicago
New Americanized Encyclopaedia Britannica (1896)
ROGER SHERMAN, Philadelphia
Encyclopaedia Britannica. Pirated (1884)
G. L. SHUMAN & CO., Chicago and Boston
Our Wonder World (1914–1927)
New Wonder World (1932–1955)
SIMON & SCHUSTER, New York (*see also* Golden Press Inc.)
The Golden Encyclopedia (1946)
Golden Book Encyclopedia (1959–1960)

J. B. SMITH CO., Philadelphia
Chambers's Information for the People (1857)
L. F. SMITH & CO., St. Louis
International Library of Reference (1899)
MAXWELL SOMMERVILLE, Philadelphia
Encyclopaedia Britannica. Pirated (1891)
SOURCE RESEARCH COUNCIL INC., Chicago (*see* Perpetual Encyclopedia Corp.)
Source Book (1935–1936)
SPENCER PRESS, Chicago (a subsidiary of Grolier Inc.)
American Peoples Encyclopedia (1948–1956)
Our Wonderful World (1955–1960)
STANDARD AMERICAN CORP., Chicago (*see also* Consolidated Book Publishers)
Standard American Encyclopedia (1937)
STANDARD AMERICAN PUBLISHING CO., New York
Standard American Encyclopedia (1899)
STANDARD BOOKBINDING CO., New York and Philadelphia
National Encyclopedia of Reference (1912)
STANDARD EDUCATION SOCIETY INC., Chicago
Standard Reference Work (1922–1927)
New Standard Encyclopedia (1941–   )
STANDARD ENCYCLOPEDIA CORP., Chicago (*see also* Standard Education Society)
New Standard Encyclopedia (1930–1939)
STANDARD INTERNATIONAL LIBRARY, New York (*see also* Universal Educational Guild)
New World Family Encyclopedia (1953)
Standard International Encyclopedia (1953–1957)
STANDARD REFERENCE WORKS PUBLISHING CO., New York (*see also* Unicorn Press)
Funk and Wagnalls Standard Encyclopedia of Modern Knowledge (1959)
Funk & Wagnalls Standard Reference Encyclopedia (1959–   )
W. H. STELLE, New York
Universal Instructor (1880–1884)
J. M. STODDART, Philadelphia
Encyclopaedia Britannica. 9th ed. Pirated reprint. (1875–1889)
F. A. STOKES CO., New York
Stokes Complete One Volume Encyclopedia (1914)
G. STRAHAN, London
A General Dictionary (1734–1741)

W. STRAHAN, London
Cyclopaedia (1778–1791)
STRAVON PUBLISHERS, New York
Children's Guide to Knowledge (1957)
Complete   Reference   Handbook
(1964–   )
H. S. STUTTMAN & CO., New York (*see
also* Unified Encyclopedia Corporation)
*Webster's Unified Dictionary and En-
cyclopedia* (1953–1961)
Unified Encyclopedia (1960–1965)
THE SUCCESS CO., New York
Continental Encyclopedia (1905)
SWAN SONNENSCHEIN, London
Little Cyclopaedia of Common Things
(1884–1906)
SYNDICATE PUBLISHING CO., Phila-
delphia and New York (*see also* World
Syndicate Publishing Co.)
International   Encyclopedia   Dictionary
(1900)
Imperial Dictionary and Cyclopaedia
(1901)
Imperial Reference Library (1901–1910)
International Dictionary and Cyclopaedia
(1901)
Twentieth Century Encyclopaedia (1901–
1907)
Current Cyclopedia of Reference (1909)
Everybody's Cyclopedia (1911–1912)
Standard Illustrated Book of Facts (1912)
People's Cyclopedia (1914)
New World Wide Cyclopedia (1918)
World Wide Cyclopedia (1919)

T. TEGG, London
The London Encyclopaedia (1829)
THOMAS, COWPERTHWAITE & CO.,
Philadelphia
Encyclopaedia Americana (1838–1849)
THOMPSON PUBLISHING CO., Chicago
and St. Louis
New Cosmopolitan Encyclopedia (1906)
TIMES SALES CO., Chicago
Times Encyclopedia and Gazetteer (1929)
R. E. TROSPER, Ann Arbor, Mich.
The Volume Library (1913)

UNICORN PRESS PUBLISHERS, New
York (*see also* Standard Reference
Works Publishing Co.)
Modern Concise Encyclopedia (1940)
*Funk and Wagnalls New Standard En-
cyclopedia of Universal Knowledge*
(1942–1943)
New Funk & Wagnalls Encyclopedia
(1949–1952)

Universal Standard Encyclopedia (1954–
1958)
UNIFIED ENCYCLOPEDIA PRESS, New
York (*see also* H. S. Stuttman Co.)
Unified Encyclopedia (1960)
UNION PUBLISHING HOUSE, Steuben-
ville, Ohio
American Home Library (1930–1953)
UNITED EDITORS ASSOCIATION, New
York and Chicago (*see also* Pacific
Newspaper Union)
*United Editors Encyclopedia and Diction-
ary* (1909)
United Editors Perpetual Encyclopedia
(1911)
UNITED EDUCATORS INC., Chicago and
Lake Bluff, Ill. (*see also* Publishers
Productions Inc.)
American Educator (1932–   )
UNIVERSAL BOOK AND BIBLE HOUSE,
Philadelphia (a subsidiary of the John
C. Winston Co.)
*New Universal Handbook of Necessary
Information* (1920–1937)
Winston's Universal Reference Library
(1930)
UNIVERSAL   EDUCATIONAL   GUILD,
New York (*see also* Standard Inter-
national Library, Readers League of
America)
World Scope Encyclopedia (1945–1958)
UNIVERSAL KNOWLEDGE FOUNDA-
TION INC., New York
Universal Knowledge (1927–1931)
UNIVERSITY OF KNOWLEDGE INC.,
Chicago (*see also* Consolidated Book
Publishers)
University of Knowledge (1937–1938)
UNIVERSITY RESEARCH EXTENSION,
New York and Chicago
Library of Original Sources (1907–1915)
UNIVERSITY SOCIETY INC., New York
(Distributors)
Modern Achievement (1904)
New Standard Encyclopedia (1906–1915)
Standard American Encyclopedia (1916)
Home University Encyclopedia (1941)

VIKING PRESS, New York
Columbia-Viking   Desk   Encyclopedia
(1953–   )
VIRTUE & CO., London
Illustrated Globe Encyclopaedia (1892–
1893)
Wonder World Encyclopaedia (1947)

WALTON EDUCATIONAL PLAN, Chicago

New Masters Pictorial Encyclopedia (c.1955)
WARD, LOCK & CO., London
The Family Cyclopaedia (1859)
Beeton's Encyclopaedia of Universal Information (1879–1881)
Universal Instructor (1880–1890)
Library of National Information and Popular Knowledge (1884–1887)
Wonder Book Encyclopaedia (1956)
Junior Pictorial Encyclopaedia (1959)
Encyclopaedia of Modern Knowledge (1965)
T. WARDLE, Philadelphia
British Cyclopaedia of Arts and Sciences (1833–1835)
FREDERICK WARNE & CO., London and New York
Nuttall Encyclopaedia (1900–1956)
WAVERLEY BOOK CO., London (*see also* New Educational Press, Educational Book Co., Odhams Press, Grolier Society Ltd.)
Waverly New Era Encyclopaedia (1920)
Waverley Encyclopaedia of General Information (1930)
Children's Home Educator and Treasury of Knowledge (1936)
New Book of Knowledge (1938–1953)
Waverley Encyclopaedia (1953)
Book of Knowledge (1959–   )
Children's Encyclopaedia (1960–   )
S. L. WEEDON CO., Cleveland
New Students Reference Work (1925–1930)
Weedon's Modern Encyclopedia (1931–1932)
WELLES BROTHERS PUBLISHING CO., Chicago and Minneapolis, Minn. (*see also* Standard Education Society, Standard Encyclopedia Corporation)
Aiton's Encyclopedia (1910)
Standard Reference Work (1913–1917)
WERNER CO., Akron (Ohio) (*see also* Saalfield Publishing Co.)
Key to the Americanized Encyclopaedia Britannica (1897)
New American Supplement to the latest edition of the Encyclopaedia Britannica (1900–1905)
New American Comprehensive Encyclopedia (1906)
Werner Encyclopedia (1909)
WHEELER PUBLISHING CO., New York and San Francisco

Standard American Encyclopedia (1912)
JOSEPH WHITAKER & SONS, London
Whitaker's Almanack (1868–   )
JOHN C. WINSTON CO., Philadelphia and Chicago (*see also* Universal Book and Bible House)
Twentieth Century Cyclopedia of Practical Information (1901)
Home Cyclopedia of Necessary Knowledge (1902)
Winston's Encyclopedia (1909)
Winston's Cumulative Loose Leaf Encyclopedia (1912–1942)
New Wonder Book Cyclopedia of World Knowledge (1954)
W. H. WISE & CO., New York
Modern Encyclopedia (1933–1937)
The Concise Encyclopedia (1937)
New Modern Encyclopedia (1943–1949)
Children's Pictorial Encyclopedia (1948)
WONDERLAND OF KNOWLEDGE CORPORATION *see* PUBLISHERS PRODUCTIONS INC.
WORLD BIBLE HOUSE, Philadelphia
The World Encyclopedia (1901)
World's Best Knowledge and How to Use It (1902)
WORLD BOOK INC., Chicago (*see also* Hanson-Roach-Fowler Co.)
World Book (1917–1918)
WORLD LIBRARY GUILD, Cleveland
Twentieth Century Encyclopedia (1930–1934)
WORLD SCOPE PUBLISHERS, New York (formerly Universal Educational Guild)
World Scope Encyclopedia (1959–1963)
WORLD SYNDICATE PUBLISHING CO., Cleveland and New York (afterwards the World Publishing Co.) (*see* Syndicate Pub. Co.)
Adair's New Encyclopedia (1923)
World's Popular Encyclopedia (1937–1942)
Comprehensive Pictorial Encyclopedia (1942–1943)
New Concise Illustrated Encyclopedia (1943)
Columbia-Viking Desk Encyclopedia (1954) (World Library Guild)

T. E. ZELL, Philadelphia
Zell's Popular Encyclopedia (1870–1875)

III

Chronology OF GENERAL KNOWLEDGE ENCYCLOPEDIAS IN THE ENGLISH LANGUAGE, PUBLISHED IN THE UNITED STATES, GREAT BRITAIN AND CANADA, SINCE 1703

. . . .

1703: *Universal, Historical, Geographical, Chronological and Classical Dictionary.* The first known alphabetically arranged reference work in English.

1704: *Lexicon Technicum.* The first of the authoritative encyclopedias in English.

1728: *Cyclopaedia.* Ephraim Chambers' great work.

1734: *A General Dictionary, Historical and Critical.* A translation from the French.

1745: *An Universal History of Arts and Sciences*

1764: *The Complete Dictionary of Arts and Sciences*

1771: *Encyclopaedia Britannica.* The first work to use the word "Encyclopaedia" in the title.

1774: *Universal Dictionary of Arts and Sciences.* Planned, but never published.

1788: *New Royal Cyclopaedia and Encyclopaedia*

1796: *Encyclopaedia Perthensis*

1802: *The English Encyclopaedia*
The New Cyclopaedia. Rees' enlargement of the work by Ephraim Chambers.

1806: *A Dictionary of Arts and Sciences*

1809: *The British Encyclopaedia*

1810: *Encyclopaedia Londinensis*

1812: *The Imperial Encyclopaedia*

1813: *Pantologia*

1816: *The Modern Encyclopaedia*

1817: *Encyclopaedia Metropolitana*

1827: *Encyclopaedia Edinensis*

1828: *Oxford Encyclopaedia*

1829: *The Cabinet Cyclopaedia*. Lardner's great compilation.
Encyclopaedia Americana. The first encyclopedia to be published in the United States.
The London Encyclopaedia

1830: *Edinburgh Encyclopaedia*
Maunder's Treasury of Knowledge and Library of Reference

1833: *British Cyclopaedia of Arts and Sciences*
Penny Cyclopaedia
Treasury of Knowledge and Library of Reference. American reprint of *Maunder's Treasury of Knowledge*.

1841: *The Popular Encyclopaedia*

1842: *Dictionary of Science, Literature and Art*

1847: *National Cyclopaedia of Useful Knowledge*

1850: *The Imperial Cyclopaedia*
Library of General Knowledge

1851: *Iconographic Encyclopaedia of Science, Literature and Art*. A revised translation of Brockhaus's *Bilder Atlas*.

1852: *Cassell's Popular Educator*

1854: *The English Cyclopaedia*

1856: *Enquire Within Upon Everything*

1857: *Chambers's Information for the People*

1858: *New American Cyclopaedia*

1859: *The Family Cyclopaedia*

1860: *Chambers's Encyclopaedia*

1862: *American Annual Cyclopaedia*

1867: *The National Encyclopaedia*. Continuation of the *National Cyclopaedia of Useful Knowledge* 1847.

1868: *Whitaker's Almanack*
World Almanac

1870: *Zell's Popular Encyclopedia*

1873: *The American Cyclopaedia*. Continuation of the *New American Cyclopaedia* 1858.
The National Encyclopedia. Colange.
The Peoples Encyclopedia. Colange.

1876: *Appleton's Annual Cyclopaedia*. Continuation of the *American Annual Cyclopaedia* 1862.
Globe Encyclopaedia of Universal Information
Johnson's New Universal Cyclopaedia

1878: *The Universal Encyclopedia*. Colange.

1879:   *Beeton's Encyclopaedia of Universal Information*
        The Encyclopaedic Dictionary

1880:   *Library of Universal Knowledge*. American reprint of *Chambers's Encyclopaedia*.
        Universal Instructor

1882:   *Little Cyclopaedia of Common Things*

1883:   *Cassell's Concise Cyclopaedia*
        Peale's Popular Educator and Cyclopedia
        Peoples Cyclopedia of Universal Knowledge
        Student's Encyclopaedia of Universal Knowledge. Re-issue of *Globe Encyclopaedia* 1876.

1884:   *Library of National Information and Popular Knowledge*

1886:   *Home Library of Useful Knowledge*. Re-issue of *Peale's Popular Educator* 1883.
        The Home Teacher

1888:   *Cassell's Miniature Cyclopaedia*
        Pocket Encyclopaedia. Low's.

1889:   *Blackie's Modern Cyclopaedia of Universal Information*
        The Century Dictionary

1890:   *Illustrated Globe Encyclopaedia*. New edition of *Students Encyclopaedia of Universal Knowledge* 1883.
        Ready Reference

1891:   *Cassell's Storehouse of General Information*
        New Cabinet Cyclopaedia and Treasury of Knowledge. American reprint of *Blackie's Modern Cyclopaedia of Universal Information* 1889.
        Ogilvie's Encyclopaedia of Useful Information

1893:   *Johnson's Universal Cyclopaedia*. Formerly *Johnson's New Universal Cyclopaedia* 1876.

1895:   *Chambers's Condensed Encyclopedia*
        Harper's Book of Facts

1897:   *Pears Cyclopaedia*
        Standard Cyclopedia

1898:   *Chandler's Encyclopedia*
        International Cyclopaedia. A revision of the *Library of Universal Knowledge* 1880.
        Universal Cyclopaedia and Dictionary

1899:   *Cambridge Encyclopaedia*. Monthly.
        Columbian Cyclopaedia
        International Library of Reference
        New National Cyclopaedia and Treasury. Previously the *New Cabinet Cyclopaedia* 1891.
        The School Encyclopedia
        Standard American Encyclopedia

Werner's Universal Encyclopedia
X-Rays of Intellectual Light

1900:   *New American Supplement to the Encyclopaedia Britannica*
        Nuttall Encyclopaedia
        Standard American Book of Knowledge
        Students Cyclopaedia
        Universal Cyclopaedia. Previously *Johnson's Universal Cyclopaedia*
            1893.
        Universal Reference Library. Previously published as the *International
            Library of Reference* 1899.

1901:   *The Century Dictionary and Cyclopaedia.* Formerly titled *The Century
            Dictionary.*
        The Current Encyclopedia. Monthly.
        Encyclopaedic Dictionary of American Reference
        Handy Cyclopedia of Common Things . . .
        Hill's Practical Encyclopedia. Same as *School Library Encyclopedia*
            1901.
        Imperial Reference Library
        New Popular Encyclopaedia. Formerly published as the *Popular En-
            cyclopaedia* 1841.
        Popular Compendium of Useful Information
        School Library Encyclopedia. Same as *Hill's Practical Encyclopedia*
            1901.
        XX Century Cyclopaedia and Atlas
        Twentieth Century Cyclopedia of Practical Information
        20th Century Cyclopedia of Universal Knowledge
        Twentieth Century Encyclopaedia
        The World Encyclopedia
        World's Book of Knowledge and Universal Educator

1902:   *American Educator and Library of Knowledge*
        Anglo-American Encyclopedia and Dictionary
        Century Book of Facts
        Collier's New Encyclopedia
        Golden Treasury of Useful Information
        Hill's Practical Reference Library of General Knowledge. Published
            in 1901 as the *School Library Encyclopedia* and as *Hill's Practical
            Encyclopedia.*
        Home Cyclopedia of Necessary Knowledge
        New Century Cyclopedia of Universal Knowledge
        New International Encyclopedia. A thorough revision of the *Interna-
            tional Cyclopaedia* 1898. One of the best encyclopedias in the Eng-
            lish language ever published.
        Students Reference Work. Formerly the *Students Cyclopedia* 1900.
        Teacher's and Pupil's Cyclopaedia. May have been in existence in
            1895.
        University Encyclopedia of Twentieth Century Knowledge

World's Best Knowledge and How to Use It

1903: *American Home Educator and Book of Universal Knowledge*
Crown Encyclopedia and Gazetteer
Imperial Encyclopedia and Dictionary
New Peoples Cyclopedia of Universal Knowledge. Formerly the *Peoples Cyclopedia of Universal Knowledge* 1883.
New Twentieth Century Cyclopaedia and Dictionary. Revision of the *XX Century Cyclopaedia* 1901.
Twentieth Century Household Library

1904: *Cassell's Cabinet Cyclopaedia*
Complete Library of Universal Knowledge. Same as *New Idea Self Instructor* 1904.
Modern Achievement
New Americanized Encyclopaedia Britannica
New Idea Self Instructor. Same as *Complete Library of Universal Knowledge* 1904.
Standard Library of Knowledge and Universal Educator
Universal Manual of Ready Reference

1905: *Continental Encyclopedia.* Previously published as the *Crown Encyclopedia and Gazetteer* 1903.
Everett's Encyclopedia of Useful Knowledge
Everybody's Everyday Reference Book for Home and Office
The Harmsworth Encyclopaedia
Home Educator in Necessary Knowledge
New and Complete Universal Self Pronouncing Encyclopedia. Previously the *XX Century Cyclopaedia and Atlas* 1901.
Pannell's Reference Book for Home and Office

1906: *Encyclopaedic Current Reference*
The Modern Cyclopaedia. Formerly the *New Popular Encyclopaedia* 1901.
Nelson's Encyclopaedia. Same as the *Harmsworth Encyclopaedia* 1905.
New American Comprehensive Encyclopedia. Previously issued as the *Anglo-American Encyclopedia and Dictionary* 1902.
New Cosmopolitan Encyclopedia. Reprint of the *New and Complete Universal Self Pronouncing Encyclopedia* 1905.
New Imperial Encyclopedia and Dictionary. Previously published as the *Imperial Encyclopedia and Dictionary* 1903.
New Standard Encyclopedia

1907: *Americana.* Re-titled edition of the *Encyclopedia Americana* 1829.
The Columbia Encyclopedia of Useful Knowledge. Published 1905 as *Everett's Encyclopedia of Useful Knowledge.*
Everybody's Encyclopedia for Everyday Reference
Everyone's Cyclopaedia
Library of Original Sources
New Century Reference Library. Previously issued as the *Continental Encyclopedia* 1905.

       New Practical Reference Library. Revision of *Hill's Practical Reference Library* 1902.

1908:   *American Home Encyclopedia of Useful Knowledge.* Same as *Columbia Encyclopedia* . . . 1907.

       Cassell's Encyclopaedia of General Information. Formerly *Cassell's Storehouse of General Information* 1891.

       The Children's Encyclopaedia. Mee's *Children's Encyclopaedia.*

       Jack's Reference Book for Home and Office. Formerly *Pannell's Reference Book* 1905.

       Standard Ditcionary of Facts

       World Wide Encyclopedia and Gazetteer

1909:   *Current Cyclopedia of Reference*

       Cyclopedia, Dictionary and Atlas of the World

       Everybody's Encyclopedia. Same as *La Salle Extension University Encyclopedia* 1909 and *Webster's Universal Encyclopedia* 1909.

       La Salle Extension University Encyclopedia. Same as *Everybody's Encyclopedia* 1909 and *Webster's Universal Encyclopedia* 1909.

       New Century Book of Facts. Previously published as the *Century Book of Facts* 1902.

       New Complete Condensed Encyclopedia

       New Students Reference Work. Revision of the *Students Reference Work* 1902.

       Practical Home Encyclopedia. Same as *New Standard Encyclopedia* 1906.

       United Editors Encyclopedia and Dictionary

       Webster's Universal Encyclopedia. Same as *Everybody's Encyclopedia* 1909 and *La Salle Extension University Encyclopedia* 1909.

       Werner Encyclopedia

       Winston's Encyclopedia

1910:   *Aiton's Encyclopedia*

       Appleton's New Practical Cyclopedia

       Modern Universal Encyclopedia

       New Teacher's and Pupil's Cyclopaedia. Formerly the *Teacher's and Pupil's Cyclopaedia* 1902.

       Routledge's Everyman's Cyclopaedia

1911:   *The Anglo-American Encyclopedia.* Apparently same as the *Werner Encyclopedia* 1909.

       Everybody's Cyclopedia

       Handy Cyclopedia of Things Worth Knowing

       Practical American Encyclopedia. Evidently the same as the *Unrivalled Encyclopedia* 1911, and the *New Teacher's and Pupil's Cyclopaedia* 1910.

       United Editors Perpetual Encyclopedia

       Unrivalled Encyclopedia. Same as *Practical American Encyclopedia* 1911.

       The Volume Library

1912: *The Book of Knowledge.* American revision of the *Children's Encyclopaedia* 1908.
Modern Encyclopedia
National Encyclopedia of Reference
Standard American Encyclopedia. Same as *New Standard Encyclopedia* 1906 and *Practical Home Encyclopedia* 1909.
Standard Illustrated Book of Facts
Standard Reference Work. Re-titled edition of *Aiton's Encyclopedia* 1910.
Winston's Cumulative Loose Leaf Encyclopedia

1913: *The Everyman Encyclopaedia.* Descended from the *Penny Cyclopaedia* 1833.
Funk & Wagnalls Standard Encyclopedia of the World's Knowledge
Home and Office Reference Book of Facts
Home and School Reference Work
The How and Why Library
The New Encyclopaedia

1914: *Human Interest Library*
Our Wonder World
People's Cyclopedia. Previously published as *Everybody's Cyclopedia* 1911.
Stokes Complete One Volume Encyclopedia

1915: *The Knowledge Book*

1916: *Pictured Knowledge*

1917: *Nelson's Perpetual Looseleaf Encyclopedia*
The World Book

1918: *The Knowledge Library.* Same as the *Knowledge Book* 1915.
The New World Wide Cyclopedia. Previously the *People's Cyclopedia* 1914 and *Everybody's Cyclopedia* 1911.

1919: *The American Educator.* Revised edition of the *New Practical Reference Library* 1907.
Bufton's Universal Cyclopaedia
Dominion Educator. Canadian edition of the *American Educator* 1919.
New Knowledge Library. Revision of the *Knowledge Library* 1918.
New World Encyclopedia. Same as *New World Wide Cyclopedia* 1918.
World Wide Cyclopedia. Same as *New World Wide Cyclopedia* 1918 and *New World Encyclopedia* 1919.

1920: *Harmsworth's Universal Encyclopaedia*
New Age Encyclopaedia
New Universal Handbook of Necessary Information
Waverley New Era Encyclopaedia

1921: *New Gresham Encyclopaedia*

1922: *The Book of Knowledge.* British edition of *Compton's Pictured Encyclopedia.*

Compton's Pictured Encyclopedia. Published in Britain as the *Book of Knowledge.*

1923:   *Adair's New Encyclopedia*
        International Reference Work. Same as *New Teacher's and Pupil's Cyclopaedia* 1910.
        National Encyclopedia for the Home, School and Library. Same as *Standard Reference Work* 1912.

1924:   *Lincoln Library of Essential Information*
        New Champlin Cyclopedia for Young Folks. Anthology of works published between 1883 and 1905.
        The Outline of Knowledge
        Source Book. Originated as the *Home and School Reference Work* in 1913.

1925:   *Concise Pocket Encyclopaedia*

1927:   *The Compact Encyclopaedia.* Based on the *New Gresham Encyclopaedia* 1921.
        Universal Knowledge

1928:   *I See All*
        New Human Interest Library. Previously the *Human Interest Library* 1914.
        New Universities Encyclopedia
        Progressive Reference Library. Formerly the *New Teacher's and Pupil's Cyclopaedia* 1910 and the *International Reference Work* 1923.

1929:   *Pocket Library of the World's Essential Knowledge*
        Times Encyclopedia and Gazetteer. Previously the *New World Wide Cyclopedia* 1918.

1930:   *American Home Library*
        Concise Universal Encyclopaedia
        New Standard Encyclopedia. Previously published as the *Standard Reference Work* 1912 and the *National Encyclopedia for Home, School and Library* 1923.
        New Universal Encyclopedia. Reprint of *Appleton's New Practical Cyclopedia* 1920.
        Twentieth Century Encyclopedia
        The Waverley Encyclopaedia of General Information
        Winston's Universal Reference Library

1931:   *American Reference Library*
        Doubleday's Encyclopedia. American adaptation of *Harmsworth's Universal Encyclopaedia* 1920.
        Funk and Wagnalls New Standard Encyclopedia of Universal Knowledge. Based to a large extent on the *New International Encyclopedia* 1902.
        Golden Pathway to a Treasury of Knowledge
        Hayward's Key to Knowledge
        Weedon's Modern Encyclopedia

1932:   *National Encyclopedia*. Collier's.
        New Standard Encyclopaedia and World Atlas
        New Wonder World. Revision of *Our Wonder World,* first published
          in 1914.
        Newnes Pictorial Knowledge

1933:   *The British Encyclopaedia*. Same as the *Concise Encyclopaedia* 1933.
        Concise Encyclopaedia. Also published as the *British Encyclopaedia*
          1933.
        The Modern Encyclopaedia. Abridged version of *Harmsworth's Universal Encyclopaedia* 1920.
        Modern Encyclopaedia for Children
        Modern Encyclopedia. American.
        New Illustrated Universal Reference Book
        New Popular Educator
        Newnes Everything Within
        Newnes Golden Treasury
        Richards Cyclopedia
        Wonder Encyclopaedia for Children
        Wonderland of Knowledge. British.

1934:   *Britannica Junior*. Revision of *Weedon's Modern Encyclopedia* 1931.
        Cambridge Encyclopaedia. Canadian edition of 1931 edition of *Everyman's Encyclopaedia*.
        Cassell's Modern Encyclopaedia
        Circle of Knowledge
        Daily Express Encyclopaedia
        Facts: The New Concise Pictorial Encyclopedia
        Golden Encyclopaedia for Children. Same as the *Wonder Encyclopaedia for Children* 1933.
        Modern American Encyclopedia. Reprint of *New Students Reference Work* 1909.
        Practical Knowledge for All
        Routledge's Universal Encyclopaedia

1935:   *British Universities Encyclopaedia*. Special edition of *Chambers's Encyclopaedia*.
        The Clear Type Encyclopaedia
        Columbia Encyclopedia
        Laurel and Gold Encyclopedia
        New Gem Encyclopedia
        New General Encyclopedia. Canadian edition of the *American Educator Encyclopedia*. Formerly the *Dominion Educator* 1919.
        New York Post World Wide Illustrated Encyclopedia
        Wonder World of Knowledge

1936:   *Children's Home Educator and Treasury of Knowledge*
        Encyclopaedia of Modern Knowledge
        Everyday Knowledge
        Hutchinson's Pictorial Encyclopaedia

International Encyclopedia and Dictionary

Library of Knowledge. Previously published in 1919 as *Bufton's Universal Cyclopaedia.*

New Outline of Knowledge. Reprint of the *Outline of Knowledge* 1924.

Wonder World Encyclopaedia

World Book Encyclopedia. British Empire Edition.

1937: *The Concise Encyclopedia.* Based on the *Modern Encyclopedia* 1933.

Modern University Encyclopedia

Nelson Complete Encyclopedia. Reprint of *Nelson's Perpetual Looseleaf Encyclopedia* 1917.

Standard American Encyclopedia

The Standard Encyclopedia

University of Knowledge

Wonderland of Knowledge. American.

World Wide Illustrated Encyclopedia. Same as *New York Post World Wide Illustrated Encyclopedia* 1935.

World's Popular Encyclopedia. Formerly the *Twentieth Century Encyclopedia* 1930.

1938: *Book of General Knowledge*

Encyclopedia of General Knowledge

Modern Marvels Encyclopedia

Modern Standard Encyclopaedia

New American Encyclopedia

New Book of Knowledge. Previously published as the *Book of Knowledge* 1922, British edition of *Compton's Pitcured Encyclopedia* 1922.

New Concise Pictorial Encyclopedia. One-volume edition of *Facts* 1934.

Universal Knowledge A to Z

University Illustrated Encyclopedia. Same as *World Wide Illustrated Encyclopedia* 1937.

1939: *Children's Everything Within*

Consolidated Encyclopedia. Commonwealth edition of the *New Standard Encyclopedia* 1930.

Richards Topical Encyclopedia. Previously published as *Richards Cyclopedia* 1933.

1940: *Modern Concise Encyclopedia.* Multi-volume version of the *Modern Encyclopedia* 1933.

Modern Illustrated Encyclopaedia. Same as *Wonder Encyclopaedia for Children* 1933 and *Golden Encyclopaedia for Children* 1934.

Modern Library of Knowledge

Nelson's Encyclopedia: Unabridged. Based on the original *Nelson's Encyclopaedia* 1906.

Nelson's New Looseleaf Encyclopedia. Re-issue of *Nelson's Perpetual Looseleaf Encyclopedia* 1917.

Webster's Columbia Encyclopedic Dictionary

1941: *Home University Encyclopedia.* Same as the *World Wide Illustrated Encyclopedia* 1937.
Webster's Comprehensive Encyclopedic Dictionary
Webster's Encyclopedic Dictionary

1942: *Comprehensive Pictorial Encyclopedia.* Revised edition of *Facts* 1934.
Encyclopedia Library. Same as *Winston's Cumulative Loose Leaf Encyclopedia* 1912.
International's World Reference Encyclopedia. Formerly copyrighted as the *Standard American Encyclopedia* 1937.
Library of Essential Knowledge. Enlarged version of *Webster's Comprehensive Encyclopedic Dictionary* 1941.

1943: *International American Encyclopedia*
New Concise Illustrated Encyclopedia. Same as *Comprehensive Pictorial Encyclopedia* 1942.
New Modern Encyclopedia. Revised edition of the *Modern Encyclopedia* 1933.

1944: *Encyclopedia for Boys and Girls*
Encyclopedic Library of Knowledge. Based on the *New American Encyclopedia* 1938.
Grolier Encyclopedia. Revision of *Doubleday's Encyclopedia* 1931.
Practical Encyclopaedia for Children

1945: *Universal World Reference Encyclopedia.* Previously published as the *Standard American Encyclopedia* 1937 and the *International's World Reference Encyclopedia* 1942.
World Scope Encyclopedia. Reprint of the *Progressive Reference Library* 1928.

1946: *The Champlin Encyclopedia.* Revised edition of the *New Champlin Cyclopedia for Young Folks* 1924.
The Golden Encyclopedia
Handy Encyclopedia of Useful Information

1947: *Information Please Almanac*

1948: *American Peoples Encyclopedia*
Austin's New Encyclopedia of Usable Information
Children's Pictorial Encyclopedia
Great Encyclopaedia of Universal Knowledge
Hutchinson's Twentieth Century Encyclopaedia
Oxford Junior Encyclopaedia
World of the Children

1949: *Children's Guide to Knowledge.* British.
Collier's Encyclopedia
New Funk & Wagnalls Encyclopedia. Based on the *Funk & Wagnalls New Standard Encyclopedia of Universal Knowledge* 1931.

1950: *American International Encyclopedia.* Continuation of *Winston's Cumulative Loose Leaf Encyclopedia* 1912 and *Encyclopedia Library* 1942.

1951:   *Everyday Reference Library.* Formerly published as *Austin's New En-
         cyclopedia of Usable Information* 1948.
         Nelson's Encyclopaedia. One-volume edition.
         New Universal Encyclopaedia. Revised edition of *Harmsworth's Uni-
         versal Encyclopaedia* 1920.
         World Home Reference Encyclopedia. Terminal edition of *Facts* 1934.

1953:   *Columbia-Viking Desk Encyclopedia.* Abridged from the second edi-
         tion of the *Columbia Encyclopedia* 1950.
         New World Family Encyclopedia. Same as the *World Scope Encyclo-
         pedia* 1945.
         Odhams Encyclopaedia
         Standard International Encyclopedia. Same as *World Scope Encyclo-
         pedia* 1945 and *New World Family Encyclopedia* 1953.
         The Waverley Encyclopaedia
         Webster's Unified Ditcionary and Encyclopedia. Based on the *New
         American Encyclopedia* 1938.

1954:   *Basic Everyday Encyclopedia*
         Consolidated Webster Comprehensive Encyclopedic Dictionary. Pre-
         viously published in 1940 as the *Webster's Comprehensive Encyclo-
         pedic Dictionary.*
         Consolidated Webster Encyclopedic Dictionary
         Illustrated Encyclopedia of Knowledge
         New Pictorial Encyclopedia of the World
         New Wonder Book Cyclopedia of World Knowledge
         Universal Standard Encyclopedia. Abridged from the *New Funk and
         Wagnalls Encyclopedia* 1949.

1955:   *Illustrated Home Library Encyclopedia.* Same as the *Illustrated En-
         cyclopedia of Knowledge* 1954.
         New Masters Pictorial Encyclopedia
         Our Wonderful World

1956:   *Illustrated Encyclopedia of the Modern World.* Revised edition of the
         New Pictorial Encyclopedia of the World 1954.
         Teach Yourself Concise Encyclopaedia of General Knowledge
         Wonder Book Encyclopaedia
         Younger Children's Encyclopaedia

1957:   *Children's Guide to Knowledge.* American.
         Children's Illustrated Encyclopedia of General Knowledge
         Modern Children's Library of Knowledge
         Modern University Encyclopedia
         New Age Encyclopaedia, World Atlas and Sports Supplement
         Pearson's Everything Within
         The Pictorial Encyclopaedia

1958:   *Illustrated World Encyclopedia.* Previously published as the *Illustrated
         Home Library Encyclopedia* 1955.

1959:   *Book of Knowledge.* British.
      The Children's Encyclopedia. Whipple.
      Funk and Wagnalls Standard Encyclopedia of Modern Knowledge
      Funk & Wagnalls Standard Reference Encyclopedia. Formerly the
        Universal Standard Encyclopedia 1954.
      Golden Book Encyclopedia
      Illustrated Encyclopedia
      Junior Pictorial Encyclopaedia
      Macmillan Everyman's Encyclopedia. American reprint of *Everyman's*
        Encyclopaedia, 4th ed. 1958.
      New Wonder World Encyclopedia. Previously the *New Wonder World*
        1932.

1960:   *The Boys and Girls Encyclopaedia*
      Caxton Encyclopaedia
      Children's Britannica
      Junior World Encyclopaedia
      Newnes Popular Encyclopaedia
      Unified Encyclopedia. Combining entries from the *Grolier Encyclo-*
      pedia 1944 and the *Richards Topical Encyclopedia* 1939.

1961:   *Black's Children's Encyclopedia*
      Caxton World of Knowledge. Same as the *Caxton Encyclopaedia* 1960.
      Golden Home and High School Encyclopedia
      Golden Treasury of Knowledge
      Junior Pears Encyclopaedia
      Knowledge
      Little & Ives Illustrated Ready Reference Encyclopedia
      The Modern Encyclopaedia. Odhams.
      Odhams Encyclopaedia for Children
      Odhams Wonder World of Knowledge

1962:   *New Wonder World Cultural Library.* Previously the *New Wonder*
      World Encyclopedia 1959.

1963:   *American Family Encyclopedia.* Formerly the *New American Ency-*
      clopedia 1938.
      Collins New Age Encyclopaedia. Previously published as the *Modern*
      University Encyclopaedia 1937.
      Cowles Comprehensive Encyclopedia—The Volume Library. Derived
      from the *Volume Library* first published in 1911.
      Encyclopedia International
      New American Encyclopedia. Continuation of *World Scope Encyclo-*
      pedia 1945.
      New Golden Encyclopedia

1964:   *American Oxford Encyclopedia for Home and School.* American adap-
      tation of the *Oxford Junior Encyclopaedia* 1948.
      Child's First Encyclopaedia

Complete Reference Handbook
New American Encyclopedia. Continuation of the *World Scope Encyclopedia* 1945.
New World Library
The World Educator Encyclopedia. Same as *New American Encyclopedia* 1964.
World University Encyclopedia. Same as *New American Encyclopedia* 1964.

1965:   *Catholic Encyclopedia for School and Home*
The Cultural Library. Formerly the *New Wonder World Cultural Library* 1962.
Encyclopaedia of Modern Knowledge
The Grolier Universal Encyclopedia. Based on the *Encyclopedia International* 1963
Hutchinson's New 20th Century Encyclopedia. Formerly *Hutchinson's Twentieth Century Encyclopaedia* 1948.
New Wonder World Encyclopaedia. British.
The Penguin Encyclopaedia

1966:   *Purnell's New English Encyclopaedia*
New Book of Knowledge. Entirely new work for children. No connection with British *New Book of Knowledge* 1938.
New Caxton Encyclopedia. Reprint of *Purnell's New English Encyclopedia* 1965.
Newnes Family Encyclopaedia
World Book Encyclopedia. International Edition.

1967:   *Everyman's Encyclopaedia*. 5th edition.
Merit Students Encyclopedia
World Wide Encyclopedia

General Bibliography

•••

• Books

AMERICAN LIBRARY ASSOCIATION
The Booklist and Subscription Books Bulletin. Chicago: American Library Assn., 1956–   .
A guide to current books published twice monthly. Preceded by *The Booklist Guide* and the *Subscription Books Bulletin,* a quarterly periodical published from 1930–36. Invaluable for its meticulous evaluations of individual encyclopedias published since 1930.

————. *Basic Book Collection for Elementary Grades.* 7th ed. Chicago: American Library Assn., 1960.

————. *Basic Book Collection for High Schools.* 8th ed. Chicago: American Library Assn., 1963.

————. *Basic Book Collection for Junior High Schools.* 3rd ed. Chicago: American Library Assn., 1960.

BALDENSPERGER, F. and FRIEDRICH, W. P.
Bibliography of Comparative Literature. Chapel Hill: University of North Carolina Press, 1950.

BARTON, M. N. and BELL, M. V.
Reference Books: a brief guide for students and other users of the library. 6th ed. Baltimore: Enoch Pratt Free Library, 1966.

BATESON, F. W. (ed.)
The Cambridge Bibliography of English Literature. 5 vols. Cambridge: Cambridge University Press, 1940–63.

BLANCK, J. (comp.)
Bibliography of American Literature. 3 vols. New Haven: Yale University
Press, 1955–   .

BONK, W. J.
The Use of Basic Reference Sources in Libraries. Ann Arbor: Campus Publishers, 1964.

BOSTON ATHENAEUM
Catalogue, 1807–71. Boston, 1874–82.

BRITISH MUSEUM. Dept. of Printed Books.
General Catalogue of Printed Books. London: Trustees, 1931–   .

BRITISH NATIONAL BIBLIOGRAPHY, 1950–
London: Council of the British National Bibliography, British Museum,
1950.

CATHOLIC LIBRARY ASSOCIATION
Basic Reference Books for Catholic High School Libraries. Haverford, Pa.:
Catholic Library Assn., 1960.

COLLISON, R. L. W.
Encyclopaedias: their history throughout the ages. 2nd ed. New York: Hafner
Publishing Co., 1966.
The only history of encyclopedias previously available. Includes foreign-
language works of reference. A primary source of information.

CRANE, R. S. and BREDVOLD, L. I., *et al.*
*English Literature, 1660–1800; a bibliography of modern studies comp. for
Philological Quarterly.* Princeton: Princeton University Press, 1950   .

DEASON, H. J.
AAAS Science Book List for Young People. Washington, D.C.: American
Association for the Advancement of Science, 1964.

EINBINDER, H.
The Myth of the Britannica. New York: Grove Press, 1964.

GOODING, L. M. (ed.)
"The 'Encyclopaedia Britannica'; a critical and historical study." Unpublished
Master's thesis, Columbia University, 1929.

HOFFMAN, H. R.
*The Reader's Adviser; an annotated guide to the best in print in literature,
biographies, dictionaries, encyclopedias, bibles, classics, drama, poetry, fiction, science, philosophy, travel, history.* New York: R. R. Bowker Co., 1964.
Earlier editions useful for out-of-print works.

KOGAN, H.
The Great EB; the story of the Encyclopaedia Britannica. Chicago: The
University of Chicago Press, 1958.
The "official" history of the largest encyclopedia in the English language

MURPHEY, R. W.
How and Where to Look It Up: a guide to standard sources of information.
New York: McGraw-Hill, 1958.
Very useful section on encyclopedias.

NATIONAL UNION CATALOG:
A cumulative author list representing Library of Congress printed cards and titles reported by other American libraries, 1953–57. Ann Arbor, Mich.: Edwards, 1958.

————. *1958–62.* New York: Rowman & Littlefield, 1963.

————. *1952–55 imprints: an author list representing Library of Congress printed cards and titles reported by other American libraries.* Ann Arbor, Mich.: Edwards, 1961.

PEABODY INSTITUTE, BALTIMORE
Catalogue of the Library. Baltimore, 1883–1905.

ROBERTS, A. D.
Introduction to Reference Books. All editions. London: Library Association.
Chapters on encyclopedias.

SANDYS, SIR J. E.
History of Classical Scholarship. New York: Hafner Publishing Co., 1958.

SHORES, L.
Basic Reference Sources; an introduction to materials and methods. Chicago: American Library Assn., 1954.
With *Subscription Books Bulletin* and Collison's work, provides more information on encyclopedias than any other source. New edition in preparation.

————. *Instructional Materials.* New York: Ronald Press, 1960.

SMITH, R.
Towards a Living Encyclopedia; a contribution to Mr. Well's new encyclopaedism. London: Andrew Daker, 1948.

UNDERBRINK, R. L.
About Encyclopedias; an annotated bibliography. Jacksonville, Ill.: Author, 1960.

UNITED STATES CATALOG, 1899–
New York: Wilson, 1899–   .

U.S. LIBRARY OF CONGRESS
A Catalog of Books Represented by Library of Congress printed cards, issued to July 31, 1942. Ann Arbor, Mich.: Edwards, 1942–46.

————. *Supplement: Cards Issued Aug. 1, 1942–Dec. 31, 1947.* Ann Arbor, Mich.: Edwards, 1948.

Library of Congress Author Catalog: a cumulative list of works represented by Library of Congress printed cards 1948–52. Ann Arbor, Mich.: Edwards, 1953.

Library of Congress Catalog. Books: subjects, 1950–54. A cumulative list of works represented by Library of Congress printed cards. Ann Arbor, Mich.: Edwards, 1955.

———. 1955–59. Paterson, N. J.: Pageant Books, 1960.

WALFORD, A. J. (ed.)
Guide to Reference Material. London: Library Association, 1959.
British equivalent of Winchell. Sections on encyclopedias particularly useful.

WALSH, S. P.
General Encyclopedias in Print; a comparative analysis. New York: R. R. Bowker Co., 1966.
Published annually.

WATT, R.
Bibliotheca britannica; or, A general index to British and foreign literature. Edinburgh: Constable, 1824.

WELLS, H. G.
"The Role of an Encyclopaedia in a Progressive Civilization" in *The Work, Wealth and Happiness of Mankind.* London: Heinemann, 1932.

———. "World Encyclopaedia", "The Brain Organization of the Modern World", "The Idea of a Permanent World Encyclopaedia" in *World Brain.* London: Methuen, 1938.

H. W. WILSON CO.
Children's Catalog. 10th ed. New York: H. W. Wilson Co., 1961.
Section on encyclopedias.

———. *Cumulative Book Index, a world list of books in the English language, 1928–32.* New York: Wilson, 1933–.

———. *Standard Catalog for High School Libraries.* 8th ed. & suppls. New York: H. W. Wilson Co., 1962.
Section on encyclopedias.

———. *Standard Catalog for Junior High School Libraries.* Suppls. New York: H. W. Wilson Co., 1965.
Section on encyclopedias.

———. *Standard Catalog for Public Libraries.* 4th ed. & suppls. New York: H. W. Wilson Co., 1958.
Section on encyclopedias.

WINCHELL, C. M.
Guide to Reference Books. 8th ed. Chicago: American Library Assn., 1967.
Earlier editions invaluable for historical material. Excellent list of criteria.

WYNAR, B. S.
Introduction to Bibliography and Reference Work. 3rd ed. Denver: Libraries Unlimited, Inc., 1966.

ZISCHKA, G. A.
Index Lexicorum; Bibliographie der lexikalischen Nachschlagewerke. Wien: Bruder Hollinek, 1959.

• **Periodical Articles**

"Buying an Encyclopedia?" *Consumer Bulletin*, v. 44 (August, 1961).

"Choosing Encyclopedias and Dictionaries; with authoritative listings from the publishers," *Senior Scholastic*, v. 72 (February 7, 1958).

"Circles of Education," *Times Literary Supplement*, (February 10, 1966).

"Current Books for the Schools; Reference Books." *Catholic School Journal*, v. 67 (February, 1967).

Dalgleish, A. "Books for Young People; facts and ideas." *Saturday Review*, (March 21, 1964).

Einbinder, H. "Our Imperfect Encyclopedias," *Progressive*, v. 25 (March, 1961).

"Encyclopedias," *Journal of World History*, v. 9 no. 3 (1966).

"Encyclopedias; Easy Payment Plan," *Credit Union Bridge*, v. 26 (June, 1961).

"Encyclopedias for Kids." *Time*, v. 88 (November 11, 1966).

Finch, H. R. "What's New in Encyclopedias?" *Senior Scholastic*, v. 86 (February 18, 1965).

"How to Pick an Encyclopedia." *Changing Times*, v. 16 (June, 1962).

Jackson, S. L. "What a History of the Encyclopaedia Could Show." *Library Review*, no. 150 (Summer 1964).

Johnston, W. T. "Encyclopedias." *Consumer Bulletin*, v. 47 (January, 1964).

Macbeth, E. and Ryan, J. "Reference Sets." *Grade Teacher*, v. 82 (November, 1964).

"Reference Sets for Home Libraries." *Library Journal*, v. 83 (April 15, 1958).

Shores, L. "The Ideal Encyclopedia," *Wilson Library Bulletin*, v. 11 (June, 1937).

Spain, C. R. "Reference Materials in the Modern School." *Education*, v. 84 (December, 1963).

Steinberg, S. H. "Encyclopedias," *Signature*, New Series 12 (1951).

Tebbel, J. "Keeping Up with Knowledge." *Saturday Review*, v. 48 (July 10, 1965).

"The Uses of Encyclopedias; past, present, future." *American Behavioral Scientist* (September, 1962).

Whalen, W. "The ABC's of Encyclopedias." *The Sign*, v. 42 (March, 1963).

"Which Encyclopedia for Your Child?" *Pageant* (June, 1963).

"Which Encyclopedias Should I Buy for My Children?" *Consumer Bulletin*, v. 42 (December, 1959).

Williatt, N. "Lucrative Learning; encyclopedias a source of profit as well as knowledge," *Barron's Magazine*, v. 39 (July 6, 1959).

Forum on Encyclopedias

A Symposium held under the auspices of the Reference Services Division at the Annual Conference of the American Library Association, Detroit, 6th July 1965

••

Our Good Encyclopedias

• BY DR. LOUIS SHORES

Dean Emeritus of the Library School, Florida State University

We are going to consider our good encyclopedias and how they can be made better. This is professionally important to us, not only as librarians but as community leaders to whom our citizens come for advice. Last year the U.S. spent nearly a quarter of a billion dollars on encyclopedias. So convinced is the parent that a good encyclopedia in the home will improve Johnny's school grades that he plans very early on this investment. Recently, an expectant mother phoned me, "We are expecting our first child in May. What encyclopedia shall I buy for him?" (All mothers seem to expect boys!) Our responsibility to the consumer has now assumed such proportions that hardly a day goes by that we are not asked to express a professional opinion on a set or to suggest how to go about the selection of an encyclopedia for the home.

But if the encyclopedia is important in the home, it is doubly so in the library. I happen to belong to the generation that had reference with the late, great Isadore Gilbert Mudge. Referring to the marked copy of the *Guide to Reference Books* I used in Library School, I find these underlined words on page 37:

> "A good encyclopedia, or collection of encyclopedias, forms the backbone of a great part of the reference work in any library".

253

With such a professional and community stake it is inevitable that the quality of encyclopedias is of critical concern to reference librarianship.

Even before the activation of the Subscription Books Committee by ALA in 1928, librarians had concerned themselves with encyclopedia evaluation. The first edition of the Mudge "Guide" I quoted was launched by Alice Bertha Kroeger in 1902 under the Houghton Mifflin imprint. The subsequent Mudge and Winchell editions, and the supplements that appeared between editions, all followed the Kroeger precedent of devoting major sections to encyclopedia study and appraisal.

By 1928 there were no fewer than 162 subscription book publishers in the U.S., many of whom were selling inferior sets, with door-to-door sales pitches that seduced defenseless homemakers. Repeated outrages against the American consumer undoubtedly precipitated ALA's activation of the Subscription Books Committee that year. But the reputable publishers were always equally concerned. Four years before SBC was activated, 31 subscription book publishers met with John F. Nugent of the Federal Trade Commission to draw up a set of 14 resolutions condemning unfair practices in subscription book publishing. In 1946 the three publishers represented here tonight and the United Educators Inc. became charter members of the ATPI Reference Book Section. It was this group of publishers which led the liaison movement with librarians which began as early as 1931 (the second year of SBC's existence) to develop creative encyclopedia standards. One of the monumental results of this liaison was the publication of the "Terminology Report" of April, 1953. The work of a joint ALA-ATPI Committee, the Report was issued as a supplement to Volume 24, No. 2 of *Subscription Books Bulletin.*

I know you will pause with me for a moment to pay tribute to John Rowe who passed away on April 7. In the past three decades no one contributed more to librarian-publisher liaison than Rowe. Single-handed he served as the catalyst who blended library-publisher efforts to make our good encyclopedias ever better.

I am convinced that today's good encyclopedias are better than ever in the long history of summarizing man's knowledge. After many years of studying and teaching most of the great examples, back to Pliny, I believe today's good encyclopedist is more aware of the scope and commitment of this monarch of reference sources than any of his predecessors. I believe, also, our leading English-language encyclopedists have contributed as significantly to encyclopedia concepts and design as any contemporaries abroad.

Of course, there are scholars in their own specialties who, suddenly confronted with requests to write or speak on encyclopedias, fortify their hasty preparation by resorting to Diderot, still a good historical reference, but a poor model for today's good encyclopedia. There are others, usually linguists, but nevertheless tyros in encyclopedia evaluation, who will celebrate *Encyclopédie Française* under the direction of L. Febvre as new-dimensional. Without taking anything away from this excellent work, the fact remains that experiments in this basic design have occurred in many non-alphabetically arranged works, and possibly most creatively in such young people's examples as the

British *Oxford Junior,* the British-American *Book of Knowledge,* the American *Our Wonderful World,* and the late M. J. Kinsella's concept for the American one-volume adult work, the *Lincoln Library of Essential Information.*

At another time I would like to present all of the data my students and I have assembled in support of the thesis that today's good encyclopedias in the English language are truly superior examples of encyclopedic concept and execution. Tonight, however, I would like to confine this introduction to some notes on the first of the basic evaluation criteria—Authority. In my opinion, one of the reasons the good American encyclopedia is now so good is because so many of us librarians have been willing to move from the sidelines of criticism to the arena of creation. There is not a good American encyclopedia today that does not have at least one professional librarian as an editorial adviser, contributor or editor. Two encyclopedias have librarians directing the editorial work. Some encyclopedias have separate library advisory boards who influence editorial policy. I believe this librarian participation as well as liaison and evaluation is one of the key reasons for the excellence of today's good encyclopedias.

U.S.'s oldest continuously published encyclopedia, the *Americana,* has not only maintained its traditional standards of excellence but innovated in several directions under the leadership of its distinguished publisher, Grolier, Inc. To Grolier, librarianship owes much for the continuous development of the British-originated *Book of Knowledge* and the American-created *Our Wonderful World* for young people, the good adult *American Peoples Encyclopedia* and the creation of the new *Encyclopedia International.*

Crowell, Collier & Macmillan, Inc. represents a merger of two century-old American publishers, P. F. Collier and New York Macmillan, as well as later subsidiaries. Before *Collier's Encyclopedia,* the former was probably best known to librarians for the *Harvard Classics,* and the latter for the *Encyclopedia of the Social Sciences,* the *Guide to Historical Literature,* and *Gone with the Wind.*

Not only because the *World Book Encyclopedia* has the largest sales, but because it represents the epitome of this alphabetic type, its publisher, Field Enterprises Education Corp., represents many of the qualities which make today's good encyclopedias superior to those that preceded it. The recent development of a new Clarence Barnhart dictionary companion is another great achievement in reference book publishing, as is the Braille edition of its encyclopedia, and the large type edition.

From each of these three great encyclopedia publishers come encyclopedists of distinction to share with us editorial considerations in making our good encyclopedias.

Before I knew the editorial director of Grolier as an encyclopedist, I knew him as a librarian, library researcher and educator. One of my memorable professional experiences is serving under his chairmanship on the committee that developed the curriculum standards by which all ALA library schools are accredited. A graduate of Lewis Institute and the University of Chicago, he went on to earn his doctorate in the graduate Library School. In the years before his present position, he served as a library practitioner in school, college and public libraries, and as a library educator at Chicago, Columbia, and Rutgers, leaving the post of dean at the last university to become vice-president of the company he represents. Dr. Lowell A. Martin has agreed to consider with us the basic criterion of scope.

During one of the five years I edited the *Library Journal's* annual list of reference books, the *New Century Cyclopedia of Names* was voted by reference librarians the best reference book published that year. You will note on the title pages of that three-volume work that the co-editor is W. D. Halsey, who before coming to his present post as editorial director and vice-president contributed significantly to the development of the *Thorndike-Barnhart* and the *American College* dictionaries. It has been professionally exciting to watch one of the most creative editors I have ever known work on so many aspects of bookmaking about which we teach in library school. He has agreed to take for tonight the assignment of "Treatment".

My association with Field Enterprises goes back to its predecessor Quarrie, and to a long line of devoted editors, among whom the name of the late J. Morris Jones must stand forever high. Morris was not only the architect of the good encyclopedia Field publishes, but he was also a master teacher of the encyclopedist's craft. One of his most distinguished disciples and indeed his right hand man in designing the *World Book* will discuss the criterion of format tonight. Bill Nault brings to his position, as Director of Editorial Research, a doctorate in education and a rich school background.

Jim Walsh is a British librarian, professionally library educated in Britain who has worked on this side of the Atlantic, first at the Akron Public Library, and next at the University of Delaware. In 1963, he first issued *General Encyclopedias in Print: A Comparative Analysis* which is now in its third annual edition, and which has been acclaimed and welcomed by reference librarians for its earnest, objective and meticulous evaluation of most of the major English-language encyclopedias. Jim Walsh is a veteran of World War II and was wounded in action. He is now at work on comparable publications for dictionaries and atlases.

Can Our Good Encyclopedias Be Made Better?

• BY DR. LOWELL A. MARTIN

Editorial Director, Grolier Incorporated

Scope in an encyclopedia presents questions similar to book selection in a library. There is first the matter of purpose and audience, then the scanning of what is available, followed by consultation of authorities, consideration of what you already have, a dark look at the question of space, and finally the decision to include or exclude. I don't want to push the analogy too far, but I do think there is some value in following this parallel between encyclopedia scope and library book selection—and value also in seeing where the analogy breaks down.

First the question of purpose. The encyclopedist, like the librarian, must reconcile himself at the outset to the hard reality that he cannot be complete and inclusive. His readers may expect anything and everything, even as the library user wants what he wants. But your libraries cannot be casually increased to millions of volumes, and your cause would not be furthered if we made encyclopedias in hundreds of volumes. And then, of course, we wouldn't sell them either.

The encyclopedia editor, like the librarian, seeks to use judgment rather than indiscriminate inclusiveness to meet the needs of his readers. It is a matter of prediction—selecting the right article for the right reader at the right time. The difficulty is that the right time, the occasion for the reader to use the material, is next week or next year, so that both the librarian and the encyclopedia editor must be something of a soothsayer.

You have no doubt engaged in discussions of just what the purposes of libraries are. Well, encyclopedia editors get into a parallel discussion over their cocktails. "A compendium of knowledge", the dictionary says of the encyclopedia. But what is knowledge? I have been brought up short by the view of the encyclopedia which our company finds as we go further into foreign markets. We early noticed that it was the topical rather than the alphabetical encyclopedia that readers wanted in countries as different as Sweden, Peru and Australia. Why? Because readers there say they want an encyclopedia to give them what they call understanding as distinct from current information or facts, which they say should be in handbooks and yearbooks and manuals. A provocative distinction here, which might be worth pursuing at another meeting of librarians and encyclopedia editors.

But already my analogy breaks down. Once the librarian has made his selection, he has an immediate feedback from readers and from seeing the book used—or unused—on the shelves. The encyclopedia editor sits in his office, and his readers are in a library a thousand miles away or in a home across the country. Our theme is how to make our encyclopedias better. One way is to get encyclopedia editors for a little time away from their authorities and their schedules and out at the point of contact. An hour with a working reference librarian would help as much with decisions about scope as an hour with a Nobel Prize-winner. And no new encyclopedia should be made without a thorough field study of the reference needs of those for whom it is intended.

We, in editorial, have our guides and sources, even as you have reviews to help in the selection process. Ours are not so much printed sources as individual advisers and experts. I am not referring here to the scholars who write the original articles, but to the non-resident faculty that each encyclopedia publisher maintains to help in deciding what goes in and what goes out. Study the roster of advisers of the several major encyclopedia publishers, and you will see a super-faculty beyond the resources of the best university in the country.

Now another difference between scope in an encyclopedia and scope in a library. In some cases there simply are not books available to meet your needs; a current example would be very readable books for adults with limited education. The librarian is not expected to acquire a book that has not been published. But the encyclopedia maker is a publisher, and cannot plead that the material is not available. It is his job to produce it.

Encyclopedia editors, like librarians, have a space problem. How do you get another book on a shelf that is already full? How do we get another entry on a page that is already crowded out into the margins? The librarian sees what can be removed, or compressed into smaller format, or relegated to little-used storage. The encyclopedia editor goes through something of the same process, except that he does not have microfilm or remote storage. But perhaps you would like an encyclopedia on microfilm, built into a corner of a drawer of your desk, with an automatic control panel to project into the desk top the particular article that you need at a given moment?

The encyclopedist also has a weeding problem. When I first studied this question shortly after shifting to encyclopedia work, I found myself wondering about the standard continuous revision policy. Of course we need constant updating in encyclopedias. But let's be realistic, I said—none of us is going deep enough into these sets; we are shifting rooms around in a structure of the past. Once I even said that every encyclopedia should be started fresh every ten years, in view of rapid changes not just in the details but down deep in the balance and emphasis and relations of knowledge. I said it with a heavy heart, because I pictured all the encyclopedias in libraries and homes becoming obsolete at intervals—and also because I did not see where the many millions of dollars would come from for periodic complete rebuilding of our major sets.

But I realize now that I was speaking within the limits of an older technology, where we set type, lay the material out on pages, and get frozen into a pattern built of metal and film. It is not so much the direct editorial costs as the typesetting and processing and plating costs that have deterred more fundamental revision. I am convinced that in a few years all the encyclopedia publishers will have their text on magnetic tape, with type automatically set and pages automatically laid out for each new printing, so that we can continuously get to the roots of our encyclopedias as well as plucking off the old flowers and this same magnetic tape may be used not only to produce the printed encyclopedia as we know it but also will be part of an information bank from which a wider range of facts, brought up to date daily, will be distributed by instantaneous transmission. This is not pie in the sky but very real research in the laboratory.

But the very last impression I want to leave is that encyclopedias will be made better solely or primarily by machines. I don't believe this will happen in our books any more than it will happen in our libraries. The heart of the matter remains the human, very human—staff member. It is editors who make good encyclopedias even as it is librarians who make good libraries. We are generalists as you are, we seek to be educators, we develop a special skill in communication. In the end, it is human judgment that determines proper scope.

I have tried not to overwork the comparison between libraries and encyclopedias, but I do see a parallel which underlines the high purpose to which we are both called. When I think of a library, I see on the one side a vast array of print and non-print materials, and on the other a group of readers needing part of these materials. The librarian's job is to bring the two together by selecting, organizing and guiding. The encyclopedia editor also is a mediator, between the world of scholars on the one side and the individual seeking information on the other, between those who know something and those who seek to know.

I can only hope that the encyclopedist makes your task as librarians a little easier, as I know your work makes ours worthwhile.

Treatment in an Encyclopedia

- ## BY WILLIAM D. HALSEY

Editorial Director, Crowell-Collier and Macmillan Inc.

I think I speak for a majority of reference-book editors and publishers in this country today, and possibly within the entire English-speaking world, when I say that the general purpose encyclopedia now finds its greatest audience among young people at school. This is not to say that any of the various excellent works now in existence are not used by adults, including advanced scholars. Indeed, I have had many letters from scholars congratulating my editors on the excellence of *Collier's Encyclopedia*. But the scholar tends to go to an encyclopedia for information in areas other than the area in which he specializes—and in these other areas the scholar is a layman.

I find this audience, ranging from the upper elementary grades into the undergraduate level at college, perhaps the most exciting group an editor or publisher can address himself to today. I doubt if there is any other segment of our population in which we can find a higher percentage of people seeking —indeed hungering for—knowledge. These people are impatient with anything which seems to them to be a barrier to knowledge. Jargon, esoteric vocabulary, ambiguity, and grammar calculated to strangle the facts rather than to reveal them—all of these are anathema to this audience.

I am sure all of us are familiar with the "Emperor's New Clothes". It is, of all the stories I know, the one which cuts most surely into one of the dreadful things which come to some human beings with age. This is the willingness to believe something, or perhaps I should say the inability not to believe something, simply because authority says it is true. As you all will recall, the emperor in the story was stark naked. And, as he walked down the street, it was a child, not an adult, who recognized and spoke the truth. This is to me the core characteristic of the audience which I have described above.

This imposes upon the editors and publishers of encyclopedias an obligation to communicate as simply, clearly and vividly as possible. The third of these adjectives, vividly, is not less important than the others. A reference work can be written in English which is simple and clear, but still be couched in a kind of English which my good friend, Eric Hodgins, once described as "encyclopedese". Perhaps there is nothing really wrong with this, but I think it is equally true that there is nothing particularly right with it. Certainly, it seems to me entirely appropriate that matter intended to be read should be made as attractive as it can be for the person who is expected to read it.

Perhaps a few instances of what I mean by the above would be helpful. Let's start first with a simple definition of the bear.

Exclusive of the necessary technical taxonomical references, a bear may be defined as a more or less carnivorous, plantigrade mammal of nocturnal habits. The bear may also be defined as a mammal that walks flat on the soles of his feet, is active chiefly at night, and eats, in addition to meat, fish and certain berries.

The two definitions mean exactly the same thing. I would believe, however, that the first one, however technically accurate, might not be particularly meaningful to the audience we address ourselves to today in encyclopedias.

As we might develop the article on the bear, it would seem to me we should bear in mind the nature of the questions about the bear which might be put to the book in question. A teenager's question about bears would be very different from those of a zoologist. Such obvious things as the variety of bears which exist, where each of these is found, how they differ from each other in size, coloration, and so on, would all be among the points which it would be obvious to cover.

Some points which might be less obvious, but perhaps not less important, could be making clear that the bear is not necessarily ferocious or ill-tempered. The child who has gained from reading fairy stories an image of the bear as an animal greatly to be feared has a right to be informed of the bears which may be seen by tourists in certain of our national parks, and which are found by most people to be amiable indeed unless teased. The bear is a mischievous animal, and some small anecdote in this connection might be appropriate.

What I am trying to do here is to describe an approach to a problem rather than to describe any single answer. Or to put it another way: I am suggesting to you the importance of thinking from the user back rather than from the writer or editor out.

But it occurs to me that I am speaking as if only words are the issue. In fact, the better reference books today recognize that communication takes place not only through words, but also, and sometimes very much more effectively, through line drawings, charts, graphs, half-tones, and the entire battery of devices which communicate on something comparable to the printed page, but in something other than words. The selection and use of these various elements of the modern reference book imposes a burden on authors, editors, art editors, designers, layout people, and every other member of the large editorial groups which now work on a year-round basis in support of every one of our major encyclopedias.

I have in my personal library several reference books dating from the 19th century, most of which were made in England, and I am always reminded when I look at them of two fairly obvious ways in which they differ from the best of their modern counterparts. They differ first in that they are evidently created for members of a fairly small group within the society of their day, and created for this group by members of the group itself. They are works written for and by the English upper-middle class. Books of today are written for literate and, hopefully, intelligent human beings, regardless of class. They are written also without the presupposition of any particular kind of formal education on the part of the user.

The second point of difference is in the physical presentation of the material. A lazy editor would have to regret the passing of the day when it was possible to produce a book by putting words one after another in a seemingly endless series of unbroken pages of black and white print. I am happy to say that my editors are not lazy, nor are any of the other professionals on my staff. I do not know whether we spend 10 or 20 or 30 more man-hours on a page today than might have been spent on an equivalent work, three, four, or five generations ago. But I am sure that we spend an amount of additional time which would be incredible to someone not familiar with the almost total change in treatment which has come about in encyclopedias.

In closing, I would like to speak of the future. I believe that relative to what we will be doing, and have to be doing, and be delighted to be doing ten years from now, the change which I have described between today and an earlier day may seem trivial. We live in an age when these things are true —and each of them is reflected in our better encyclopedias—the amount of knowledge which must be known to the people who use our books has accumulated and is accumulating at a staggering rate. And the means by which this knowledge is communicated to its users are diverse and ingenious. The good editor today is, and will be even more so in the future, the one who can use these various means appropriately, simply, and gracefully.

Evaluating the Format of an Encyclopedia

• BY DR. WILLIAM H. NAULT

Executive Director of Research, Field Enterprises Educational Corporation

Speaking on a topic like format reminds me of the story of the bishop who attended a dinner where the waiter spilled a cup of hot soup in his lap. The bishop leaped up in pain and looking desperately around said, "Will some layman say something appropriate to the occasion!"

Because format includes so many aspects and truly involves a number of highly controversial elements, I had to, like the good bishop, think of what would be appropriate to this occasion. This is particularly so because many book designers, production men, and editors do not agree on all problems of format. For that matter they often disagree—and markedly so!

It is my belief, and I'm sure that librarians share this view, that format is an important evaluative criteria, although in my opinion, it ranks down the hierarchical ladder below the items just discussed by my fellow encyclopedists.

For if a reference work lacks authority, if it lacks proper scope, if it lacks readability, if it lacks objectivity—no format including an abundance of lavish illustrations, realistic color, or even dramatic Trans-Visions will make the work an effective reference tool!

To make sure that we're thinking in the same terms—what do we mean by "format"? The general format means the design or plan of the book—its shape, size, binding, type face—in short, its whole arrangement. To be sure, many poorly designed books are read and used, particularly if the information contained is vital to the user. However, keep in mind that this type of publication assumes a highly-motivated user—one for whom the information has special or great significance—and one who is probably not the typical person using a general encyclopedia.

It is an axiom of good writing, I believe, that an author must have in mind the audience for which he is writing. Good communication assumes a knowledge of the intended receiver. Knowledge of the intended audience is critical too, in assessing the various aspects of format. For example, the encyclopedia publisher interested in producing a reference work for general family use or a reference set designed for children and youth may have to pay special attention to certain dimensions of format. Those producing a set for an adult market or for a scholarly audience may not have to feel restricted in the same way. The important point, however, in assessing the format of an encyclopedia is to ask—*who* is the *primary* audience for the reference work?

Let's begin this discussion by examining the question of the relationship of text to illustration. In other words, how heavily is the encyclopedia illustrated? A picture is worth 10,000 words has become a tedious phrase and yet it drives home the point that many ideas can be communicated most efficiently and effectively through illustrations—photographs, charts, diagrams, schematics, etc. But the critical reviewer is concerned with not only how many illustrations, but more importantly: (1) do the illustrations contribute to an understanding of the subject by showing visually those ideas which the mind can grasp more readily when aided by a visual image? (2) are the illustrations placed physically near the related text? (3) do the illustrations supplement the text? (4) do the illustrations attract the reader and motivate him to read the material? (5) do the illustrations emphasize the important or significant aspects of the subject? (6) are the illustrations truly functional or are they included *primarily* to make the volumes attractive? (7) are teaching captions included to help guide the reader in getting the most out of the visual aids?

Most would agree, I am sure, that the ratio of text to illustrations should vary from encyclopedias intended for young readers to those prepared for an adult audience; and that within any given encyclopedia the ratio should vary from subject to subject. A topic like philosophy probably does not need as many illustrations as articles on architecture, animals, or painting. Generally, a book designed for a scholar would not need the same degree of illustration as one having the layman as its central audience. The encyclopedia I know best has about one-third of its space devoted to illustrations. Keep in mind also that the editorial budget has a direct relationship to the amount of illustration a book can carry. As my colleagues can attest, fine photographs in black and white or in full color are frightfully expensive and creative art work puts a heavy burden on the debit side of the ledger. The costs of engraving and printing have also soared in recent years making it necessary for the editor to use illustrations with great care and discretion.

One aspect of illustration that I was asked to mention, and it is one of considerable interest, is the use of bleed illustrations and the pros and cons of the technique of bleeding. A bleed page, you'll recall, is designed without a margin; the page is trimmed so that the illustration goes to the edge or edges of the page and there is no white margin. The advantages of the bleed page are: (1) illustrations can be made larger by using the space normally consumed by the margin, (2) more space is made available for textual material when illustrations are moved to the margins; and (3) more flexibility in design of the page is possible when illustrations are released from the formal boundaries of the usual page format.

Bleeding the illustrations also has disadvantages. First of all, there are increased costs caused by a greater paper allowance, the need for larger printing plates, and additional ink coverage. Overuse of bleed can also reduce the amount of white space needed to rest the eye and the amount of white space needed for contrast with the illustrations. And, from a practical point of view; page numbers, running heads (or guide words), and titles may be displaced or completely lost.

The disadvantages of an excess of bleed pages brings up an important format issue for publishers of educational or reference publications: when the *aesthetic* conflicts with the *effectiveness* of the page or the over-all *ease of use* of the work, which aspect takes precedence? In other words, the editor must, in the final analysis, decide if the guide word on a specific page or spread is more or less important than an attractive bleed illustration. Or to say it another way, the reference quality of the work should take precedence over the artistic or aesthetic. He might also have to decide whether a good teaching illustration should be used instead of one that is striking, beautiful, and contributes little in a substantive way to the purposes of the article.

Next, let's consider the matter of color. Why color? How much? What kind? Color should add an aesthetic value to a book while *functioning* as a teaching tool. Color is a powerful vehicle if used properly and can clarify a process, emphasize a point, or dramatize an operation by leading the eye with directional lines or arrows. Color can separate items or groups of items in a chart or graph. It serves to emphasize a vital element when used in parts of an illustration or when used in the text material itself. It makes photographs and drawings more realistic and is invaluable in the correct identification of such things as flags, birds, snakes, rocks, and minerals.

Can there be too much color? In one sense—NO—particularly in terms of appearance and use. We live in a world of full color and a book should be an extension of our environment. But, black and white pages provide contrast and relief for the eye. Complete color can tend to become neutralizing in effect. And, as we all know, black and white photographs and drawings can be powerful and dramatic. They can make the pages more exciting by their contrast to the color.

Can there be too much color? YES—in terms of cost and time. The cost and time necessary to make four-color illustrations triples and quadruples that needed for black and white illustrations. If a publication has a limited editorial budget and too much of that budget is committed to color, something else suffers—is it accuracy, authoritativeness, scope, readability?

The intelligent editor then uses color when it serves a significant purpose—a purpose that generally transcends the mere "dressing up" of the publication—and he uses it to create the greatest possible impact—educationally speaking—on the reader.

And, returning to illustrations for a moment, the good editor uses illustrations when they are the most efficient and effective way to communicate a point. He uses a variety of visual aids and uses each kind for the purpose it serves best. Whether it be a map, a chart, a diagram, a pictograph, or a Trans-Vision—whether it be in black and white, in two color—in four color—or in full color—it must be appraised critically in terms of the contribution it makes to comprehension of the subject.

It is somewhat surprising to note that even though the printed page is now—and probably will continue to be—a basic and primary source of communication, relatively little organized research exists on what makes a printed page easy to read. Unquestionably, a great body of tradition has grown up around type usage and this tradition—plus the judgment and artistry of typographers—has dictated choices in this vital format area. Much work needs to be done in both theoretical and empirical research and a number of publishing firms have initiated exploratory studies with university specialists, book designers and communication experts.

But let's consider certain factors that usually go into type selection. Most students of the graphic arts would agree that legibility and ease of reading depends on (1) size of type, (2) amount of spacing or leading between lines, (3) weight of type face (density of ink), (4) width of column line, and (5) type style. Let me emphasize here that the *size* of the type, in and of itself is not a good measure of the readability of the page. It is important only when seen in terms of the other criteria just mentioned.

A well-designed format requires also that the type elements be in harmony. In other words, the type styles of text, running heads, captions, page numbers and section heads must be kept within a single design concept. If the combinations of type faces, styles and sizes are not kept within strict limits, a hodgepodge results and the book does not give a pleasing appearance.

Another important element in the over-all format of the encyclopedia is the type, quality and weight of the paper. Here, too, the main audience for the book is of significance. A volume to be used primarily by school children will require a paper that is strong and capable of withstanding heavy usage.

The weight and strength of the paper is measured by the weight of 500 sheets of a standard size, normally 25 x 38 inches. *World Book* uses a 50-pound paper or stock which means that 500 sheets of our paper measuring 25 x 38 inches weigh 50 pounds. We use a machine-coated paper which means that a coating of clay and adhesives in liquid form is applied to the paper on the paper-making machine. This smooth glossy surface is required for the reproduction of the fine-line half-tone photographs and full-color illustrations.

Although a smooth glossy surface is needed for good art reproduction, the paper should not be too glossy or it will produce a glaring effect which annoys the reader and impedes his ability to continue his reading. In evaluating the paper it is important, therefore, to observe just how much glare occurs when the light strikes the page from a variety of angles.

If the paper is too thin and lacks sufficient weight and body, one may observe what we call "show through". If "show through" occurs, the reader sees the backside of the material which is on the other side of the paper. A "show through" condition is both annoying and frustrating to the reader and undoubtedly impedes effective reading. "Show through" should be avoided in books published for all levels of readership.

Encyclopedias are printed either by the letterpress or offset methods. Some utilize a combination of the two, using letterpress for some sections of the volume and offset for others. When printers get together—or even when editors from various firms meet—arguments begin on the pros and cons of letterpress versus offset and vice versa. These discussions are quite technical and we should not get into this area of controversy today. But to show that my company feels both methods to be excellent ones for producing quality publications, let me say that we have used letterpress for many, many years. It has long been considered *the* printing method for fine color reproduction. Note, for example, that publications like *National Geographic, Life* and *Time* use the letterpress method exclusively. On the other hand, my firm is now involved in the Herculean task of converting to the offset method, primarily because of new major developments in offset equipment. Our manufacturing experts tell us that our new web-offset presses will print more efficiently and in better detail than our present letterpress equipment. Because offset inks are "heat set", the printing can be immediately and quickly dried in large driers (or ovens) producing a dry sheet that can be folded at the end of the printing press. These inks have a high degree of gloss and brightness. All our tests and research indicate a superior print quality with bright crisp-looking illustrations.

For years I had taken the letterpress side of the arguments and now I must join my colleagues who use the offset method of printing.

Now we have the text and the illustrations (in proper ratio) we've the paper, and the presses are rolling (either letterpress or offset). I guess now we're about ready to bind our books. But what method of binding shall we employ? Again the audience we are to serve is critical. Books designed for rough wear and tear generally use the McCain method of binding. It is simply sewing through the side of the book, through all the pages at once, rather than section by section or signature by signature. The resulting backbone of the book is rigid and solid. The McCain method is the strongest binding available and it is probably not surprising to learn that most school textbooks use McCain binding.

But like most methods, McCain has a disadvantage. Because the pages are so strongly sewed and securely bound, the McCain bound book will not lay flat when opened like a Smyth-sewn volume. Your large unabridged dictionary, by the way, is a good example of a Smyth-sewn book. It lays flat when opened but will not take the physical abuse—dropping, etc.—that a McCain bound book will.

And before we leave binding of the books, don't forget to examine the binding cloth. Is it a high quality fabric? Will it withstand grime, dirt, perspiration and abuse? Can it be cleaned?

Let's now discuss briefly one more format consideration. How large should the volumes be—both in page size and thickness, and the weight of the individual volumes? Again the intended audience partially answers the question. Books for children should probably not be too large nor too heavy for convenience and ease of use. Also, if the volume is too thick it cannot be bound by the McCain method and a weaker binding system must be used. Books intended primarily for an adult market can undoubtedly enjoy a wider variation in size of page and in thickness or weight of the volume, than is true of those designed primarily for children and youth.

In the brief time I've had today, I have attempted to shed light on the various aspects of evaluating the format of encyclopedias. I've emphasized throughout the importance of evaluating the various dimensions of format in terms of who the volumes are intended for. Keep in mind, I've said the purpose for which the book is to be used and who is to use it. Ask yourself, is the format design functional? And I've said that format *is* important, but it's important *only* if the books are worth printing in the first place.

The Evaluation of Encyclopedias

• BY S. PADRAIG WALSH

Editor, General Encyclopedias in Print, R. R. Bowker Co.

The theme of this symposium is "Can Our Good Encyclopedias Be Made Better?". But this is by no means a simple question and is, in fact, two questions wrapped up in one, because, whichever way you answer—yes or no—you certainly have to follow up with a "how" or a "why".

But let us begin with a straight answer to the basic question. Yes, indeed, I do believe that our good encyclopedias can be made better. But more than that, they will be made better. This is as inevitable as night follows day. It just has to be. Everything (anyway, almost everything) in our modern technological society can be made better and will, in the natural course of events, be improved. For example, our automobiles do get better, safer and more efficient with each passing decade, even though we may feel at times that they occasionally take a step backwards to achieve a further advance. And so it is with most of our modern conveniences and so it will be with educational media, not least of which will be our leading encyclopedias and tools of reference.

The bigger, wealthier and more enterprising publishers, such as those represented here tonight have already conducted considerable research into the future, and their plans are far reaching. And let there be no doubt that the competition between them is a splendid and healthy incentive, ensuring that they and their various publications will be kept abreast of the times and the ever changing needs of the times. Just what form the encyclopedia of the future will take is a matter of conjecture right now. Almost certainly, computers will play an increasingly important part, and it is not at all difficult to visualize the time when an encyclopedia will be produced almost entirely from the data fed into computers at a speed and with an accuracy beyond anything previously accomplished. But, of course, a computer can only produce what is programmed into it, and can never, in itself, entirely replace the printed book. I am reminded here of a story which I came across a short while ago, which surely provides a moral.

This concerns two clocks, one of which was broken and did not go at all, while the other gained a matter of seconds each day. This information was fed into the computer to determine which clock was the more accurate. Quite logically, I suppose, the answer given was that the broken clock was correct twice each day, whereas the clock that gained a few seconds daily was correct only once in 100 years.

Obviously, therefore, a computer, accurate though it may be, does not, and cannot, replace commonsense. So, while a computer may produce an encyclopedia which is technically accurate, the human factor cannot be obviated.

Having answered "yes" to the basic question, we are immediately faced with the second part, how can our good encyclopedias be made better? There are two aspects to this—the technical and the applied. I am sure that we can safely leave the technical preparation of a major reference work to those highly competent editors and compilers who are already producing such fine tools in the face of incredible difficulties in the way of cost and other limiting factors. But, insofar as we, as librarians, are concerned, we really need to know only the basic fundamentals of encyclopedia compilation and production, just sufficient for us to know how to use these works of reference to their maximum advantage. We do not, for example, need to know how a telephone or a computer works from an engineering aspect, but we most certainly do need to know how to use them for maximum efficiency and profit, and so it is with encyclopedias and other works of reference. But, at the same time, we should be aware of the tremendous problems which confront the present day editors and publishers. As we all know, knowledge is expanding at an ever accelerating rate, doubling itself at least each ten years. But, while human knowledge is itself expanding, the encyclopedias cannot burst out of their confines, if only on the grounds of cost alone. An encyclopedia cannot double in size to keep pace with the knowledge explosion, and we must always remember this when we are called upon to use one, or, for that matter, to advise upon one. A century ago, it was feasible for a relatively medium-sized work to encompass a major portion of man's accumulated knowledge, but the same work today can cope with but a small percentage of the social, scientific and technological developments within that period. Indeed, just look at the momentous events of our own time—these alone could easily fill any of today's larger encyclopedias.

If, therefore, we leave the technical improvement of our good encyclopedias to those with the necessary know-how, there still remains the question of what we, as librarians, can contribute to the same cause, and there is much that we can and should do, and our role is no less vital than that of the editors and the publishers. In the first instance, we should be conversant with, at least, all our good encyclopedias. We should know just how authoritative they are, what age group they cater to, the extent of their subject coverage, their methods of arrangement, etc.,—in short, the basic criteria for all encyclopedias. But is this enough? Preferably, in my opinion, we should be almost equally conversant with those encyclopedias which are not good, and I would even go so far as to say that it is our bounden duty to be even more aware of the many works (unfortunately) of poor quality. We, in the United States (and Canada) are fortunate in that we have a choice of several encyclopedias, probably the best in the English language, and certainly a wider range of good encyclopedias than any other country. But, before we start congratulating ourselves, let us also be aware of the fact that we are equally unfortunate in that we are the unwilling hosts to just as many spurious works of reference.

At the present time there are in print more than 30 encyclopedias of general knowledge published in the United States, ranging in size from one volume to 30, and in word coverage from 1 million words to almost 40 million. But of these, only half can be considered to be acceptable, and then from these, only a bare handful can be considered as being in the top drawer. We have what I would say are five proven top quality encyclopedias, i.e., the multi-volume works, with another two knocking on the door, just awaiting the test of time to gain admission to the elite. Then again, there are two junior encyclopedias in preparation by two of our major publishers which, from what I have seen of them, are likely candidates for top honors. In this group of some 16 or 17 acceptable works, approximately half are what may be termed "fringe" works, hovering on the edge of the abyss and liable, if they are unable to keep up with their wealthier brothers, to drop out of the race altogether and, because of their lack of resources, it seems likely that they will eventually have to concede the field to the leaders. But this still leaves us with a substantial number of really sub-standard works, never likely to climb above a degree of mediocrity, and I believe that these are the sets with which we should be most seriously concerned.

These are the works which have given, and are giving, the encyclopedia publishing industry a bad name. These are the works which are the cause of discontent and disappointment to those unfortunate enough to purchase them. To be sure, some people buy the right set for the wrong audience, but these are usually mistakes of their own making. I am speaking now of those people who have been deliberately duped into paying a considerable sum of money for a virtually worthless product, and there are, unfortunately, very many of them. Bear in mind that more than 90% of the encyclopedias and allied works sold in this country are vended to families—to the average family who knows little or nothing about reference works and who, unversed as it is in the basic criteria of encyclopedia evaluation, is easy prey for the outwardly attractive works of internally shockingly poor quality. I know of one instance at the present time of a work which originated in 1895, which has changed title no less than thirteen times and which is today being sold under three different titles at a wide variation in cost. Admittedly, the work has changed beyond all recognition from the original issue of 1895, but it was a bad work to begin with, and although changed, has improved little since then. There- fore, since about half of the encyclopedias published in the United States are of what we consider a sub-standard quality, it is axiomatic that a very great number of families are being swindled—and I use the word without apology— out of their hard earned dollars, paying a lot of money for very little. Some of our wiser citizens, to be sure, are astute enough to consult their local library but these, regrettably, are in the minority.

This is the area of encyclopedia publishing in which I believe our role can be a vital one. If I may use an analogy at this time to more clearly illustrate my meaning: We do not have to be keen gardeners to know that useful fruits and vegetables cannot thrive in an orchard choked with weeds. If they are to attain full maturity, that orchard must be carefully tended to deal with the weeds, pests and parasites which would hinder and even destroy these useful products. Can we not be the gardeners in the field of encyclopedia publishing? Can we not weed out the choking growths, the pests and the parasites which feed on the reputation of our good encyclopedias? Let us, as librarians, as professionals and advisers to the reading public, endeavour to assist in the future advancement of our major reference works by warn- ing against the undesirables, by attempting to eliminate the pests and the parasites, and keep on weeding them out. Relax our vigil and back they will come, just as surely as we allowed them to clutter up the field through com- placency in the initial instance. If we do this, we really will be providing a service, not only to the community which we are all dedicated to serve, but to the editors and the publishers who are really striving to provide us with the best possible works of reference.

No one body, no one person, can do this. It is up to all of us. At the present time we have, of course, the expert advice of the Subscription Books Committee and there can be no doubt that the evaluations of this body of expert and dedicated librarians are of incalculable value. But, and I say this not with criticism, but with regret, the evaluations of the Committee, metic- ulous though they are, appear, as a general rule, long after a spurious work has been put on the market, and by that time the damage has been done, and the offending publisher has already marched off with a substantial profit. The time to crack down on inferior encyclopedias (and other expensive works of reference) is before, if at all possible, but at least as soon as possible after publication. The late Lawrence Hart, despite many adverse criticisms, and despite the lack of official recognition, did do a little towards this end. Un- fortunately, he was not really qualified to undertake such a responsibility. One of his criteria, for example, was the cost per million words for each encyclopedia, but such a criteria cannot be applied to all and sundry. This would be valid only if all the sets were of otherwise equal merit. But let us be fair. Lawrence Hart was a thorn in the side of many publishers and he did a great deal to oppose the multiplication of inferior works.

There is much, much more which could be said on the evaluation of encyclopedias, but in an address which must, of necessity, be confined to essentials, let me summarize by saying again: Yes, our good encyclopedias can be made better and yes, we can play a vital role in ensuring that they are made better. And this we can and must do by cleaning up the rubbish with which we have been plagued for so long. May I conclude by saying: This forum was concerned with the theme "Can Our Good Encyclopedias Be Made Better?"—can we continue it on the theme of "How Can We Get Rid of Our Bad Encyclopedias?"